Shadow of Spirit

By illuminating the striking affinity between the most innovative aspects of postmodern thought and religious or mystical discourse, *Shadow of Spirit* challenges the long-established assumption that contemporary western thought is committed to nihilism.

This collection of essays by internationally recognized scholars from the humanities and social sciences explores the implications of the fascination with the 'sacred', 'divine', or 'infinite' which characterizes much contemporary thought. It shows how these concerns have surfaced in the work of Derrida, Levinas, Baudrillard, Lyotard, Kristeva, Irigaray and others. Examining the connection between this postmodern 'turn' and the current search for a new discourse of ethics and politics, it also stresses the contribution made by feminist thought to this unexpected intellectual direction.

The editors: Philippa Berry is a Fellow and Lecturer in English at King's College, Cambridge. She has written *Of Chastity and Power: Elizabethan Literature and the Unmarried Queen* (Routledge 1989). Andrew Wernick is a Professor of Cultural Studies at Trent University, Canada, and is the author of *Promotional Culture: Advertising, Ideology and Symbolic Expression* (1991).

The contributors: Mark C. Taylor, Gillian Rose, John Milbank, Joanna Hodge, Toby Foshay, Rowan Williams, Don Cupitt, Jonathan Bordo, Gad Horowitz, Eve Tavor Bannet, Shannon Bell, Robert Magliola, John O'Neill, Regina Schwartz, Geraldine Finn, Carl Raschke, Patricia Klindienst Joplin, Philippa Berry, Andrew Wernick.

Shadow of Spirit

Postmodernism and Religion

Edited by Philippa Berry and
Andrew Wernick

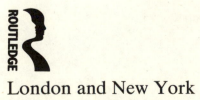

London and New York

First published 1992
by Routledge
11 New Fetter Lane, London EC4P 4EE

Simultaneously published in the USA and Canada
by Routledge
a division of Routledge, Chapman and Hall Inc.
29 West 35th Street, New York, NY 10001

Typeset in 10/12 pt Times by Florencetype Ltd, Kewstoke,
Avon
Printed in Great Britain by Butler & Tanner Ltd, Frome and
London

British Library Cataloguing in Publication Data
Shadow of Spirit: Postmodernism and
Religion
  I. Berry, Philippa II. Wernick, Andrew
  291.2

Library of Congress Cataloging-in-Publication Data
Shadow of spirit : postmodernism and religion / edited by
Philippa Berry and   Andrew Wernick.
      p. cm.
   Most of the papers collected in this volume were given at
a conference held at King's College, Cambridge in July
1990.
   Includes bibliographical references.
   1. Postmodernism—Congresses.
   2. Religion—Congresses.
I. Berry, Philippa, 1955–. II. Wernick, Andrew, 1945–.
B831.2.S42 1992
190′.9′04—dc20   92-12225

ISBN 0-415-06638-7
ISBN 0-415-06639-5 (pbk)

For Michael and Lilith

Wir aber verweilen,
ach, uns rühmt es zu blühn, und ins verspätete Innre
unserer endlichen Frucht gehn wir verraten hinein.
(Rilke, *Duino Elegies*, no. 6)

A storm is blowing from Paradise; it has got caught in his wings
with such violence that the angel [of history] can no longer close
them. This storm irresistibly propels him into the future to which
his back is turned, while the pile of debris before him grows
skyward. This storm is what we call progress.
(Walter Benjamin, *Theses on the Philosophy of History*)

Contents

Illustrations

Contributors

Shannon Bell has just completed her doctorate 'Reading, Writing and Rewriting the Prostitute Body', in Political Science at York University, Ontario. Her publications include 'Feminist Ejaculations', in Arthur and Marilouise Kroker (eds), *The Hysterical Male – a New Feminist Theory* (1991), and 'The Political-Libidinal Economy of the Socialist Female Body: Flesh and Blood; Work and Ideas', in *Dialectical Anthropology*, vol. 15 (1990).

Philippa Berry is a Fellow and Lecturer in English Literature at King's College, Cambridge. She is the author of *Of Chastity and Power: Elizabethan Literature and the Unmarried Queen* (1989), and of essays in the fields of Renaissance literature and feminist theory. She is currently working on two projects: a feminist reading of Shakespearean tragedy, and a book on French feminism entitled *Dancing in Space: The Turns of Feminist Theory*.

Jonathan Bordo is an Associate Professor of Cultural Studies at Trent University, Canada. He is the author of essays in cultural theory and the visual arts including, most recently, "Aesthetic Monumentality, Technology and the Renaissance Origins of Modern Picturing" in Coward, *Worldviews and Cultural Policy* and is at work on a book concerning modernity and the sublime.

Don Cupitt is a Lecturer in Theology at the University of Cambridge, a Fellow of Emmanuel College, Cambridge, and an Anglican priest. He is the author of many books, including, most recently, *Creation Out of Nothing* (1990), *What is a Story?* (1991) and *The Time Being* (1992).

Geraldine Finn is Associate Professor of Cultural Studies at Carleton University, Ottawa, Canada. A philosopher by training, she has published articles in many journals and collections, on a wide range of issues related to feminism and contemporary cultural critique. She is currently working in the area of feminist musicology and the relationship between philosophy and fiction. Her publications include *Feminism: From Pressure to Politics* (co-edited with Angela Miles, 2nd edn 1989), *Limited Edition: Voices of Women, Voices of Feminism* (as editor, 1993) and *Feminism and the Politics of Postmodernism* (forthcoming 1993).

Toby Foshay teaches critical theory and modern literature in the Department of English, University of Victoria, Canada. Recent work includes *Wyndham Lewis and the Avant-Garde: The Politics of the Intellect* (1992) and *Derrida and Negative Theology* (co-edited with Harold Coward, 1992).

Joanna Hodge studied for her first degree at the University of Oxford. She wrote her doctoral thesis on Martin Heidegger, working for it in Oxford, Heidelberg and Berlin. She is now a Senior Lecturer in Philosophy at Manchester Polytechnic.

Gad Horowitz is Professor of Political Science at the University of Toronto. He is the author of *Canadian Labour in Politics* (1968), *Repression: Basic and Surplus Repression in Psychoanalytic Theory* (1977) and 'The Foucaultian Impasse: No Sex, No Self, No Revolution', in *Political Theory* (February 1987).

Patricia Klindienst Joplin has taught literature and feminist studies at Yale University. She is currently finishing a book on Virginia Woolf, *The Mind's Natural Jungle*.

Robert Magliola (Ph.D., comparative literature, Princeton University) was co-chair of the doctoral programme in Philosophy and Literature at Purdue University, and is now Distinguished Chair Professor at the Graduate School of National Taiwan University. Specializing in philosophical, Christian and Buddhist hermeneutics, he has published *Phenomenology and Literature* (1977) and *Derrida on the Mend* (1984). His next book is entitled *Cross-Hatching the Buddha*.

John Milbank is University Lecturer in Divinity at the University of Cambridge. He has published two books to date: *Theology and Social Theory: Beyond Secular Reason* (1990) and *The Religious Dimension in the Thought of Gianbattista Vico* (1991). At present he is working on a book on Trinity and selfhood in western theology and philosophy.

John O'Neill is Distinguished Research Professor of Sociology at York University, Canada, and an External Associate of the Centre for Comparative Literature at the University of Toronto. He is also a Fellow of the Royal Society of Canada. He is the author of, among other works,

The Communicative Body: Studies in Communicative Philosophy, Politics and Sociology (1989) and *Plato's Cave: Desire, Power and the Specular Functions of the Media* (1991). He is presently at work on *The Domestic Economy of the Soul*, a study of Freud's principal five case histories.

Carl A. Raschke is currently President of the American Association for the Advancement of Core Curriculum. He has served as Director of the Institute for the Humanities and Professor of Religious Studies at the University of Denver, where he has taught since 1972. He received his Ph.D. from Harvard University and is a former Director of the American Academy of Religion, the national professional society for college instructors and research in religion. He has also served as a member of the chairman's advisory board of the National Endowment for the Humanities in Washington, and was recently invited to join a panel assembled by the top federal funding agencies in Washington, DC, to discuss the reform of higher education. He is a contributor to the *New Handbook of Christian Theology* (1988).

Gillian Rose is Professor of Social and Political Thought in the Department of Sociology, University of Warwick. Her most recent book is *The Broken Middle: Out of our Ancient Society* (1992). Her other books include *Dialectic of Nihilism: Post-Structuralism and Law* (1984), *Hegel contra Sociology* (1981), *The Melancholy Science: An Introduction to the Thought of Theodor W. Adorno* (1978) and *Judaism and Modernity: Philosophical Essays* (1993).

Regina Schwartz is Associate Professor of English and Religious Studies at Duke University, where she teaches Renaissance literature, theory and theology. She is the author of *Remembering and Repeating: On Milton's Theology and Poetics* (1988, reprinted 1992), the editor of *The Book and the Text: The Bible and Literary Theory* (1990), co-author of *The Postmodern Bible* (forthcoming, 1993), and co-editor of *Border Crossings: Psychoanalysis and the Renaissance* (1992). She is currently writing a book on monotheism and identity.

Eve Tavor Bannet's publications include *Structuralism and the Logic of Dissent: Barthes, Derrida, Foucault, Lacan* (1989) and *Postcultural Theory: Theories for the '90s* (forthcoming). She is presently teaching at the University of South Carolina.

Mark C. Taylor is the Preston Parish Third Century Professor of Religion at Williams College, Williamstown. A specialist in modern theology, philosophy of religion and cultural studies, his most recent books include:

Altarity (1987), *Tears* (1990) and *Disfiguring: Art, Architecture, Religion* (1992) and *Nots* (forthcoming).

Andrew Wernick is Professor of Cultural Studies at Trent University in Canada and Director of its graduate programme in Methodologies for the Study of Western History and Culture. He is the author of *Promotional Culture: Advertising, Ideology and Symbolic Expression* (1991), and co-editor, with Mike Featherstone, of *Images of Ageing* (forthcoming). His current work focuses on contemporary media theory and the commodification of music.

Rowan Williams was born in Wales, studied theology at Cambridge and researched Russian religious thought at Oxford. He has published a number of books on the history of Christian theology and spirituality (most recently a study of Teresa of Avila) and articles on the frontiers of philosophy and theology (including some recent essays on Simone Weil). He was Professor of Divinity at Oxford from 1986 to 1992, and is now the (Anglican) Bishop of Monmouth.

Acknowledgements

Most of the papers collected in this volume were given at a conference held at King's College, Cambridge, in July 1990, entitled 'The Shadow of Spirit: Contemporary Western Thought and its Religious Subtexts'. We would like to express our sincere appreciation to the Provost and Fellows for their kind support of that venture, and to thank the King's College Research Centre in particular, whose Managers agreed to contribute substantially towards the funding of the event. We also want to thank the British Academy and the Cambridge University Faculties of Divinity and Social and Political Sciences, each of whom likewise contributed generous grants. We are especially grateful to Martin Hyland and Rosemarie Baines of the King's College Research Centre for their constant patience and support at all stages of this project. Thanks also to the *Journal of the American Academy of Religion* for permission to republish Carl Raschke's paper 'Fire and Roses: Or, the Problem of Postmodern Religious Thinking', which appeared in 58, iv, Winter 1991 pp. 671–89. Regina Schwartz's essay has appeared in *'Not in Heaven': Literary Readings of Biblical Texts*, Indiana University Press, 1991 and in *Critical Inquiry*, Fall 1992. At Routledge, the enthusiastic support and guidance of Jane Armstrong, Helena Reckitt and especially of Rebecca Barden were invaluable. Fiona Wilson and Rosemarie Baines gave loving and careful attention to different versions of the manuscript. Among the many friends and colleagues whose inspiration and enthusiasm have helped to bring this book into being, we would like to thank in particular Ralph Yarrow, Franc Chamberlain, Teresa Brennan, Tony Giddens, Don Cupitt, and Phillip Blond. Philippa would also like to thank Frank Payne for his love and support during her work on this project. The collaboration and friendship between the co-editors would have been impossible without a sabbatical grant from Trent University, which brought one of us, for a while, back to Cambridge. The spirit of that place, we like to think, has left its traces here.

AW and PB

Introduction

Philippa Berry

Thoughts are not the fruits of the earth. They are not registered by
areas, except out of human commodity. Thoughts are clouds. . . .
Thoughts never stop changing their location one with the other. When
you feel like you have penetrated far into their intimacy in analysing
either their so-called structure or genealogy or even post-structure, it is
actually too late or too soon. One cloud casts its shadow on another, the
shape of clouds varies with the angle from which they are approached.

(Jean-François Lyotard, *Peregrinations*)

It seems strange to acknowledge, as this century draws to a close, that in
several important respects twentieth-century thought is still positioned as it
was at its inception. For much intellectual activity in the humanities and
social sciences apparently continues to occupy the disturbing twilight zone
which was evoked by Nietzsche in 1888, in *The Twilight of the Idols*: that
indeterminate moment which ostensibly marks the limit of the bright day
of the Enlightenment. In a sense, this intellectual hesitation is inevitable;
since deconstruction has taught us to view both endings and beginnings
with scepticism, it seems that there is now no other place to think than
amidst the dereliction of former ideas. None the less, it still appears
somewhat odd that for postmodernism, as for modernism, a shadowy in-
between realm – a no-man's-land of thought – has continued to figure our
long-drawn-out moment of cultural decline. For modernist poets such as
Eliot and Pound, of course, this waste land, whether as purgatory or
inferno, ostensibly imaged a transitional state, the promise of a fantasized
ending and subsequent renewal of western culture. But for those who have
lost both the poetic innocence of origins and (given the declining influence
of orthodox Marxism) a faith in the teleology of history, this strange and
indeterminate intellectual position can now lead precisely nowhere, unless
it facilitates the directionless, 'nomadic' mode of intellectual wandering
recommended by Gilles Deleuze and Felix Guattari.[1] Such an acceptance
of philosophical stasis, however, pessimistic as it might seem, is currently
producing some rather surprising fruits. For while much contemporary

thought is now characterized by a disturbing 'waylessness', what are continuing to change are the ways in which we choose to view our perplexingly unspecific intellectual location.

As we begin to assimilate the wider philosophical implications of the crisis of humanist subjectivity – that crisis which Jacques Lacan in particular compelled us to acknowledge, but whose culmination is now often attributed to phenomenology as well as to psychoanalysis – so we appear to be discovering a different way of perceiving our philosophical dilemma.[2] Although our collective 'overcoming' of our former notions of subjectivity is clearly still incomplete, the process has undoubtedly begun to undermine western philosophy's implicit oculocentrism: a perspective which, as Michel Foucault pointed out, was based on a naive yet extremely dangerous equation between seeing and knowing.[3] For a darker, more obscure way of seeing and thinking – a perspective which is perhaps more appropriate to the twilight regions where philosophy now finds itself – appears gradually to be replacing our long-established visual drive to power and truth. In consequence, much intellectual attention is currently focussed on those figurative shadows which an earlier thinking, in its oculocentric vision, either forgot or marginalized. Such shadows, for example, are a persistent theme in the thought of Luce Irigaray, who has written of the survival of an oculocentric stance in even Nietzsche's work: 'Your noon leaves in the darkness the other side of the earth, and its inside, and the depths of the sea.'[4] Irigaray's 'dark' feminist thinking stresses the affinity between philosophy's shadows and its refusal, since Plato, to incorporate a bodily or experiential model of knowledge.[5] Given their mutual debt to phenomenology, it is perhaps not surprising that Irigaray's perspective has certain features in common with that of the later Heidegger, who stressed the ambiguous and dark character of *alētheia* or truth: 'self-concealing, concealment, *lēthē*, belongs to *alētheia*, not just as an addition, not just as a shadow to light, but rather as the heart of *alētheia*'.[6] Indeed, although Heidegger himself has often been criticized for his incomplete rejection of the philosophical concepts of presence or *parousia* which he tried so hard to subvert, David Michael Levin has recently suggested that the discovery of a genuine 'dark' mode of thinking is actually inseparable from that critique of a metaphysics of presence which is fundamental to both deconstruction and postmodernism:

Western metaphysics has forgotten, has suppressed, this *other* vision, this vision without the presence, the *parousia*, of the light of day: a vision which understands (the ontological significance of) the *absence* of light and is open to learning from the greatness – even the terror – of the night.[7]

Yet an interest in philosophy's shadows is having some unexpected effects upon the character of postmodern thinking. Not only does it often tend (in a manner which is arguably consistent with Nietzsche's concept of the eternal return) to efface temporal differences, such as those formerly clear-cut distinctions between past, present and future thought upon which previous accounts of the history of western philosophy depended. It is eroding too the many rigid distinctions between opposites which were fundamental, not only to the Enlightenment, but also to earlier western thought. It is precisely because of this confusion, of course, that so many categories and concepts formerly designated as 'other' can now be reassessed. It has proved extremely difficult, however, to move beyond a naive reversal of the hierarchies inscribed in such binary couplings. It is arguably only in the last few years that we have begun to elaborate 'other' ways of thinking that alterity which philosophy formerly consigned to the marginality of darkness. Probably one of the most unexpected results of this changed perspective has been to revive interest in those once-tabooed aspects of 'otherness' which can broadly be termed spiritual or religious. Indeed, by focussing on the unexpected emergence of religious motifs and themes in both deconstruction and postmodernism, some recent work in the humanities and social sciences offers new insight into Nietzsche's curious comment that nihilism is the 'uncanniest of all guests'.[8]

Among a number of commentators who have contributed to our changing view of Nietzsche's legacy of nihilism, Maurice Blanchot has emphasized Zarathustra's distress in understanding that he will never definitively go beyond man's inadequacies, or that he will only be able to do this, paradoxically, by a movement of return. Blanchot commented of this Nietzschean turn or return:

> It affirms that the extreme point of Nihilism is precisely where it is reversed, that Nihilism is reversal itself: it is the affirmation that, in passing from the *no* to the *yes*, refutes Nihilism – even though it does nothing other than affirm it, at which point Nihilism is extended to all possible affirmations. From this we conclude that Nihilism would be identical with the will to overcome Nihilism *absolutely*.[9]

As if in confirmation of Blanchot's comments, several recent assessments of postmodern thought have directly or indirectly reminded us that Nietzsche himself anticipated the eventual emergence of what he called '*a divine way of thinking*' from the intellectual tradition which he helped to form.[10] Probably one of the most publicized, and certainly one of the most controversial aspects of this debate is concerned with the obscure relationship of Derridean deconstruction to various religious or mystical treatments of negation and absence, whether these appear in the *via negativa* of Christianity, in Lurianic Kabbalism or in Buddhist metaphysics.[11] While such readings of Derrida seem superficially to be 'against the Derridean grain', as it were, their preoccupations have been obliquely encouraged by

Derrida's own continuing meditation upon this aspect of his work: for example, in the essays 'Of an Apocalyptic Tone Recently Adopted in Philosophy,' and 'Comment ne pas parler'.[12] Simultaneously, comparable themes in the work of other thinkers associated with postmodern thought have begun to be emphasized. Thus a developing interest in the extensive debt of deconstruction to the thought of Heidegger has foregrounded the precarious balance between secular and sacred themes which characterizes his later thought.[13] At the same time, a new enthusiasm for the writings of Emmanuel Levinas and Luce Irigaray, two broadly postmodern thinkers who have alluded frequently – if unobtrusively – to religious or spiritual themes for some years, has seemingly accelerated the emergence of this changed perspective on postmodern thinking.

It now seems plausible that the deconstructive style of thinking which was initiated a century ago, in Nietzsche's twilight, has subtly and unobtrusively dissolved the clear-cut distinction between secular and religious thinking which Kant and the Kantian tradition had carefully secured. Hence the question which was implicitly asked by the conference where most of these papers were first presented: could an apparently nihilistic tradition of thought – a thought ostensibly *shaped* by that darkness of *angst*, of meaninglessness and abjection, which shrouds the 'end' of the modern era – paradoxically have acquired a new religious or spiritual dimension?[14] For Heidegger, the encounter with nothing is ultimately pervaded by 'a strange kind of peace', 'a spellbound calm'. The papers which are gathered together here suggest that the paradox is a real one. For while the contributors to this collection differ significantly in their accounts and interpretations of this curious phenomenon, all of their essays imply that now, in this in-between and shadowy intellectual region which we have inherited from Nietzsche and others, 'the gods', 'the divine', 'God', may perhaps be thought differently: or, as Levinas has expressed it, 'otherwise'. In this endeavour, as the rest of the academy begins to interrogate the assumptions upon which its secularism formerly depended, so too the contributions currently being made by many theologians to the changing orientation of postmodern thought appear to herald the end of theology's long intellectual marginalization.

All of these essays testify, however, to the problems of terminology which the question presents; words or phrases such as 'spirit', 'the holy', 'the divine', 'God', 'the infinite', and so on, have accumulated associations of presence or transcendence which make it extremely difficult to redefine them. What would it mean, then, in the words of Levinas, 'to hear a God not contaminated by Being', or to recover, in the formulation of Mark C. Taylor, 'the nonabsent absence of the holy'?[15] While this style of thinking is centrally concerned with issues of alterity, a frequent theme in such discussions presents a new understanding of spirit, not as the opposite term of a binary couple, but rather as facilitating a wholly new mode of awareness, which not only invites the thinker to abandon their residual attachment to dualistic thinking, but also offers a potent challenge to their desire for subjective mastery and knowledge. Interest in the implications of such a non-dual perspective is apparent in some recent feminist investigations of the preconceptual relationship to the world of the child before the Lacanian mirror-stage and Oedipalization; perhaps significantly, there is an insistence upon the *bodily* dimension of this knowledge in such formulations. Yet the result of a recovery – or discovery – of this understanding, as variously explored by thinkers such as Levinas, Irigaray, Levin or Edith Wyschogrod, appears to be the attainment of a new capacity for ethical action – whether this is described in terms of love, compassion, altruism or care. As articulated by writers such as Levinas and Wyschogrod, this postmodern ethics proposes a new dismantling of the long-established dichotomy between Judaic and Hellenic thought; at the same time, in the works of Irigaray, Levin and others, it rejects a much wider distinction between eastern and western styles of thinking. What results from this bricolage of multiple religious and philosophical perspectives is a distinctively non-dogmatic mode of intellectual inquiry.

For Wyschogrod, the new mode of existence which this stance implies is impossible to describe in terms of modern notions of subjectivity. It can best be compared either to premodern concepts of Christian saintliness or to the Buddhist figure of the Bodhisattva, who defers her or his own blissful enlightenment in the endless assistance of others:

> A postmodern altruism must appeal to radical saintly generosity, to a benevolence that will not be brought to a close. Such saintliness is not a nostalgic return to premodern hagiography but a postmodern expression of excessive desire, a desire on behalf of the Other that seeks the cessation of another's suffering and the birth of another's joy.[16]

Wyschogrod's *Saints and Postmodernism* stresses the intimate links between the new religious or spiritual thematics of postmodernism and its search for an ethical stance which can fill the extensive gap left by the dismantling of Marxism. Yet it also testifies to the many epistemological uncertainties which mark this new direction. In particular, Wyschogrod suggests that the relationship of this 'radical altruism' to the concepts of desire and *jouissance* which have figured prominently in so much postmodern thought is both fundamental and also extremely problematic; in fact, she argues that the new quasi-religious discourse which is emerging within postmodernism is split 'along a fault-line', with the 'ecstatics' (among whom she includes Deleuze, Guattari and Julia Kristeva) on one side and the 'philosophers of difference' (especially Derrida, Levinas and Blanchot) on the other. This is because she considers that the themes of *ek-stasis* which so often appear in this new phase of postmodern thought tend towards a narcissistic quietism, and that they could consequently subvert the emergent altruistic impulse, in an effective disengagement from history which threatens to repeat the unforgivable political error of Heidegger. In contrast to these 'ecstatic' thinkers, Wyschogrod praises the engagement of the 'philosophers of difference' with the function of alterity in language, since it is this work, she contends, which has enabled a new, postmodern, understanding of the ethical demands of communication. In her view, it is those in this second category of thinkers who should be regarded as the true trail-blazers of a 'saintly' postmodern ethics.

But the essays collected here extend across the 'fault-line' demarcated by Wyschogrod. Not only does it seems inappropriate, in the context of a discourse in which the deconstruction of opposites is so pervasive, to accord priority to yet another binary divide; the distinction that Wyschogrod proposes is not in fact wholly defensible. In the first place, her account of the 'ecstatic' thinkers omits to note the frequent ethical or political concerns which appear in their work: for example, she fails to discuss the radical redefinition of love as *agape* attempted in Kristeva's *Tales of Love*; she also overlooks the radical political agenda of Deleuze and Guattari. And in the second place, Wyschogrod's wish to control desire, by excluding an unreasonable *ek-stasis* from her saintly discourse, seems to refuse that radical deconstruction of that subject which she herself has acknowledged to be necessary to the emergence of a new way of thinking, and a new altruism. This implication of a continuing attachment to the authoritative subject of modern thought flaws her otherwise compelling account of a saintly postmodernism.

In contrast to Wyschogrod, we would contend that it is those feminist, or feminist-influenced, thinkers whom she placed on the inferior or 'faulty' side of her 'fault-line' who have actually attempted some of the most radical and valuable rethinkings of subjectivity or identity in postmodern thought. As Rosi Braidotti has recently argued: 'If feminist thought is clearly situated in the field of modernity, in the critique of the subject, it is because women's struggles are one of the facets of the same "crisis", and act as one of its deepest theoretical and political rhizomes or roots.'[17] Our view of the need to accord equal importance to both sides of Wyschogrod's putative 'fault-line' is reflected in the organization of this collection, which, after a group of key introductory essays offering diverse 'maps' of the terrain of this new discourse, is subdivided into two groups of essays. These are concerned, on the one hand, with ethics, morality and politics; on the other, with questions of gender, subjectivity and textuality. In fact (in further confirmation of the partiality of Wyschogrod's division), none of the essays concerned falls neatly into either category, but we have chosen to reapply this rather artificial distinction in order to stress the *complementary* character of both emphases within this new field of intellectual possibility. In our view, a combination of both perspectives is needed in order to

begin to demarcate the 'groundless ground' of the new kind of thinking: ✓
that apparently empty space which Levinas has called the infinite, and
Irigaray, the divine.

NOTES

1 See Gilles Deleuze and Felix Guattari, *A Thousand Plateaus: Capitalism and
   Schizophrenia*, trans. Brian Massumi, London, Athlone Press, 1988.
2 See, for example, Jean-Luc Marion, 'L'interloqué', in Eduardo Cadava, Peter
   Connor and Jean-Luc Nancy (eds), *Who Comes after the Subject?*, London,
   Routledge, 1991, pp. 236–45.
3 Foucault wrote in *The Birth of the Clinic: An Archaeology of Medical
   Perception*, trans. Alan Sheridan, New York, Random House, 1975, of the
   'sovereignty of the gaze . . . the eye that knows and decides, the eye that
   governs' (p. 89).
4 Luce Irigaray, *Marine Lover: Of Friedrich Nietzsche*, trans. Gillian C. Gill,
   New York, Columbia University Press, 1991, p. 8.
5 See in particular Luce Irigaray, *Speculum: Of the Other Woman*, trans. Gillian
   C. Gill, New York, Columbia University Press, 1985, *passim*.
6 Martin Heidegger, *Der Satz vom Grund* (The Principle of Ground), Pfullingen,
   Neske, 1957, p. 78, trans. in David Michael Levin, *The Opening of Vision:
   Nihilism and Postmodernism*, London, Routledge, 1988, p. 423.
7 Levin, op. cit., p. 351.
8 Friedrich Nietzsche, *The Will to Power*, trans. Walter Kaufmann and R.J.
   Hollingdale, New York, Random House, 1968, I, 1.
9 Maurice Blanchot, 'The Limits of Experience: Nihilism', in David B. Allison
   (ed.), *The New Nietzsche*, Cambridge, Mass., MIT Press, 1985, pp. 121–8.
10 Nietzsche, op. cit., I, 15. For examples of this trend, see David Michael Levin,
   The Body's Recollection of Being, London, Routledge, 1986; *The Opening of
   Vision*, op. cit.; and *The Listening Self*, London, Routledge, 1990; Mark C.
   Taylor, *Erring: An A/Theology*, Chicago, University of Chicago Press, 1984;
   Altarity, Chicago, University of Chicago Press, 1987; and *Tears*, Albany, State
   University of New York Press, 1990; John Milbank, *Theology and Social
   Theory: Beyond Secular Reason*, Oxford, Blackwell, 1990; Edith Wyschogrod,
   Saints and Postmodernism, Chicago, University of Chicago Press, 1990.
11 See, for example, Harold Bloom, *Kabbalah and Criticism*, New York, Seabury
   Press, 1975; Susan Handelman, *The Slayers of Moses: The Emergence of
   Rabbinic Interpretation in Modern Literary Theory*, Albany, State University of
   New York Press, 1982; Robert Magliola, *Derrida on the Mend*, West Lafayatte,
   Purdue University Press, 1984; Kevin Hart, *The Trespass of the Sign:
   Deconstruction, Theology and Philosophy*, Cambridge, Cambridge University
   Press, 1990; Harold Coward and Toby Foshay (eds), *Derrida and Negative
   Theology*, Albany, State University of New York Press, 1992.
12 Jacques Derrida, 'Of an Apocalyptic Tone Recently Adopted in Philosophy',
   trans. John P. Leavey Jr, *Semeia*, 23 (1982), pp. 63–97, and 'Comment ne pas
   parler', in *Psyché: inventions de l'autre*, Paris, Galilée, 1987, pp. 535–96.
13 See in particular Herman Rapaport, *Heidegger and Derrida: Reflections on
   Time and Language*, Lincoln and London, University of Nebraska Press, 1989;
   Graham Parkes, (ed.), *Heidegger and Asian Thought*, Honolulu, University of
   Hawaii Press, 1987; John D. Caputo, *The Mystical Element in Heidegger's
   Thought*, Athens, University of Ohio Press, 1978.

14 'The Shadow of Spirit: Contemporary Western Thought and its Religious Subtexts', held at King's College, Cambridge, from 21 to 25 July 1990.
15 Emmanuel Levinas, *Otherwise than Being or beyond Essence*, trans. Alphonso Lingis, Dordrecht, Kluwer, 1991, p. xlii; Taylor, *Tears*, op. cit., *passim*.
16 Wyschogrod, op. cit., p. xxiv.
17 Rosi Braidotti, *Patterns of Dissonance: A Study of Women in Contemporary Philosophy*, Oxford, Polity Press, 1991, p. 11.

ACKNOWLEDGEMENT

I would like to thank Andrew Wernick for the many stimulating discussions which helped to inspire this essay. Thanks also to Eve Tavor Bannet, George Pattison and John Millbank for their comments on an earlier version of the text.

Part I

Maps and positions

Chapter 1

Reframing postmodernisms

Mark C. Taylor

Why is LA, why are the deserts so fascinating? It is because you are delivered from all depth there – a brilliant, mobile, superficial neutrality, a challenge to meaning and profundity, a challenge to nature and culture, an outer hyperspace, with no origin, no reference points. . . . The fascination of the desert: immobility without desire. Of Los Angeles: insane circulation without desire. The end of aesthetics.

(Jean Baudrillard)

I have come from the desert as one comes from beyond memory.

(Edmond Jabès)

Frames: Desert; Dessert. One word that is at least two – one spelling, two pronunciations; two spellings, one pronunciation. Desert; Des(s)ert. After dinner desserts – just or otherwise. Neither dinner nor not dinner, but a supplement. Something like a frame that repeats, while inverting, the hors d'oeuvre. No longer before but after the *repas*. *Le repas*: what is a *pas* that is a *re-pas*? Does the doubling of the k/not bind or rebind – *ligare* or *religare*? Desert . . . Des(s)ert . . . Des(s)erts. What is des(s)erted in the desert? Desert(s): site or non-site of wandering, erring – Vegas . . . *vagus*. Delivery *from* all depth . . . lights, pure light, absence of shadow? Or delivery *to* a certain *re-pas* that is beyond . . . *le pas au-delà*, where the absence of shadow is the shadow of spirit?

'Postmodernism' is, of course, a notoriously problematic term. As students of religion have become involved in debates about postmodernism, confusion has proliferated. For some postmodernism suggests the death of God and disappearance of religion, for others, the return of traditional faith, and for still others, the possibility of recasting religious ideas. I will not try to explain what postmodernism is, for it is not one thing. Indeed, from a postmodern perspective nothing is simply itself and no thing is one thing. Rather, I will contrast two postmodernisms in such a way that their differences become clear. I will approach this task by way of painting. More precisely, I will consider three examples of the painter/critic relationship: Barnett Newman and Clement Greenberg, Andy Warhol and Jean

Baudrillard and, finally, Anselm Kiefer and Maurice Blanchot and Jacques
Derrida. The contrasting aesthetic positions established by these painters
and critics suggest alternative theological and religious perspectives. I am
convinced that recent developments in the visual arts create new possibilities for the religious imagination.

Postmodernism, which is not simply an additional epoch or era following
modernism, is inseparably bound to the modern. The term 'modernism' is
as complex and as contradictory as postmodernism. The meaning of
modernism changes from context to context and field to field. For example,
while modern philosophy is generally thought to have started with
Descartes' work in the middle of the seventeenth century, the beginning of
modern theology is usually dated from Schleiermacher's *Speeches on
Religion* in 1799. In the visual arts, modernism emerged during the closing
decades of the nineteenth and opening decades of the twentieth centuries.
Though an extraordinarily diffuse movement, different versions of
modernism share a will-to-purity and will-to-immediacy that implicitly or
explicitly presupposes a philosophy or theology in which being is identified
with presence. The critic who raises the artistic methods of modernism to
the level of self-consciousness is Clement Greenberg. In a highly influential
essay entitled 'Modernist Painting', Greenberg writes:

> I identify Modernism with the intensification, almost the exacerbation,
> of this self-critical tendency that began with the philosopher Kant.
> Because he was the first to criticize the means itself of criticism, I
> conceive of Kant as the first real Modernist. The essence of Modernism
> lies, as I see it, in the use of the characteristic methods of a discipline to
> criticize the discipline itself – not in order to subvert it, but to entrench it
> more firmly in its area of competence.[1]

So understood, modernism is, as Habermas continues to insist, an extension of the Enlightenment project. To be enlightened is not only to be
critical but, more importantly, to be self-critical. 'The task of self-
criticism', Greenberg continues,

> became to eliminate from the effects of each art any and every effect
> that might conceivably be borrowed from or by the medium of any other
> art. Thereby each art would be rendered 'pure', and in its 'purity' find
> the guarantee of its standards of quality as well as of its independence.
> 'Purity' meant self-definition, and the enterprise of self-definition, and
> the enterprise of self-criticism in the arts became one of self-definition
> with a vengeance.[2]

Another term for the purity established by self-criticism is autonomy.
An art form is pure when it is determined by nothing other than itself and
thus is perfectly self-reflexive.[3] From Greenberg's point of view, modern
art achieves aesthetic autonomy through a process of abstraction in which

there is a gradual removal of everything that is regarded as inessential in a particular medium. In painting, the result of such abstraction is pure formalism in which all ornamentation and representation disappear. In semiotic terms, ornamentation and representation are signifiers that obscure pure form, which is, in effect, the transcendental signified. In other words, authentic art erases the signifier in order to allow the signified to appear transparently.

The will-to-purity that characterizes Greenberg's aesthetic theory assumes a variety of forms in twentieth-century painting. For many artists, the search for aesthetic purity is actually a spiritual quest. Nowhere is the coincidence of painterly and spiritual concerns more evident than in the work of Barnett Newman. Newman's signature canvases are monochromes that are interrupted by one or more vertical lines or 'zips'. His titles underscore his spiritual preoccupations: *Onement, Dionysus, Concord, Abraham, Eve, The Stations of the Cross, L'Errance, Moment, Not There – Here, Now, Be, Vir Heroicus Sublimis*. The last five titles suggest an intersection of themes that recurs throughout Newman's corpus: Moment, Here, Now, Being and the Sublime. In what might be regarded as his personal manifesto, 'The Sublime Is Now', Newman maintains that 'man's natural desire in the arts [is] to express his relation to the Absolute'.[4] The goal of Newman's artistic endeavour is to provide the occasion for the experience of the sublime. To experience the sublime is to enjoy the fullness of Being Here and Now – in the Moment. This moment is the Eternal Now, which, paradoxically, is simultaneously immanent and transcendent. It can be reached only through a process of abstraction in which the removal of figuration or representation creates the space for presentation of the unfigurable or unrepresentable. The (impossible) representation of the unrepresentable is sublime.

As is well known, Kant distinguishes the mathematical from the dynamic sublime. In both of its forms, the sublime is excessive; it marks the boundary between reason's demand for totality and the imagination's inability to deliver it. Anticipating the romantic preoccupation with nature, Kant argues that the dynamic sublime is encountered in the overwhelming power of nature. The dynamic sublime exceeds all forms. 'In what we are accustomed to call sublime in nature', Kant argues,

> there is such an absence of anything leading to particular objective principles and forms of nature corresponding to them that it is rather in its chaos or its wildest and most irregular desolation, provided size and might are perceived, that nature chiefly excites in us the ideas of the sublime.[5]

Newman translates the Kantian dynamic sublime from nature to culture by reinscribing the power of formlessness in the purely formal experience of paint as such. Consider, for example, *Vir Heroicus Sublimis*. This immense

Figure 1.1 Barnett Newman, *Vir Heroicus Sublimis*, 1950–1, Museum of Modern Art, New York.

canvas[6] is painted a brilliant red, with five vertical stripes ranging in colour from cream and white to shades of pink and crimson. Newman intended his paintings to be viewed at close range. When one stares at *Vir Heroicus Sublimis* closely, the painting creates an halluncinatory effect in which it seems to engulf the viewer. The sense of direct participation in the experience of redness is deepened by the absence of any frame. Like many other modern painters, Newman leaves his canvases unframed. It is as though he wants to remove the frame to allow viewer and painting to become one. The perfect union of subject and object is the sublime experience of Onement. When Newman 'seeks sublimity in the here and now', Lyotard explains,

> he breaks with the eloquence of romantic art but does not reject its fundamental task, that bearing pictorial or otherwise expressive witness to the inexpressible. The inexpressible does not reside in an over there, in another world, or another time, but in this: in that something happens. In the determination of pictorial art, the indeterminate, the 'it happens' is the paint, the picture. The paint, the picture as occurrence or event, is not expressible, and it is to this that it has to witness.[7]

In the event of painting, the will-to-purity becomes the will-to-immediacy.

This immediacy is the aesthetic version of the unitive experience that is the telos of negative theology. For Newman, the negation entailed in painting is, of course, abstraction. As I have suggested, abstraction removes every vestige of form and figuration in order to reach the formlessness of the unfigurable or unrepresentable. While the presence of figure is the absence of oneness, the absence of figure is the presence of oneness. Newman's use of abstraction as a method of negation repeats one of the most important strategies employed by early Greek philosophers in their search for the original One from which all emerges and to which everything longs to return. Developing insights advanced in Plato's *Parmenides*, Speusippus proposes a novel way of negation, which he labels *aphairesis* or abstraction. Aphairesis is intended to be an alternative to the well-established *apophasis*. Apophasis, the form of negation used in traditional negative theology, negates by stating an opposite. Complete identification would require an infinite series of negations. Aphairesis, by constrast, negates by abstracting or subtracting particular qualities from an entity. The penultimate aim of aphairesis is the essence of the entity under consideration; its ultimate aim is the essential One that underlies the many that comprise the phenomenal world. By moving from the world of appearance to the realm of essence, aphairesis functions like a 'ritual purification'[8] that allows the initiates to draw near the purity of the origin.

When Newman's theoaesthetic project is placed in this context, it becomes clear that his work is a painterly version of one type of negative theology. As Harold Rosenberg points out, Newman attempts to 'transform the canvas into the signified thing'.[9] The pure signified, from which all signifiers have been removed, is nothing less than the Absolute. Newman conceives this Absolute in ontotheological terms that are characteristic of western philosophy and theology. The Absolute is the One in which Being is presence that is fully realized in the present.

Newman's paintings not only suggest important parallels with negative theology but, if read somewhat differently, bear unexpected similarities to dialectical or neo-orthodox theology.[10] During the first half of this century, Karl Barth and his followers developed an influential reformulation of Calvinist theology. Calvinism is, of course, rigorously iconoclastic; the transcendent God cannot be represented in images. In Barth's theology, Calvin's God reappears as the 'Wholly Other' who completely transcends nature and culture. In Barth's early and more important work,[11] the only way to relate to God is negatively, i.e. by denying the religious validity of all natural and cultural forms. Barth's 'No', however, harbours a 'Yes'. The negation of nature and culture is at the same time the affirmation of the God who is Other. Barth's strategy of negation, which, it is important to note, he formulates at the precise moment non-objective painting appears, mirrors Newman's method of abstraction. For Barth and Newman, the negation of representation is the affirmation of the unrepresentable. There is, of course, an important difference between Barth's theology and Newman's art. For Barth, the will-to-purity does not involve a will-to-immediacy. Complete union with the transcendent One is never possible and is forever delayed.

Abstract art and dialectical theology suffer a similar fate. The movement of negation or abstraction leads to a separation or even opposition between the aesthetic and the religious on the one hand, and, on the other, society, culture and history. Abstraction gradually becomes empty formalism. The aesthetic autonomy definitive of modernism can be understood as a variation of the 'other-worldliness' characteristic of dialectical theology. When carried to completion, non-objective art and dialectical theology undergo a radical reversal; the former prepares the way for Pop art and the latter leads to the death of God. Though not immediately apparent, Pop art is the aesthetic embodiment of the death of God, and the death of God is the theological ground of Pop art.

In the wake of Abstract Expressionism, figuration returns with a vengeance . . . but also with a difference. As we have seen in our consideration of Newman's work, for many twentieth-century painters, representation is a problem to be overcome rather than an ideal to be realized. The bifurcation of signifier and signified creates a tear that must be mended, a fault that must be covered, a wound that must be healed. Abstract painters attempt to attain truth in painting by erasing signifiers in order to expose the pure signified. Pop art reverses this process. In Pop, the transcendental signified disappears and all that remains is an infinite play of signifiers. Images image nothing – nothing but other images. When representation returns in the work of Rauschenberg and Johns it differs from classical mimesis. Instead of depicting nature or independent objects, Rauschenberg and Johns paint *signs* that are quite literally signs. Consider, for example, Johns' famous targets and flags. The object represented is a thing that is a sign; the painting, in other words, is the sign of a sign. Art does not represent an independent reality but enacts a play of signs in which nothing (or everything) is in-sign-ificant.

What Rauschenberg and Johns begin, Warhol completes. From one point of view, Pop art breaks with modernism by destroying the autonomy of the aesthetic object. Warhol creates the space for the return of what modernism represses: image, representation, popular/low culture, kitsch and every other imaginable 'impurity'. For Warhol, the very notion of originality is suspect. Having started his career as a commercial artist, he borrows or steals images from the consumer culture that surrounds him. As if taking Walter Benjamin's 'The Work of Art in an Age of Mechanical Reproduction' as his programmatic guide, Warhol sets up what he calls 'The Factory' in which artistic reproduction simulates industrial production. The fabricated work of art does not merely mimic the mass-produced object but actually becomes a commercial product whose worth is its exchange value. In Warhol's art, Johns' targets multiply in a flurry of silk-screened photographs, soup cans and Brillo boxes. Pop art is utterly superficial – it is all surface and no depth. Shades of difference give way to sameness without shadow. Light, not dark; light, not heavy. Nonetheless, there is a certain spirituality in Warhol's superficiality. The surface of his art displays the shadowlessness of spirit. Spirit is shadowless when every trace of altarity has been elided.

To discern the spirit playing on the surface of the work of art, it is helpful to return to Kant's analysis of the sublime. While Newman's theoaesthetic quest can be interpreted in terms of Kant's dynamic sublime, Warhol's superficial art can be understood as an extension of Kant's mathematical sublime. In contrast to the dynamic sublime, which involves the experience of pure form that is finally formless, the mathematical sublime arises from the infinite proliferation of forms. Seeking to satisfy reason's desire for 'absolute totality', the mind is 'pushed to the point at which our faculty of imagination breaks down in presenting the concept of a magnitude, and proves unequal to the task'. In this moment of failure, one experiences a feeling of 'the inadequacy of his imagination for presenting the idea of a whole within which the imagination attains its maximum, and, in its fruitless efforts to extend this limit, recoils upon itself, but in so doing succumbs to an emotional delight'.[12] While Newman's sublime arises from the elimination of figure, Warhol's sublime presupposes the endless repetition of figure. So understood, Warhol's excessive images displace Newman's transcendent sublime with a radically immanent sublime.

Figure 1.2 Andy Warhol, *Campbell's Soup*, 1965, Museum of Modern Art, New York.

The sublimity of immanence becomes possible with the death of God. It is no accident that Pop art and the death of God theology emerge at the same historical moment. From one point of view, the death of God abolishes the otherness that implies a difference between appearance and reality. As in the Christian drama of redemption, death leads to rebirth, so in the death of God theology, the disappearance of the transcendent Other leads to the realization of the Parousia.[13] When negation is doubled, it yields affirmation. By negating transcendence, the death of God leads to the total presence of Being here and now. In semiotic terms, the death of God is the abrogation of the transcendental signified. In the absence of the signified, only signifiers remain. Pointing to nothing beyond themselves, these freely floating signifiers stage a play in which transcendence gives way to an immanence that is no longer merely apparent but now is real. In the wake of the death of God, the reality of the sign is all we can experience or know.

Though not customarily understood in terms of Warhol's work, many analysts associate postmodernism with the semiology inherent in Pop art. Through a misunderstanding and misappropriation of Derrida's claim that 'there is nothing outside the text', critics interpret postmodernism as a pantextualism that is, in the final analysis, indistinguishable from the absolute idealism implicit in high modernism. The specularity of idealism reappears in what Guy Debord labels 'a society of spectacle' where appearance and reality become one. Jean Baudrillard extends the analyses of Debord and other Situationists to the consumer culture of late capitalism. In post-industrial society, the token, as well as the object of exchange, is information and image rather than the thing itself.[14] The thing itself is absorbed in the sign system. As electronic media invade every corner of consciousness and activity, 'reality' becomes image. Baudrillard cites his version of verses from Ecclesiastes in the epigraph to his influential essay, 'The Precession of Simulacra':

> The simulacrum is never that which conceals the truth – it is the truth which conceals that there is none.
>
> The simulacrum is true.

The simulacrum is not secondary to a more primordial or original reality that is antecedent to, and independent of, the structure of signification. To the contrary, 'reality' is always already coded; the sign is always the sign of a sign.

'Abstraction today', Baudrillard writes,

> is no longer that of the map, the double, the mirror or the concept. Simulation is no longer that of a territory, a referential being or substance. It is the generation by models of a real without origin or reality: a hyper-real. The territory no longer precedes the map, nor survives it. Henceforth, it is the map that precedes the territory – PRECESSION

OF SIMULACRA – it is the map that engenders the territory, and if we were to revive the fable today, it would be the territory whose shreds are slowly rotting across the map. It is the real, and not the map, whose vestiges subsist here and there, in the deserts that are no longer those of the Empire, but our own. *The desert of the real itself.*[15]

In a certain sense, Baudrillard discovers what might be called 'God' in the desert of the real itself. The God of Baudrillard's desert is the God who dies only to be reborn in images as the image itself.

'The iconolaters', Baudrillard argues,

> were the most modern and adventurous minds, since underneath the idea of the apparition of God in the mirror of images, they already enacted his death and his disappearance in the epiphany of his representations (which they perhaps knew no longer represented anything, and that they were purely a game, but that this was precisely the greatest game – knowing that it is dangerous to unmask images, since they dissimulate the fact that there is nothing behind them). . . . All of western faith and good faith was engaged in this wager on representation: that a sign could refer to the depth of meaning, that a sign could *exchange* for meaning and that something could guarantee this exchange – God, of course. But what if God himself can be simulated, that is to say, reduced to signs that attest to his existence? Then the whole system becomes weightless, it is no longer anything but a gigantic simulacrum – not unreal, but a simulacrum, never again exchanging for what is real, but exchanging in itself, in an uninterrupted circuit without reference or circumference.[16]

This weightlessness is the unbearable lightness of *Being*. Every form of postmodernism that presupposes an immanence of the sign like that embodied in Pop art and its architectural equivalent[17] is actually an extension of modernism. The sign that is the sign of a sign is self-referential and thus self-reflexive. Though incorporating the domain of representation, the product of Pop art is every bit as autonomous as the work of abstract art. While inverting the abstractions of modernism, Pop art fails to subvert the longing for presence that motivates the will-to-immediacy. Pop art's reversal of abstraction is the realization of Baudelaire's classical definition of modernity. In his prescient essay, 'The Painter and Modern Life', written in 1863, Baudelaire explains: 'By "modernity" I mean the ephemeral, the fugitive, the contingent, the half of art whose other half is the eternal and the immutable.'[18] For Warhol, presence can be fully realized in the present only if there is nothing other – nothing beyond appearance. Contrary to expectation, the opposite paths of Warhol and Newman lead to the same goal: the immediacy of experience in which Being is totally realized in the Moment.

There is, however, a dark side to this experience of at-onement. As if to parody Newman's insistence that 'the sublime is now', Warhol proclaims:

'Money is the MOMENT to me.' Elsewhere he explains that 'Pop art is liking things.'[19] The things that Warhol likes are commodities. When he paints a series of dollar bills, Warhol literalizes the commodification of the work of art. Art is money. Warhol confesses: 'I don't understand anything except GREEN BILLS.'[20] In Warhol's vision, the world has become the realized 'Utopia' of consumer capitalism that parodies the idealistic Utopias imagined by avant-garde artists. In the absence of anything other, he calls upon us to embrace what IS. In the perpetual present of ever-proliferating images, everything constantly changes and yet everything remains the same. Without altarity, experience becomes vacuous, our landscape a desert.

The desert in which Warhol and Baudrillard err is none other than the desert of Las Vegas – the very same Las Vegas that provides the images and material for the text that inaugurates postmodern architecture: Robert Venturi's and Denise Scott Brown's *Learning from Las Vegas*. In this desert there are no shadows, only lights, bright lights. Baudrillard concludes his provocative book, *America*, with the following words:

> Gambling itself is a desert form, inhuman, uncultured, initiatory, a challenge to the natural economy of value, a crazed activity on the fringes of exchange. . . . Neither the desert nor gambling are open areas; their spaces are finite and concentric, increasing in intensity toward the interior, toward a central point, be it the spirit of gambling or the heart of the desert – a privileged, immemorial space, where things lose their shadow, where money loses its value, and where the extreme rarity of traces of what signals to us there leads men to seek the instantaneity of wealth.[21]

Is the wager of Warhol and Baudrillard the only remaining possibility? Can we imagine a different wager – a wager that would open us to an 'immemorial space' where things do not lose the shadows that mark shades of difference? Might one who approaches this immemorial space come from a different time, another past? 'Come from the desert as one comes from beyond memory?' Beyond, *au-delà*, memory . . . the immemorial . . . *le pas au-delà* that leads to the 'outside of time in time'.[22] Were we to make such a wager, we would not discover 'the instantaneity of wealth'; we would be left not richer but poorer, infinitely poorer. Destitute. Devastated. In the midst of this desert lurks a different postmodernism.

Anselm Kiefer is obsessed with the desert. His desert is not, however, the shadowless desert of bright lights; it is a dark, shadowy landscape in which the earth is burnt, even scorched. The canvas does not merely represent but actually embodies the desert. Kiefer's obscure canvases are covered with lead, dirt, straw, sand and ashes. Ashes . . . always ashes. Traces of a disaster that can never be wiped away. Ashes that appear and reappear in the poetry of Paul Celan, whose *Todensfuge*, written in a concentration camp in 1945 (the year of Kiefer's birth), inspires some of Kiefer's most moving paintings.

Ash.
Ash. Ash.
Night.
Night-and-night.[23]

The disaster whose immemorial trace is ash opens a wound that can never heal.

All the names, all the
names burnt up
with the rest. So much
ash to bless.[24]

Blessure . . . bless-ure . . . b-less-ure . . . b-less-ur-e. . . .

The infernal desert traced on Kiefer's canvases is, at one level, the European wasteland created by world war. The sites are unmistakable: March Heath, Nuremberg, The Bunker. Sometimes criticized, sometimes praised for reviving previously repressed memories of Germany's militaristic past, Kiefer is engaged in an endless interrogation of the devastation his country has unleashed. In *The Ways of Worldly Wisdom*, he suggests that this tragedy is a product of Germany's intellectual and cultural heritage. It would be a mistake, however, to limit Kiefer's concerns to cultural developments and historical events. In an effort to grasp what seems to be incomprehensible, Kiefer repeatedly returns to ancient myth and religion: Babylonian and Nordic mythology, as well as Christian and Jewish theology.

In a particularly impressive series of sixteen paintings entitled *Departure from Egypt*, executed between 1984 and 1987, Kiefer presents unusually powerful images of the desert. Appropriating the postmodern methods of layering images, he paints on photographs. To the paint and photographs he adds layers of dripping lead.[25] The result of this interplay of images is very different from a postmodern pastiche. The work of art is neither transparent nor superficial; though not exactly deep, it is strangely obscure. Rather than clean and pure, it is dirty, almost contaminated; rather than bright and shadowless, it is dark, almost a world of shades; rather than self-referential and self-reflexive, framed or almost unframed. However, in eleven of the sixteen paintings in *Departure from Egypt*, the trace of a frame is painted on the canvas itself. Furthermore, in several of the works, the title, which is a kind of frame, is inscribed within the painting. Instead of removing or erasing the frame, Kiefer seems to draw attention to it. Why? A question to be set aside, in the margin, near the frame. But it will return.

In his exploration of the desert, it is Aaron and not Moses who fascinates

Figure 1.3 Anselm Kiefer, *Seraphim*, 1983–4, Guggenheim Museum, New York.

Kiefer. Aaron, of course, is, among other things, the idolater whose infidelity causes Moses to shatter the tablets that bear the original writing of God. In worshipping the golden calf, Aaron worships an image. Idolatry – the love of image that mistakes it for the real or absolute – is always the temptation of the painter. It is this temptation to which modernism and certain forms of so-called postmodernism succumb. Modernism and modernist postmodernism are not simply secular but involve a dialectical reversal through which the secular becomes sacred. In the realm of aesthetics, art becomes spiritual. From the Romantics, through Nietzsche, down to Kiefer's teacher, Joseph Beuys, the artist is regarded as a priest or shaman who brings salvation. In paintings like *Icarus – March Sand*, *Wayland's Song*, *Tree with Palette*, *Palette with Wings*, *To the Unknown Painter* and many others, Kiefer explores the soteriological role of art. His canvases reflect considerably less certainty about the healing power of art than is evident in the work of many of his precursors. Kiefer's doubts are most obvious in his troubling *Iconoclastic Controversy*.[26]

Idolatry or, in Baudrillard's terms, iconolatry is not merely an aesthetic or religious issue; it is a serious political problem. With National Socialism's aestheticization of politics and politicization of aesthetics, the power of the image became demonically effective. The multiple layers of Kiefer's work suggest the multiple layers of the interrelated problems of iconolatry and iconoclasm. Kiefer again employs the technique of painting over a photograph. In this case, superimposed photos represent the wooden floor of his earlier atelier and a brick wall in his current studio.[27] Between the wooden floor and the brick wall, there is a stretch of sand, in the midst of which there is a hollow whose bottom is fissured by intersecting cracks. Around this pit, three tanks armed with large guns face each other. Over these images Kiefer paints a huge palette with lines emanating from, or returning to, the central hole. On the surface of the palette, flames from battle, sacrifices, funerals, ovens or something else erupt. In the lower right-hand corner of the painting, the title: *Bilder-Streit*. This scene is, indeed, a desert and the desert is the scene of devastation . . . the scene of a catastrophe . . . a holocaust . . . a disaster.

The political message of *Iconoclastic Controversy* is clear: when the relative is absolutized, when criticism gives way to adoration, the consequences are disastrous. Moreover, the intersection of tank and palette implies a problematic complicity between politics and art. When art loses its critical edge, it becomes not merely advertising but propaganda for systems of power that are repressive. The complexity of Kiefer's work cannot, however, be reduced to such a direct message. Something else, something other, is at stake in this unsettling painting.

Kiefer, like Warhol, rejects abstraction. But unlike Warhol, he does not absolutize the image as such. *Iconoclastic Controversy* is itself iconoclastic. The canvas is tattered, torn, wounded. Like Moses confronting the golden calf, Kiefer shatters images. The tear of the canvas tears asunder the aesthetic autonomy of the art object. Heterology, not autonomy, is Kiefer's concern. He neither eliminates nor sacralizes figure; rather, he uses figure to figure the unfigurable. In other words, Kiefer stages the *failure* of representation in and through the strife of images. The disaster his works depict implies another disaster, a more ancient disaster.

'The disaster', Blanchot writes,

> ruins everything, all the while leaving everything intact. It does not touch anyone in particular; 'I' am not threatened by it, but spared, left aside. It is in this way that I am threatened; it is in this way that the disaster threatens in me that which is exterior to me – an other than I who passively become other. There is no reaching the disaster. Out of reach is he whom it threatens, whether from afar or close up, it is impossible to say: the infiniteness of the threat has in some way broken every limit. We are on the edge of disaster without being able to situate it in the future: it is rather always already past, and yet we are on the edge or under its threat, all formuations that would imply the future – that which is yet to come – if the disaster were not that which does not come, that which has put a stop to every arrival.[28]

On the edge . . . the edge of the disaster or under its threat.

Return to *Bilder-Streit*. The centre of the painting, which is also the centre of the palette, is a hole created by faults in the earth. Above the hole a flame flickers that bears an uncanny resemblance to a memorial flame. This flame, which seems to recall the 'memory of the immemorable',[29] is, perhaps, a memorial to the immemorial. In this case, the immemorial is not an eternal presence or present but is the 'outside of time in time' that forever displaces presence and interrupts the present. Never present without being absent, this 'outside' that is 'inside' is an exteriority that cannot be re-presented. It draws near – but no more – at the limit, margin, edge of experience.

'We are on the edge of disaster . . .'. The edge *of* disaster 'is' the edge *as* disaster. The edge is, of course, the frame. The frame of *Iclonoclastic Controversy* is an edge that is outside/inside the image as *Bilder-Streit*. The site of the strife, struggle, conflict, battle is the frame. But what is a frame? Does a frame exist? What does a frame do or not do? How do frames work? 'Where', Derrida asks, 'does the frame take place. Does it take place. Where does it begin. Where does it end. What is its internal limit. Its external limit. And its surface between the two limits.'[30]

The frame as such does not exist; nor is it non-existent. Its site, which is really a non-site, is the neither/nor of the between . . . *l'entre-deux*. The frame works by allowing appearances to appear, representations to be represented, and images to be imagined. As the condition of the possibility of presentation, the frame is forever *hors d'oeuvre*, perpetually *désoeuvrement*. It is unpresentable, unimaginable . . . not proper but indecent –

unpresentable. Its scene is an ob-scene that is, in a certain sense, sublime. In this case, the sublime is neither here nor now but always withdraws under the limen [*sublimis*: *sub* + *limen*].

Andrew Benjamin correctly points out that 'the inscription of the problem of nonpresence within the frame indicates that the question at hand concerns how the presence of that nonpresence is to be understood'.[31] Alternative responses to the question of how the presence or, more precisely, the non-absent absence, of non-presence is to be understood distinguish modernists, modernist postmodernists and postmodernists, *sensu strictissimo*. In *The Postmodern Condition*, Lyotard writes:

> I shall call modern the art that devotes its 'little technical expertise', as Diderot used to say, to present the fact that the unpresentable exists. To make visible that there is something that can be conceived and that can neither be seen nor made visible: this is what is at stake in modern painting. . . . The postmodern [by contrast] would be that which, in the modern, puts forward the unpresentable in presentation itself; that which denies itself the solace of good forms, the consensus of a taste that would make it possible to share the collective nostalgia for the unattainable; that which searches for new presentations, not in order to enjoy them but in order to impart a stronger sense of the unpresentable.[32]

The sense of the unpresentable that haunts all presence and every presentation is sublime. The postmodern sublime, however, is not an extension of either Kant's dynamic or mathematical sublime. It results from neither the erasure nor the multiplication of form, image and representation. The sublime that is neither the fullness of the signified nor the plenitude of signifiers lies – always lies – between, in the differential strife of images. This strife is, in Jean-Luc Nancy's terms,

> an infinitely subtle, infinitely complex operation, and, at the same time, it is the most simple movement, the strict strife of the line against itself in the motion of its tracing: two borders in one, union 'itself', it is no less necessary for all figure. Every painter, every writer, every dancer has knowledge of it. It is presentation itself, but it is no more presentation than an operation of a (re)presentation producing or exhibiting a (re)presented. It is presentation *itself* to the point where it is no longer able to say 'itself', it is the instantaneous sharing/parting [*le partage*] of the limit, by the limit, between figure and illumination, one against the other, one on the other, one toward the other, coupled and detached by the same movement, the same incision, the same strife.[33]

This incision, this strife is the wound that cannot be healed, the tear that cannot be mended, the tear that cannot be wiped away. This limen, I believe, creates the impossible possibility of reframing the sacred in our postmodern worlds. In the fissures of Kiefer's canvases, at the edge of

Blanchot's disaster, along the margin of Derrida's *différance*, opens a space – an immemorial space – for religious reflection. It is to this deserted space that we are called by an Other we can never name.

Our course has been circuitous: from religion, to art, to . . . With Blanchot, we finally must ask:

> But where has art led us? To a time before the world, before the beginning. It has cast us out of the power to begin and to end; it has turned us toward the outside where there is no intimacy, no place to rest. It has led us into the infinite migration of error.[34]

Errance . . . Erring in the desert . . . always the desert . . . the other desert. The infinite migration of error is the non-place of exile where we are forever destined to dwell.

> *The unsayable settles us in those desert regions that are the home of dead languages. Here, every grain of sand stifled by the mute word offers the dreary spectacle of a root of eternity ground to dust before it could sprout. In the old days, the ocean would have cradled it. Does the void torment the universe, and the universe in turn vex the void? Roots buried in sand keep longing for their trees. The deepest weep for their fruit. They are reborn of their tears.*[35]

Reborn of tears . . . of tears.

NOTES

1 Clement Greenberg, 'Modernist Painting', in Gregory Battcock (ed.), *The New Art: A Critical Anthology*, New York, Dutton, p. 101.
2 ibid., vol. 1, p. 102.
3 For a highly influential reformulation of Greenberg's position, see Michael Fried, *Absorption and Theatricality: Painting and Beholder in the Age of Diderot*, Chicago, University of Chicago Press, 1980.
4 Barnett Newman, 'The Sublime Is Now', in David Shapiro and Cecile Shapiro (eds), *Abstract Expressionism: A Critical Record*, Cambridge, Cambridge University Press, 1990, p. 325.
5 Immanuel Kant, *The Critique of Judgement*, trans. James Meredith, New York, Oxford University Press, 1973, p. 40.
6 It measures $95\frac{3}{8}$in × $313\frac{1}{4}$in.
7 Jean-François Lyotard, 'The Sublime and the Avant-Garde', in Andrew Benjamin (ed.), *The Lyotard Reader*, Oxford, Blackwell, 1989, p. 199. Lyotard interprets Newman's paintings through Heidegger's notion of *Ereignis*. At some points Lyotard associates the sublime with modernism and at other points with postmodernism. It is not always clear whether he intends the modern and postmodern sublimes to differ significantly. As will become apparent in what follows, I insist on an important difference between the effort to represent the unrepresentable in modernism and in postmodernism.
8 Raoul Mortly, *Word to Silence: The Rise and Fall of the Logos*, vol. II, Bonn,

Hanstein, 1986, p. 42. Mortley's study presents a very helpful analysis of different types of negative theology.

9 Harold Rosenberg, *Barnett Newman*, New York, Abrams, 1985, p. 75.

10 It is important to point out that Newman was interested in and influenced by the Kabbala. Some of his paintings directly invoke Kabbalistic themes. Newman's relation to the Jewish tradition is a complex topic that deserves more extensive consideration than I can give it here.

11 See especially Karl Barth's epoch-making book, *The Epistle to the Romans*, trans. Edwyn Hoskyns, New York, Oxford University Press, 1968.

12 Kant, op. cit., pp. 90, 100.

13 The theologian in whose work this is most evident is Thomas J.J. Altizer. See, for example, *The Self-Embodiment of God*, New York, Harper & Row, 1977; *Total Presence: The Language of Jesus and the Language of Today*, New York, Seabury, 1980; and *History as Apocalypse*, New York, State University of New York Press, 1985.

14 For an elaboration of the aesthetic implications of post-industrial capitalism, see, *inter alia*, Frederick Jameson, 'Postmodernism and Consumer Society', in Hal Foster (ed.), *The Anti-Aesthetic: Essays on Postmodern Culture*, Port Townsend, Bay Press, 1983, pp. 111–25.

15 Jean Baudrillard, *Simulations*, trans. Paul Foss, Paul Patton and Philip Beitchman, New York, Semiotext(e), 1983, p. 2.

16 ibid., pp. 9–10.

17 Postmodern architecture as it is usually understood is the architectural equivalent of Pop art. Venturi and Brown repeatedly draw parallels between their work and Pop art. The return of ornamentation in modernist postmodern architecture repeats Pop art's use of figure.

18 Charles Baudelaire, *The Painter and Modern Life and Other Essays*, trans. Jonathan Mayne, New York, Da Capo Press, 1964, p. 13.

19 Andy Warhol, *The Philosophy of Andy Warhol*, New York, Harcourt Brace Jovanovich, 1975, p. 146.

20 ibid., p. 129.

21 Jean Baudrillard, *America*, trans. Chris Turner, New York and London, Verso, 1988, p. 128.

22 Maurice Blanchot, *Le Pas au-delà*, Paris, Gallimard, 1973, p. 8.

23 Quoted by Jacques Derrida, 'Shibboleth', in Geoffrey Hartman and Sanford Budick (eds), *Midrash and Literature*, New Haven, Yale University Press, 1986, p. 336.

24 ibid., p. 334.

25 Lead plays an important role in medieval alchemical practices. The most inert element, it is often the material alchemists attempt to turn into gold. Kiefer is fascinated by alchemy and sometimes suggests parallels between alchemical practice and painting. It is also important to note that lead is associated with Saturn, the god who presides over the Saturnalia and also represents Cronus and Baal.

26 Kiefer paints two versions of *Iconoclastic Controversy* in 1976–7. For reproductions of these works, see Mark Rosenthal, *Anselm Kiefer*, Philadelphia, Philadelphia Museum of Art, 1987, pp. 77, 79.

27 The straw and bricks in Kiefer's paintings carry a variety of connotations. During their captivity in Egypt, the Israelites were forced to gather straw for their captors to use in making bricks. The association of bricks with ovens is too obvious to require comment.

28 Maurice Blanchot, *The Writing of the Disaster*, trans. Ann Smock, Lincoln,

University of Nebraska Press, 1986, p. 1.
29 ibid., p. 6.
30 Jacques Derrida, *The Truth in Painting*, trans. Geoff Bennington and Ian McLeod, Chicago, University of Chicago Press, 1987, p. 63. Derrida raises these questions in the context of his analysis of Kant's Third Critique. *The Critique of Judgement*, Derrida argues, functions as something like a frame between the First and the Second Critiques. In the course of his consideration of 'The Parergon', Derrida develops his most complete account of the sublime.
31 Andrew Benjamin, 'Anselm Kiefer's *Iconoclastic Controversy*', in Christopher Norris and Andrew Benjamin, *What Is Deconstruction?*, New York, Academy Editions/St Martin's Press, 1988, pp. 48–56. Benjamin is, to my knowledge, the only other critic who has noted the similarities between Kiefer's work and poststructuralist criticism.
32 Jean-François Lyotard, *The Postmodern Condition: A Report on Knowledge*, trans. Geoff Bennington and Brian Massumi, Minneapolis, University of Minnesota Press, 1984, pp. 78, 81. Lyotard's comment is particularly helpful, for it indicates the way in which the postmodern inhabits the modern instead of constituting an era following the modern.
33 Jean-Luc Nancy, 'L'Offrande sublime', *Du Sublime*, Paris, Berlin, 1988, p. 59.
34 Maurice Blanchot, *The Space of Literature*, trans. Ann Smock, Lincoln, University of Nebraska Press, 1982, p. 244.
35 Edmond Jabès, *El, or the Last Book*, vol. VII, *The Book of Questions*, trans. Rosmarie Waldrop, Middletown, Wesleyan University Press, 1984, p. 77.

Chapter 2

Problematizing the secular: the post-postmodern agenda

John Milbank

I

What is the crucial thought that has inspired the agenda of this book? I suspect that it is somewhat as follows: 'modernity' has been characterized by the critique of religion, in the name of liberating autonomous, purely human realities, goals and desires. If we are now in a phase of 'postmodern' thought and experience, then must not our attitude to the validity of this critique have somewhat shifted? Perhaps the arena of 'purely human' judgement is as great an illusion as the transcendent court of appeal which it replaced; perhaps the sacred was never as secular as it appeared to be; perhaps the secular never really disappeared, never really can disappear . . .? But along with this crucial speculation goes a more impressionistic observation: the practitioners of postmodern theorization appear to incorporate quasi-religious thematics into their texts. There then arises out of both the speculation and the observation the following question: does not postmodern thought somehow redefine the critical enterprise so as to make it no longer one conducted on behalf of the 'human', in opposition to the illusory intrusions of the sacred?

However, this question already exposes to view the great tension that must exist between, on the one hand, a *hyper*-critical attitude, which fulfils modernity's project beyond its own humanist limitations, and, on the other hand, misty intimations about a 'return of the sacred'. For on one construal of the postmodern outlook, it does not at all abandon or qualify the enterprise of critique of religion, but, on the contrary, is constituted by the will to pursue this critique to the very limit. Thus Lyotard, for example, may talk about 'lessons in paganism', but he also declares that the most important lesson it teaches us is 'the need to be godless in things political'.[1] The crucial point here is that the critique of humanism, and of the deriving of a universal human project from the postulate of human autonomy, depends since Nietzsche on the insight that the notion of the self as subject is derivative from the notion of God as substance, such that the coherence of the self collapses when it is no longer referred to stable transcendent goals, and the redemptively unifying reclamations of divine grace. The death of humanity is involved with the death of God, but the import of the latter, as Nietzsche suggested, has but slowly filtered through. Postmodernism, on this account, is but evidence of modernity's long delay, its persistent self-deception.

Yet if this is the case, how then do we explain the presence of quasi-religious thematics in postmodernist texts, or at least elements of greater respect for religious phenomena? The answer is, I think, twofold. First of all, one must pay attention to a difference in the 'modes of suspicion' exercised by modern and postmodern thought respectively. Characteristically, modern thought seeks to reduce the burden of what it identified as 'irrational' phenomena by showing that they are traceable to an error, a failure of reason, or else that they secretly subserve rational purposes: for example, Freud traced pathological mental phenomena to failures of self-recognition, but also showed how irrational manifestations help us to cope with the subjectively intolerable. Yet Nietzsche and his contemporary French followers do not, on the whole, seek to show that the apparently strange and arbitrary is not purely arbitrary. On the contrary, they seek to demonstrate almost the reverse: that apparently rational, common-sense assumptions about self-identity, motivation and moral values themselves disguise historically instituted mythological constructs. So, for example, the whole complex of attitudes to do with free will and guilt is but a rationalization of a low degree of power, and plebeian *ressentiment*. Where modernity lifted the burden of power and obscurity in favour of a light-travelling reason, postmodern hyper-reason makes arbitrary power into the hydra-headed but repetitious monster whose toils we can never escape, yet whom we should joyfully embrace.

What happens, though, to 'obscurity', by which I mean the religious? To be sure, obscurity is here regarded as itself a ruse of power, but since power will always operate through ruses and self-disguisings, and half-concealed inventions of mysterious new creeds, one can no longer will the *end* of religion. For every socially instituted creed and code of practice must lack foundations beyond the essence that it creates through its own self-elaboration. Religion will not depart, because *all* social phenomena are arbitrary and therefore 'religious'. Quite clearly, these conclusions will tend to suggest affinities between postmodernism and those kinds of sacrality which lay stress of the wilfulness of God, the positivity of revelation, the total and absolute inaccessibility of the divine unity beyond the always divisive manifestations of this unity in time. I should like, at this point in my essay, already to note that I find the issue validation versus non-validation of the sacred to be a more or less spurious and uninteresting one. What is more important is the *mode* of sacrality, the logic of a particular theological articulation.

This first reason – concerning different 'modes of suspicion' – for apparent religious subtexts in postmodern discourse, has to do mainly with the

attitude of postmodernism towards historical religious phenomena. The
view, however, that one cannot ever wish religions – as 'local discourses' –
away does not at all mean, for Lyotard and other kindred theorists, that
our public language of adjudication, of the distribution of physical and
linguistic resources, must itself be 'religious' or 'mythical'. On the contrary, what Lyotard calls legitimation by 'paralogy' is 'godless' in that it
does not, like modernist attempts at totalization, itself construct a 'grand
narrative', and neither does it seek a dialectical convergence upon a focal
point: a single forum of reason at the centre of the human city. Instead, it
tries to promote the proliferation of local – one might say 'religious' –
narratives, allowing them to mutate and compete endlessly, but with the
proviso that the 'rights' of a particular narrative discourse to compete must
be respected, along with all the pragmatic instances of narration: the
positions of narrator, narrated, narratee.[2]

For Lyotard, as for all the heirs of Nietzsche, including Heidegger, one
might say that the ineradicable human impulse, identified by Kant, to
shape metaphysical speculations will always determine the character of any
human institution; but on the other hand, these institutions are but pearls
on a string of transitions, whose aleatory character is registered not by a
religious or metaphysical discourse, but by a discourse which remains non-
metaphysical, critical and even 'true', whether we call this 'genealogy',
'fundamental ontology', 'deconstruction' or 'paralogy'.

However, the second reason for the presence of religious subtexts in
postmodern discourse no longer concerns its approach to religious content,
but the apparently religious overtones of its language of critical decoding.
To give some examples: the resemblance of deconstruction to Valentinian
or Marcionite thematics (more so, I think, than to more orthodox 'negative
theology');[3] the identification made by Deleuze of perfect 'deterritorialization' with a Spinozist Absolute;[4] Heidegger's talk about 'Being' as if it
bestowed grace; finally the way in which Nietzsche, like Spinoza before
him, converted a standpoint of critical indifference towards reality, which
purged it of all values, relative comparisons and teleologies, into a new
intuition of an 'eternal' standpoint, regarded after all as the attainment of
something valuable and, indeed, salvific.

All these instances are, I think, striking and impressive, and merit our
profound consideration. We can only, I want to suggest, comprehend
them, if we slightly modify the historical picture which I presented earlier
in the paper. There I claimed that current anti-humanism can be read as
but a deepening of the anti-metaphysical, anti-religious project of modernity. However, to preserve this chronology, to perceive the postmodern as
what must come *after* modernism, as its sequel and completion, could be in
itself to remain within the confines of a modernist perspective, and its need
to see history as the unfolding of necessary stages. (Incidentally, I do not
think that any of the major *penseurs* dubbed 'postmodern' identify it in any

straightforward sense with an epoch; this is why so many of them rebut the term.) It is not at all clear that the dominant modern project of humanism straightforwardly preceded what we now dub 'postmodernism', any more than it is clear that the commodification of 'useful' goods happened entirely prior to an invasion of the realm of taste by the speculative norms of 'fashion', and the reduction of public discourse to a system of formally equivalent 'signals'.[5] Where a strict order of priority is maintained, and postmodernity is too closely defined as an epoch, it becomes all too easy to offer Marxist 'explanations' of postmodernist thought as mere passing fashion, in general terms of an ontological priority of the economic and the productive, and specific terms of the profit-driven needs of capitalism to invade the cultural sphere. This over-glibness ignores precisely 'postmodernist' underminings of such a priority, which deconstruct the metaphysics of a material 'base', and demonstrate historically how capitalism was from its inception a discursive as much as an economic order, even if many aspects of 'culture' for a long time remained resistant to commodification.[6] Somewhat analogously, the assumption that modernist humanism preceded anti-humanism can foster the view that the latter is but a later and deeper ruse of a capitalism represented as in part a process which realizes 'essential' human freedoms, and in part one which suppresses and denies them. This again begs the questions which anti-humanism poses about the existence of any human 'nature', and the possibility of regarding autonomous freedom as basically benign. Precisely because it is in no real sense a 'successor' to humanist critique, anti-humanist critique is 'critical' in an entirely different manner.

This latter point is well made by the episode in *Thus Spake Zarathustra* involving 'the ugly man' who is responsible for 'the death of God'. The ugly man has not *disclaimed* God for critical or elevated reasons – on the contrary, he has murdered God out of *ressentiment* because he could not tolerate God's constant gaze upon his weaknesses and failures.[7] Here humanist anti-religiosity is identified by Nietzsche with a bourgeois refusal of the great and noble, precisely of the *ubermenschliche*, which Nietzsche in his notebooks identifies with the religious impulse itself.[8] Refusal of God in the name of some sort of human normativity is *not* regarded by Nietzsche as critical. Similarly, Gilles Deleuze refuses to see the 'turn to the subject' as the historically crucial inauguration of the critical enterprise, because it merely mirrors, in the subjective depths, the attempt to secure, in the transcendent heights, some 'underlying' point of fixity beneath the flux and aimlessness of patterns of relating and affecting which alone constitute 'reality'. One can argue that the 'turn to the subject', in both its Cartesian and Kantian forms, was a reaction against the sceptical implications of Renaissance thought, which had abandoned essentialism and hylomorphism, and so made dynamic interrelationship, and self-forming and creating matter, the ultimate ontological principles. On this view, as

Deleuze puts it, the critical revolution did not consist in putting things back where they belonged, in returning negatively alienated realities to the human depths, but in denying both depth and height, in favour of a surface, or a self-forming 'plane of immanence', where nothing 'belongs', but everything appears and fades away, yet at the same time abides in an intensive, 'complicated' eternity which we can intuit.[9]

The crucial word here is *immanence*. 'Postmodern' thought is the legatee of a version of critique founded on an assumption of immanence, which Yirmiyahu Yovel, in a recent book, has argued is at least as constitutive (in a line of descent from Spinoza) of modernity as the Kantian outlook.[10] The difference between the two can be spelled out in two specific ways: first of all, Kantian critique is not founded upon a refusal of transcendence, so much as on the reduction of transcendence to an empty but overwhelmingly sublime horizon, whose threatening unfathomability and inscrutable violence are tamed through assimilation to our own postulated and unknowable freedom, which is then turned (despite its unpromising vacuity) into the very principle of moral order and propriety. Knowledge, for Kant, is secured within the bounds of the knowledge possible for the knowing subject – yet at the borders of this space, and providing its regulations *in practice*, remains the empty yet fearful gaze of God.[11]

By comparison, the immanentist version of critique begins with a refusal of transcendence, and an affirmation of the self-sufficiency, not of God, nor of humanity, but of nature or nature-in-process. This latter qualification contains the crucial difference between the two critical idioms. They both speak in the name of finitude, but Kantian critique associates the finite with the limited, with a distinction that can be validly made, for all time, between possible and impossible knowledge. By comparison, the immanentist critique associates finitude with indeterminability, so fulfilling, more genuinely than Kant, the Copernican turn which made infinitude a property of the material universe. As the human subject is a compound of temporary alliances, affiliations and resistances, the categories of its understanding are never fixed, and do not relate to the possibilities of empirical truth, but are rather 'expressions' (to use a Spinozan word later adopted by Herder and the Romantics) in the mode of thought, of ontological dispositions which are also physical.

This form of relativism would appear to remove us still further from any form of metaphysical or religious affirmation than the subject-based criticism of Kant. However, to make that judgement may still be to think of the immanentist critique as an *intensification* of the Kantian project, whereas it manifestly is not. Against such a judgement one can observe that, in a philosophy which decomposes the 'human' in favour of some larger ontological process beyond human control, there will be a tendency to 'deify' this process. Thus there is a clear line of continuity from Spinoza's 'pantheism' to Nietzsche's postulation of an ultimate cosmic distribution beyond chance and necessity, and Heidegger's talk of 'Being' which 'happens' through its self-concealment in the instance of beings. This is not to say that Spinoza thought that he could fully comprehend the *Deus-Natura*, nor that Heidegger thought that he could grasp Being as an object (clearly his point was that he could not). However, in both cases, the relativizing perspective upon particulars, and, more especially, a moral indifference in relation to 'modes' or to 'beings', can only be ontologically upheld by a claim to grasp the manner of transition from mode to mode, being to being, as a manifestation of an *ultimate* indifference. Such that, in regarding *this* particular transition, *this* particular differentiation, one affirms that here one grasps, literally and *univocally*, a part of God, a real advent of Being, and at the same time one is aware of its utterly non-hierarchical, non-teleological relation to everything else. One understands perfectly, both some 'parts' of ultimate reality, and also the law of indifference of ultimate reality with respect to these parts, lying beyond our usual contrasts of order and disorder. (Notice here that, regarded from both directions, seventeenth-century rationalism and postmodern 'anarchism' are not perfect opposites: the distributive divine *mathesis* proposed by Spinoza is already said by him to operate beyond the level of any 'order' in the usual sense as imagined by purposing, desiring or feeling. On the other hand, to identify 'difference' with transcendental truth – like Heidegger, Derrida and Deleuze – is precisely to repeat, albeit in an anarchic mode, the rationalist claim that truth coincides, not with essence, but with the always differentiating occurrence of being, down to the infinitely small last particular.)

What follows from all this is that it scarcely seems appropriate – particularly from a theological point of view – merely to 'celebrate' the religiosity of postmodern thought, or its reinvocation of all sorts of interesting and necessarily empty mysteries. On the contrary the point is to notice how its religious overtones are linked to the project of founding critique in immanence, and then to ask, does immanent criticism somehow legitimate religiosity, or is this supposed critique rather itself reducible to a positive, 'religious' construction, and therefore to be regarded in its claims to be the (last) legatee of the project of reason, as illegitimately transgressive and metaphysical? In the course of the widespread reaction against Heidegger and Nietzsche which has arisen in France during the past decade this is an accusation which has been variously made, notably by Luc Ferry and Alain Renaut, in their book *La Pensée '68*, where they claim that to focus one's vauntedly critical thought in an unmediated fashion upon the ontological difference is in fact to be totally uncritical. Genuine critique, they claim, must always traverse the subject, and ground itself on a Kantian schematization of *a priori* categories of thought.[12]

This retreat into humanism, however, can scarcely be upheld: Ferry and Renaut do not comprehend why Heidegger's *ontological* account of the historical situatedness of human knowledge within the temporal happening of language cannot be reduced to mere epistemological schematism. In terms of such an account, 'schematizing' does not serve to provide determinate sense, but dissolves such determination in favour of the necessity of an imprescribable interpretation. Moreover, given that temporal linguisticality provides 'categories' as well as a 'scheme' for human understanding, there really exists no subjective surplus 'to be schematized', and therefore Heidegger gradually came to conclude that there is no *a priori* space for a subjective projection of an open 'horizon', nor for an exercise of 'interpretation', as these are illusory doublings of the movement of Being itself as the incidence of 'meanings'.[13] Against Ferry and Renaut, it is more genuinely 'critical' to recognize that 'indeterminate openness' is directly recognized in the constitutively 'originary' opening of the ontological difference, than in some supposed private perspective which we have upon reality – however much this may seem to augment our sceptical dilemmas.

Ferry and Renaut claim that, by eliding the necessarily foundational moment of critique in subjectivity, Heidegger also loses the Kantian possibility of turning indeterminacy into the basis for morality, by treating it formalistically and intersubjectively. However, this is not to reckon with Hegel's contention that the upholding of subjective autonomy alone cannot provide us with concrete social norms, but rather 'subjects' us to the merely empty negativity of an endless striving for a never fully attained freedom – which is likely to visit incessant terror on the always persisting modes of heteronomy, without ever substituting a materially realized autonomous order. If, by contrast, we reject both Kantian foundational epistemology, and the Kantian attempt to ground law on the formal analysis of freedom, then we must accept that in both cases immanentist critique is able to operate as a 'meta-critique' of the critique associated with the subject.

Nevertheless, Ferry and Renaut do have a point when they argue that any claim to characterize, however elliptically, the ontological difference, must be illegitimately metaphysical. The point needs to be rephrased, not in terms of a plea on behalf of a subjectively grounded critical distinction between the knowable and the unknowable, but rather in terms of a meta-critique of immanentism itself, pointing beyond the characteristic norms of 'postmodern' discourse in its poststructuralist variety. One can ask whether the claim to adjudicate transitions sceptically in an indifferent fashion, and in this manner to grasp or mediate the ontological difference, whether as arbitrary assertion, or as unavoidably violent self-concealment, is not itself uncritical and questionable. It is precisely at this juncture that a project of 'problematizing the secular' might want to part company with postmodernism, and claim that it attains to perspectives which the latter is unable to arrive at.

For what I have now implied is that the two forms of critique which variously compose the modern project – subjectivism and immanentism –

are equally, at certain points, intellectually vulnerable. This implication might now cause us to attend to the manner in which both, despite their diversity, have been means whereby the secular has sought to define and maintain itself. We have recently grown accustomed to the realization that there is no 'purely human' space which stands disclosed once we are free of the burden of religious illusion. However, a more important consideration may be that there is no purely *secular* space, outside the constitutive opposition of this term to that of 'the sacred'. The 'real' secular is no more disclosed in the immanentist discourses of naturalism, (post)structuralism, fundamental ontology, and so forth, than in the language of humanism. On the contrary, the secular as a self-regulating, immanent space – what Guy Lardreau and Christian Jambet call 'the world' – is something sustained only by a conventional symbolic coding, and only (to use Lacanian termi- nology) by 'imaginary' identification do we take this space for the real itself.[14]

The quickest way to intimate this point is to give some examples of how the secular is in fact composed out of rearranged fragments of religious discourse, which are not its 'subtexts', but rather make up its whole substance. Let me mention the following three instances, all relating to early modern Europe. The first two will be dealt with very briefly; the third will be given more extended treatment in the second section of this essay.

First of all, the need which finds its expression in Machiavelli, Bodin and Spinoza to discover a *non-Christian* political practice was not to do with lay liberation from religious tutelage, but rather a protest against the Christian divorcing of sacrality from the power and disciplined violence of city life. Thus Machiavelli tried to invent a new political religiosity, and therefore not so much to 'free' the secular, but almost to *resacralize* an arena whose cultic status, along with its claims to define a field for the exercise of virtue, was perceived to be denied. He is later imitated in this respect, albeit in a very different fashion, by Spinoza.[15]

Second, it is equally clear that early modern science – the normative mode of modern knowledge – did not emerge in a space vacated when people ceased to invoke divine causality. As Amos Funkenstein and Michael Buckley have made abundantly clear, something more like the opposite is true: from Duns Scotus onwards, a 'univocal' treatment of divine and human attributes – reaching its *acme* in Spinoza's immanentism – encouraged a new discourse, at once both 'scientific' and 'theological', which sought to explain the world and to prove God's existence, by invoking God as an 'immediate' and not remote cause of finite realities, operating on the same level as these realities themselves.[16] Variants of this are seen in Descartes' *creatio continua*, Malebranche's occasional caus- ality, Leibniz's pre-established harmony, Newton's divine *sensorium* and even (I would want to claim, beyond Funkenstein) the hidden hand of the political economists, Kantian things-in-themselves (which though inscrutable and spiritual, directly sustain both empirical objectivity and a freedom surmounting causality) and De Bonald's 'divinely created' (not merely legislated) social order, which later gets inverted as Durkheim's 'society is God'.[17] The prestige of this discourse can only be comprehended if one realizes that, in the circumstances of the decay and disintegration of Christendom, 'science' was able to establish itself not simply as a new possibility of controlling nature, but also as a new religion of reason whose self-sufficiency and non-heteronomy with respect to revelation were appropriate to a rational devotion to the increasingly compound totality of God/Nature.

II

The autonomy of 'science' was required by a construal of its object of study, nature, as legible and self-explanatory: therefore as *immanently* comprehensible. A God entirely beyond nature, enshrining an eminent and mysteriously inaccessible level of causality, became increasingly redundant. However, for my third example, I now want to show how the self-founding autonomy of immanentism itself disguises a new metaphysical positing of transcendence.

The new secular religiosity of the seventeenth century, associated with the 'new science', invented a new theological idiom, which Leibniz finally dubbed 'theodicy'.[18] One might suppose that what one has here is a rationalist attempt to do justice to the perennial theological problem of evil. However, it is clear that evil and disorder were only regarded, in antiquity, as a 'problem' (rather than just as facts, or facts unproblematically explicable) within stoic philosophy, which affirmed precisely the necessary rationality and order of the whole cosmos.[19] The revival of stoic immanentism in the seventeenth century leads to a revival of the question how, within order, can there none the less be disorder? But this problem fundamentally disturbed, as it had for the stoics, the security of a monistic outlook. This is particularly clear in the case of Spinoza, whose monistic aspirations were the most extreme.

For Spinoza, there exists no negativity, sadness, passion or conflict at the level of *Deus-Natura*, which includes the entire positivity of being. But short of denying the reality of finite duration, or else its necessitated character, Spinoza must still regard the negative and illusory phenomena of subjective sadness, lacerating passion and anger, as none the less inevitable.[20] Two near contradictions arise from this contrast between a temporal perspective and that of eternity, into which we have some intuitive insight in 'the third kind of knowledge'. First, at the finite level, sadness cannot quite be pure illusory negation, because the transition from joy to sadness is itself a real positive act, involving the partial dissolution of one finite power by another, greater one.[21] In so far as a consciousness of 'selfhood' remains, sadness records an objective disintegration. Second, this residue of positive ill in turn introduces a descriptive contrast between the level of *Deus-Natura* and the level of duration in terms of their essential characteristics (pure affirmation on the one hand, real denials endured on the other), so placing duration in some sense 'outside' eternal substance, despite the fact that this is supposed to be an all-encompassing totality.[22] At this point Spinoza's destruction of a metaphysics of transcendence, and of morality in the usual sense (as assuming such a metaphysics), itself comes under threat, in the following manner.

By abolishing transcendence as a locus of moral norms, Spinoza claims to have exposed as fictional all narratives of subjective progression, all dramas of guilt and redemption: such things are the illusory result of thinking in terms of *genera*, whereas our subjective condition in the present is no more properly compared with a higher or lower state of our own activity in the past or future than with a finite thing like a stone, which is indeed less active than us, yet fully active according to its own degree of perfection.[23] However, the fissure of *disorder* within this non-moral and 'non-ordered' order, which is constituted by the fact of religious and metaphysical illusion concerning advance and regression within a single *genus*, itself requires the *reinstatement* of transcendence, hierarchy and a dramatic narrative of transcendence, by imposing a new moral imperative to overcome the sad passions and become more purely joyful, active and assertive. Already, before Nietzsche, value is first denied by Spinoza, but then necessarily transvalued. *Amor fati* constitutes a paradoxical exercise of preference: we should leave behind all the illusions of non-necessity, so as to arrive at a true vision of God. Within the *lacuna* of this paradox, there opens up the gap between Spinoza's naturalistic and apolitical ethics on the one hand, where the injunction of resignation can be realized, and the sphere of politics on the other, which he takes to be a form of life we cannot evade, and yet one constitutively *defined* by the persistence of religious illusion.[24] For to repeat, Spinoza does the reverse of secularizing politics. While the philosophically wise élite know that politics aims to achieve at least a simulacrum of the positive harmony of relations which is the real underlying reality, none the less the necessitated character of the sad passions means that human religious illusions, and the need to govern people through the manipulation of these illusions, will always remain. Spinoza purports to overcome Platonic transcendence: yet, as Christian Jambet indicates, the 'modern' turns out to be the (non-Judaic) ancient after all: just as for Plato, so for Spinoza, the wise can never fully communicate their vision of justice to the time-bound masses.[25]

From Spinoza the trail to Heidegger, Lacoue-Labarthe and their kin is clear.[26] Although his contemporary successors collapse even the eternal vision into the sequence of necessary illusions, this perfecting of non-ordered order, non-legal law, as 'crowned anarchy' – that which *ordains* the necessarily arbitrary – equally enshrines the inevitable return of irrepressible transcendence.[27] And the affirmation of transcendent chaos preserves Spinoza's repetition of a Platonic pessimism in politics: for the 'truth' of the inevitable substitution of one ruse of power for another (one pretence of 'presence', or of consistent subjectivity) can never quite appear *as* political power, presence or citizenship, without being once more lost sight of.

However, I do *not* wish simply to denounce Spinoza and Nietzsche's transvaluation of ethics. On the contrary, I submit that both, in identifying the good with power and actuality, parody a post-antique transvaluation *already carried out* by Neoplatonism, Judaism and Christianity.[28] For example, in the thought of Augustine, Aquinas and Maimonides, if God is the Good, then the Good is no longer a Platonic idea beyond being, or a limit (*peras*) above the flux of time, but rather is to be equated with the infinity of being in its power, strength and mutually affirming interrelationship. Evil, by contrast, is simply privation, the inhibition of an active reality which could be present. Spinoza inherits this view of evil as privation, and accordingly insists that as there is nothing negative in the Good, it follows that sadness and sickness, and even guilt, hope and redemption – tainted as they are with melancholy – are not fully good, although they can act as points of transition into a state of real activity.[29]

If this is what is meant by virtue as 'will-to-power', virtue as 'non-moral', but rather coincident with whatever is uninhibitedly alive, then Augustine, Aquinas and Maimonides were close to such an affirmation, just as for St Paul, faith and hope, unlike charity, *do not remain*. But one can go further: while it may be possible to read the will-to-power as the most radically consistent thinking through of evil as *privatio boni*, it may also be the case that in another respect Spinoza and Nietzsche, compared with the medieval thinkers, cannot adequately persist in the thought of the negativity of evil. For their immanent necessitarianism demands that at the temporal level negation remains permanently inscribed in the inevitable violent overcoming of one being by another. In Spinoza this renders state violence, and a justice founded on the rights of *de facto* power, unsurpassable.[30] And kindred ontologies foster the reign of pure resignation and pessimism in postmodern political reflection.

For Spinoza, to be an individual willing subject, to be a political subject, and to be a subject who conceives himself as innocent or guilty before God, all amount to the same thing. For to be a subject is to be locked into agonistic conflict. If subjects are perceived to relate harmoniously in a 'good order' (beyond order and disorder), then this is only by way of a collapse into the dissolving ether of totality. Repentance and regret are, for Spinoza, in the end not virtues, not simply because of their negative residue, but because what is done remains, foreordained and irretrievable, in its positivity of violent disturbance.

By contrast, for Christian and Jewish tradition, the equation of negativity with a 'pure' free will, a free will which only exists in this surd and absurd form as *refusal* of divine necessity, opens up a reduction of nature to artifice – to what has been, contingently, interfered with and mismade by perversely willing creatures. This, in turn, allows the possibility of an undoing of this mismaking, of repentance that is indeed not virtue – since it still includes the self-cancellation of evil, negation of the negation, rebounding of violence upon its perpetrator – but none the less the *opening* upon virtue. Such repentance occurs through the recognition of evil as ·mere destruction, repetition of a uniquely impotent and sheerly self-referring (so self-cancelling) act of denial, [31] negative refusal of the fullness of being, or of aesthetic harmony (the non-teleological *telos*, as Kant appropriately describes it in the *Critique of Judgement*).

For this vision, there is transcendence, as there is also, I have argued, for Spinoza and his successors; in both cases a transcendent perspective which is that of an infinite, non-ordered order. There is also – as for Spinoza, against his affirmed desire – dualism: we inhabit this 'other' world of successive difference and the play of oppositions. Yet, by contrast with Spinoza, there is a refusal of univocity: for in this case transcendence is not a 'truer' perspective *within* the world, the perspective of the whole; a version of transcendence which renders dualism absolute in terms of the non-mediability of the absolute over against the realm of subjective conflict (which therefore appears as naturalized, just as sheerly 'given' as chaotic primal matter in the thought of antiquity). For Christian theology the world is indeed fully contained in God, yet in an 'eminent' sense which always exceeds the world as the state of perfection in which it should be, will be and always already is. The world in its createdness 'outside' God does not occupy a space of exclusion, nor even of subordination, but the space of an infinite tensional progress towards its own eminence, the infinitely actual realization of all its moments. Precisely the affirmation that what is transcendent is more than the whole – but rather a fullness of being independent of the contingencies of the world, which constantly replenishes those contingencies – ensures that there need be no rivalry of perspective between time and eternity, nor between the 'present' moment and the differential process. Transition from time to eternity, which is identical with the passage of time itself, or the passage from moment to moment, involves no jettisoning of temporarily necessary illusions, because the imperative demand of the transcendent God is not that we adopt the point of view of the whole, but rather that we continue to embrace new and unexpected contingencies. Paradoxically, we can only *remain* with the unsurpassability of temporal difference, with mundane 'political' reality, where we affirm a giver of difference in excess of the totality of differences happening in time.

Where we must remain with temporal, 'political' difference, there also we must remain with preference, value, choice, taste and attempted integration: with differences in *relation*. For faith in a creative transcendence forbids us the metaphysical luxury of claiming to unveil a transcendent indifference. Rather, our hazily correct 'preferences' and 'integrations' are held to be eminently confirmed in the unknowable transcendent source. Inversely, it is also the case that pure affirmation and harmonious coexistence are no longer the prerogative of an apolitical vision: whether of the 'third kind of knowledge' or of the 'eternal return'. Temporal progress into its own eminence is rather regarded as in its original reality both affirmative and harmonious. This progress is, indeed, temporarily thwarted, distorted, by evil, which means negation, powerlessness, self-wounding; and yet the sequence of negation can *in principle* be wholly abandoned via the contradictory gates of repentance. Not in favour of a refusal of temporality, but for another temporality, the real temporality constituted by the continuous gift of divine creation.

Hence transcendence as envisaged by the doctrine of creation *ex nihilo* does indeed imply dualism, and yet a kind of perpetually self-cancelling dualism. This is the nearest we can get to non-dualism, certainly as compared to the vaunted claims for non-hierarchization enshrined in the tradition of 'immanentism'. For firstly, the transcendent that is 'beyond' this world as its source does not subordinate the moments of the world to the process of the world; and secondly, it preserves at an 'eminent' level the reality of a non-violent temporal process, whose persisting promise indicts actual violence of contingency, and *insufficient* actuality and strength. In this way 'creation and fall', the speculative elements of a self-cancelling dualism, still open before us a space of political hope, a hope for absolute justice, remembering that justice is indivisible.

This third, extended example was not, however, intended simply to indicate how theology might help us overcome the political *aporias* of modernity, but also to illustrate how a problematizing of the secular might surpass the 'postmodernist' idiom, in demonstrating how the tradition of immanentism, as well as the 'modernist' tradition of subjectivism, is constituted through the erection of a new but concealed symbolic order, a new religiosity and a new version of transcendence. Whereas, for 'postmodernism', a metaphysical imperative is unavoidable and constitutive of human culture, and yet a 'master discourse' is still able to unmask and narrate its aberrations, the new agenda which is the 'problematizing of the secular' would abandon even the claim to attain to such anarchic mastery. This does, indeed, tend to put postmodernisms on a level with the great religious discourses of the world, which are not, be it noted (as postmodernists might fondly imagine), anything like 'local' discourses, but already imperial attempts to construct, albeit not necessarily on any 'foundations', grand narratives and universal ontologies which construe precisely the transitions from one historical or geographical locality to the next. Beyond postmodernism – but always with and before it – lies the *immanently* non-adjudicable battle of human creeds.

NOTES

1 Jean-François Lyotard, 'Lessons in Paganism', in Andrew Benjamin (ed.), *The Lyotard Reader*, Oxford, Blackwell, 1989, pp. 122–55.
2 Jean-François Lyotard, *The Postmodern Condition*, Manchester, Manchester University Press, 1986, pp. 60–7; *The Differend*, trans. Georges van den Abbeele, Manchester, Manchester University Press, 1988. pp. 151–61.
3 This comparison arises because the necessary 'violence' of erasure of absent meaning in Derrida is akin to the idea of a 'fall' or loss which accompanies the original cosmic creation. Similar claims can be made in relation to Heidegger; I am indebted to discussions with Jean-Pierre Faye on this matter.
4 Gilles Deleuze and Felix Guattari, *A Thousand Plateaus*, trans. Brian Massumi, London, Athlone, 1988, pp. 509–10:

> We could say that the earth, as deterritorialized, is itself the strict correlate of D [deterritorialization]. To the point that D can be called the creator of the earth – of a new land, a universe, not just a reterritorialization. . . . This is the meaning of 'absolute'. The absolute expresses nothing transcendent and undifferentiated. . . . It expresses only a type of movement qualitatively different from relative movement.

This very Spinozistic passage should be related to my remarks about Spinoza later in the essay: my queries against Spinoza are also queries against Deleuze.
5 See Jean Baudrillard, *The Mirror of Production*, trans. Mark Foster, St Louis, Telos, 1975.
6 See, for example, David Harvey, *The Condition of Postmodernity*, Oxford, Blackwell, 1989.
7 Frederich Nietzsche, *Thus Spake Zarathustra*, trans. R.J. Hollingdale, Harmondsworth, Penguin, 1969, pp. 275–9.
8 Giorgio Colli and Mazzino Montinari, eds, *Nietzsche Werke*, vol. VIII, part 3, Berlin, W de Gruyter, 1972, pp. 98–100.
9 Gilles Deleuze, *The Logic of Sense*, trans. Mark Lester with Charles Stivale (ed.), Constantin V. Bourdas, London, Athlone, 1990, pp. 127–33; *Spinoza: Practical Philosophy*, trans. Robert Hurley, San Francisco, City Lights, 1988.
10 Yirmiyahu Yovel, *Spinoza and Other Heretics: The Adventures of Immanence*, Princeton, Princeton University Press, 1989.
11 See Howard Caygill, *Art of Judgement*, Oxford, Blackwell, 1989, pp. 284–393.
12 Luc Ferry and Alain Renaut, *La Pensée '68: Essai sur L'anti-humanisme Contemporain*, Paris, Gallimard, 1985, pp. 263–87.
13 See John D. Caputo, *Radical Hermeneutics*, Bloomington, Indiana University Press, 1987, pp. 95–120.
14 Christian Jambet and Guy Lardreau, *Le Monde*, Paris, Grasset, 1978, pp. 9–23.
15 See John Milbank, *Theology and Social Theory: Beyond Secular Reason*, Oxford, Blackwell, 1990, chapter 1.
16 Amon Funkenstein, *Theology and the Scientific Imagination*, Princeton, Princeton University Press, 1986, pp. 3–202.
17 Milbank, op. cit., chapters 2, 3.
18 G.W.F. Leibniz, *Theodicy*, trans. E.M. Huggard, Lasalle, Open Court, 1985;

see also Kenneth Surin, *Theology and the Problem of Evil*, Oxford, Blackwell, 1987, chapter 1.
19 See Jambet and Lardreau, op. cit., pp. 234–61.
20 Baruch de Spinoza, *Ethics*, trans. R.H.M. Elwes, New York, Douer, 1981, Part I, props XXIX, XXXI; Part III, props V–XIII, XX, XXXI; 'General Definition of the Emotions'; Part V, props XVIII, XX, V, XXXIX; Deleuze, *Spinoza*, op. cit., pp. 94–7.
21 Spinoza, op. cit., Part III, props V–XIII; Deleuze, *Spinoza*, op. cit., pp. 30–43.
22 Deleuze, *Spinoza*, op. cit., pp. 51–2, 91–2.
23 Baruch de Spinoza, *Correspondence*, trans. R.H.M. Elwes, New York, Douer, 1981, letter XXXVI (XXIII); Deleuze, *Spinoza*, op. cit., pp. 17–29, 30–43, 71–3.
24 Spinoza, *Ethics*, op. cit., Part IV, prop. XXXVII, n. 2; *A Theologico-Political Treatise*, trans. R.H.M. Elwes, New York, Dover, 1981, chapters XIV, XV, XVI, XIX.
25 Jambet and Lardeau, op. cit., p. 274.
26 See Philippe Lacoue-Labarthe, *Heidegger, Art and Politics: The Fiction of the Political*, trans. Chris Turner, Oxford, Blackwell, 1990.
27 Here I find myself in some measure of agreement with Gillian Rose in her *Dialectic of Nihilism*, Oxford, Blackwell, 1984.
28 This train of thought was sparked off by Gillian Rose and Howard Caygill's suggestion to me that the 'will-to-power' is connected with the Aristotelian and Thomist *actus purus*.
29 Spinoza, *Correspondence*, op. cit., letters XXXI–XXXVIII (XVIII–XXVII); Deleuze, *Spinoza*, op. cit., pp. 30–43.
30 Spinoza, *Tractatus*, op. cit., chapters XVI, XIX, XX; *A Political Treatise*, trans. R.H.M. Elwes, New York, Douer, 1981, chapters I, V, XI.
31 See Regina M. Schwartz, *Remembering and Repeating: Biblical Creation in 'Paradise Lost'*, Cambridge, Cambridge University Press, 1988, chapter 4, pp. 91–110, for an illuminating account of Milton's presentation of this theme in terms of the fall of Satan.

Chapter 3

Diremption of spirit

Gillian Rose

Postmodernism, theological and a/theological, however 'framed' or 'reframed' – whether as ecstasy or as eschatology – is a *trahison des clercs*. For the current sceptical reception of religion is analogous to the former critical reduction of religion: it repeats a historical and political diremption which it refuses to think.

The current sceptical reception of religion, as expressed in the portentious title and subtitle of the original conference out of which this paper grew, has its roots in the erstwhile critical reduction of 'religion'. In both cases the object is 'given'; religion is given as a positivity. To the critical reduction, positive religion is given; to the sceptical reception, positive religion*s*. In effect, the critical reduction knows and posits its reductee – 'religion'; while the sceptical reception, although it has renounced knowledge, nevertheless posits integral objects – 'religions'. Criticism, *Kritik*, was quasi-transcendental in its inquiry into the preconditions or possibility of its object, but it was restricted to independently specifiable conditions, not to the formation of the object; and it was, of course, negative and destructive. It did not produce a *speculative* exposition of the historical separation of the institutions of Caesar from the institutions of God, which would require neither a sociology nor a philosophy of religion, but investigation into the changing relation between meaning and configuration, revelation and realization.

Since the original, lyrical title with its academic and expatiatory subtitle resonates with the imbedded ethos of postmodernity, they warrant an initial consideration. What do they give us to work with? First, the SHADOW: the shadow of spirit – not the substance, even less the light or, more significantly, the darkness. Second, what casts this shadow – this shadow OF SPIRIT? 'Spirit' is to remain weightless, without *gravitas*, where formerly we discovered the gravity of the material base. Third, 'RELIGIOUS subtexts' takes religion*s* as given, and posits them as epithets not as substantives, as epithets of subtextuality, not even textuality, even less, actuality. Fourth, SUBtexts: 'sub', does this allude to secret or suppressed predominance – substance not shadow? This would be to reduce the apparently non-religious to a religious substructure. Fifth, subTEXTS: this ontology of the 'text' posits 'Contemporary Western Thought' as its superstructure. It characterizes textual Being as discursive, shying away from its potentiality and its actuality – pardon my metaphysics – that from which it arises and that which it effects.

O Shadowy Spirit – whereto your Substance?
O protean and ghoulish Subtext – what is your Text?
O multiple opacity – what is your Actuality?

The postmodern ontology of the text and ethos of the subtext claims that it is sceptical in its acknowledgement of the demotic plurality of discourses. Yet, I shall show that postmodern scepticism *completes itself* as political theology. The structure of this paradoxical reversal may be rendered explicit by comparing the way in which postmodern theology (Milbank), a/theology (Taylor), post-theology (Cupitt) and rediscovered Judaism at the end of philosophy (Strauss, Levinas, Steiner) construe their relation to tradition.

Taylor's postmodern 'a/theology' and Milbank's postmodern 'Beyond Secular Reason' offer Christian New Jerusalem for old Athens.[1] These authorships provide evidence of that prodigious, omniscient 'western' intellectuality that would crown postmodern theology or a/theology – 'queen of the sciences'. Each self-declaredly 'postmodern', their work is comprehensive while decrying comprehension: it disrespects and breaks down further the already lowered barriers between philosophy and literary criticism in the one case, between philosophy and social theory in the other, which are then gathered up and completed as postmodern a/theology or theology. Thereby is vidicated an old prognostication: that if we fail to teach theology – we will usurp it. Or, to cite the very words of John Henry Newman himself from 1852, in *The Idea of a University*: 'supposing Theology be not taught its province will not simply be neglected but will be actually usurped by other sciences'.[2]

In spite of their shared comprehensive scope and fervent ambition for postmodern a/theology or theology – what do these two bodies of thought have in common? Nothing – where sources, style, tone and method are apparent. Working closely with Nietzsche and Derrida on that 'shifty middle ground *between* Hegel and Kierkegaard',[3] Taylor inserts Heidegger and recent French thought into the terrain: while Milbank's argument covers the development of secular politics to classic sociology from Malebranche to Durkheim and Weber, from Hegel and Marx to Catholic Liberation Theology, classical philosophy and medieval theology, all oriented, however, by recent French thought, as *trivium* to its ultimate ecclesiology. Stylistically, they are even more diverse: Taylor offers a montage of text and illustration, accruing grammatical, phonetic and gra-phological juxtapositions and complications, learned, it would seem, from

Finnegans Wake; Milbank offers a treatise, four books in one, with sober, sustained argumentation, paced temporally and spatially from beginning to end. In tone, Taylor is masked, ironic, transgressive and extravagant; Milbank is straight, logical – in spite of his ontology of narration – severe, authoritative and original. Yet, we are explicitly offered, by the one, a deconstruction of theology; by the other, a deconstruction of classical and modern secularity; by the one, a deconstructive a/theology; by the other, 'Difference of Virtue, Virtue of Difference'.

In *Erring*, Taylor deconstructs 'Death of God', 'Disappearance of Self', 'End of History', 'Closure of the Book', which are translated into deconstructive a/theology in four paratactic 'moves': 'Writing of God', 'Markings', 'Mazing Grace', 'Erring Scripture', to culminate in Dionysian 'joy in suffering'.[4] 'The "Yes" of anguished joy breaks the power of the law and fissures the "Notshall" of history',[5] while 'The unending erring in scripture is the eternal play of the divine milieu', for, in play, 'which is interplay', 'the entire foundation of the economy of domination crumbles'.[6] In *Altarity*, the middle ground between Hegel and Kierkegaard is no longer occupied by Nietzsche but by Heidegger and recent French thinkers. Yet the whole is framed by Hegel as 'Conception' and Kierkegaard as 'Transgression', titles of the opening and concluding chapters. Hegel is expounded as the identity of difference and identity, Kierkegaard as the Abrahamic transgression of the ethical from *Fear and Trembling*. Every other author is then locked into this opposition between knowledge and faith which Taylor nevertheless knows Kierkegaard invented for his pseudonym, *de Silentio*. No transgression occurs, for Abraham's arm is stayed by an angel, but the work concludes by affirming the opposition between 'the Law' and 'the Call of the Other', an erring in time, where *Erring* offered a nomadicism in space.

In *Theology and Social Theory: Beyond Secular Reason*, Milbank demonstrates, by a generic-archaeological reconstruction, that 'secular discourse' is constituted by its opposition to orthodox Christianity as 'pagan' theology or anti-theology in disguise.[7] In four 'sub-treatises' the complicity of secular reason with an 'ontology of violence' is rehearsed: first, in eighteenth-century politics and political economy; second, in all nineteenth-century sociology which is presented, including Weber, as a positivist church; third, in Hegel and in Marx, whose impulse towards the non-secular is 'indecently recruited' for secular science; this equivocation evident to Milbank is itself, with indecent alacrity, recruited to 'a gnostic plot about a historically necessary fall and reconstruction of being with a gain achieved through violence undergone'.[8] These two treatises conclude with attempts to terminate the dialogue between theology and sociology and between theology and liberation, respectively. Finally, at the threshold to the last great treatise, Milbank disentangles his self-declared nihilistic voice from his Greek–medieval voice to complete nihilism with Christian logos and virtue which know 'no original violence'.[9] Not the difference of nihilism nor the virtue of the Greeks, not liberal, of course, but equally 'Against "Church and State" ',[10] that is, without natural rights and without natural law, 'transcendental difference' is 'encoded' as a 'harmonic peace' beyond the circumscribing power of any totalizing reason.[11] Without violence or arbitrariness, yet with difference, non-totalization and indeterminancy, without representation, the Augustinian 'Other City' is 'advocated' as 'the continuation of ecclesial practice', 'the imagination in action of a peaceful, reconciled social order, beyond even the violence of legality'.[12] The active imagination of 'the *sociality* of harmonious difference'[13] (emphasis in original) sketches the peaceful donation of 'the heavenly city' where 'beyond the possibility of alteration 'angels and saints . . . abide in a fellowship [whose] virtue is not the virtue of resistance and domination, but simply of remaining in a state of self-forgetting conviviality'.[14] Between this heavenly city and the sinful city founded on the murder of Abel of the *saeculum*, 'the interval between the fall and final return of Christ',[15] God sends a salvation city, the City of God, 'on pilgrimage through this world' which does not exclude anyone but 'provides a genuine peace by its memory of all the victims, its equal concern for all its citizens and its self-exposed offering of reconciliation to enemies',[16] 'its salvation . . . "liberation" from political, economic and psychic *dominium*'.[17]

This explication of pilgrimage and inclusivity effectively destroys the idea of a city: its inclusive appeal deprives it of limit or boundary that would mark it off from any other city and their different laws; while its task of salvation deprives it of site: 'the city of God is a nomad city (one might say)'.[18] The otherwise always indicted features of gnostic demiurgic soteriology in this messenger city, and the precondition of violence in this 'peace coterminous with all Being whatsoever' should be noted in this 'encoded narrative'.

Now the new Jerusalems have emerged: postmodern a/theology as nomadic ecstasy – Dionysian joy; postmodern theology as nomadic ecclesial eschatology – harmonious peace; both breaking the frame in their antinomianism, and both reinstating the frame in their dependence on law transgressed – joy 'breaks the power of law',[19] or law subdued – peace 'beyond even the violence of legality',[20] Taylor with joy but without sociality; Milbank with sociality and glimpses of angelic conviviality; both converge on the acknowledgement of difference, but in so doing reinstate the *age-old* oppositions between law and grace, knowledge and faith, while apparently working without the *modern* duality of nature and freedom.

Replacing old Athens by new Jerusalem involves consigning the opposition between nature and freedom to one of any number of arbitrary, binary, metaphysical conceits – instead of recognizing it as the index and indicator of the tension between freedom and unfreedom – and then proceeds to complete such 'deconstruction' in holiness. This founding and consecrating of holy cities inadvertently clarifies how that discarded opposition made it possible to reflect: the *critique* which is disqualified by its disappearance. Furthermore, those two Christian holy cities – Protestant (Taylor), Catholic (Milbank) – arise on the same foundation – antinomian and ahistorical – as the Davidic cities of Leo Strauss and Emmanuel Levinas.

These authorships – Strauss and Levinas – embrace the paradox in presenting Judaic theologico-political prophecy or ethics in *philosophical* terms as the *end of the end* of philosophy. There are, of course, two proclaimed 'ends' to philosophy: the end of 'metaphysics' from Kant to Nietzsche and Heidegger which may well found a 'new thinking'; and the end of 'philosophy' from Hegel and Marx to Adorno which raises the question of the *realization* of philosophy. By *the end of* the end of philosophy, I mean the discovery in the long debate between Judaism and philosophy – understood in relation to the Greek quest for the beginning, principles, causes – of the missing middle, the *tertium quid*, ethics, which finds itself always within the imperative, the commandment, and hence always already begun.

Strauss and Levinas present Judaism as solving the theological-political or the ethical problem *without* the opposition between nature and freedom: Strauss is *contra* nature; Levinas, *contra* freedom. Consequentially, both represent Judaism or Jewish history eschatologically: for Strauss, in *Philosophy and Law*, however, 'the prophet is the founder of the [ideal] Platonic state',[21] and while the 'era that believes in Revelation/is *fulfilled*', this is not because of the belief but because what is revealed is a 'divine Law/a simple binding Law/a Law with the power of right'.[22] For Levinas, while the face to face traumatically disturbs the presence of consciousness to itself, this awakening to responsibility for the Other occurs 'beyond being', understood as beyond rationalism, beyond violence – 'war' – in *Totality and Infinity*, beyond the history of the world.[23] In this Judaic Manichaeism Levinas has learned from Rosenzweig's *Star of Redemption*, where Judaism is presented liturgically as 'the holy community' in opposition to the Christian mission of world-imperium.[24]

These philosophical presentations of Judaism which have made Judaism accessible and available to rediscovery at the end of the end of philosophy, *die Ironie der Ironie*, for the religion historically denigrated as superseded, are, nevertheless *deeply* misleading. They misrepresent the rationalism or knowledge against which they define themselves; they misrepresent Judaism; and they misrepresent the history and modernity in which they are implicated. Strauss misrepresents Greek rationalism and ignores the connection between the birth and development of philosophy and earlier strata of pre-Olympian Greek religion.[25] If philosophy begins 'in wonder' then it is not a response to what is wonderful, but to what is awe-ful: it begins too, even apotropaically, in fear and trembling.[26] Levinas assimilates different philosophical accounts of 'knowledge', while alternating between Kantian consciousness as self-contained and Husserlian reduction (*epoche*) of intentionality which presents and describes processes of knowing in opposition to Kantian deduction of validity, that is, without epistemology.[27] By means of this feint, Levinas is able to avoid the struggle between universal and aporia as it is evident from Kantian judgement to Hegelian speculative experience, and thus does not acknowledge the predicament of universal and local jurisprudence which characterizes modern philosophy as much as modern Judaism.

Both Strauss and Levinas misrepresent Judaism. The 'Talmudic argument' rehearses a rationalism which is constantly exploring its own limits – the oral law, which was also revealed at Sinai, gives rise within Halachic Judaism to a never-ending commentary on the written law, according to which knowledge and responsibility are *in effect* renegotiated under the historically and politically changing conditions of both. Yet Strauss and Levinas present Judaism as unchanging and without a history; internal and external, as commentary, as law, as community. Strauss gives priority to medieval Judaism, while Levinas' decision to give priority not to 'the relation of ethics and halacha' 'but rather [to] the passage from the non-ethical to the ethical', arguing that the latter 'is truly the necessity of our time' when all authority and morality are called into question, draws attention systematically away from the mainstream debate within Judaism over ethics and halacha (*halacha* means the legal passages of the Talmud, distinguished from *aggada*, non-legal; or law and lore), which, far from being specialized to Judaism, shows the mutual difficulty shared by Jewish and non-Jewish thinkers in the conceiving of law and ethics. It is this evasion which permits postmodern philosophy to allude to a Judaism, taken from Rosenzweig, Buber or Levinas, as an open jurisprudence, a holy sociology, instead of confronting the configuring and conceiving of law and ethics in the shared context of modern legality and morality.

Within halachic Judaism there is fundamental disagreement over the relation between ethics and halacha, a disagreement which partakes in and reveals the breakdown in the conceiving of law and ethics 'outside' Judaism. Paradoxically, the orthodox inquiry into an ethic independent of halacha which is couched in terms of tradition (Lichtenstein)[28] defends and develops equity in its flexibility by demonstrating from the Talmudic sources a situational or contextual morality which supplements, 'beyond the line of the law', by balancing universal and local factors and not assimilating cases to a strict deduction; while the reform inquiry (Borowitz),[29] suspicious of this supra-legality, seeks to import a categorical Kantian ethic with its unconditional and formal character into Judaism in the attempt to make questions not of *equity* but of *equality* unavoidable.

Whether based on the apparent unconditioned immediacy of the face to face or on the idea of halachic contestation which offers an open jurisprudence and no end to history, recent philosophical 'representations' of Judaism overlook the contestation within Judaism over law and ethics as they overlook it outside Judaism. The rediscovery of Judaism at the end of the end of philosophy can be witnessed, therefore, as a convergent aspiration without a third, a middle, on which to converge.

However, these nomadic, Christian, and jurisprudential, Davidic, holy cities, consecrated in the shifting sands of ahistoricism and antinomianism, may be compared in the terms made explicit by the two Christian ones as *postmodern political theologies*. First, they are 'political theology' because they offer a complete solution to the political problem: for Taylor, economies of domination will crumble;[30] for Milbank, salvation must mean 'liberation' from political, economic and psychic *dominium*, and therefore from all structures belonging to the *saeculum*.[31] Second, they are 'postmodern' because their politics and their theology are explicitly developed without the prevalent, guiding, modern contraries of nature and freedom, nature and law, nature and convention. This disqualifies the possibility of *critique* – of recognizing such contraries as indicating the tension of simultaneously possessing freedom and unfreedom. Not therefore representable, they can only be presented as 'holiness': for Taylor, 'the coincidence of opposites extends the divine milieu'; while for Milbank, ecclesial practice extends to the divine.[32] Significantly, both lay claim to the middle: Taylor joins 'the eternal play of the divine milieu', while Milbank distinguishes his ontology from Levinas' by denying that 'mediation is necessarily violent'.[33] So, third, then, the *agon* of postmodernisms: within the holy play, the holy city, holy nomads – beyond nature and law, freedom and unfreedom – they resonate with and claim to do justice to – the unequivocal middle. But where is this middle? Neither ecstatic affirmation vaunting its 'totally loving the world', nor eschatological peace vaunting its continuity with untarnished ecclesial practice, display any middle.[34] There are no institutions – *dominium* – in either: Taylor offers no exteriority; Milbank offers no interiority. Without command and without revelation, Taylor's ecstatic affirmation remains exiled in an interior castle; whereas, with Milbank's latinity of 'sociality' and 'charity', how could 'peace' bequeathed as 'harmonious' arise without acknowledging the polis intruding into such vague sociality, and without acknowledging *eros* and *agape* intruding into such tamed 'charity'? In both cases, without anxiety, how could we recognize the equivocal middle? In fact we have here middles *mended* as 'holiness' – without that examination of the *broken* middle which would show how these holy nomads arise out of and reinforce the unfreedom they prefer not to know.

The dispute between Don Cupitt and George Steiner, which was staged at the original conference,[35] displayed the same asymptote. Both Cupitt and Steiner declaim their visions in the prophetic mode – the one, prophet of dynamic pluralism; the other, prophet of ancient justice, of a justice which is proclaimable even when unrealizable. The one presents himself as a holy celebrant of the market place, the other as the zealous guardian of monotheistic absolutism. Yet what they represent displays an inversion: Cupitt glorifies markets – for commodities, languages, political interests and religions – as plural and labile. But the market thus enthroned in the middle is a remorseless and authoritarian universal. In high dudgeon, Steiner conjures Deutero-Isaiah for the sake of our futurity – and yet such ferocity in the name of transcendence allows expression to our anxiety and anger and hence releases intimations of salvation.

However, these contrary prophecies converge in a powerful complacency which, whether apparently whole-heartedly embracing modernity or stern-heartedly refusing it, reduces modernity to the ineluctable and promiscuous market, which prophecy refuses to know or to criticize. Prophetic exhortation, whether by post-theology or in the name of biblical antiquity, converges with postmodern theology in laying claim to a holy middle elevated without equivocation, and without examination of *the broken middle* which they hold in righteous disdain. This very converging corrupts – for in figuring and consecrating holy cities, such 'holiness' will itself be reconfigured by the resource and articulation of modern domination, knowable to these postmodern ministers only as mute and monolithic sedimentation.

Postmodernism is submodern: these holy middles of ecstatic divine milieu, irenic other city, holy community – face to face or halachic – and the unholy one of the perpetual carnival market, bear the marks of their unexplored precondition: the diremption between the moral discourse of rights and the systematic actuality of power, within and between modern states. And therefore they will destroy what they would propagate, for once substance is presented, even if it is not 'represented', however 'continuous' with practice, it becomes procedural, formal, and its meaning will be configured and corrupted within the prevailing diremptions of morality and legality, autonomy and heteronomy, civil society and state. Mended middles and improvised middles betray their broken middle: antinomian yet dependent on renounced law; holy yet having renounced 'ideals'; yearning for nomadic freedom yet having renounced nature and freedom. This thinking concurs in representing its tradition – reason and institutions – as monolithic domination, as totalitarian. It overlooks the *pre*dominance of form, abstract legal form, as the unfreedom *and* freedom of modern states, and falls into the trap, not of positing another totalitarian ideal, but of presenting a holy middle which arises out of and will be reconfigured in the prevalent broken middle.

This holiness corrupts because it would sling us between ecstasy and eschatology, between a promise of touching our ownmost singularity and the irenic holy city, precisely without any disturbing middle. But this 'sensual holiness' arises out of and falls back into *a triune structure* in which we suffer and act as singular, individual and universal; or, as *particular*, as represented in institutions of the *middle*, and as *the state* – where we are singular, individual and universal *in each position*. These institutions of the middle *represent* and configure the relation between particular and state: they stage the agon between the three in one, one in three of singular, individual, universal; they represent the middle; broken between morality and legality, autonomy and heteronomy, cognition and norm, activity and passivity.[36] Yet they stand and move between the individual and the state. It has become easy to describe trade unions, local government, civil service, the learned professions – the arts, law, education, the universities, architecture and medicine – as 'powers'. And then renouncing knowledge as power, too, to demand total expiation for domination without investigation into the dynamics of configuration, of the triune relation which is our predicament – and which, either resolutely or unwittingly, we fix in some form, or with which we struggle, to know, and still to misknow and yet to grow. Because the middle is broken – because these institutions are systematically flawed – does not mean they should be eliminated or mended.

This will be the unintended consequence when the tradition is construed as 'Platonism' or 'Monotheism', or as any age-old domination of binary oppositions. It becomes impossible to distinguish between the intellectual tradition – whose resources, nevertheless, are being drawn upon at the very point of their indictment – and the institutional inversions which attend reformations of the kind being attempted yet again here. It becomes impossible to know which of these two paradoxes represents domination and which emancipation.

An analogy drawn from the history of architecture may illustrate this. Le Corbusier is the scourge of the Modern Movement, held responsible for its anti-humanism, its functionalism, its rationalization, apparently captured by his infamous dictum: 'A house is a machine for living in.' But what did he intend? He intended, as he also declared, *to liberate women from furniture*.[37] Since the much-vaunted scepticism of postmodernity indicates *nolens volens* an ethical impulse to overthrow the 'idealizing narratives' of the 'western intellectual tradition', it will suffer the same fate as Le Corbusier's good intention if it simply represents the tradition as unequivocal domination instead of attempting to comprehend how ideals and anti-ideals may be reconfigured in their historical and political realization. Postmodernity may, as it were, continue earnestly to try and liberate women from furniture, and invent new, unanticipated lumber in so doing.

Holy middles corrupt because they collude in the elimination of the broken middle by drawing attention away from the reconfiguration of singular, individual and universal at stake. Cupitt, for example, calls for voluntary associations, for plural politics 'of issues and causes', without mentioning that civil society is the Janus-face of the state. This is to draw attention away from the ways in which under the promise of enhanced autonomy – whether for individuals or communities – the middle is being radically undermined in a process of *Gleichschaltung* which, unlike the Nazi version, is quite compatible with the proclamation and actuality of civil society, with the proclamation and actuality of plurality, with the proclamation and actuality of postmodernity.

> This public person, so formed by the union of all other persons, formerly took the name of *city*, and now takes that of *Republic* or *body politic*; it is called by its members *State* when passive, *Sovereign* when active, and *Power* when compared with others like itself.[38]

Before we reorient our theology, let us reconsider the city and philosophy. Neither politics nor reason unifies or 'totalizes': they arise out of diremption – out of the diversity of peoples who come together under the aporetic law of the city, and who know that their law is different from the law of other cities – what Rousseau called 'power' and we now call 'nation'. Philosophy issues, too, out of this diremption and its provisional overcoming in the culture of an era. Without 'disowning that edifice', philosophy steps away to inspect its limitations, especially when the diremptions fixated in the edifice have lost their living connections.[39] We should be renewing our thinking on the invention and production of edifices – cities – apparently civilized within, dominion without – not sublimating those equivocations into holy cities. For the modern city intensifies these perennial diremptions in its inner oppositions between morality and legality, society and state, and the outer opposition, so often now inner, between sovereignty and what Rousseau called 'power' and we call 'nations and nationalism'; and which recurs, compacted and edified, in Levinas as 'war', as the spatial and temporal nomad in Taylor, as the nomadic city which 'remembers all the victims' in Milbank.

A final look at the labyrinth, setting of this spatial and temporal nomadicism: on the cover of *Erring* we look down on a maze, and are placed not in joyous disempowerment but in panoptic dominion, even though in the text the maze is celebrated as 'the horizontality of a pure surface', and we are situated 'in the midst of a labyrinth from which there is no exit'.[40] Towards the end of *Theology and Social Theory* we are told that the nomad city means that 'space is revolutionized' and no longer defensible.[41] It is worth looking more closely at these festive vulnerabilities. Taylor has put a unicursal maze on his cover – which offers no choice of route – as opposed to a multicursal maze – with choice of route. In either case, it is the beginning and the end which give authority to the way, and meaning to being lost – especially to any conceivable relishing of being lost. If the beginning and the end were abolished, so that all were (divine) middle – *Mitte ist überall* – we would not achieve joyful erring; nor pure virtue 'without resistance'; we would be left helpless in the total domination of

the maze, every point equally beginning and ending. We encounter not
pure freedom but pure authority and become its complete victim.

We cannot think without freedom because we are thought by freedom
and unfreedom, their insidious, dirempted morality and legality. Let us not
be holy nomads; let us invent no theologies, mend no middles – until we
have explored our own antiquity. Otherwise we blandish a new idolatry –
unholy cities, idols of the theatre, masking the idol of the market place.[42]

NOTES

1 Mark C. Taylor, *Erring: A Postmodern A/Theology*, Chicago, University of
  Chicago Press, 1984; John Milbank, *Theology and Social Theory: Beyond
  Secular Reason*, Oxford, Blackwell, 1990.
2 John Henry Newman, *The Idea of a University*, (ed.) Martin J. Svaglic, Notre
  Dame, Indiana University Press, 1982, p. 74.
3 Taylor, op. cit., p. 99.
4 ibid., p. 182.
5 ibid., p. 169.
6 ibid., p. 134.
7 Milbank, op. cit., p. 3.
8 ibid., p. 4.
9 ibid., p. 5.
10 ibid., pp. 406f.
11 ibid., pp. 6, 5–6.
12 ibid., p. 6.
13 ibid., p. 5.
14 ibid., p. 391.
15 ibid., pp. 391–2.
16 ibid., p. 392.
17 ibid., p. 391.
18 ibid., p. 392.
19 Taylor, op. cit., p. 169.
20 Milbank, op. cit., p. 6.
21 Leo Strauss, *Philosophy and Law: Essays towards the Understanding of
  Maimonides and his Predecessors* (1935), trans. Fred Baumann, Philadelphia,
  Jewish Publication Society, 1987, p. 105.
22 ibid., pp. 110, 106.
23 Emmanuel Levinas, *Totalité et infini: essai sur l'exteriorité* (1961), The Hague,
  Martinus Nijhoff, 1980; trans. Alphonso Lingis as *Totality and Infinity*, The
  Hague, Martinus Nijhoff, 1979, pp. 21–30.
24 Franz Rosenzweig, *Der Stern der Erlösung* (1921, 2nd edn 1930), *Gesammelte
  Schriften II*, The Hague, Martinus Nijhoff, 1976; trans. William W. Hollo as
  The Star of Redemption, London, Routledge & Kegan Paul, 1971, Part 3, pp.
  265ff.
25 See, for example, F.M. Cornford, *From Religion to Philosophy: A Study in the
  Origins of Western Speculation* (1912), Brighton, Harvester, 1980, pp. 124–53.
26 See Jane Harrison, *Prolegomena to the Study of Greek Religion* (1903),
  London, Merlin, 1980, pp. 1–31.
27 Emmanuel Levinas, 'Ethics as First Philosophy' (1984), in *The Levinas Reader*,
  trans. Sean Hand, Oxford, Blackwell, 1989, pp. 76–87.

28 Aaron Lichtenstein, 'Does Jewish Tradition Recognize an Ethic Independent of Halacha?', reprinted from Marvin Fox (ed.), *Modern Jewish Ethics: Theory and Practice*, Athens, Ohio University Press, 1975, pp. 103–6.
29 Eugene B. Borowitz, 'The Authority of the Ethical Impulse in "Halakha" ' (1981), in Norbert M. Samuelson (ed.), *Studies in Jewish Philosophy*, Lanham, University Press of America, 1987, pp. 489–505.
30 Taylor, op. cit., p. 134.
31 Milbank, op. cit., p. 391.
32 Taylor, op. cit., p. 169; Milbank op. cit., p. 6.
33 Taylor op. cit., p. 134; Milbank op. cit., p. 306.
34 Taylor, op. cit., p. 169; Milbank, op. cit., pp. 6, 433–4.
35 See Cupitt, infra, pp. 149–55.
36 For elaboration of this argument, see Gillian Rose, *The Broken Middle: Out of our Ancient Society*, Oxford, Blackwell, 1992.
37 See Le Corbusier, *Towards a New Architecture* (1923), trans. Frederick Etchells, London, Architectural Press, 1982, pp. 210–47.
38 Emile Rousseau, *Du contract social, ou principes du droit politique* (1762), ed. C.E. Vaughan, Manchester, Manchester University Press, 1962, p. 14, trans. pp. 89–90.
39 See Hegel, *Differenz des Fichte'schen and Schelling'schen System der Philosophie* (1801), Hamburg, Felix Meiner, 1962; trans. H.S. Harris and Walter Cerf as *The Difference between Fichte's and Schelling's System of Philosophy*, Albany, State University of New York Press, 1977, pp. 12–13, trans. pp. 89–90.
40 Taylor, op. cit., p. 168.
41 Milbank, op. cit., p. 392.
42 Francis Bacon, *The New Organon and Related Writings* (1620), ed. Fulton H. Anderson, Indianapolis, Library of Liberal Arts, 1979, pp. 47–50.

Chapter 4

Post-Marx: theological themes in Baudrillard's *America*

Andrew Wernick

> My point of view is completely metaphysical. If anything, I'm a meta-
> physician, perhaps a moralist, but certainly not a sociologist. The only
> 'sociological' work I can claim is my effort to put an end to the social.
>
> (Baudrillard, '*Forget Baudrillard*')

PARIS/BAUDRILLARD/RELIGION

At the moment of death, so it is said, your whole life flashes before you.
No surprise, then, as we glide – comfortably, some of us, yet dystopically –
towards the turn of the second millennium, a movement shadowed by
foreboding, but even more by the collective sense of becoming-dead, of –
socially speaking – entropic dissolution, that contemporary western culture
should be saturated by nostalgia for what is irredeemably past. Nor that it
should be haunted – or rather revisited – by archaic metaphors that have
welled up from our sedimented pre-industrial imaginary.

It is in such terms, at least, that we might plausibly account for the
recently revived interest in religion – an interest manifest not only in
popular fundamentalism, but also, and more paradoxically, in the preoccupation with the mystical, the spiritual and the religious that has surfaced
within the new postmodernist (and therefore post-post-Enlightenment)
theoreticians of the secular intelligentsia. As markers, we may think of
Derrida's *Of Spirit*, of the Buddhist conception of (not-)self which can be
detected in the work of Foucault and others, as underlying the subject's
'de-centring', and, in more ecclesiastical mode, of Althusser's crypto-
Comteian attempt to turn Marxism-Leninism into the heir of Catholicism.
To these we may also add: Lyotard and Deleuze's concern with the
sublime, Levinas' and Irigaray's with alterity and (an instance which I will
come to in a moment) the resolutely disenchanted sociologizing of Jean
Baudrillard.

Even this partial list makes one thing clear. In its primary authors and
texts, whatever their international resonance, the strange resurfacing of
'the religion question' in the heart of secular thought has been a largely

Parisian affair. This is not just to make a cheap point about localism and the vagaries of academic fashion. The French rationalist tradition, in the medium of whose partly dismantled inheritance the drama of 'the *post*' has largely taken place, bears a privileged historical relation to the modern story of the death of God. Its rationalism was formed (at first as theology) in the very womb of revealed religion. Even – and perhaps especially – in Reason's post-medieval rupture, autonomization, and ambition to build a new, certain foundation, the marks of this earlier formation have persisted, both in the inherited architecture of French theory's meta-categories and, more explicitly, in its lingering preoccupation with the evacuated space of the foundational itself, a centre which a reason that wants no illusions has (with the aid of linguistic self-consciousness) finally reasoned away.

Behind Derrida, that is, lies Descartes, and behind Descartes, Abelard and Anselm. And between these peaks can be traced the locus of a *ratio* which, through all its adventures, has remained deeply joined – in relations of both reconciliation and antagonism – to its transcendental and fideistically conceived opposite. In modern rationalism's (politically) radical moment the polarity becomes absolute. *Ecrasez l'infâme*: let emancipated reason show the way to a real paradise of earthly happiness and moral good. In its reconstructive phase, a more orderly mission was placed on the agenda. Reason, positivized, industrialized, aligned with the post-revolutionary needs of the Republican state, and in the teeth of Catholic reaction, would establish the basis for a new faith, a new religion and a new theology. Hence, at the cusp of the Third Republic, a neo-Kantian reception, Durkheimian sociology, the sacralization of the human, the civic and the social, and the institution of all this as official doctrine ('moral education') within the secularized schools of the state.[1]

Viewed from within, as its theoretical successor, it is, indeed, not just substantive rationality in general, but precisely this counter-Catholic edifice, whose roots can be seen in St Simon and Comte, and which was, in a final Althusserian burst, fantastically married to Marxism, which deconstruction has dissolved. In this latest stage, the sceptical conscience that has always been the other side of a would-be constructive rationality has not only returned to do battle with updated illusions. It has become increasingly absolute – a disintegrative movement that can be traced from the aporias of Durkheim, Mauss and Lévi-Strauss to the existentialist and phenomenological irruption, to the post-structuralist dissolution of logocentric thought as such.

Altogether, then, what we can call (in reference to this abbreviated genealogy) modern French thought has not only lived, at first hand, and without the mitigating bridge of Protestant individualism, the whole post-medieval dialectic of religion and enlightenment. From its corner in the latter, it has virtually lived that dialectic to death. In the nineteenth century, allied with a resurgent Scholastic passion for systematicity, it sought to replace God by Humanity and the Social, only to suffer in the twentieth – and partially by its own hand – the extinction of these as well. Put simply: the 'French' faith in reason – the self-sustaining drive for the apodictic that has driven its discourse along – has ended its adventure by utterly unravelling both faith and reason, abjuring in both respects (can we call them Subject and Object? atman and brahman?) any notion of an absolute which, in any case, has absolutely eluded its grasp.

But this ending – at root, perhaps, only the dissolution of the particular intellectual paradigm which produced all these symbolic deaths as its 'reality effect' – has been compounded by another. The postmodern is also the post-Marxist – and more generally a wave of farewell to the whole oppositional project represented by revolutionary socialism. While western Marxism as a theoretical tradition has certainly gone through an efflorescence (and even here, disintegrative trends are now well advanced), the revolutionary impulse whose revival brought this about has plainly passed from the scene. At the frenzied peak of the mobilization, history itself seemed to be validating Marxism's most radical insights and horizons. But then, just as totally, the moment passed, leaving the inescapable thought that the radical carnival of the 1960s and 1970s was a blow-out rather than a pre-revolutionary situation, the beginning of the end not for capital but for the Left itself.

For those who most identified with it, and notwithstanding the various movements generated in its wake, May '68 (Aron's *revolution introuvable*)[2] left behind an intense enigma and an intense disappointment. Of course, a similar set of circumstances was repeated throughout the west. But in France the upheaval of the 1960s was peculiarly lived as a 'Marxist' moment, peculiarly thwarted by a peculiarly Stalinist Communist Party and peculiarly condensed – a cultural and political explosion that came and went in the twinkling of an eye. There was in France, accordingly, a particularly sharp pathos to the theoretical and ideological demolition of Marxism which ensued, a demolition which had already begun, which was taken to the limit, and which was largely conducted (by Baudrillard and others) from within.

The story-line, then, seems clear. In the latest (I will not say final) vicissitude of French theorizing, beneath the hankerings for the transcendental that motivate the symptom of that transcendental's obsessive deconstruction, can be sensed the profound disillusionment – and unease – of a foundationalist tradition that has been confronted with the impossibility of what it has all along been seeking to do. In the atavistic stirrings of former gods (and of a former hiddenness) we may even suspect something worse: a death-bed conversion, a straightforwardly retrograde movement (doesn't Althusser prove it?) from disillusion to belief, an end to the agony of deferral through a premature closure, even if that closure, and the absolute on which it closes, is the non-closure of deferral itself.

Nevertheless the tone of 'new French theory' is not simply one of despair. In Derridean free play, in Deleuze's flux of desire, in Barthes' *jouissance*, in Baudrillard's 'ecstasy' and 'dizziness', there is also a note of intoxication, one that is marked, moreover, as a positive term. It is not exactly that postmodern theory has expected to find anything in the black hole where meaning used to be. But wilfully sliding there at least offers the promise – or thrill – of a little forward motion. In the bleak absurdism of this will, indeed, there might even be the basis for a new (self-)affirmation.

Of course, we know the once 'untimely' name which marks this spot. If the postwar period saw a fleeting postponement of total disenchantment through a return to Marx (and the metaphysics of revolution), it also saw (after a lifting of the anti-Nazi ban, and at first through the Sadian writings of the mad Bataille) a return to Nietzsche. For many in the left intelligentsia, indeed, Nietzsche has outlived Marx. And not surprisingly: the death throes of the Enlightenment's humanist God, the God of the individual, of Society and History, have provided a new present – a second death of God – from which to stage afresh the Nietzschian project of transvaluing values. Nietzsche's ecstatic *amor fati* has provided, as well, a powerful counter-lure to any continuing pull of teleology – which is why, despite its catastrophism, the 'post-history' of those for whom, with May '68, history (in the willed sense) came to an end is not at all apocalyptic. In the stasis of the Dionysian dance, the bomb has already dropped. The revolution has already happened. There is no rupture to fear or hope for. We are left only with the eternal present of late capitalism, a febrile recurrence of the Same from which there has never been, nor ever could be, any but an imagined escape.

It is against the background of these contextual understandings that I would like to approach the question promised in my title: how to decipher the religious subtext that has begun to surface in the recent writings of that most profane, and profaning, of ex-Marxist sociologists, Jean Baudrillard.

I should immediately make clear that I am not using the term 'religious' in any traditional or restricted sense. My point is not that Baudrillard's lapsed Catholicism is waiting to grab him from the wings. If I speak of Baudrillard's theorizing as 'theology', it is a theo-logy in which the first term, and indeed the second as well, should be understood as *sous rature*. My excuse for this semantic stretching is straightforward: it corresponds to an actual stretching of the religious domain, both in everyday life and as a topic for theory; we need a terminology if we are to talk about all this; and Baudrillard's own term 'metaphysics' (which misleads Kellner,[3] in his otherwise reasonable critique, into ignoring Baudrillard's 'esoteric side') is both too narrow and too shamefaced to indicate the field of issues and positions onto which Baudrillard's ironic meditation on the dissolved absolutes of a once progressivist reason actually opens out.

I have in mind three particular texts. The first is a remarkable series of interviews that Baudrillard gave to Sylvere Lottringer in 1984–5 (It was published in English by Semiotext(e) as 'Forget Baudrillard', and offered as a companion piece to *Forget Foucault*.) Of special interest is chapter 4, in which, with rare candour, Baudrillard articulates the idea of theorizing to which his work aspires. The others, whose production overlapped with the interview, are the most recently translated: *America* and *Cool Memories*. They are companion pieces. *Cool Memories* – a kaleidoscope of aphorisms, *obiter dicta* and rhapsodic reflections set in diary form (every entry an October, from 1981 to 1985) – provides an existentially reflexive framework for interpreting *America*; while *America* – a travelogue through the New World which depicts its astral hyper-reality from the confessed angle of a European imaginary – provides a kind of macro reality-map within which to contextualize the scattered insights of *Cool Memories*.

The tone is ruminative, the procedure indirect. In fact, as Baudrillard explains, both works were driven rather than designed. *America* – 'a certain number of fragments, notes and stories collected over a given time' – 'starts out from the certainty that everything is already there and it will be sufficient simply to find the key'.[4] As for *Cool Memories*: 'This journal develops, as its title indicates, over the course of time. However, it is haunted by something which preceded it, the secret underlying event.'[5] Overall, then, we have a shrouded quest, serendipitously pursued in the conviction that its meaning will spontaneously emerge.

The key to the meaning, I want to suggest, is provided by various scattered, oblique and apparently marginal comments in Baudrillard's later writings which reference his project, analogically at least, to certain traditional themes in the history of western religious thought. But why, in the context of puzzling about the contemporary relation of religion and thought, should Baudrillard claim our attention at all? The answer – I have been hinting at it in the foregoing remarks – is threefold: (a) because he gives us – despite everything – a 'real' scenario within which to think some aspects of the larger question; (b) because his writings are intimately and explicitly bound up with the conjoint deaths of sociology and Marxism, of society and history, and thus with the 'second death of God' which traverses that scenario; and (c) because, in the shadow of these secondary deicides, and under the extreme conditions he speculatively posits as actual, he has something to say about what Plato termed the ' "virtue" of theory'.[6]

ASTRAL AMERICA

Baudrillard's 'America', like Tocqville's, to which it alludes, is a self-consciously Old World projection, an occasion for reflecting (frequently from a car window) not only about the contemporary United States, but also about certain differentiating features of Europe itself. As Europe's

'other', America is also its horizon: the extrapolation of modern civilization trends taken to their fullest extent; an extravagant development,
which has been neither mediated nor checked by surviving traces of how
things were before the colonizers' New World project got under way.

The resulting ultra-capitalism – the site of a cancerous accumulation, of a
sidereal circulation whose image is the freeway intersection, of an endless
simulation in which the real movie begins outside the movie-house – is
captured in all the familiar Baudrillardian terms. 'America' at this level is
just a spectacular figure for general exchange and the 'third order of the
simulacrum'. It is the vanishing point at which the 'postmodern scene',[7]
petrified by deterrence and stockage, confounded with its representations,
its sociality imploded, utterly collapses into the objectal obscenity it has
become.

For readers of Baudrillard such a characterization is hardly novel. Still,
the argument does advance, which perhaps we can see if we consider the
movement within the complex of attitudes he brings to bear.

Let us note first that, as the residue of an activism manqué, Baudrillard's
'America' is grasped in quasi-dialectical terms, albeit that what is grasped
(on the place of actuality) as its essence is an amputated dialectic within a
totality which pointedly lacks a negative-critical pole. Just as with pre-
Habermasian critical theory, in fact, what focusses Baudrillard's attention,
here as elsewhere, is precisely the absence of that immanent, system-
threatening contradiction which earlier critics of an earlier capitalism had
posited as the foundation of transformist hope. In the first instance, this
absence is socio-political: the evacuated space of what various strains of
Marxism have posited as the revolutionary subject. But the departed
proletariat and its successors are also subsumed by an absence still more
general and profound. For Baudrillard, the implosive reversals of late
capitalism have eliminated any and every source of neg-entropic opposition – not just from the structurally engendered play of interests, but also
from the repressed forces of desire, from the anthropological impossibility
of tolerating unfreedom, and from symbolic traditions (religious, aesthetic,
intellectual) capable of generating a resistance that points to an achievable
better world.

Baudrillard is not content, though, just to let the dialectic rest in peace.
He is haunted by what has disappeared. Hence, from the very depths of
that disappearance, and against the grain of the fatalism it engenders, his
continual quest for a counter-principle. At first this is provided by 'symbolic exchange', a primal dynamic illustrated by agonic gift-giving (the *pot-
latch*), which inheres in the ontology of the social and which irrepressibly
opposes itself to the whole de-ritualized order of economic change. In the
clash of these logics, transgression replaces determinate negation, while
the category of opposition is itself rethought as the duelling movement of a
counter-gift.

With the postulate of the 'death of the social' which overhangs his later writings, such opposition loses all positivity. Yet even here some version of the dialectic continues to shadow his account. Thus, he argues,[8] while entrenched tendencies towards political withdrawal and mass apathy may be lamented by the romantics of the activist Left, these are precisely the ways in which radical opposition expresses itself these days. Indeed, the collective suicide of the subject is the only counter-gift that a serialized populace can validly offer to a vampiric order whose all-powerful circuitry of unilateral communication obliterates the effectivity of any 'banal' (i.e. non-sacrificial) form of response. Hence, finally, Baudrillard's rationale for his own paradoxical line of critique: a 'fatal' reversion in which a simulative theory offers itself back to the triumphant 'system of objects' in the only coin which cannot be tolerated – one that expressly simulates the seductive skull painted on its face.

But Baudrillard's 'America' is not just an automatic product of modern capital. Or rather, the fact that it appears so is overdetermined by the enthusiasm by which this destiny is culturally embraced. It is an 'achieved Utopia'. Why? Because of a superb, but historically contingent, fit between the Republic's eighteenth-century founding ideals – Lockeian/Protestant/pragmatic – and the objectification of these in the globalizing commercialism America has spread to the world. In the American case, then, a capitalist formation's charter revolutionary myths have been totally integrated into its contemporary imaginary. And beyond this horizon, whose one-dimensional optimism both feeds and feeds off the self-perpetuating energy of capital itself, no alternative future can be conceived.

The contrast with Europe is clear. Its Revolution, trailing both pre- and trans-capitalist longings, has never assumed flesh. Worse: in view of the actual future shown in the mirror of America itself, Old World Utopianism has increasingly revealed itself as hopelessly trapped in the past. Thus, while 'Theirs is the crisis of an achieved utopia, confronted with the problem of its duration and permanence', 'ours is a crisis of historical ideals facing up to the impossibility of their realization'.[9]

It is this double conjuncture that contemporary theory – culturally transatlantic on both sides of the pond – has been given to ponder. Overall: a kind of complementary agony of the ideal. No wonder that *Cool Memories* opens with a meditation on melancholy, a 'melancholy (e.g. in dialectics) which is gaining the upper hand today, though in ironically transparent forms'.[10]

In line with the apparent bleakness of what he projects into the space of the postmodern, Baudrillard's thought has a Manichean, even gnostic, strain. The subject must die in order to triumph over the powers of the world. Yet, as if in perverse adherence to the negated negation of the negation in which we are apparently stuck, Baudrillard refuses to demon-

ize either the catastrophic and socially evacuated hyper-reality he describes
– the 'evil demon of images' – or the national-imperial entity – America –
identified with it. 'I shall never forgive anyone', he says, 'who passes a
condescending or contemptuous judgement on America'.[11] Hence the
enthusiastic tone in which we are enjoined, following Venturi, to learn
from Las Vegas – and, indeed, from New York, Chicago, Salt Lake City
and Los Angeles. This is consistent, too, with Baudrillard's more general
perspective on the postmodern. In the pleasure dome of excrescent
semiurgy the only pleasure available is that of being perpetually seduced.
Moralists will condemn and resist. But there is a certain wisdom, not to
mention a certain psychedelic pleasure, to be gained from going with this
flow; that is, from submitting to the seductions of the obscene, from
immersing oneself, in a gesture of supreme moral indifference, in the
vertiginous ecstasy of the image.

Hovering here, against the grain of any merely justice- or praxis-based
critique, is an attraction towards 'America' (= postmodernism incarnate)
as a figure for what Jameson has summarily called 'the postmodern sublime'.[12] This category – which expresses that aspect of contemporary
sensibility that is astounded and awed by a globality it cannot grasp – has
been articulated in a variety of ways. With Baudrillard, whose starting
point was the confounding of sign and commodity, what is emphasized is
the unutterables of infinite circulation and of infinite imagistic regress. In
its implosion of subjectivity, and complete flattening of the social landscape, this sublimity is even physically echoed in the literal landscape in
which America's humanly constructed habitat is set. America's 'nature' (or
the south-west's, anyway) is the desert: a barren surface whose refusal of
meaning mirrors the sidereal speed and indifferent imagescape of the
endless urban itself.

The suspicion that we properly bring to bear on all academic production
will no doubt see in Baudrillard's post-critical move something self-serving:
a position that – in the daring of its amorality – outpositions all the others;
an instance, more banally, of self-advertisement and bad faith. But it is a
position, none the less, which at least has the virtue of avoiding the
ultimate end-game of lament. Openness to the American sublime, to the
unimaginable carnival into which the 'real's big numbers' of 'power, economy, sex'[13] have dissolved, at once provides immediate success to an
experience (giddy, hallucinatory) that transports us beyond the dreadful
immanence of the hyper-real itself, as well – more coolly – as providing an
appreciation of just what it is, in the words of the English Pop artist
Richard Hamilton, 'which makes today's home so attractive, so
appealing'.[14]

Moreover, for all the comatose immobilism Baudrillard pronounces
irreversible, this turn, this flight into the black sun of postmodern capitalist
culture, this fascinated absorption into the gaze of Medusa, even offers the

possibility of a strategy. It is, to be sure, a strange one: opposition through acceptance, immersion as critical distance, a transfiguration of nihilism through its full-blooded embrace. The Nietzschian strain is evident, yet there is also a whiff of the other-worldly. For it is not the noonday of our coming to our senses, but the American sublime, the unrepresentatable (and unspeakably demonic) experience of identifying with the seductive vortex of its surfaces, which is offered as a beacon of hope. By allowing ourselves to be summoned towards it, it seems, we can secure a redemptive escape – an escape, moreover, not only from the integrative ideality of 'America' itself, but also from the impossibly nostalgic ideality of the 'Europe' from which Baudrillard himself self-confessedly speaks.

THE SECOND DEATH OF GOD

Baudrillard's project traverses the space of a double emptiness. It is unintelligible, indeed, if we fail to see that what it seeks to take account of is that Nietzsche's original death of God has been compounded by a second. If the first disappearance (in Carlos Fuentes' phrase) left a God-shaped hole, the second has left a Marx-shaped one. It is this second hole with which Baudrillard, the disillusioned Situationist, is immediately concerned. Yet in this very preoccupation he cannot avoid the first. The evacuations are not just linear and successive. Their sites overlap; and through the clear void at their transcendental centre, their overlapping emptiness, which reverberates with the collapse of subjectivity as such, is identically the same.

Baudrillard, to be sure, is not just a spectator at this wake. His early works (from *Le Système des objets* to *Vers une critique de l'économie politique du signe*) consisted of a triple deconstruction in which he set against themselves the would-be scientific categories of Marx, Saussure and Mauss.[15] Depth models, ontologies of the social, illusory consolations, all came tumbling down. Just as with Nietzsche himself, then (though not in so isolated an endeavour), Baudrillard presents himself both as an active participant in the destruction of contemporary 'idols', and as an heroic inheritor of the chaos that results.

Baudrillard's description of this situation is striking:

> Nietzsche grappled with the death of God, but all we have to deal with is the disappearance of politics and history. The disappearance may take on a degree of pathos (as in May '68) but that will no doubt be the last time. May '68 marked the onset of a long eventless process. That is why those who did not live through it can never understand what is happening today in a diluted form, just as those who never lived through the death of God can understand nothing of the convalescence of values.[16]

At first sight, since 'what is happening today' is only doing so in a 'diluted form', the second death is less far-reaching than the first. Indeed, while this was precisely a 'death', what has happened to the transcendentals conjured up by the terms 'politics and history' is only a 'disappearance'. Yet the phrasing is deceptive.

To begin with, and notwithstanding the enlightened secularity in whose midst it has occurred, the 'disappearance of politics and history' does not register with Baudrillard as a merely secular – i.e. post-death-of-God – development. This is clear from the awestruck tone in which he alludes to the 'event' – May '68 – which 'marked its onset'. Within the Baudrillardian theatre something mighty is certainly at stake. It is as if, the first time, God did not really yet die. To put it differently: with the reversal of capital from explosion to implosion, with the end of history, what has gone, whether in its liberal meliorist or radical Utopian form, is no less than the modern version of what has long been (I am inclined to say for two and a half millennia) the west's sometimes buried, and sometimes open, transcendental wish. That is: the myth of human history itself as the ground and vehicle for redemption from our accumulated individual and collective discontents. Gone, in short, and even in the disguised form of secular ideologies, is that sense of what Christians have called the Holy Spirit and Jews *ruach*.

In its most mystical-revolutionary form, via Joachimite heresy, rabbinical and Kabbalistic messianism, and apostolic hopes for a second coming, it is this sense which has fed the tradition of millennarian upheaval documented by Norman Cohn[17] and which, in a more politically ambiguous way, came to underpin Hegel's own notion of dialectical transcendence. It is this sense, too, I would argue, which the exhausted Utopias of the eighteenth century and the impossible ones of the nineteenth, themselves, for a while, sustained. And vice versa, for the we-experience rekindled at the heart of every enthusiastic rebellion has continually given the subterranean canon of transformist images and slogans a new lease on life. It was, of course, a commonplace of early nineteenth-century radical thought that the spiritual continuity between biblical religion and the humanist project of freedom and progress was the hermeneutic secret of both. With the present-day expiry of the latter, then, an entire religious epoch appears to have reached its end.

But what Baudrillard calls the disappearance of politics, the social and history has not been only a matter of eroded faith. With the confounding of the real with its image (a process he associates with the rupture brought about by mechanical reproduction, and thus with a constitutive feature of late capitalism) the transcendental signifieds of society and history really have disappeared. In its illusoriness, the very upheaval of the late 1960s which promised to resuscitate them only confirmed the irrevocable extent to which that had occurred. Nor is it only ideologies of the Left which have consequently lost their hold. The dissolution of the social and the effacement of the individual before the brute, if fascinating, destiny of the object have deprived even Nietzschean transvaluation of its material grounds. The eternal recurrence of late capitalism is only a parody of that idea. It provides no foothold for the will. Nothing happens any more.

Altogether, then, with the second death of God, the consequences of the first death have returned with a vengeance. The vertiginous sense of loss and displacement associated with the first dawning of fully fledged disbelief has recurred in the new context of the variously formulated death of 'Man'. But this time the nihilism is complete. There is no prospect of a replacement, no Dionysian promise that God's death could, should and would lead to human self-overcoming, and thence to a divine re-empowerment.

THEORY TOWARDS A STATE OF GRACE

So what, in this implacably post-Marxist, but also post-Nietzschian, conjuncture, does Baudrillard propose?

Certainly not a renewed attempt to legislate into being a new table of values. Such voluntarism has been swept from the board. In addition, Baudrillard remains Marxisant enough to reserve such counter-tendencies for the determined contradictions of the real – even in the realization that Marxism itself was only ever an internal critique of political economy, and that the dialectic (increasingly complicated and attenuated) that Marxists have posited has lost all historical force. Nor, however, does Baudrillard's strategy of reversal have anything to do with a neo-Marxist critical theory, even of an Adornoesque kind. For, by insisting on a mimetic counter-seduction (through which he aims to lure the 'big reals' of postmodernity into their own trap) he refuses precisely the singular negativism of such a stance.

The form of theory which Baudrillard offers, in fact, though profoundly dissatisfied in spirit, seems only tenuously related to any kind of practical aim. Self-consciously pitting its own 'fatality' against that of capital, it simply sets about staging its own death. Or rather – for 'this is the real trick' – it aims to disappear.

'You know', Baudrillard observes (in the Lottringer interview),

> my way is to make ideas appear. But as soon as they appear I immediately try to make them disappear. That's what the game has always consisted of. Strictly speaking, nothing remains but a sense of dizziness, with which you can't do anything.[18]

On one level, this epistemological game of hide-and-seek has a straightforward justification. By 'rigorously cutting itself off from any system of reference', theory will 'at least be current, on the scale of what it wishes to describe'.[19] But by taking this tack, Baudrillard also positions himself towards the hyper-real in a manner remarkably similar to that which, in the Counter-Reformation, was adopted by the Jesuits towards the second-order simulations of their own day. It was in that context, Baudrillard tells us,[20] that the Jesuit iconolaters penetrated the dark secret of divine non-existence. From which angle, the Protestant iconoclasts were simply naive. For Baudrillard himself, those who hanker after a truth beyond the evil demon of images have similarly missed the point. For him, as for the Machiavellian cadres of the seventeenth-century Society of Jesus, 'The secret of theory is that truth doesn't exist.'[21]

But this is not all. In the constant self-demolition through which such theory proceeds, in its 'art of disappearing', lies the possibility of its assuming a virtually sacred role. Through that ploy, as Baudrillard puts it, theorizing might be modulated finally 'into a state of grace'.[22] Two senses can be given to this remarkable term. On the one hand, the 'grace' of theory can be read as akin to Plato's virtue of theory – the discipline of a practice which, to be faithful to itself, must be faithful to truth. Today, to be sure, there is no singular or originary Truth to be found. But there remains, in a manner to be rigorously uncovered, at least the truth of this non-truth. On the other hand, however, if theory, in fidelity to its cognitive interest, must these days adopt the pose of a deconstructive simulation, it is not only meditative. Even as such, that is to say, as a kind of non-representational *mimesis*, Baudrillard's ideal practice of theory is performative as well as constative. It is 'both simulation and challenge'.[23]

'Theory', he elaborates,

> is a challenge to the real. A challenge to the world to exist. Very often a challenge to God to exist. But there is more than theory. In the beginning, religion, in its former heretical phase, was always a negation – at times a violent one – of the real world, and this is what gave it strength. After that, religion became a process of reconciliation rather than a pleasure or reality principle. This can hold true for theory as well: a theory can attempt to reconcile the real with theory itself.[24]

In Adorno, and in much of contemporary postmodern theorizing, we can see a transposition of negative theology and its apophatic search for the hidden God. With Baudrillard, what seems to be a similar enterprise is much more despairing, and much more radical. Its aim, indeed, premised on the understanding that simulacra precede the real, is well-nigh magical. The utterances of Baudrillardian theory, premised on an identification with the fallen but sacred horizon of appearances, whose ruses will be used against it, are a cosmic dare. Through the eliciting reversals of seduction, they would force the disappeared deity, or messianic moment, to reappear, to come (back) into being.

It is extraordinary, perhaps, to find this archaic homoeopathy at the obscure heart of a message delivered by one whom the *New York Times* (quoted on *Cool Memories*' cover) has described as 'a sharp-shooting lone ranger of the post-Marxist left'. Yet this very provenance provides its own key.

In thoroughly magical, yet thoroughly disenchanted form, Baudrillard's writings hint at a recovery of the prophetic voice; at a recovery, that is, of what the Left, for a century and a half, has (without knowing how to acknowledge this without self-contradiction) taken over from western religiosity as its own. This voice, I should immediately clarify, is not that of the soothsayer. It is not predictive. Baudrillard foretells nothing, and certainly not (unlike the revolutionary he may once have been) the Messiah, the Apocalypse, or the Second Coming. His is the prophecy, rather, of one who toys with the idea that the signifier can produce the signified; that through the Word (or rather: through the seductive wiles of a game in which theory challenges the more-than-real to a duel to the death) these impossibles can be made flesh. But only toys, because to fixate on any spot, to abandon the aleatory *jouissance du texte*, would risk being sucked into the flattening machine of pure opinion, pure dogma, pure moralism. Besides, as he notes in a reference (in *Forget Foucault*) to Kafka's Messiah, who only turned up the day after he was needed, the God who is successfully challenged into being may come too late.

In the end, then, Baudrillard remains suspended between a playfully immoral stoicism and the hope that something redemptive may yet appear. With regard to the former, his theorizing is constative and resigned. With regard to the latter, he is performative and ecstatic. We might want to say that only this second strand in his thinking – inclined specifically as it is towards the 'missing' transcendental – is, properly speaking, a religious attitude. But that, as I have suggested, would be to take too narrow a view of the religious, in whose medium this whole contradictory drama is enacted. Even the first moment of his stance can be construed as piety before an intimation of the sublime. In any case, Baudrillard's attitude to the God-shaped, Marx-shaped hole which preoccupies him is not simply and absolutely ambivalent. Its poles of repulsion and attraction coexist within a lofty and aristocratic irony which disdains the false closure of a choice. Baudrillard's contradictoriness is irreducible and constitutive. It is at once, and with deliberate undecidability, a movement towards and a movement away from what seduces him in all the depthlessly obscene surfaces he delights to depict: the hiddenness of his – and our – hidden God.

NOTES

1 I have elaborated this view in 'Structuralism and the Dissolution of the French Rationalist Project', in J. Fekete (ed.), *The Structural Allegory: Reconstructive Encounters with the New French Thought*, Minneapolis, Minnesota University Press, 1985, pp. 130–49.

2 R. Aron, *La révolution introuvable: réflections sur la révolution de mai 1968*, Paris, Fayard, 1968.
3 D. Kellner, *Jean Baudrillard: From Marxism to Postmodernism and Beyond*, Cambridge, Polity, 1989; especially chapter 8.
4 Jean Baudrillard, *Cool Memories*, trans. Chris Turner, London, Verso, 1990, p. 219.
5 ibid., p. 192.
6 Plato, *Protagoras and Meno*, London, Penguin, 1964, pp. 115–57. Of course Baudrillard's own theory is not apodictic, and it aims to know the forms not of the real, but of the hyper-real.
7 The term has been widely disseminated by Arthur Kroker. See, for example, A. Kroker and D. Cook, *The Postmodern Scene: Excremental Culture and Hyper-Aesthetics*, Oxford, Oxford University Press, 1986.
8 The argument is elaborated in Jean Baudrillard, *In the Shadow of the Silent Majorities*, New York, Semiotext(e), 1983. The silence of the masses, he observes (p. 22), 'is paradoxical – it isn't a silence which does not speak, it is a silence which refuses to be spoken for in its name. And in this sense, far from being a form of alienation, it is an absolute weapon.'
9 Jean Baudrillard, *America*, trans. Chris Turner, London, Verso, 1989, p. 77.
10 Baudrillard, *Cool Memories*, op. cit., p. 4.
11 ibid., p. 209.
12 F. Jameson, *Postmodernism, or the Cultural Logic of Late Capitalism*, Durham, Duke University Press, 1991.
13 Jean Baudrillard, *Forget Foucault*, New York, Semiotext(e), 1987, p. 46.
14 Hamilton's 1956 collage, exhibited as part of the Future Exhibition in London, depicts a mid-1950s domestic interior, complete with ideal couple. It is entirely made up of cut-outs from ads of the period.
15 In *L'Echange symbolique et le mort*, Paris, Gallimard, 1976, Baudrillard also deconstructs the Freudian category of desire. As an aspect of his rejection of productivism he has constantly criticized Deleuze and Guattari's attempt to thematize the 'libidinal economy'.
16 Baudrillard, *Cool Memories*, op. cit., p. 186.
17 N. Cohn, *The Pursuit of the Millennium*, London, Secker & Warburg, 1957.
18 Jean Baudrillard, 'Forget Baudrillard', in *Forget Foucault*, op. cit., p. 127.
19 ibid., p. 131.
20 Baudrillard's reference to the seventeenth-century Jesuits, as a foreshadowing of the postmodern 'third order of the simulacrum', is a constant theme in his writings. The following two passages may be taken as representative. The first is from *Simulations*, New York, Semiotext(e), 1983, p. 9:

> It can be seen that the iconoclasts, who are often accused of despising and denying images, were in fact the ones who accorded them their actual worth, unlike the iconolaters, who saw in them only reflections and were content to venerate God at one remove. But the converse can also be said, namely that the iconolaters were the most modern and adventurous minds, since underneath the idea of the apparition of God in the mirror of images, they already enacted his death and disappearance in the epiphany of his representations (which they perhaps knew no longer represented anything, and that they were purely a game, but that this was precisely the greatest game – knowing also that it is dangerous to unmask images, since they dissimulate the fact that there is nothing behind them). This was the approach of the Jesuits.

The second is from *Seduction*, London, Macmillan/New World Perspectives,

1990, p. 176:

> The Jesuits were already famous for having returned the throngs to the bosom of the Catholic Church by the worldly and aesthetic seduction of the baroque. . . . And they were relatively successful. It is entirely possible that, once the austere charms of political economy and producer capitalism have been swept away, a Catholic and Jesuit era will begin, with a soft technology of seduction and a soft, rosy semiurgy.

21 Baudrillard, 'Forget Baudrillard', op. cit., p. 130.
22 ibid., p. 128.
23 ibid., p. 133.
24 ibid., p. 124.

Chapter 5

Hegel and the gods of postmodernity

Rowan Williams

As this ludicrously ambitious title indicates, I shall be offering no more than a sketch for an argument which I hope may turn out to be worth pursuing more carefully; an argument which attempts to identify an area of ambiguity in certain kinds of theological reception of Derridean themes, and to raise, yet again, the overworked spectre of Hegel in order to question and explore this ambiguity. My attention will be directed not so much to the primary texts of deconstruction as to certain discussions of their problematic by writers in theology and religious studies; but my final aim is to raise an issue for some of the rhetoric of postmodern performance itself.

Briefly then: in spite of Derrida's disclaimers, it has proved very hard for religious writers *not* to read the language of trace and *différance* as a negative theology. For Derrida himself, it is reasonably clear that 'God' is an 'effect of the trace': to speak of God is to try to put a face upon that which haunts language – what is over the shoulder, round the corner, what is by stipulation not capable of being confronted, being *faced*. Thus to speak of God is to try and erase the genuine trace; and negative theology (like the negativity of all dialectic) simply affirms the possibility of a state devoid of this haunting, since it *identifies* trace and *différance* with a kind of subject, with what is ultimately, despite all theological evasions, presence. However, the response of a good many writers (J.D. Crossan,[1] John Caputo,[2] and, most recently, Kevin Hart,[3] among others) has been to say, in effect, that Derrida has assumed too hastily that negative theology is a merely dialectical move in an unreconstructed metaphysical (or, if you insist, onto-theological) framework. Negative theology, as practised by an Eckhart or a John of the Cross, is a prohibition against *any* thematizing of divine presence, any ultimate return to an analogy of being between God and the subject. Kevin Hart, in particular, at the end of his admirably clear study, suggests that a negative theology that has learned its proper task under Derridean probing is the only thing capable of stopping theology's constant and compulsive sliding back towards a metaphysic of presence.

Hart and Caputo – and I think Joseph O'Leary[4] as well – repudiate a theology of divine presence but seem eager to hold to a theology of divine *grace*. Other theological or quasi-theological receptions of Derrida evidently see this as a failure to understand the seriousness of Derrida's challenge. Cupitt's reading of Derrida[5] supports what still appears as a powerfully voluntarist account of the speaker's confrontation with the world, and pays little attention to the question of trace; since nothing in Cupitt's writing can be put down to carelessness, we must suppose that this is a conscious strategy to block any attempt at slipping an 'objective' God in through the back door of the *via negativa*. In other words, he rejects in advance the retrieval and radicalization of negative theology by Caputo, Hart and others. Mark Taylor, on the other hand, has tackled the question directly, and – notably in his recent *Tears*[6] – developed an aesthetic of 'non-absent absence' (Blanchot's term), the inscription (not representation) of *différance* in a manner which does in some sense make of *différance* an occasion of 'grace'. The art of 'non-absent absence' is the art of the sacred; taking the sacred to be the interruption of ordinary 'exchange', 'the circulation of knowledge'.[7] Thus, for art to be grace-full, it must *defer* presence; which means deferring, indefinitely, the end of time, and thus dissolving time as *a* system or *a* story. In Taylor's own idiom, his a/theology is 'anachronistic': it is the refusal alike of origins and ends. The grace or gift of art, what it is that locates this or that work in the arena of the sacred, is an overthrowing of the normally prevailing alliance of time and understanding. Time as history is spoken of as a linear movement; it cannot avoid the suggestion of ends, and so of *parousia*, the manifestation of what's hidden. It is thus appropriately bracketed with understanding, whose task is 'reducing difference to identity and returning otherness to same'.[8] The sacred interrupts as 'Absolute Paradox' (Taylor is here working through Kierkegaard's *Philosophical Fragments*); yet, although it is a rupture it is also the desire of understanding itself. Language wills its own downfall: this is what it is to say with Derrida that language itself announces the non-originary origin, *différance* as such, that without which (only it is not an 'it' or a 'that') there would be no speech.

What interests me in all this is the clarity with which the sacred, the order of grace or liberation, is assimilated to absence, rupture. Taylor is more consistent here than the negative theologians, for whom some sort of gracing agency seems still to be in the background: for Taylor, who is here, I think, profoundly faithful to Derrida, grace can only be the effect of the irruption, both unpredictable and unavoidable, of the empty purity of *différance* 'surrounding' the practice of speech. For Derrida, of course, it is *writing itself* that irrupts, breaks through the presence of the spoken word. There are no *words* of grace, except in so far as the writer or, for Taylor, artist deploys signs in the direction of the saving absence, the trace; nor can there be a narrative of grace, since the holy is the timeless – not simply the *discontinuous* in time, but the pure negation of successiveness as such, chronological successiveness and the 'succession' of thinking and speaking. There is the world of exchange, in which (to pursue the figure of 'exchange') utterances are convertible, in that they provide material for a hearer's or reader's utterance in response; and there is pure, unanswerable 'tearing'. (I suspect that 'exchange' is being given more malign connotations as well, in terms of the endless substitutability of signs in an advanced credit-economy.) It is hard to avoid the conclusion that the exchange of language, as a communal and temporal practice, is necessarily an extinguishing of true or final otherness: the otherness of linguistic intercourse inevitably falls under the condemnations of totalizing dialectic, the other becoming *my* other, defined in relation to my(self-) presence, a resolvable, confrontable difference. And this in turn bears out Peter Hodgson's judgement in a recent book[9] that the theology or a/theology of postmodernism is fundamentally tragic and ironic: it leaves the speaker and what speech cannot master eternally divided. Writing/art remembers what speech forgets, precisely by *dis*membering (the idiom is infectious) direct utterance, speech coming from a tangible source. It 'reminds' speech of its contingency, of the illusoriness of presence, transparency, authorship/authority.

Writing for Derrida, the art of dismemberment and silence for Taylor, are occasions of grace presumably because they constitute an end to illusion by locating language vis-à-vis what makes language what it is – which is not a cause or source, an *archē*, but the very fluidity and play of language itself. Direct, 'convertible' utterance conceals this. My question here, chiefly to Taylor but to some extent also to Derrida, is to do with the *pathos* of this model, the pathos of the 'veiled truth', of a diurnal or primitive perception in need of dismantling. A string of dualisms opens up in the background: the intelligible and the mysterious, speech and silence, the inside and the outside, the apparent and the real, the speaking ego and the speechless void, even – dare I evoke it? – spirit and nature. The sacred, the liberative, is here the second set of terms – the ineffable, the outside, the eternal. My anxiety is to do with the relegation to profanity of the temporal, the communicative, the implied devaluation of 'exchange', or, to adapt an idea of Hodgson's, 'followability'. If the sacred is innately alien to 'exchange', the tragic quality of such thinking is not only a matter of abstract dualism between speech and void but also affects the valuation of human corporateness. Take 'exchange' to designate the whole range of *negotiated* human activity, from plain conversation to political activity, all those contexts in which resistance and misunderstanding have to be overcome, concealed interests and agenda drawn out and confronted, the implicit or explicit refusal of a voice to an interlocutor overturned, and a concluding position, not simply determined by one speaker, arrived at; what are the implications of treating this as the primary locus of illusion or unfreedom?

The fear expressed is of totalization: all negotiation moves inexorably towards identity, all exchange presupposes an attainable sameness or equivalence. The otherness of negotiation is, *ex professo*, temporary. What this anxiety underrates, however, is the degree to which the identity towards which negotiation or dialect moves is a construction not simply determined by either of the identities present at the start; it can only be described as '*returning* otherness to same' by a violent abstraction from the fact that this otherness is constituted substantially by the passage of (irreversible) time. Time and understanding do indeed belong together. The suspicion proper to understanding is not directed against the communicative/negotiating process itself but against *specific* distortions and evasions that show themselves in the conduct of the process. The liberation sought for or required is not from a global illusion about linguistic exchange, but from whatever conditions hinder the movement to a jointly accepted mode of continuing. Fear of totality, of the tyranny of identity, would be appropriate if such an accepted 'mode of continuing' were regarded as an end of all negotiation, rather than being itself in turn a negotiable position – i.e. if it were absolutized against possible criticism; it might also be appropriate if each phase of dialectic, each act of negotiating, systematically ignored its location in a history of exchange, believed its positions to have no past, no process of construction. Indeed, such a prior commitment to ahistorical truth would be precisely one of those claims to power that dialectic's business is to dismantle, or at least to put to the test.

Which brings me – at last – to Hegel. It is of course true that Hegel believes there to be only one story to tell of the life of the mind (or of followable speech, to give it a less self-condemning designation); but it is emphatically not a story of *return* to the same. His disagreement with Fichte is normally held to turn on this point, and it is what decisively marks him off from Neoplatonist thought. Absolute spirit is characterizable as ultimate self-presence, but (despite all the disastrously misleading trails laid by Hegel's philosophy of history) it is at least debatable whether, in the Hegelian system, it could actually make any sense to claim that Absolute Spirit was realizable as the term of any specific historical process.[10] It is possible in Hegel's terms to talk about the term towards which all acts of understanding (all negotiations) intrinsically move – the 'actuality' (as the *Logic* has it)[11] in which concrete presence and intelligible structure are no longer separate in the subject's engagement in the world; in this sense, there is and must be a teleology in reflection. But the *telos* is not *representable* (not present) in the structure of any given historical consciousness or set of consciousnesses, not *a* meaning which a speaker or writer could articulate as a piece of communicable information (no one would need to know it; no one could learn it by being told it as an external state of affairs). Therefore all that is *said* about this *telos* has a necessarily quasi-fictional character: it has the negative force of insisting that we don't take for granted *any* level of dualism between self and world, the perceived and the real, the concept and the 'brute fact', and so on. Derrida complains that the negative moment in Hegel is simply 'contradiction'; the cancelling of what is there, to be cancelled in its turn by the negation of the negation which (re-)establishes identity. But – as Deborah Chaffin has shown in a remarkable essay on Derrida's Hegel[12] – the structure of Hegel's dialectic is meant to challenge the all-sufficiency of the polarity of simple identity and simple difference. Reflection does not work with such symmetries, it requires the plain opposition of positive and negative (presence and absence) to be left behind. What is thinkable is so precisely because thinking is not content with the abstraction of mutual exclusivities, but struggles to conceive a structured wholeness nuanced enough to contain what appeared to be contradictories. Once again: time and understanding belong together; language constantly remakes itself in the fact of what is not yet understood, criticizes itself unceasingly. Its problem (if that's the right word) is not a timeless shadow of pure alterity, but the otherness engendered in a temporally shifting situation. To talk here in Derridean fashion of différance as such is to say something with only tangential relation to the processes of concept formation as they show themselves in language. What is strange to reason moves around in the field of cognition: we can indeed abstract to the trace of a perpetual shadow (though in so far as this supposes a fundamental contingency in language it misses Hegel's central concerns), but this shadow *can only 'appear'* in the historical process of making (communicable, communal) sense, in the 'following' of discourse.

I am genuinely not sure how far this would represent a model acceptable to Derrida himself; that is, as Chaffin intimates, a very large question.[13] My present interest is to return to the question of God and the sacred in Derrida's theological commentators. Hegel does not use 'the sacred' as a category; but it is perfectly plain that the meaning of 'God' for Hegel is bound up with the making of sense. God is – ultimately – the actuality in which concreteness and intelligibility coincide; the life of God is therefore, in temporal terms, the movement towards that coincidence, the movement towards a kind of action that is the proper consummation, the bringing to sense, of the world's process, the movement towards non-dualistic understanding, the movement towards 'rational' (just and natural) communalty, and so on. Grace (not a particularly Hegelian word, I know) is in the making of rational connections, the overcoming of otherness not by reduction to identity but by the labour of discovering what understanding might be adequate to a conflictual and mobile reality without excising or devaluing its detail. Liberation here is liberation from a sterile and reductive adhesion to a fixed perception of fixed states of affairs. The holy, the graceful, is not interruption, the timeless overthrowing of process and purpose, but is inseparable from the labour of making – which is necessarily, for Hegel, the labour of finding: hence its innate and massive *difficulty*, its distance from voluntarist play.

A Hegelian version of negative theology would thus be neither Taylor's a/theology nor a merely conceptual moment in the clarification of ideas about God – 'dialectical' in a rather cheap or trivial sense. It would be a move away from the hope of 'merely conceptual' clarification as such, towards an actuality in which the dualisms of self and world, thought and deed, were sublated. It would be, in more conventional terms, a moral and spiritual dispossession and recreation, inseparable from the process of a corporate making of sense. Seen in these terms, it actually stands rather closer to the negative way of John of the Cross and others (notably also to the definitions of apophatic theology in modern eastern Christian writers like Lossky[14] and Yannaras[15]) than to the negative graces of art celebrated by Taylor. It seems that both radical and fairly orthodox theological readers of Derrida have too hastily assumed that the 'anachronism' of the Derridean trace is the proper mode of a Christian apophaticism, and that what has to be done to reconcile Derrida with the negative theology he is both fascinated and alienated by is a sharpening of the anti-metaphysical thrust of apophaticism – whether in the direction of a conscious retrieval of Eckhart and Aquinas (as in Caputo) or in the direction of the nameless space of holiness, as in Taylor. But the question remains of whether the negative strain in Christianity – or, indeed, other faiths, including Buddhism – can be read so exclusively as an anti-metaphysical strategy, as opposed to a discipline interwoven with others in a general project of what Hodgson calls 'transfigurative praxis'.

The risk of a negative theology in abstraction, the identification of the sacred with the void, is the purchase it gives to a depoliticized – or even anti-political – aesthetic, in which there is a subtle but unmistakable suggestion that the social and linguistic order (as opposed to this or that particular and questionable order) is what we need to be delivered from, and that a particular kind of artistic praxis can so deliver. The 'meaning' which our unillusioning about language offers is the anti-meaning of time-lessness, the empty and endless space of pure difference. To revive a question posed many years ago by Gerald Graff,[16] how is this to avoid a basically dishonest rhetoric of risk or cost, 'redescribing resignation as heroism'? Is there a *labour* of the negative here? To turn to Hegel for help in formulating this challenge is not to endorse the Hegelian system in all its ambition and complexity, but only to ask whether certain Hegelian themes may help to undermine a sacralizing of absence and inception at the expense of the work of social meaning. Gillian Rose's comment on the antinomies of sociology has pertinence here: 'If actuality is not thought, then thinking has no social import.'[17] Translated into our present context, this implies that to look for liberation to what is not thought is to miscon-ceive the entire project of human reflection and to bar the way to an authentically critical philosophy.

Hegel's structuring narrative is, of course, that of incarnation – more specifically of incarnation as understood in the Lutheran framework in which the humanity of God incarnate is not a 'picture' of the divine power, but the enacting of divine resource in the poverty, pain and negativity of a life and death which could not by any stretch of the imagination be held up as natural symbols of divine identity. The point, for our purposes, is threefold. Hegel assumes that what we might call the 'interests' of God and the reasoning subject are not alien or in competition: the sacred is our fruition not our annihilation. *But*: the merging of human and divine interest in any kind of static pantheism can only have the effect of dehistor- icizing (derationalizing) the human project; there is no identity *yet to be found* in the endless exchanges of speech and understanding. *Thus*: the union of divine and human interest must be affirmed and understood at just that point where the sheer historical vulnerability of the human is most starkly shown, where unfinishedness, tension, the rejection of meaning and community are displayed in the figure of a man simultaneously denied voice or identity by the religious and the political rationalities of his day.[18] To understand the (historical) cross as God's is to understand the negative 'speculatively' – the negative not as absence or mystery but as the denial of human spirituality in oppression, suffering and death. And it is the *concrete* character of the negative here that makes the Hegelian sublation some- thing quite other than a return to the same: we are discussing the historical denials of spirit, the lack of meaning or closure not as a verbal/conceptual aporia but as the denial and death of persons; so that the 'identity' lying beyond can only be a new set of conditions for thought in which the concrete denial of spirit is overcome. Hence, for Hegel, the nexus linking the cross with the 'spiritual community'.

Whatever is at issue here, it is not the negative as a detour on the road from simple identity to simple identity. The negative, as it appears in the cross, is the destruction of human valuation, and so the collapse of commu- nicative practice itself;[19] more than a formal polarity set against affirma- tions of presence, etc. In a sense, it is just as much a breach in language, an interruption of exchange, as the 'trace' in Taylor's aesthetic; what is different is that it cannot, in Hegel, stand as a timeless space for the holy. Because it is the negation of the human itself, it demands to be *thought* if the project of communication is to continue. If it is *not* to continue, then, in Hegelian terms, there is no liberation from that partial or pre-reflective or fetishistic practice that turns violently on spirit itself in the negation which the cross represents (and this, incidentally, is why Hegel would not be able to see the Shoah as a *unique* interruption of the project of spirit, or as a kind of ontological barrier to the possibility of communicative practice; what would have to be said here is, of course, authoritatively opened up in Edith Wyschogrod's *Spirit in Ashes*).[20]

So I am reluctant to settle too rapidly for a theological retrieval of negative theology along Derridean lines. I am suspicious of the sacred as the void. In so far as the Derridean critique of dialectical negation warns us of the dangers of a glib historicism – such as Hegel's rhetoric does not always avoid – and a reduction of the apophatic dimension to a play of concepts, it is of crucial significance. If we are steered away from a metaphysics of anthropomorphic divine subjectivity and recalled to the recognition that the God of Christian theology is not *an* agent among agents, well and good. If we learn to look warily at systematic claims to overcome the plural and conflictual character of our speech and world, we shall have profited. But I am left with my questions: does the Derridean construal of the arbitrariness or contingency of communication actually do justice to the linguistic essence of the human and so to the bodily constraints on what is sayable? And does such a construal remove from language its critical and liberative possibilities? Is 'exchange' profane? Postmodern theological receptions of this problematic seem to suggest so; but my aim has been to invoke Hegel's shade to help put the question of whether this in fact dissolves the complex differentiations of a religious tradition committed to both divine liberty and divine 'commitment' to a historical life and a social practice, whose mark of godliness is self-critical vigilance (what used to be called repentance, I think).

NOTES

1 J.D. Crossan, 'Difference and Divinity', *Semeia*, 23 (a special issue on 'Derrida and Biblical Studies', ed. Robert Detweiler), 1982, pp. 29–40. Crossan distinguishes negative theology, 'conceived as a simple alternative strategy within ontotheology', from an apophaticism genuinely marginal to the mainstream of theological metaphysics – a refusal of the questions, not only the answers, of that tradition, which is properly comparable to Derridean différance (pp. 38–9).
2 John Caputo, 'Mysticism and Transgression: Derrida and Meister Eckhart', in Hugh J. Silverman (ed.), *Derrida and Deconstruction*, London and New York, Routledge, 1989, pp. 24–39, suggesting that Eckhart's apparent 'metaphysics of the one' is not an ontological claim but 'just a way of making the prevailing onto-theo-logic tremble' (p. 38). The aim is the mind's dispossession, not a new *theory*. Cf. Caputo's earlier studies, *The Mystical Element in Heidegger's Thought*, New York, 2nd edn, 1986, and *Radical Hermeneutics: Repetition, Deconstruction and the Hermeneutic Project*, Bloomington, Indiana University Press, 1987.
3 Kevin Hart, *The Trespass of the Sign: Deconstruction, Theology and Philosophy*, Cambridge, Cambridge University Press, 1989, especially section III. This book is the most substantial essay in the area so far in English.
4 Joseph O'Leary, *Questioning Back: The Overcoming of Metaphysics in Christian Tradition*, Minneapolis, Winstan Press, 1985, a very important attempt to bring Augustine into the discussion.
5 Especially in Don Cupitt, *The Long-Legged Fly: A Theology of Language and Desire*, London, SCM Press, 1987, and *The New Christian Ethics*, London, SCM Press, 1988, where the intense insistence on the *creation* of values seems still to slip towards the idea of a voluntary imposing (individual or corporate) of

meaning on the Void which is at least as much post-Kantian as postmodern.
6 Mark C. Taylor, *Tears*, Albany, SUNY Press, 1990.
7 ibid., p. 119.
8 ibid., p. 182.
9 Peter Hodgson, *God in History: Shape of Freedom*, Nashville, Abingdon Press, 1989, p. 88.
10 See, for example, Charles Taylor, *Hegel*, Cambridge, Cambridge University Press, 1975, chapter 15, especially pp. 419–21, 426–7.
11 'Actuality is the unity, become immediate, of essence with existence, or of inward with outward' – *Hegel's Logic*, trans. William Wallace, Oxford, Clarendon Press, 3rd edn, 1975, prop. no. 142.
12 Deborah Chaffin, 'Hegel, Derrida and the Sign', in Silverman, op. cit., pp. 77–91.
13 ibid., pp. 83–4, 90–1.
14 Vladimir Lossky, *The Mystical Theology of the Eastern Church*, London, James Clarke, 1957; see also R. Williams, 'The Via Negativa and the Foundations of Theology: An Introduction to the Thought of V.N. Lossky', in Stephen Sykes and Derek Holmes (eds), *New Studies in Theology*, vol. I, London, Duckworth, 1980, pp. 95–118 (on the use of apophaticism as more than a merely dialectical tool); and Tomasz Weclawski, *Zwischen Sprache und Schweigen: Eine Erörterung der Theologischen Apophase im Gespräch mit Vladimir N. Lossky und Martin Heidegger*, Munich, Minerva, 1985.
15 Christos Yannaras, *De l'absence et de l'inconnaissance de Dieu*, Paris, Cerf, 1971.
16 Gerald Graff, *Literature against Itself: Literary Ideas in Modern Society*, Chicago and London, University of Chicago Press, 1979, especially chapters 2, 3; p. 62 on learning to 'redescribe resignation as a form of heroism'.
17 Gillian Rose, *Hegel contra Sociology*, Cambridge, Cambridge University Press, 1981, p. 214.
18 Hegel, *Lectures on the Philosophy of Religion*, vol. III, *The Consummate Religion*, ed. Peter C. Hodgson, Berkeley, Los Angeles and London, University of California Press, 1985, pp. 124–31.
19 ibid., p. 130: 'Since the dishonoring of existence has been elevated to a position of highest honor, all the bonds of human corporate life are fundamentally assaulted, shaken and dissolved'; p. 131: 'everything ethical, everything commonly viewed as having authority was destroyed'.
20 Edith Wyschogrod, *Spirit in Ashes: Hegel, Heidegger and Man-Made Mass Death*, New Haven and London, Yale University Press, 1985, especially pp. 205–11 on the tension between language and violence.

Chapter 6

Resentment and apophasis: the trace of the other in Levinas, Derrida and Gans

Toby Foshay

Referring to Nietzsche's description, in the first chapter of *The Geneology of Morals*, of Judaeo-Christianity as *ressentiment*, as a 'slave morality' founded on resentment of the weak for the strong, Eric Gans observes in his essay 'The Culture of Resentment' that resentment 'does not have what might be called a good press'. Both Nietzsche, he says, and Max Scheler (whose notion of resentment Gans calls 'a ponderous and timid caricature of Nietzsche's') characterize resentment as 'the evil cause of an evil modernity'.[1] Nietzsche distinguished between active and reactive will to power. '[C]hange, and becoming', Nietzsche says,

> can be an expression of overfull, future-pregnant strength (my term for this is, as one knows, the word 'Dionysian'), but it can also be hatred [i.e. resentment] of the undeveloped, needy, underprivileged who destroys, who *must* destroy, because the existing, and even all existence, all being, outrages and provokes him.[2]

The 'bad press' which Nietzsche's notion of resentment has encountered is typified in the Marxist Fredric Jameson's position respecting it:

> In a world dominated by the weak and their various slave ethics, Nietzsche's own position must necessarily be reactive; indeed, the bitterness with which the 'phenomenon' of *ressentiment* is inevitably evoked – and it is the fundamental conceptual category of all late-nineteenth and early twentieth century counterrevolutionary literature – suggests that, as an explanatory category, *ressentiment* is always itself the product of *ressentiment*.[3]

Eric Gans, however, offers what he considers a more radical formulation than Nietzsche's of the idea of resentment:

> Resentment is indeed the fundamental precondition of modern Western culture, via Christian morality and its sources in Judaism. But it is equally the precondition of Greek culture, and of high culture as such.

In the view I shall attempt to defend, resentment is precisely the 'late' variety of desire that high-cultural phenomena reveal and transcend.[4]

Gans acknowledges the reactive and negative character of resentment. 'Resentment', he says, 'is surely a form of revelation, but it is a negative revelation. . . . But', he goes on to say,

> the point is precisely that resentment in itself is not a source of falsification, but a means of discovery – the only means, indeed, by which we as readers are called upon to put into question the founding oppositions by means of which texts signify'.[5]

My concern in this paper is with resentment as negative revelation and with the tradition of apophatic thought as a revelation of and through the negative. Apophatic thought as is well known takes its traditional and most explicit form in negative theology. In an important recent article addressing the relation of his thought to negative theology, Derrida characterizes negative theology and the continuity of the apophatic movement of thought in the western tradition up to and including deconstruction:

> Suppose, by a provisional hypothesis, that negative theology consists of considering that every predicative language is inadequate to the essence, in truth to the hyperessentiality (the being beyond Being) of God; consequently, only a negative ('apophatic') attribution can claim to approach God and to prepare for a silent intuition of God. By a more or less tenable analogy, one would thus recognize some traits, the family resemblance of negative theology, in every discourse that seems to return in a regular and insistent manner to this rhetoric of negative determination, endlessly multiplying the defenses and the apophatic warnings: this which is called X (for example, text, writing, the trace, différance, the supplement . . . etc.) 'is' neither this nor that, neither sensible nor intelligible, neither positive nor negative . . . neither present nor absent. . . . Despite appearances, then, this X is neither a concept nor even a name; it does *lend itself* to a series of names, but calls for another syntax, and exceeds even the order and the structure of predicative discourse.[6]

Derrida has always refused this 'more or less tenable analogy' between negative theology and deconstruction, from the 1968 essay 'Différance' up to the 1987 essay from which this quotation is taken. This recent essay, 'How to Avoid Speaking: Denials', bears in its very title Derrida's struggle with the challenge to his thought presented by negative theology and by the many attempts of critics to assimilate deconstruction to it. He, of course, anticipated this problem as early as the essay 'Différance', where he cautions:

> The detours, locutions, and syntax in which I will often have to take

recourse will resemble those of negative theology, occasionally even to the point of being indistinguishable from negative theology. . . . And yet those aspects of *différance* . . . are not theological, not even in the order of the most negative of negative theologies, which are always concerned with disengaging a superessentiality beyond the finite categories of essence and existence.[7]

And yet, from the time of the first oral presentation of 'Différance' at the Sorbonne, when he was accused in the question period of being a negative theologian,[8] Derrida has been subject to this contention that he was merely turning the tradition of ontotheology on its head, and so was as contained within the dialectical play of logocentric rationality as the thinkers he purported to deconstruct.

Derrida refuses the title of negative theologian, he says, because negative theology is not negative enough, is not rigorously apophatic. Negative theologies[9]

are always concerned with disengaging a superessentiality beyond the finite categories of essence and existence, that is, of presence, and always hastening to recall that God is refused the predicate of existence, only in order to acknowledge his superior, inconceivable, and ineffable mode of being.[10]

At the same time, Derrida has always professed his fascination for negative theology,[11] so that, he says in 'How to Avoid Speaking',

I objected in vain to the assimilation of the thinking of trace or différance to some negative theology, and my response amounted to a promise: one day I would have to stop deferring, one day I would have to try to explain myself directly on this subject, and at last speak of 'negative theology' *itself*.[12]

To speak of negative theology itself is, of course, he implies here, a contradiction in terms. What could be the negative *as such*, the essence of the negative? It can have neither being nor non-being, and can be known only as an effect of language, 'an attitude toward semantic or conceptual determination'.[13] Is there any such *thing* as negative theology, or: 'Is one not compelled to speak of negative theology according to the rules of negative theology, in a way that is at once impotent, exhausting, and inexhaustible? Is there ever anything other than a "negative theology" of "negative theology"?'[14] We can see the allure of this question for Derrida, for it embodies the internal completeness of logocentric reason and the ontotheological tradition, and situates his own attempt to escape conceptual discourse while recognizing that the very language of our supposed escape is formed by reason itself. The question of Derrida's title – 'How to Avoid Speaking: Denials' – then, embodies the quandary of a necessity to address the question of negative theology and the concomitant necessity to avoid speaking a language of being, of essence, and of their simple negation that will have been thoroughly anticipated by negative theology itself. While his difference with negative theology cannot be indefinitely deferred, at the same time his attempt to address it in the present must avoid the framework of the metaphysics of presence over which negative theology presides as its negation and transcendence.

But Derrida names another avoidance in 'How to Avoid Speaking': his refusal to discuss apophaticism in Jewish and Islamic thought. Regarding this he acknowledges that 'How to Avoid Speaking' is 'the most "autobiographical" speech I have ever risked',[15] and that his silence on the question of the Jewish and Islamic context of his own Algerian childhood and education is an inherent function of the need to avoid speaking of essences, identities and 'things in themselves'. In other words, Derrida can allow himself, he implies, to speak of the Platonic and Neoplatonic heritage of negative theology, but not of the Jewish or Islamic, which are closest to him and, as it were, identical with him. He cannot altogether avoid speaking of the analogy and isomorphism of apophaticism and deconstruction, but he can defer mere personal and 'attitudinal' questions of identity.

For, as Derrida points out, ' "negative theology" has come to designate a certain typical *attitude* towards language, and within it, in the act of definition and attribution, an *attitude* toward semantic or conceptual determination'.[16] This distinction between attitudinal response and categorial thinking, between affectivity and conceptuality, can be seen to organize the relationship between the thought of Emmanuel Levinas and that of Derrida. In an early essay, 'Violence and Metaphysics', Derrida challenges Levinas' thought precisely on the grounds of its residual negative theology, of an apophaticism that remains analogically and metaphorically implicated in the ontology which it claims to transcend.[17] And it is Levinas himself who describes his project as the articulation of an other than being that transcends the circularity and auto-reflection of ontological thought. Levinas asks:

> Can there be something as strange as an experience of the absolutely exterior, as contradictory in its terms as a heteronomous experience? In the affirmative case, we will, to be sure, not succumb to the temptation and the illusion that would consist in finding again by philosophy the empirical data of positive religions, but we will disengage a movement of transcendence. . . . We will also put into question the thesis according to which the ultimate essence of man and of truth is the *comprehension of the being of beings.*[18]

Levinas marks off his project, then, both from positive religions, and from the tradition of ontological thought that has grounded philosophy and affirmative, cataphatic theologies. In the words of the title to his major work, the other which he seeks to articulate is 'otherwise than being or beyond essence', and also other than the classical Judaism of his own heritage. Neither an ontology nor a theology, it is termed by him a metaphysics of the trace, rooted in the priority of attitude over category: 'The heteronomous experience we seek would be an attitude that cannot be converted into a category, and whose movement unto the other is not recuperated in identification, does not return to is point of departure.' This movement towards the other which escapes the circularity of rational reflection is likened by Levinas to the difference between Abraham and Ulysses, the Jewish and the Greek heroic archetypes:

> To the myth of Ulysses returning to Ithaca, we wish to oppose the story of Abraham who leaves his fatherland for ever for a yet unknown land, and forbids his servant to even bring back his son to the point of departure.[19]

At the end of 'Violence and Metaphysics', Derrida also employs the Judaic/Hellenic typology to question Levinas' project of a heteronomous metaphysics: 'But if one calls this experience of the infinitely other Judaism . . . one must reflect upon the necessity . . . to borrow the ways of the unique philosophical logos, which can only invert the "curvature of space" for the benefit of the same.'[20] 'Violence and Metaphysics' is a reading of Levinas' *Totality and Infinity*, a work subtitled 'An Essay on Exteriority',[21] in which Levinas attempts to define a notion of exteriority beyond the inside/outside polarity of Greek metaphysics, with its primary dependence on spatial metaphors. 'Why', Derrida asks,

> is it necessary still to use the word 'exteriority' . . . in order to signify a nonspatial relationship? Why is it necessary to *obliterate* this notion of exteriority without erasing it . . . by stating that its truth is its untruth, that *true* exteriority is not spatial, that is, is not exteriority?[22]

Thus Derrida points to the apophatic structure of Levinas' thought, which, he says, inhabits the spatial metaphor of ontology as a 'metaphor in ruins'.[23] Derrida finds Levinas' apophaticism inconsistent, not because of its negation of categories, but because it clings to the categories of metaphysics while at the same time negating their ontological significance; it appeals to an other beyond categories by attempting to redefine categorial terms as being rooted primarily in attitudes arising from experiential encounter with the Other. But, unlike the classical negative theologian, Levinas insists on the centrality of language as the medium of the experience of alterity. 'Negative theology', Derrida says, 'was spoken in a speech that knew itself failed and finite, inferior to God's understanding. Above all, negative theology never undertook a Discourse with God in the face to face . . . of two free speeches.'[24] So that, at the close of 'Violence and Metaphysics', Derrida characterizes Levinas' thought as an empiricism, a position, he says, which 'has always been determined by philosophy, from Plato to Husserl, as *nonphilosophy*: as the philosophical pretension to nonphilosophy, the inability to justify oneself'.[25] We can see Derrida poised in this early essay between the extremes of attitude and category which, with Levinas, he casts as Jewish and Greek:

> Are we . . . *first* Jews or *first* Greeks? And does the strange dialogue between the Jew and the Greek . . . have the form of the absolute, speculative logic of Hegel, the living logic which *reconciles* formal tautology and empirical heterology? . . . Or, on the contrary, does this [dialogue] have the form of infinite separation and the unthinkable, unsayable transcendence of the other?[26]

The extremes of Jew and Greek, of empirical and therefore unsayable heteronomy and of the transcendental dialectic, are obviously unworkable for Derrida and he goes on in his 1968 essay 'Différance' to articulate a sayable heterology that escapes both classical negative theology and the metaphorical heterology of Levinas, while at the same time acknowledging that 'the thought of *différance* implies the entire critique of classical ontology undertaken by Levinas'.[27] And yet, as already mentioned, it is with 'Différance' that Derrida's own obligation to speak directly on negative theology becomes explicit, an obligation finally taken up in 'How to Avoid Speaking'. In this latter essay, the problem of negative theology is addressed as the necessity to speak about the negative itself, the necessity to speak about what essentially is not, is not any essentiality, and which must be articulated in another syntax, a different language. To address negative theology is for Derrida to speak of différance and to render it present, and so he likens his task in the essay to the revelation of a secret, an element which the thought of différance shares analogically with the classical discourse of negative theology, for example, in Pseudo-Dionysius. 'To avoid speaking', Derrida says, 'is to delay the moment when one will have to say something and perhaps acknowledge, surrender, impart a secret, one amplifies the digressions. . . . Under this title, "how to avoid speaking," it is necessary to speak of the secret.'[28] The secret is what cannot be by its very nature fully articulated in language, and in Pseudo-Dionysius it of course designates the transcendent and numinous divinity itself, which imparts itself only to the elect capable of passing beyond the idolatrous forms equally of Scripture and of affirmative philosophical theology.

But what of the negative itself, the language of the unsayable? 'Here Dionysius evokes', says Derrida, 'a double tradition, a double mode of transmission; on the one hand unspeakable, secret, prohibited, reserved, inaccessible or mystical, "symbolic and initiatory"; on the other hand, philosophic, demonstrative, capable of being shown.'[29] Both these modes are recognized by Dionysius to intersect and by Derrida that the place of intersection, or 'symploke', situates also the relation of his own discourse to that of Dionysius. This intersection necessarily precedes and makes possible the two modes of preserving the secret and naming the secret. One has to speak of the secret without divulging the secret, and for Derrida he must address the relation of the thought of différance to negative theology without articulating that relation in a language that would distort the thought of différance. This oscillation between preservation and divulgence of the secret Derrida names denegation or denial:

> There is a secret of denial and a denial of the secret. The secret as such, as *secret*, separates and already institutes a negativity; it is a negation that denies itself. It de-negates itself. This denegation does not happen to it by accident; it is *essential and originary* (my emphasis) . . . [and] gives no chance to dialectic.[30]

This passage on denegation seems to me pivotal in 'How to Avoid Speaking'. Derrida goes on to pursue in the essay certain problems in the thought of Plato and of Heidegger, and says little more about denegation. And one can speculate why, for it seems curiously akin to Levinas' attempt to define exteriority as beyond the inside/outside dialectic of ontology. To say that the self-negation of the negative places it beyond the negative/positive dialectic and that this 'beyond predication' is 'essential and originary' seems as classically apophatic a formulation as one could desire, and its articulation in the language of category merely an assertion of the greater appropriateness of the Greek that in no way improves on Levinas' evocation of the typically Hebraic relation between self and other as one primarily of attitude.

Derrida's discussion of the 'secret' in 'How to Avoid Speaking' emerges from a commentary on the relation between interior and exterior *topos* in Dionysius. *Topos* is both rhetorical and political in that the secret place of God's dwelling beyond being is reached and pursued within the context of the unknowing described and enacted in apophatic discourse. But this discourse itself is situated within the community of an elect constituted by this secret knowledge beyond knowledge. These interior/exterior, rhetorical/communal elements Derrida names 'the topolitology of the secret', and his discussion is itself situated as a response to those who describe deconstructionists as a cabal of negative theologians. But the point to be emphasized is that Derrida locates his treatment of the secret as denegation and denial primarily in the interior and rhetorical space of the subject as constituted individually, as it were, in language:

> I refer first of all to the secret shared *within itself*, its partition 'proper,' which divides the essence of a secret that cannot even appear to one alone except in starting to be lost, to divulge itself, hence to dissimulate itself, as secret, in showing itself: dissimulating its dissimulation. There

is no secret *as such*; I deny it. And this is what I confide in secret to whomever allies himself to me.[31]

It is as if the secret itself, as the limit structure of predication, both constitutes and deconstitutes the subject through its allure, its revelation and its simultaneous and necessary withholding, defining its relation both to itself and to others as and in language. And we can pause to note how very Greek and categorial Derrida's emphases are here, over and against the political and ethical emphasis of Dionysius' Judaeo-Christianity on which he is commenting.

But Derrida earlier introduces his discussion of the secret by considering it as indeed a definitive trait of distinctively human consciousness and language. While Derrida qualifies these reflections as perhaps naive, 'one may nevertheless observe', he says, 'that animals are incapable of keeping or even having a secret, because they cannot *represent as such*, as an *object* before consciousness, something that they would then forbid themselves from showing'. Derrida puts this problem of the secret as definitively human aside because:

> Above all, it would be necessary to re-elaborate a problematic of consciousness, that thing that, more and more, one avoids discussing as if one knew what it is and as if its riddle were solved. But is any problem more novel today than that of consciousness?[32]

In his essay 'Differences', Eric Gans delineates in an early form, but directly in relation to Derrida's thought, the theory of consciousness and representation that he fully elaborates in his 1985 book *The End of Culture: Toward a Generative Anthropology*.[33] In 'Differences', Gans criticizes what he sees as Derrida's too metaphysical notions of différance and the trace, the 'always already' character of language that is anterior to all representation and therefore to consciousness. 'But', says Gans, 'Difference "always already" exists, in a form that Derrida refuses to recognize. . . . The original difference is precisely that of life itself, which from its own problematic origin has distinguished structurally, if not conceptually, between the organism and its appetitive objects.'[34] Employing a developed version of Girardian mimetic desire, Gans locates the origin of representation in the difference and deferral that enable human communities to avoid conflict and to co-operate rather than compete in the gathering of food and other needs of material survival. The founding gesture which necessarily constitutes human community, for Gans, must be an act of renunciation:

> That is why the first cultural act, the act of representation, must originate in an *aborted* act of appropriation. It is when fear of conflict leads man to *designate* this object rather than grasp at it that the deferral of conflict by the differentiation of the object can be adequate to its task.[35]

Thus the deferral and differentiation of the founding act of representation, Gans says, also constitute the community in its presence to itself, so that difference and presence are seen by him as coterminous.

'Derrida', Gans asserts, 'fails to see that although the origin of consciousness must itself be conscious, it should not be expected to possess a *concept* of this consciousness.'[36] Gans sees the emergence of cultural from appetitive desire to be structured by this originary act of renunciation. The founding gesture of renunciation leads to the *imaginary* representation of what is inaccessible to appetite. This is the paradox of a consciousness constituted by a founding gesture of renunciation: an *imagined* fulfilment of desire that is not problematic is not significant, since *real* satisfaction is in the realm of appetitive desire. Like Levinas, then, Gans sees significance as arising from an ethical attitude rather than an ontological conception, an attitude that places the welfare of the community above that of the self, but he is more radical than Levinas in rooting human significance in the renunciation of appetitive desire rather than in Levinas' presumption of a transcendental ethics. In presenting significance as originating in empirical appetite, Gans generates what he calls an anthropology which is able to account for the paradoxical relation between the private and public spheres of desire as mediated in language. The high cultural expressions of desire in art, philosophy, religion and science, he says, are structured by the hierarchical distribution of material power that emerges from an earlier egalitarian and reciprocal economy. Since significance and signification are ultimately rooted in an ethics of renunciation, the emergence of hierarchical material differences leads to the resentment that Nietzsche notices in Christianity, but which Gans sees as characteristic of high culture in general, both Hebraic and Greek.

Unlike Nietzsche's moralistic preference for Dionysian over Apollonian desire, Gans' theory of resentment is able to account for both the moral negativity of resentment and its ethical positivity. 'Resentment', Gans says,

> may be defined as the scandal of the peripheral self at the centrality of the other which transforms the equality of the original scene of representation into an absolute polarity of significance. It differs from envy in being directed not at contingent but at communally significant and hence ethically necessary differences. It is thus a necessary evil.[37]

But Gans sees the necessity of resentment as the basis of a new solidarity that escapes the communal normativity of the ritual environment now necessarily frustrated by hierarchical relations. This new solidarity is the basis of secular culture and it expresses itself in secular art, philosophy and science where 'resentment is demystified and abolished'.[38] Whereas ritual creates communal solidarity around the common ritual possession of the symbolic object, aesthetic otherness creates an imaginative representation in which the desired object is acknowledgedly *inaccessible* to all equally. Such a fictive universe, says Gans, is one 'in which the individual spectator can imagine himself, secure in his awareness that the desiring imagination of his fellow spectators is no less unrealizable than his own'. Thus, the negative structure of both ritual and secular desire: deferral to the next world and renunciation in this. The Hebrew and Greek, the 'ritual and secular . . . are poles rather than incompatible essences'.[39] The movement typified by Abraham for Levinas, the '*attitude irreducible to a category*', is not to be able to slip away from responsibility, not to have a hiding place in inwardness in which one can return into oneself,[40] a movement which he otherwise names 'liturgy'.[41] For Derrida,

> [a] conscious being is a being capable of lying, of not presenting in speech that of which it yet has an articulated expression: a being that can avoid speaking [the secret]. . . . To keep something to oneself is the most incredible and thought-provoking power.[42]

But, of course, he says: 'There is no secret *as such*: I deny it. And this is what I confide in secret to whomever allies himself to me.'[43]

Levinas' emphasis on the self's movement towards the other and Derrida's focus on its paradoxical residence and captivation within itself are seen to be equally sacrificial and renunciatory, equally the product of resentment and equally a response to inequities: for Levinas, the ethical objection to the abuse of power; for Derrida, the intellectual challenge to the presumptive claim to knowledge. Both trace for Levinas and différance for Derrida arise from an immemorial past, a past before any historical past that can be recuperated in a language which presumes its adequacy to being. Even the most rigorously apophatic discourse for Derrida is imprinted by this rhetorical 'place' or 'event' of language:

> Even if one speaks and says nothing, even if an apophatic discourse deprives itself of meaning or of an object, it takes place. . . . The possible absence of a referent still beckons, if not toward the thing of which one speaks (such as God, who is nothing because he takes place, *without place*, *beyond being*) at least toward the other (other than Being) who calls or to whom this speech is addressed. . . . The most negative discourse preserves a trace of the other. A trace of an event older than it.[44]

'Thus', Derrida concludes, 'at the moment when the question "How to Avoid Speaking?" arises it is already too late. There is no longer any question of speaking. Language has started without us, in us and before us.'[45] Thus, Gans' Rousseauian project of a 'generative anthropology', conceiving language as the origin of culture, in its presentation of a hypothetical scene of origin simultaneously of representation and of distinctively human society – and presented by him as a genuinely scientific construct – would be clearly presumptive in Levinasian or Derridean terms. But Gans' materialized and fully historicized hypothesis is capable of thinking both of simultaneous and deferred structures of difference and of presence and of its own emergence within this historical and material unfolding of religious and secular institutions and discourses. The emergence of secular artistic, philosophical and scientific discourse from ritual practices and sacred conceptions is part of the process of a self-differentiation that is primarily ethical for Gans. And this ethical desire, rooted in material survival and driven on by the material and psychic necessity of its own self-differentiation and necessarily increasing self-appropriation, remains material while unfolding the full range of cultural institutions and practices. Resolution is presented not in religious or ontological constructs *or* in their attempted apophatic devolvements – neither, that is, in apotheosis nor in kenosis, but in a hypothesis to be tested both by its internal plausibility and its capacity to explain the phenomena of culture and its systems of representation, not the least of which is its own emergence within discourse and in relation to it. The resentment between knowledge and power, Gans says, can only be resolved by a knowledge *of* power and of the necessary and necessarily conscious renunciation of appetitive instinct to domination. Gans' theory of resentment, unlike Nietzsche's, avoids hypostasizing resentment as an other and so repeating it, but rather acknowledges and accounts for resentment's presence in its very impetus to know and to theorize itself. Gans' theory knows itself as an attitude resolving itself through its representation as category, grounded in a theory of the relation between difference and presence that accounts for the tension which holds them together in identity and without dissolving the *différance* coextensive with their material embodiment.

NOTES

1 Eric Gans, 'The Culture of Resentment', *Philosophy and Literature*, 8, 1984, p. 55.
2 Friedrich Nietzsche, *The Gay Science*, quoted in Walter Kaufmann, *Nietzsche: Philosopher, Psychologist, Anti-Christ*, Princeton, Princeton University Press, 3rd edn, 1968, pp. 374–5; Kaufmann's interpolation.
3 Fredric Jameson, *Fables of Aggression: Wyndham Lewis, the Modernist as Fascist*, Berkeley and London, University of California Press, 1979, p. 131.
4 Gans, op. cit., p. 56.
5 ibid., p. 64.
6 Jacques Derrida, 'How to Avoid Speaking: Denials', in Sanford Budick and Wolfgang Iser (eds), *Languages of the Unsayable: The Play of Negativity in Literature and Literary Theory*, New York, Columbia University Press, 1989, pp. 3–70.

7 Jacques Derrida, 'Différance', in *Margins of Philosophy*, trans. Alan Bass, Chicago, University of Chicago Press, 1982, pp. 1–27.
8 Jacques Derrida, 'The Original Discussion of "Différance" (1968)', in David Wood and Robert Bernasconi (eds), *Derrida and Différance*, Evanston, Northwestern University Press, 1988, pp. 83–95.
9 See Derrida, 'How to Avoid Speaking', op. cit., pp. 3–4 and p. 63, n. 1, on the plurality of the negative theological project.
10 Derrida, 'Différance', op. cit., p. 6.
11 See Derrida, 'The Original Discussion', op. cit., p. 85; 'Letter to John Leavey', *Semeia*, 23, 1982, pp. 61–52; and 'How to Avoid Speaking', op. cit., p. 12.
12 Derrida, 'How to Avoid Speaking', op. cit., p. 12.
13 ibid., p. 4.
14 ibid., p. 13.
15 ibid., p. 66, n. 13.
16 ibid., p. 4; my emphasis.
17 Jacques Derrida, 'Violence and Metaphysics: An Essay on the Thought of Emmanuel Levinas', in *Writing and Difference*, trans. Alan Bass, Chicago, University of Chicago Press, 1978, pp. 79–153.
18 Emmanuel Levinas, 'The Trace of the Other', in Mark C. Taylor (ed.), *Deconstruction in Context: Literature and Philosophy*, Chicago, University of Chicago Press, 1986, pp. 345–59.
19 ibid.
20 Derrida, 'Violence and Metaphysics', op. cit., p. 152.
21 Emmanuel Levinas, *Totality and Infinity: An Essay on Exteriority*, trans. Alphonso Lingis, Pittsburgh, Duquesne University Press, 1969.
22 Derrida, 'Violence and Metaphysics', op. cit., p. 112.
23 ibid., p. 152.
24 ibid., p. 116.
25 ibid., p. 152.
26 ibid., p. 153.
27 Derrida, 'Différance', op. cit., p. 21.
28 Derrida, 'How to Avoid Speaking', op. cit., p. 16.
29 ibid., p. 24.
30 ibid., p. 25.
31 ibid., p. 26.
32 ibid., p. 17.
33 Eric Gans, *The End of Culture: Toward a Generative Anthropology*, Berkeley and London, University of California Press, 1985.
34 Eric Gans, 'Differences', *Modern Language Notes*, 96, 1981, pp. 792–808.
35 ibid., p. 804.
36 ibid., p. 801.
37 Gans, *The End of Culture*, op. cit., p. 174.
38 ibid.
39 ibid., p.175.
40 Levinas, 'The Trace of the Other', op. cit., p. 354.
41 ibid., p. 350.
42 Derrida, 'How to Avoid Speaking', op. cit., pp. 17–18.
43 ibid., p. 26.
44 ibid., p. 28.
45 ibid., p. 29.

Chapter 7

Fire and roses, or the problem of postmodern religious thinking

Carl Raschke

Down the passage we did not take
Toward the door we never opened
Into the rose-garden . . .
      (T.S. Eliot, 'Burnt Norton')

I

At the conclusion of Umberto Eco's *The Name of the Rose* – considered by many critics one of the so-called 'postmodern' novels – what has proceeded all along as a murder mystery suddenly turns into a revelation concerning the workings of language, and the adventure of signs.

The 'discovery' of the perpetrator of a string of baffling, and heinous, crimes inside a late medieval abbey becomes the occasion for what today might be termed a 'deconstructive' literary covert operation. The murders in the monastery turn out to be the artifice of the fanatical friar Jorge, who has connived and conspired to protect a mysterious book in the secret chambers of the abbey. The 'book', of course, is Aristotle's legendary 'lost' treatise on laughter.

Jorge defends his crime by arguing that the opening of such a book to the learned would transvalue all the values of classical learning and of Christian civilization. It would unleash the spirit of levity. In addition, it would set going the process of destruction for the entire metaphysical architectonic upon which holy 'faith' has been erected as the capstone. 'I have been the hand of God,' protests Jorge to his inquisitor William of Baskerville. Jorge insists that the hand of God must conceal, and that 'there are boundaries beyond which' the probe of language 'is not permitted to go'. But William replies: 'God created the monsters, too. And you. And He wants everything to be spoken of.'[1]

The saying of the unsaid, the reaching towards the unreachable, the naming of the unnamed name – all signified by the rose – is literally 'the end of the book'. *The Name of the Rose* concludes with a fire that burns down the monastery and its enormous library. We may read into the fire an eschatological event – the apocalyptic capsizing of a metaphysical era in which God's secrets have remained closeted in forbidden books. From a philosophical point of view, the 'naming' of the rose is at the same time its dissolution; it is the semantic displacement of the signified by the act of signification. Signification is seen as disruption, a violation of context, a transgression.

The term 'postmodern' has itself come of late to serve as a kind of clandestine intrusion into the kingdom of signification. The word concomitantly baffles, bedazzles and enrages – principally because it neither denotes nor intimates anything other than an incursion across the borderland of sensibility. Heidegger is generally regarded as the first postmodern thinker because of his declarations about the 'overcoming' of metaphysics and the 'end' of philosophy. At the 'semiotic' level – that is, in the distinctive space where language performs no longer as code or syntax, but as a skein of tracings, as the movement of complex and ephemeral modules of signification that cannot be repeated or circumscribed – so-called 'postmodernity' means much more than some ill-defined time period.

Postmodernity amounts to a redescription of logic as 'aesthetics', of message as medium, of communication as dramatics, of truth as embodiment. Postmodernity is the transcendence, or 'overcoming', of all archaic or 'legendary' orders of significance that have underwritten cultural discourse. Understood superficially, the 'postmodern' represents a transition from the highly formalized, or 'modern', understanding of things to the 'carnival' of popular culture. But this defection is less a revolution in taste than a reappropriation of the theory of meaning itself. The idea redounds upon what Eco in one of his semiotic treatises refers to as 'carnivalization'. The study of carnivals – Brazil's *escloa de samba*, New Orleans's *Mardi Gras*, the ancient Roman *saturnalia* – offers a glimpse into the origin of language itself as an assault upon the hegemony of silence. 'Carnival', says Eco, 'can exist only as *authorized* transgression.'[2] With its ornate pageantry of music and sensual dancing, the exhibition of costume and colour, the exposure of bodies, the enactment of folk drama, 'carnival' creates a 'scene' in which the achievement of the 'signifier' no longer depends on language as social interaction, but emerges through the very distension of the grammar of culture. The inquiry into popular culture – at least from the standpoint of formal semantics – has always been a 'dangerous liaison'.

The term 'postmodernism' has burgeoned, crowded and suffused academic conversation during the last decade. Once strange and unfamiliar, if not disarming, locutions like 'subtext', 'discursivity', 'meta-narrative' and 'alterity' have become their own sort of patois within the humanities. It is as though a philosophical irredentism had been set in motion, dislodging the once seemingly immovable sovereignty of Germanic thought in a more-than-century-long 'Franco-Prussian' war of methods, phraseologies and notions.

Gallic preciosity and rhetorical sportiveness appear to have triumphed over Teutonic global rationality, or any probing into what Hegel termed the 'depths of Spirit'. The distinction, as well as the antagonism, can be espied in Jurgen Habermas' waspish dismissal of Derrida as a *nicht argumentationsfreudiger Philosoph* – literally a 'philosopher who does not enjoy argumentation'.[3] Postmodern works of scholarship, however, have deliberately avoided 'argumentation', because they are regalia of a 'style' more than a discipline. In this respect 'postmodern' reflection – particularly the philosophical and theological kind – stands in relationship to its earlier twentieth-century antecedents as Renaissance 'humanism' compared with the earlier religious scholasticism. In the 'humanism' of the *quattrocento* rhetoric supplanted Aristotelian logic, eloquence displaced inference, the performative took precedence over the referential. Indeed, it is the *power of performance* that appears to have emerged as the common denominator among the variegated 'postmodernisms' of art, philosophy, theology, textual criticism, and the like.

When Derrida in *Of Grammatology* proclaimed the end of the 'age of the sign', he most likely did not intend to claim that the event of signification was now impossible. But Derridean 'deconstruction', once shorn of its metonymic excesses and its tropic diffusions, is precisely the philosophical reversal of Roland Barthes' semiotics of the everyday. The point can be easily overlooked, inasmuch as Barthes' recognition that 'to signify' means to *disconnect* the token from the object in the generation of a sign-system anticipates the 'deconstructive' view that textuality is inseparable from temporality, from the self-erasure of language as action. The sometimes maddening penchant of 'deconstructionists' for word-games and punning bespeaks an unselfconscious mimesis of the semiotic enterprise.

Barthes' semiosis of reading, encapsulated in the slogan the 'pleasure of the text', would appear to be the schema for Derrida's 'supplement' of writing. Nonetheless, Barthes' *jouissance*, as a sense of the libidinous freedom and *revelatory* aesthetics of sign-production, is transfigured by Derrida into a 'joyless' chain of paralogisms, which turn out to be transgressions without conquests, wounds without healings, lesions without disclosures. The irony is captured in Derrida's own 'parapractical' re-reading of Heidegger's discussion of the 'work of art'. Whereas for Heidegger Van Gogh's 'peasant shoes' can be 'seen' in terms of an ontological manifestation, a 'worlding', through the pen of Derrida they become the utter negativity of *différance* – the 'disparity of the pair', a 'separateness' that is 'in itself, in the word, in the letter, in the pair'.[4]

Derrida himself has failed to intuit his own nihilism, the nihilism of an ongoing textual commentary no longer capable of signification. Instead Derrida has elected to mythify his own 'total eclipse' of the power of signs in terms of the chaos mother, the Great Kali of Hinduism, who abrogates even the archetypal form of 'female' in the primal and eternal recurrence of darkness. 'No woman or trace of woman . . . save the mother, that's understood. . . . Everything comes back to her, beginning with life.'[5] But any mythopoesis of life is also a mask for death, as Jean-François Lyotard, today's pre-eminent philosopher of *postmodern culture*, has reminded us. The 'postmodern' is, he says, 'that which searches for new presentations, not in order to enjoy them but in order to impart a stronger sense of the unpresentable'.[6] In a later work Lyotard tells us that the 'unpresentable' is 'Auschwitz'. It is the 'differend' of the silent victims. The differend, as the bare negativity of concealed violence, constitutes the ultimate limits of a logocentric universe. It is, to employ Edith Wyschogrod's terminology, 'spirit in ashes'.[7]

The differend is the antonym of the referent; but is also something much more, and far stranger, than what Paul Ricoeur and others have termed as 'plurisignificative', the unlimited semiosis that characterizes fluid and allusive language. The differend is the pure unvocalizable that quivers not only at the boundaries of discourse, but at the fringes of existence. Like the Heideggerian *nihil*, Lyotard's *differend* is both limit and horizon. It is the 'line' circumscribing signification beyond which a new and more fundamental occasion for 'semiophany' becomes possible. The end of the age of the sign, disclosed in the *differend*, in the silence, is at the same time an overture to what is genuinely postmodern, understood at last as a total presence, an eschatological fullness, a *parousia* – after the fashion of Heidegger – of the very sign-universe.

II

The problem with the recent stampede into 'postmodern' discourse throughout the study of religion, and in religious thought, however, is that its 'semiotic' overtones are too often overlooked. The fascination with so-called 'deconstructionism' has led ironically to what might be dubbed an old school or 'late' modernist cast of thought that has wrongly been described as postmodern. The expressions 'modernism' and 'postmodernism' were originally contrived to identify styles and trends in the arts and architecture. Modernism refers to a preoccupation with the conditions of aesthetic creativity as well as the problem of composition, contrasting with an interest in artistic content and the methods of representation. The anti-representationalism and extreme textualism of putative 'postmodern' philosophers and critics amount, in fact, to a recycling of earlier modernist concerns under the aegis of the humanities, compelled by many of the same attitudes that captivated visual artists in the early years of this century. The 'painterly' self-scrutiny of the modern artist – the Fauvist's prevision with colour, the minimalist's reduction of the work to shapes and surfaces – is transposed into the 'grammatology' of the text.

Authentic 'postmodernism', on the other hand, involves a recovery of the richness of 'natural' signifiers, if not a return to the 'naturalism' or 'realism' of the late classical era. In art, so-called 'postmodernism' has actually meant a 'return to content', as Charles Jencks has so aptly put it, along with a rediscovery of 'historical continuum and the relation between past and present'. This renaissance of classical figuration, proportionality and stylized elegance has at the same time take place within the 'modernist' setting of cultural pluralism and representational heterogeneity, so that postmodernism generates narratives without plots as part of a world of 'divergent significations' compelling 'multiple readings' of the familiar.[8] Postmodern style enfolds within itself tradition without canonicity, form without formality, beauty without monumentality, coherence without symmetry. The two most popular and powerful editions of visual 'postmodernism' – pop art and so-called 'earth art' – have been self-cognizant efforts to revive the aesthetics of signification, the one through the commercial replication of popular culture icons and the other through an almost magico-ritual expression of earth lines, geometries and energies. If, from a semiotic point of view, there is a deeper-lying 'postmodern' principle of interpretation, it is simply that the world glitters with signs, and the signs belong to an encompassing and polyvalent harmony of semantic sighs and whispers.

Unfortunately, postmodernism as a religious, or theological, libretto has all too often been assimilated to what are patently at best modern, and at worst *pre*modern, types of discursivity. The crypto-modernism of what purports to be postmodernism can be inferred from the ideological continuity between 'deconstructionism' and late-1960s death-of-God theology, which in turn derived from the postwar fashions of European religious existentialism.

Another 'postmodern' feint has also been devised for what is *prima facie* a premodern gnosticism, or 'perennialism'. Huston Smith, as an illustration, has characterized the 'postmodern' mind in almost archaicist terms. The genuine 'postmodernist' is the devotee of the 'sacred unconscious'; he or she is an oriental adept on the path to an enlightenment, a *jivamukti*, one who 'lives in the unvarying presence of the numinous'.[9] The same leanings can be glimpsed in the 'postmodern' theological programme of David Griffin, which is little more than process thought – a modernist metaphysic – leavened with the politics and eco-mysticism of the ageing 1960s counterculture.

More recently, as the word 'postmodernism' has come to refer to poststructuralist kinds of philosophical and literary arguments, Smith has turned his wrath against the concept itself. In a plenary address to the American Academy of Religion at Anaheim, California, in late 1989 Smith has dismissed 'postmodernism' as merely a degenerate form of modernism,

which arose when science and empiricist epistemology supplanted revelation and what Smith calls 'the wisdom of the ages' as the fountainhead of
truth. The sin of postmodernism, according to Smith, is its denial of
'ontological transcendence', by which he means the hierarchical metaphysics of religious esotericism tracing back to ancient Vedantism and hermeti-
cism. Smith has urged that 'postmodernist' impulses be judiciously
dislodged by 'a return to the truth claims of our field as impounded in the
world's great traditions'.[10]

The upshot of all of this, however, is that a serious postmodernism has
not left its stamp on religious thought. The impasse may have more to do
with the poverty of academic theology than with the 'theological' promise
of postmodernism *per se*. If the theological thinking is not a task but an
oeuvre, or a 'work' in the Ricoeurian sense, then in order to become
postmodern, it must become what Eco dubs the 'open work'. In the open
work, according to Eco, 'the signs combine like constellations whose
structural relationships are not determined univocally, from the start, and
in which the ambiguity of the sign does not . . . lead back to reconfirming
the distinction between form and background'.[11] The capaciousness of
postmodern theological thinking would, like the artwork itself to which
Eco applies such a hermeneutic, be both 'informal' and 'cultural' in a
comprehensive sense. It would no longer emanate strictly from arcane
conversationalists, who claim to be avant-garde and trend-motivated, but
who in actuality have contrived a curious, convoluted and overdetermined
scholasticism of the academic Left. It would become 'popular' in the sense
that pop art, which in many respects launched postmodernism, has served
as an aesthetic idiom of mediation between familiar representational systems and the imagism of urban folk culture. Just as the movement over a
generation ago from abstraction to 'pop' can be construed as a revolt
against the discreet nihilism of purely formal painting, so postmodern
religious thinking no longer takes as its 'texts' the recondite writings of the
so-called 'deconstructionalists'.

The strategy can be adduced in part from the theory of culture advanced
by Jim Collins in his insightful study of what empirically falls under the
heading of 'postmodernism'. Collins faults what he terms the 'grand hotel
theory' concerning mass culture, which has been a whipping boy for
choleric western critics from the Frankfurt School on down through the
existentialists. Grand hotel theory is a kind of surrogate canon for those
intellectuals who despise the 'canonism' of the classical humanities. It
looks down upon the whole of popular culture as crude exploitation and
the purveyance of alienation, all the while ignoring the subtle modes of
intelligibility inherent in its different functions and genres. As Collins
notes:

When the punk rocker tears holes in her jeans and closes them with safety pins, or when the fashion designer adds a mink collar to a purposely faded denim jacket, both construct specific signs with quite divergent ideological values – but in each case, the meaning produced is predicated on the violation of the sign's earlier incarnations.[12]

In other words, the notion of the 'popular', according to Collins, suffers from 'oversimplification'. Popular culture, as opposed to the image of the 'grand hotel' in which cultural élites dominate over a consumer population of untutored kitsch-mongers, can be viewed as a multi-centred dynamic in which sign-manufacturing and semiotic performance have the effect of both expressing and differentiating. Semiotics, therefore, should be understood as a veiled praxis of 'liberation', whereby deeper values of freedom can be decoded from the would-be vulgarisms, or even the apparent 'crass commercialism', of quotidian social representations. It is in this connection that we can begin to understand the hostility of Frankfurt School followers towards the very idea of 'postmodernism'. For postmodernism no longer presumes an 'avante-garde' of cultural opposition in much the same way that the post-Marxist politics of eastern Europe today has dispensed handily with the paradigm of the party as the 'vanguard' of revolutionary change.

For example, in his influential *Theory of the Avante-Garde*, the German philosopher of culture Peter Bürger dismisses what we have called postmodernism as 'commodity aesthetics' designed to 'enthral' and concoct 'a false sublation of art as institution'.[13] From the semiotic standpoint the postulate of postmodernism unmasks the hidden, and one might even go so far as to say 'hypocritical', élitism in the conventional 'grand hotel' reading of the role of cultural élites. A social semiotics needs no longer to presuppose that signification *equals* oppression, that is invariably a vertical imposition of symbol-controllers upon the mass, but that it may also be a kind of *cri de coeur* of the disenfranchised. The horizontal dissemination of sign-performances through a 'decentred' popular culture does not necessarily legitimate either their moral or ontological character, but reframes their purpose, primarily in terms of the categories of regimentation, subversion, 'ceremonial' articulation and ideological oscillations. According to the sociologist Erving Goffman, who in his more recent work has co-opted the semiotic method, the 'commercialism' of so much popular culture can best be considered a complex set of typifications that are not so far distant from ritualized, everyday language and behaviour.[14] Sign-events cluster around 'displays', which in turn coalesce around different social codings, not to mention *codings of difference*, which may or may not be co-ordinate with the insignia of class.[15]

In the postmodern context the sign becomes, to use Lyotard's term, more 'presentation' than representation. The semiotics of presentation demands the *differend*, which in turn yields a query more than a direct, 'metaphysical' statement – even if it be the sort of metaphysics that masquerades as critical sociology. 'In the differend', says Lyotard, 'something "asks" to be put into phrases, and suffers from the wrong of not being able to be put into phrases in the right way.'[16] The differend is, in effect, the Heideggerian 'unsaid', or at a deeper, 'speculative' level, the 'unthought'; it is the speaking of the unspoken that writhes towards articulation in the wilderness of contemporary culture. It is the 'semiotic' reminder of social contradiction that reveals itself in the face of the homeless wanderer at the New York Port Authority. It lingers in the midnight offer of the street walker in Guadalajara. It is both Moral Majority and MTV (the American rock music TV network). It is the death of an abused child. It is the 'Velvet Revolution' in Prague. It is, also, strangely, Mickey Mouse and Goofy. But it is the crystal draped around the neck of a Santa Fe socialite, and the blood on the back of a Native American *penitente* as he follows the 'stations of the Cross'.

The so-called 'postmodernism' of certain contemporary theological writers who have somehow cornered the word, therefore, is but shadow ballet. When someone like Griffin asserts that 'postmodern theology rejects the extreme voluntarism of supernaturalistic theism and the atheistic naturalism of modernity, replacing both with a naturalistic form of theism',[17] he is not brushing oils on the canvas of a genuine postmodernism, but merely hooking on a voguish label to the kind of standard, American 'empirical theology' that has been current for many generations. Similarly, in the book of essays by diverse authors entitled *Spirituality and Society: Post-Modern Visions*, 'postmodernism' becomes nothing more than a buzzword for the sort of 'New Age' Utopianism spun from the cerebra of many California dreamers during the 1960s – a folio of themes and notions that are almost now a generation outdated.[18]

The contribution of a semiotician like Eco, however, to an authentic postmodern idiom lies in his recognition of the intimate linkage between 'theological' reflection and aesthetics. Eco laid the groundwork for his postmodernist, aesthetic 'hermeneutic' in an early work entitled *Art and Beauty in the Middle Ages*. It is the task of historical analysis, Eco points out, to scrutinize how a particular epoch 'solved for itself aesthetic problems' within the syntax of its own cultural organization.[19] Whereas medieval thought has often been regarded as inordinately 'metaphysical' and obsessed with questions of supersensible cognition at the expense of intramundane concerns, the inward legacy of the culture itself was always, according to Eco, the search for a plausible 'ontology of concrete existence'. Such an ontology Eco finds in the medieval emphasis on the power of colour, proportion and symbol. The grandeur of Chartres Cathedral, the scientific interest in the properties of natural light and the effects of luminosity, the detailing of both the sublime and the grotesque in what have wrongly come to be treated as 'fanciful', clerical accounts of both geography and natural history – these 'aesthetic' preoccupations were actually the philosophical subcode for a later grammar of signs and modes of signification which flowered in both Renaissance humanism and the style of artistic expression known as 'mannerism'.

The twelfth-century School of Chartres, for example, held that God is essentially an artist and that the world could be conceived as a grand artwork. Intellectual contemplation was compared to aesthetic appreciation. The notion of 'beauty' was closely connected to the classical ideal of the 'good'. In the words of Albert the Great, 'non est aliquid de numero existentium actu, quod non participet pulchro et bono'.[20] ('There is no existing being that does not share in beauty and goodness.') For Eco, one of the great theoreticians of cultural 'postmodernism', the aesthetic consciousness is wrapped up with a philosophical grasp of the ability and evanescence of sign-activity. Texts are no longer bare runes to be puzzled over. They are at once an intricate braid of the latent and the manifest, of form and function, of intimation and opacity, of word and image, of grapheme and difference. Indeed, *textuality* and *culture* – regarded in the primitive sense of all that is somehow 'indicative' – now emerge as reciprocal constructs.

III

The pre-eminence of an aesthetic 'postmodernism' is underscored not simply by the origin of the word in contemporary art criticism, but by the striking similarity between the new artistic values and certain strategies of interpretation in the humanities. The so-called 'conceptual art' that flourished in the 1970s disengaged the effort at aesthetic creation from its actual output, much in the same way that 'authorship' and writing were separated within the deconstructionist movement. Postmodern architecture has been characterized in one recent historical account as by its 'colour, variety and capriciousness' that is not so much decorative as texturally light and elusive.[21] If postmodernism as a discursive design is marked in Lyotard's terminology by the 'end of grand narrative', then as cultural episode it is what Julia Kristeva has called the *théorie d'ensemble*, an 'intertext' of heterogeneous, yet *significant*, moments of disclosure. According to David Carroll, postmodernism can be summed up in the German term *Begebenheit*, which may be translated as 'givenness', albeit in the dynamic sense. Another rendering is 'mere occurrence'.[22] Postmodern discourse itself 'is concerned with theorizing the historical moment'.[23] According to David Levin, postmodernism constitutes the 'critical deconstruction of the essence still at work in the modernist'. It is a weave of 'aesthetic moments', each of which performs as a 'critical commentary' on past aesthetic moments.[24]

Levin distinguishes between the 'analytic postmodern' and the 'metaphoric postmodern'. The analytic postmodern should be construed as the formalist reappropriation of the anti-metaphysical propensities within modernist culture and thought. When, for instance, Stephen Moore brands Mark Taylor as a thoroughgoing 'modernist' installed as an apostle of the postmodern because of the latter's undue attention to 'horizontality' and 'surfaces',[25] he is inadvertently acknowledging that postmodernism itself rests on an interior act of reinscription covering all that has been 'modern' in the most fruitful sense of the word. One problem with Taylor's work, and with the now expiring fashion of 'deconstructionism' in religious writing for that matter, is that it has reached a seemingly insurmountable impasse, so far as the critical task is concerned, largely as a result of its inability to embrace the 'metaphoric postmodern', which ultimately harks back to the desire of Nietzsche's Zarathustra to *dance*. The metaphoric postmodern rests on a profound post-metaphysical insight – what the Czech novelist Milan Kundera has called the 'unbearable lightness of being'. The metaphoric postmodern is Eco's 'travels in hyper-reality'. It is the transcendence of nihilism – a nihilism that is the hidden agenda behind what Derrida calls the 'truth in painting', the emptiness of all frames and representations, including the dys-representative entropy of the decon-structive campaign.

The end of deconstruction, strangely enough, is not the freedom of the text, but a totalizing twilight, a *Götterdämmerung* in which philosophy and theology no longer paint even a grey on grey, but recede into the ice-entombed, ink-black night of exhaustion. Deconstruction constitutes the universal 'closing time' that Heidegger has termed the 'end of philosophy'. It is the veritable *summa* of the analytical postmodern. It is the reduction of the sign to an anonymous exterior, to the uni-dimensional word-canvas upon which its cracked and discoloured oils have left their crepuscular impression.

The metaphoric postmodern, on the other hand, arises phoenix-like to recover the power of signification in an even more radical fashion. The metaphoric postmodern can best be described as a *fundamental ontology of the body* where metaphysics, now dismembered and disassembled, can be 'rewritten' as pure somatology, as the deciphering of the 'aesthetic' or sensate markings we know as *world* and as *culture*. As Jencks notes with respect to postmodern architecture, it is an aesthetic incorporating 'orna-ments and mouldings suggestive of the human body' that also 'humanizes inanimate form as we naturally project our physiognomy and moods onto it'.[26]

Eco's understanding of semiotics as 'carnival' in the sense of ribald and 'polyform' aesthetic display anticipates such a *hermeneutic* of the meta-phoric postmodern. But the same presentation more appropriately can be identified with what Kristeva has spiritedly termed 'Giotto's Joy', the dissolution of the space-segregating signifier and signified in the painting, or image-texture. The racinatory visual symbolism of Giotto constitutes a *narrative* of the incarnate signifier, of semiology as aesthetic encounter and appreciation. It is also proleptic with respect to the postmodern revelation of the body. Just as Giotto's joy is derived from the holy yearning of the supplicant for immanent fulfilment, so the metaphorical postmodern hinges upon what Kristeva acknowledges as the ontology of 'desire' that grounds not just aesthetic discourse, but the signifying act itself. Whereas Kristeva's somatology is, unfortunately, still circumscribed within a late psychoanalytic grid-language of paternal wish, displacement, substitution, transgression and repression, the codings for her own version of a meta-phoric, postmodern grammatology of both masculine and feminine are inherent in her own semiotics. Semiotics, for Kristeva, is 'polylogue' – where the 'speaking subject' is unmasked as body, as 'bursts of instinctual drive – rhythm', as 'heterogeneous strata . . . that can be multiplied and infinitized'.[27]

The concept of 'body' in the postmodern context, of course, refers to something more than the mere physical agent. 'Body' itself becomes a 'metaphor' for the metaphoric postmodern; it connotes both the region of alterity, of the 'outlandish' and the *outré*, with respect to the Cartesian, metaphysical subject; it becomes the pre-discursive horizon for all possible significations that transcend the logic of linguistic acts and their appli-cations. 'Body' is a basal, 'aesthetic' metaphor in so far as it correlates with Kristeva's infinity of sign-moments, with mutability, with a kind of 'music'. Body becomes a metaphor for the dance of signification. The 'dance' of the metaphoric postmodern – and of the body as infinite sign-ensemble, as 'semio-text', as the cipher of culture – surpasses all implicit modernisms to the extent that it belies the privatized subjectivities of the old metaphysics, and the old aesthetics. The body as metaphor contravenes the totalizing force of ideological belief systems – even the many neo-Marxist and crypto-metaphysical kinds of political romance that employ the rhetoric of the postmodern. It works against the temptation, so prevalent in the contem-porary agonism of the 'cultural politics' that also calls itself 'postmodern', of 'hyperrealizing the social', as Steven Connor has put it.[28] A postmodern somatology would in this sense serve as a genuine, transfinite semiotics which is not simply a rhetorical double for Marxist criticism, or for 'decon-structionist' badinage. The language of the body, together with the ontolo-gical category of 'embodiment', tracing the origin of that peculiar polylogical style of communication that embraces psychology, philosophy, theology and aesthetics, thus emerges as its own distinctive *lingua franca* for 'postmodernist' conversation.

Ironically, the somatic emphasis in the development of a postmodern, aesthetic sensibility, including what might be described as a distinctive postmodern *religiosity*, brings us into the realm of 'popular culture'. Many recent theoreticians of popular culture have concentrated on what might be described as the different modes of 'body signification', and the different styles of somatic repression and expression that characterize the *signa populi*.

Popular culture by its very nature is 'exhibitionist'. It seeks to idealize certain iconic representations of the human *figura* – shamans in colourful costume, kings and queens in their finery, popes with their tiaras, rock stars in their outrageous and often half-naked get-ups, the present-day postmillennial 'Madonna' whose hit song 'Like a Prayer' outrages the church because it is concomitantly hierophantic and crudely sensual – and to invoke these presentations as exemplary patterns for identification and enactment. In short, popular culture, as anthropologists have been telling us for generations, is held together by the power of multiple, and often ambiguous, significatory functions. Texts and other types of discursive formalities – even the highly sophisticated 'meta-textual' operations of deconstructionist readers – provide us with only a stylized, and one might even go so far as to say 'neo-metaphysical', rendering of what persists down through the ages as 'book culture'.

From this standpoint Derrida's proclamation of the 'end of the book' is but a reinscription of the old textual ideology. A true postmodern closure of the book would involve not just an exercise in what has become the weird, new fashion of Derridean scholastics, but a 'cultural' or 'semiotic' turn to fill out and finalize the earlier 'linguistic turn' which overshadowed an earlier era in philosophy and theology. A semiotician is interested not just in religious thought, but also in the religious context out of which the discursive ensembles of 'thought' are crystallized. In the same way that a Mick Farren can interpret the whole of twentieth-century culture through the iconics of the 'black leather jacket',[29] so a theological thinker privy to the aesthetics and the poetics of the postmodern can begin to envision 'sacrality' not simply as a complex of stock theological emblems or representations, but as a veritable marquee flashing with the evanescent tokens and hints of religious sentimentality in the twentieth century. The intertwining of religious aspiration and popular culture as a peculiar variant on postmodern aestheticism can be seen in what have wrongly been termed 'new religious movements' or 'New Age' religion. So much would-be 'new religiosity' – whether we are talking about channelling, 'satanic rock', crystal madness or the pop metaphysics of Shirley Maclaine, J.Z. Knight and Barbara Marx Hubbard – is nothing new at all. It is simply old-time esotericism, and in many instances archaic superstitions or dangerous obsessions, repackaged for present-day consumer tastes and employing the semiotic conveyances of popular culture.

New Age religion may in many respects be described as the *commodification of the arcane and obscure*, but we must comprehend its 'materiality' not with the raw ideological slant that allegedly postmodern 'political economists' adopt, but as a showing of embodied sign-contents. Sexuality

and popular religion, for instance – including even the scandals of Jim
Baker and Jimmy Swaggart – cannot be disentangled from each other
because of their very 'carnivality' (in Eco's sense), or 'in-carnality' from a
broader semiotic perspective. The materiality of the postmodern, aesthetic
mode of meaningfulness, therefore, must not be understood according to
some subtextual stance of metaphysical dualism in which an 'authentic'
sacrality stands as a sceptre of austere judgement over its popular formats.
Although a responsible 'cultural politics' does, in fact, require a self-
conscious distinction between canonical works and the fleeting products of
collective consumption, a postmodern aesthetical hermeneutics of culture
– embracing the various subdisciplines of the 'study of religion' – must tear
down the long-standing, scholarly Maginot lines barring religious thinking
from penetrating the 'otherness' of its own democratic milieu. The
Tillichean with its passion for workings of 'Spirit' in the night of *Existenz*
must displace the Eliadean with its historical preservationist bent for
dusting off and displaying behind glass the ancient, golden calves. A
Tillichean 'theological thinking' concerning culture comes once more to
the forefront.

The postmodern era, no matter what the concept implies diachronically,
can best be understood as the unveiling of a new epoch in the historicity of
Being, as Heidegger would claim. Yet we must now seriously consider
taking several, giant philosophical steps beyond both the Heideggerian
programme of 'fundamentally' re-reading the western tradition and two-
dimensional Derridean wordgrams with their curious, Dadaist messages of
inconsequentiality. If, as Ferdinand Saussure and Eco both stress, signs
'work' exclusively because they set in motion the play of differences, then
'deconstruction' can be freed from Derrida's hidden modernist semantics
of surface.[30] The moment of difference now discloses the transcendental
backlighting of immanent everydayness; it is the *signature* of a pure
presencing.

The 'age of the sign' must no longer be conceived, as Derrida once
proposed, as merely 'theological'. Postmodernly speaking, it is also the
time of *parousia*. *Parousia* is both the closing time of modernist metaphysics and the final naming of the rose whereby the all that has remained
unspoken during the long exile of signifier must at last struggle towards
speech. Most recently, Derrida himself has alluded to the end of deconstruction itself within his cryptic discussion of 'spirit' as 'fire'.[31] Or perhaps
we must uncover the essential meaning in the end of T.S. Eliot's *Four
Quartets*, which some commentators regard as the first 'postmodern' poem
of the twentieth century.

Four Quartets is 'postmodern' because it is a sweeping poesis disclosing
not jewels in the lotus but 'sapphires in the mud', a genuine Heideggerian
'worlding of the world' through the movements of signification that suddenly appear like a 'thousand points of light' (Wordsworth) across the

craggy terrain of 'mass culture'. The closure of the poem, however, is not about the 'naming' that takes place through discourse, but about fire. The discourse of the world is set aflame. As we discover at the conclusion of *The Name of the Rose*, the end of the book is also the end of the world. The representation of the metaphysical aeon burns up. For 'our God is a consuming fire'.

The concluding words of *Four Quartets*, therefore, are more than mildly prophetic: 'We only live, only suspire/Consumed by either fire or fire.' AND, our task, as Eliot directs us, 'will be to know the place for the first time'. It shall be, semiotically speaking, 'a condition of complete simplicity'. WHEN: 'All manner of thing shall be well/ When the tongues of flame are in-folded/ Into the crowned knot of fire/ And the fire and the rose are one.'[32]

NOTES

1 Umberto Eco, *The Name of the Rose*, trans. William Weaver, New York, Harcourt Brace Jovanovich, 1980, p. 583.
2 Umberto Eco, 'Frames of Comic Freedom,' in Umberto Eco, V.V. Ivanov and Monica Rector, *Carnival!*, ed. Thomas A. Sebeok, Amsterdam, Mouton, 1984, p. 6.
3 The remark appears in Jurgen Habermas, *Der philosophische Diskurs der Moderne*, Frankfurt, Suhrkamp, 1985. For a discussion of the problem Habermas raises, see Rodolphe Gasché, 'Postmodernism and Rationality', *Journal of Philosophy*, 85, October 1988, pp. 528–38. See also Sabine Wilke, 'Adorno and Derrida as Readers of Husserl: Some Reflections on the Historical Context of Modernism and Postmodernism', *Boundary*, 2, 1989, pp. 77–90; and Ulrich Schönherr, 'Adorno, Ritter, Gluck, and the Tradition of the Postmodern', *New German Critique*, 48, 1989, pp. 135–54.
4 Jacques Derrida, *The Truth in Painting*, trans. Geoffrey Bennington and Ian McLeod, Chicago, University of Chicago Press, 1987, p. 352.
5 Jacques Derrida, *The Ear of the Other: Otobiography, Transference, Translation*, Lincoln, University of Nebraska Press, 1988, p. 38.
6 Jean-François Lyotard, *The Postmodern Condition: A Report on Knowledge*, trans. Geoffrey Bennington and Brian Massumi, Minneapolis, University of Minnesota Press, 1984, p. 81.
7 The similarity between Lyotard's and Wyschogrod's argument is exemplified in the following quotation: 'Just as the sheer existence of language points phantastically to its non-violent character, the birth of the death event in our time opens up a new phantasmatic meaning borne by the speaker, one that accompanies all discourse' – Edith Wyschogrod, *Spirit in Ashes: Hegel, Heidegger, and Man-Made Mass Death*, New Haven, Yale University Press, 1985, p. 214. Wyschogrod's brilliant treatment of the origin of postmodern thinking in Hegel and Heidegger, however, is distinguished by her call at the end for a 'transactional' communitarian self, which may be described more as a modernist concern than a postmodern one.
8 Charles Jencks, *Post-Modernism: The New Classicism in Art and Architecture*, New York, Rizzoli, 1987, p. 338.
9 Huston Smith, *Beyond the Postmodern Mind*, New York, Crossroad

Publishing, 1982, p. 182.

10 Huston Smith, 'Postmodernism's Impact on Religious Studies', plenary address before the American Academy of Religion in Anaheim, California, 1989.

11 Umberto Eco, *The Open Work*, trans. Anna Cancogni, Cambridge, Mass., Harvard University Press, 1989, p. 86.

12 Jim Collins, *Uncommon Cultures: Popular Culture and Post-Modernism*, London and New York, Routledge, 1989, pp. 17–18.

13 Peter Bürger, *Theory of the Avante-Garde*, trans. Michael Shaw, Minneapolis, University of Minnesota Press, 1984, p. 54.

14 Erving Goffman, *Gender Advertisements*, New York, Harper & Row, 1979, p. 84.

15 Heinz-Güter Vester, in 'Erving Goffman's Sociology as Semiotics of Postmodern Culture', *Semiotica*, 76, 1989, pp. 191–203, has insightfully and effectively analysed Goffman's contribution to 'postmodern discourse'. 'Our understanding of a sign, a sign system, or a text is a developing process of unlimited semiosis' (p. 191). The theory of unlimited semiosis through cultural elaboration – a key element in the framing of a postmodern schema of interpretation – is made possible, according to Vester, through the 'playfulness' and 'intertextuality' of popular productions, as Goffman analyses them.

16 Jean-François Lyotard, *The Differend: Phrases in Dispute*, trans. Georges Van Den Abbeele, Minneapolis, University of Minnesota Press, 1988, p. 13.

17 David Ray Griffin, *God and Religion in the Postmodern World*, Albany, State University of New York Press, 1989, p. 138.

18 David Ray Griffin (ed.), *Spirituality and Society*, Albany, State University of New York Press, 1988.

19 Umberto Eco, *Art and Beauty in the Middle Ages*, New Haven, Yale University Press, 1986, p. 2.

20 Quoted in Wladyslaw Tatarkiewicz, *History of Aesthetics*, vol. II, The Hague, Mouton, 1970, p. 288.

21 Bruce Cole and Adelheid Gealt, *Art of the Western World: From Ancient Greece to Post-Modernism*, London, Summit Books, 1989, p. 333.

22 See David Carroll, *Paraesthetics: Foucault, Lyotard, Derrida*, New York, Methuen, 1987. For other recent philosophical, or theological, attempts to epitomize the postmodern, see George James, 'The Postmodern Context', *Contemporary Philosophy*, 22, 1989, pp. 1–5; David Crownfield, 'Postmodern Perspectives in Theology and Philosophy of Religion', *Contemporary Philosophy*, 22, 1989, pp. 6–13; Robert Morris, 'Words and Images in Modernism and Postmodernism', *Critical Inquiry*, 15, 1989, pp. 337–47; and Paul Jay, 'Modernism, Postmodernism, and Critical Style: The Case of Burke and Derrida', *Genre*, 21, 1988, pp. 339–58.

23 Robert Merrill, 'Simulations: Politics, TV, History', in Robert Merrill (ed.), *Ethics/Aesthetics: Post-Modern Positions*, Washington, Maisonneuve Press, 1988, p. 151.

24 David Levin, 'Postmodernism in Dance: Dance, Discourse, Democracy', in Hugh J. Silverman (ed.), *Postmodernism – Philosophy and the Arts*, New York, Routledge, 1990, p. 221.

25 Stephen Moore, 'The "Post-" Age Stamp: Does It Stick?', *Journal of the American Academy of Religion*, lvii, 3, 1989, p. 548.

26 Jencks, op. cit., p. 336

27 Julia Kristeva, *Desire in Language: A Semiotic Approach to Literature and Art*, trans. Thomas Gora, Leon Roudiez and Alice Jardine, New York, Columbia University Press, 1980, p. 186.

28 Steven Connor, *Postmodernist Culture: An Introduction to Theories of the Contemporary*, Oxford, Blackwell, 1989, p. 61.
29 See Mick Farren, *The Black Leather Jacket*, New York, Abbeville Press, 1985.
30 Says Eco:

> the elements of the signifier are set in a system of oppositions in which, as Saussure explained, there are only differences. The same thing with the signified. . . . The correlation between expression-plane is also given by a difference: the sign-function exists by a dialectic of presence and absence, as a mutual exchange between two heterogeneities.
>
> (*Semiotics and the Philosophy of Language*, Bloomington, Indiana University Press, 1984, p. 23)

The enhancement which Eco's philosophical linguistics achieves in relation to Barthes' relatively naive 'poststructuralism' cannot be understated. Eco's notion of semiosis as the revelation of a kind of 'unsaidness', in contradistinction to Derrida's detextualizing *différance*, also puts the original aims of 'deconstruction' back on a sounder philosophical, and ontological, footing.
31 Jacques Derrida, *Of Spirit: Heidegger and the Question*, trans. Geoffrey Bennington and Rachel Bowlby, Chicago, University of Chicago Press, 1989.
32 T.S. Eliot, *Four Quartets*, New York, Harcourt Brace Jovanovich, 1971, p. 59.

Part II

Ethics and politics

Chapter 8

The politics of spirituality: the spirituality of politics

Geraldine Finn

> Happiness occurs when people can give the whole of themselves to the moment being lived, when being and becoming are the same thing.

These are the words of John Berger. They are from an essay he wrote on the recent political changes in eastern Europe which was published in *The Guardian* newspaper earlier this year.[1] The essay was accompanied by a large tinted photograph of the faces of people at a mass demonstration in eastern Europe, of the kind we got used to seeing on our TV screens and in our newspapers in the Fall of 1989. This picture, Berger tells us, was taken in Prague, but it could just as well have been Warsaw, Leipzig, Budapest or Sofia. The people were standing shoulder to shoulder, in winter clothes, looking up and over each other in the direction of the camera. Their faces are grave and attentive, expectant and concerned, tense and eager, yet calm and self-contained. They seem to be energized for collective action yet-to-be-determined and united in a shared experience yet-to-be-articulated – one which is neither fear nor joy, triumph nor despair. Nobody is talking or gesticulating and there is scarcely a hint of a smile on any of the approximately 350 faces in the picture. This is clearly not a football crowd, nor even a demonstration for peace.

I like this picture a lot. I find it moving and compelling and inspiring in its singularity, particularity and detail. In its otherness. In its opaqueness to easy or familiar interpretation, in its resistance to common sense – to *sens commun*. I like it because it both affirms and performs what it shows, and because what it shows nourishes me: the truth of the ethical encounter with the other (to use Levinas' terms), of the movement when 'being and becoming are the same thing' (to use Berger's).[2] What this photograph shows, affirms and performs is the relationship with others as a responsibility that does not refer to (my) freedom (to my 'will' or my political status), i.e. the relationship with others as an alliance, a 'neighbouring' that was not chosen. It shows, affirms and performs the encounter with the *face* of the other in particular as a singularity: as a 'trace' outside all categories, which puts me into question as well as the relationship, the world and the 'common sense' we share. It shows and affirms the face of the other as a

'signification beyond all intentionalities': all phenomenological consti-
tutions and socio-political constructions; the face of the other as a visi-
tation, a 'transcendence', an epiphany, an imperative which demands and
commands me. It reveals the other as an exteriority which cannot be
integrated into the (old Imperialisms of the) Same, which is and must
therefore be the starting point of philosophy in the best sense, i.e. of *parole
originaire* and, as I hope eventually to demonstrate, *politique originaire*.[3]
This is the imperative – the demand, the command, the responsibility and
the promise of the picture and the event(s) it commemorates: to think and
be anew, to risk being 'otherwise than being' what we have already known
and become.[4]

This is not an encounter I expect to have when I read the newspaper,
watch TV, do the groceries or even engage in political or philosophical
debate(s). Though I have come to expect it from the likes of John Berger
and it is one I constantly seek and seek to produce in my relations with
others and in my own intellectual work as a reader, writer and teacher. I
used to think of this desire of mine for what I now (following the letter,
though perhaps not the spirit, of Levinas) am calling the *ethical* encounter
with others (with otherness), this seeking for being-otherwise-than-being
simply a member, a re-presentative of a category or class (man, woman,
child; Catholic, Protestant, Jew; bourgeois, aristocrat, prole') as a form of
intellectual snobbery. Since it led me away from not only the everyday
taken-for-granted discourse, practices and alliances of my colleagues and
peers but also away from the more sophisticated but still formulaic and
predicative posturings of the church and state and the equally predicative
clichés of the spiritual and political movements which would oppose them –
into the arcane and increasingly esoteric and always shifting, unresolved
and disputatious worlds of literature, philosophy and art.

Eventually, it became clear to me however that what I had been identifying as 'intellectual' desires, preferences, commitments, pleasures and pains
(and chastising myself for) were really *political* desires, preferences, commitments, pleasures and pains (of which I could be proud). That what I was
really seeking in both my work and my personal life was the possibility of a
being-in-the-world-with-others which was not always already pre-dicated,
pre-determined and pre-scribed – and thereby foreclosed – by language
and the various institutionalized political relations which organize its
meanings and *sens*, and thereby the meanings and '*sens*' of both our
consciousness and our lives. I was seeking to inhabit the space of becoming, to use Berger's terms: the *space between* experience and expression,
reality and representation, existence and essence: the concrete fertile pre-
thematic and an-archic space *where we actually live*: the space of sensibility
and affect, of undecidability and chance, of being-otherwise-than-being a
man, a woman, a Christian, a Jew, a mother, daughter, father, son, etc. I
was seeking, that is, to establish relationships with others in 'excess' of

(beyond and between) the categories which render us knowable and/or already known (as re-presentations of the Same, the familiar); relationships beyond and between the categorical imperatives predicated upon our being-as a man, a woman, a Christian, a Jew; relationships beyond and between the classifications and identities which pre-empt the specifically *ethical* encounter with others *as other*: as otherwise-than-being man, woman, Christian, Jew, etc.

This space between representation and reality, text and context, expression and experience, language and being is the necessary and indispensable space of judgement and critique, creativity and value, resistance and change. It is the ground of the critical intentions and originating experiences which enable us to call the political status quo into question and challenge the already-known universe and its organization into and by the predicative and prescriptive categories of 'practical reason'. As such, it is *the* ethical space – the space of the specifically ethical relation with others – and the only place from which the conventionality, the contingency (the 'arbitrariness') of reality (of political positivities and identities) can be seen and challenged. Managing this silent but nevertheless signifying/*signifiant* space between the pre-thematic an-archical-ethical and the categorical hier-archical-political encounter with others, this space of the otherwise-than-being a re-presentative of a category or class is absolutely central therefore to the exercise of political power and to the organization of our subjection to it. It is absolutely central, that is, to our 'subjectivity': to our being as subjects of experiences and actions which 'count', of sentences which make sense in the *polis*. (Which should give us pause in claiming our 'subjectivity' as 'woman', 'black' or 'gay', for example – as anything other than an always strategic political identity deployed provisionally for and against particular political ends.)

Categorical schemas and institutionalized discourses (the discourses of politics, philosophy, science, sex, literature and art, for example) work towards this end of managing – and in our own society, suturing, though this need not be the case – this vital space between representation and reality, language and being. They channel the affective, anarchical-ethical experience of 'wild being' (Merleau-Ponty), of being-as-becoming (Berger), of being-otherwise-than-being (Levinas) into articulated, hierarchical, predicative meanings, intentionalities and desires compatible with and amenable to the controlling interests of prevailing political powers. The task, however, is never accomplished. For the contingent and changing concrete world always exceeds the ideal categories of thought within which we attempt to express and contain it. And the same is true of people. We are always both more and less than the categories which name and divide us. More and less that is than a woman, a man, a Christian, a Jew, a lesbian, a mother, a wife. More and less than what we stand for in the *polis* and what stands for us. More and less than anything that can be said about us. Our lives leave remainders (they say more than they mean) just as our categories leave residues (they mean more than they say). Lives and categories precipitate, that is, an-archical *sens/significance* which exists beyond and between given categorical frameworks, beyond and between the knowable and the already known, as an always available (re)source of difference, resistance and change, of being-otherwise-than-being.

Politics speaks directly to this an-archic 'precipitate' of being and thought, this (re)source of *différance* and change, this space-between being and being-as: this fertile, disruptive, unpredictable space of the relation with an otherness which ex-ceeds established categories of predication and control. Conservative politics speak to this space in order to contain, deny or negate its excesses: to recuperate is deviations and *différance* into and for the hegemonic categories and relations which constitute the status quo. Radical, progressive and/or revolutionary politics speak to and from the same 'precipitate' (the same space between category and experience, representation and reality) to *affirm* it: to inhabit and expand it, and to organize it for political resistance and change. At least radical politics must *begin* there as any critical moment must, in the *space between* category and reality, language and experience: in the space of excess and disjuncture, deviation and *différance*; the space from which the 'arbitrariness' of political divisions and classifications and the incommensurability of being and thought (of my being and my being a woman, a lesbian, a black, a Jew . . .) are both visible and lived, visible because lived. Radical politics must originate this way, in the as-yet-untamed 'precipitate' (the residues and remainders) of languages and lives, and take its inspiration and direction from the an-archical *ethical* relation with others/otherness which occurs there, between and beyond the categorical imperatives of regulated institutionalized thought. But it seldom recognizes or acknowledges that fact or the place of its origin (not surprisingly, since we are systematically bereft of an adequate language with which to do so) nor therefore the implications of that space of its own origination for its own would-be 'alternative' political praxis. As a consequence, radical politics tend towards the same kind of political positivities and 'final solutions' as the 'conservative' regimes they purport to resist, transform, subvert or replace, with their categorical assertions of competing imperatives, identities and ends. (The identities and ends of 'women', 'blacks', 'minorities' or 'gays', for example.) Would-be radical politics thereby collude with the powers that be and bind us all the more securely to our assigned identities and political destinies (as woman, black or gay) by obscuring once again that experience of excess – of the space between reality and representation, being and being-as – from which they can be deconstructed and resisted.

I once thought of this tendency in the theories and practices of would-be radical politics (of the politics of feminism and postmodernism, most recently, for example) as an abdication of *politics*: as an abdication of the space of political judgement and critique, of political self-consciousness and reflection, of having to take a stand and acknowledge responsibility for it – for the place from which you have *chosen* to speak (*as* a woman, a man, a black, a lesbian . . .) and for what, therefore, is spoken from it. But I have recently come to see it as an *abdication of ethics for politics*; as a flight into the relatively safe categorical (familiar, known and predetermined) space of the '*polis*' – of the political relation with others – away from the risky, uncertain, creative, accountable and responsible *space-between* of the an-archic *ethical* relation.

Which brings me back to the Prague photograph, John Berger's essay on it and the relationship between *spirituality and politics* which is the focus of this paper. For Berger takes the same flight path from the ethical to the political but *by way of the spiritual* in this article: away from the place of the in-between, of excess, contingency, undecidability and chance, of *parole* and *politique originaire*, back to the familiar and safe place of the *polis*, of necessity and identity and more of the Same, and all in the name of systematic and fundamental change! The language of spirituality mediates this flight from ethics to politics while at the same time obscuring it and thereby its own relationship to politics and to the ethical encounter with others/otherness which, I have been arguing, politics both organizes and obscures; organizes to obscure. This deployment of 'spirituality' against 'ethics' in the service of 'politics' is, I believe, inherent in the discourses and practices of 'spirituality' itself in our culture and not some deviation or aberration from it, or from some purer version of it, on John Berger's part – as the analysis which follows is intended to show.

Berger argues that the picture from Prague bespeaks a (re)turn to spirituality in eastern Europe following the demise of Communism and what he refers to as the 'materialist' philosophy which fuelled it. And he sees the (re-)emergence of religious and nationalist movements as harbingers of this (re)turn to spirituality. This is how he makes the connections:

> Independence movements all make economic and territorial demands, but their first claim is of a spiritual order . . . all of them want to be free of distant, foreign centres which, through long, bitter experience, they have come to know as soulless. . . .
>
> The spiritual, marginalized, driven into the corners, is beginning to reclaim its lost terrain. . . . The old reasoning, the old common sense, even old forms of courage have been abandoned, unfamiliar recognitions and hopes, long banished to the peripheries are returning to claim their own. This is where the happiness behind the faces in the photo starts. . . .
>
> nothing is finally determined. The soul and the operator have come out of hiding together. All are back in the human condition.

Well, yes and no. It all depends on what he means by soul and spirit, the human condition and, elsewhere in the article, 'transcendent vision' and 'enclaves of the beyond' of 'materialist explanations'. These are abstract and contentious categories, mere slogans as long as their meanings are not made clear and concrete – slogans which, like democracy, freedom and progress, have been used to support a lot of rather nasty political practices in their time. And when they are linked both historically and conceptually – and indiscriminately – as they are here, to the affirmation and promotion of religious and nationalist movements (the Catholic Church in Latin America, Islam in the Middle East, the Irish, the Basques, the Kurds, the Kasovans, the Azerbaijanis, the Puerto Ricans, the Latvians) because of their commitment to bringing 'social justice' to the poor, the landless, the exiled and those 'treated as historical trash' (does this extend to women, do you think?) . . . Well! I begin to feel not only nervous, but disappointed, cheated and angry. I feel nervous about what is being promoted in the name of 'spirituality' and the return to the 'human condition'. I feel cheated of the promise of difference and change, of the possibility of *parole* and *politique originaire*, of the truth of the anarchical-ethical relation which the Prague photo testifies to. And I feel angry at the obfuscation, the mystification, the falsification, the recuperation, the pre-emptive and premature reduction of that promise *yet again* by one of our would-be oppositional and (I would argue not coincidentally) white male intellectuals, into the ancient and familiar *political* categories and ends of good old patriarchal praxis: nationalism and religion – paraded in this case under the purportedly non-materialist flagship of 'spirituality', 'soul' and the 'human condition'.

I am not of course opposed *a priori* to the various liberation movements which are organized by and in the name of religion and nationality (or any other 'identity': to women's, gay or black liberation, for example) but rather to that in the name of which and ultimately, therefore, for the sake of which they are organized and made practical and concrete: 'identity' itself. In this case, the tribal identities of particular patriarchal religions, particular patriarchal nation-states. I am objecting, that is, to the particular political ends (though not all political ends) to which the originally non-aligned, anarchic-*ethical* experience of and desire for being-otherwise-than-being a representative or member of a class, i.e. for being *beyond* political determinations, are repeatedly subordinated. And to the language of *spirituality* in particular, which in this case, as I fear in most in our culture, colludes in that process of subordination of the ethical to the political: recuperating the aspiration to being-beyond as being-as, *parole originaire* to *parole parlée*, *politique originaire* to *politique secondaire*.[5]

I have always been uncomfortable with the language of spirituality and its tendency to 'other-worldliness' in particular; that is, with its presumption of and aspiration to a being-otherwise-than-being *in and of the ma-*

terial world – to a being beyond 'materialist interpretations' as Berger puts it in this article. This tendency to 'other-worldliness' sets up an opposition, a separation, an hiatus between 'spiritual' and 'material' being, between 'spirit' and 'flesh' and 'soul' and 'body' from which depend a whole series of autogenous binary oppositions by means of which relations of ruling are rationalized and reproduced (personal/political, self/other, mind/body, particular/universal, etc.). The differentiation of 'spirit' from 'matter', for example, both mystifies and falsifies the complex reality of material being by splitting off from it its most creative and potentially subversive possibilities and effects and syphoning them off into and for some 'transcendent' space of other-worldliness, of the *immaterial*: of God, the soul and/or the human spirit. This postulate of an immaterial and 'transcendent' soul, spirituality or 'Otherness' secures the 'quiddity' of the material world *as it is* and at the same time the safety of the political status quo which organizes it. It thus abandons us to politics – and politics to politicians – by appropriating the mundane ethical experience of and motivation towards otherness, to being-otherwise-than-being the realization of a pre-existing category or class, for a 'spirituality' which is 'out of this world'.

The experiences, knowledges, values, aspirations and desires characteristically claimed for a transcendent 'spirituality' do not, I believe, require nor are they well served by 'other-worldly' and/or would-be 'non-materialist' interpretations: I mean experiences of the 'beyond' and the 'ineffable', for example, of 'transcendence', 'oneness', the 'absolute' and 'God', and of the humility, grace, fear, love, sin or guilt which living in 'God's presence' can entail. All of these can, I think, be understood in terms of the particular and specific contingencies, complexities and necessary mysteries of our existence as particular and specific, contingent and complex material beings: beings who can think and speak but always only from a spatio-temporally particular and partial point of view: beings who live in a particular and specific contingent and complex material world which thinks and speaks through us. The experience of so-called 'spiritual' transcendent and necessary realities like 'God', for example, can be understood as and in terms of the experience of the necessary excess of being over thought (and vice versa): as and in terms of experiences of the necessary and inevitable incommensurability of thought and that of which it is the thought, for thinking beings and beings thought (*that think in us*) that are neither dead nor complete – if complete, then dead.[6]

This experience of both the mystery and necessity of the incommensurability of being and thought, this apprehension of both reality and experience as *more than* what appears, more than what we know or can ever know, as that which exceeds any cognitive or practical grasp we have of it; this experience of 'being-beyond-being', if you like, has been claimed for 'God' by traditional religions and institutionalized discourses of spirituality, i.e. it has been claimed for a spirituality which transcends the material world. I want to claim it back for our material experience of the material world which in its contingency and temporality always exceeds any and every consciousness we have of it and any and every organizing structure we impose upon it. Just as we exceed every and any particular category which names us, and our categories exceed any and every particular application of them. The language of 'transcendence' (of a 'spirituality' which 'transcends' the material world) misrepresents (mystifies and falsifies, obscures and obfuscates) this vital, dynamic and always ambiguous negotiated and negotiable relationship of excess (of the necessary and constant movement of convergence and divergence between being and otherwise-than-being) with its implicit or explicit hypostasis of a division in human being, in Being itself, which is absolute, constitutive and irremediable. On the contrary, so-called 'spiritual' experiences, aspirations and values do not refer to a reality (or Being) beyond the material world but to a reality (or being) beyond its categorical frameworks and any particular apprehension or *sens/significance* we may have of it. They refer, that is, to what I have been calling the *space-between* category and reality, text and context, language and being; the space which is also the condition of possibility (and necessity) of both our ethical and political relations with others (with otherness). I said earlier that managing, and in our own case suturing, this space-between is absolutely central to any and every political system, and that categorical schemes and institutionalized knowledges work towards this end by organizing and interpreting our experience into meanings and activities which preserve and reproduce the interests and instrumentalities of the powers that be. Institutionalized religions and discourses of spirituality are part of this management process, part of the apparatus of ruling. They pick up the 'slack' of the secular categorical schemas, the residues and remainders of languages and lives which are potential resources for *parole* and *politique originaire*, for disaffection and resistance, and work them up into supplementary systems of authorized meanings which reconcile us to the status quo while offering us the illusion of negotiating ourselves a better deal within it. The consumer economy, and the discourse of commodities and needs which fuels it, does the same thing. It too speaks to the excess of being over being-as, to our experience of this excess and to our desire to have this experienced excess, this *space-between* category and reality, acknowledged, valued and inhabited. But the consumer economy and the discourse of commodities do so by re-covering and re-cuperating this excess all the more securely into the old systems of meanings for more of the Same: the same old identities, meanings, loyalties, relations, realities and values of family, sexuality, self, freedom, modernity, masculinity, femininity, identity, progress, etc.

It saddens me to see contemporary would-be critical theorists of the modern and/or postmodern condition (like Berger here) doing the same thing: speaking to and from the *space-between* which is the condition of possibility of their critical speech as it is of all (radical/ethical) judgement and critique, only to obfuscate that space of *parole* and *politique originaire* under familiar political categories of traditional identities, nationalities and religions (here masquerading as an immaterial 'spirituality'), and thereby denying the significance of the ethical relation, of the space-between, as a (political) reality, experience or value worth fighting for. This is precisely how would-be radical progressive and/or revolutionary political movements lose their radical, progressive and/or revolutionary edge and end up reproducing the systems they set out to critique and/or offer alternatives to. Contemporary struggles within and about feminism and postmodernism, for example, tend to assume the terms and relevancies of the politics they purport to reject – the ancient and familiar categories of subjects and objects, self and other, identity and difference, man and woman, freedom and necessity, for example – as if these categories of thought were commensurate with the contingent and concrete realities they organize and describe, and as if the categories, the realities and especially the *relationship between* them were unambivalent and transparent. It is as if we are afraid to 'come out' from the categories which – uncomfortable and contradictory as the lives they afford us may be – at least supply us with a place in the *polis*, i.e. with the appropriate mask of 'objective' authoritative knowledge and a voice that will be heard as, and because, it is 're-presentative' of an identifiable category or class: as the voice of Québec, or Canada, or black women, or gay men or whatever. Organizing under and identifying with the category which organizes our position in and exclusions from the *polis* (with the category of woman, lesbian, Jew, black or native, for example) may be necessary for winning for ourselves (as women, lesbians, Jews, blacks or natives) more and better space within it. But if this is as far as the political gesture goes, if it stops with the institutionalized categories themselves, then it is not really subversive of the politics with which it is engaged. Our lives exceed the categories which organize our relationship to power and to each other. Claiming that excess against the category which names and contains us broadens the political scope of the category and thus the political scope of our lives. But it leaves the category and the 'class' system it articulates intact and available for recuperation and control by and for the ruling apparatus if this is all it does. If it does not at the same time challenge the politics and practices of representation itself: i.e. the organization of experience and affect into discrete and exclusive categories of being (identities) through which our encounter with the world and others is mediated as always-already predicative and pre-scriptive, and thereby irresponsible to the otherness of others and the possibilities of fundamental difference and change, of *parole* and *politique originaire*. If politics is 'merely' politics, i.e. if political struggle fails to acknowledge or inhabit the space-between of the *ethical* relation with others, then no matter how radical or subversive its claims and self-conscious ends, it will always reproduce the instrumentalities and ends of its 'point du départ', of the regimes it purports to oppose. As I have argued elsewhere, the politics of postmodernism in its most visible and increasingly hegemonic (and productive) manifestations does this.[7] It takes modernist representations of reality at face value and proceeds to reject or reform them, all the time speaking not from the *space-between* reality and representation, context and text which permits the critique in the first place, but from the places prescribed by modernism itself, from the spaces of the modernist text.[8] It thus binds us all the more securely and narrowly to and within the sedimented meanings, instrumentalities and ends of the modernist status quo: to and within, that is, the increasingly atomized, volatilized, fragmented and impoverished categories of subjective/ subjected being upon which the contemporary version of the 'modernist project' depends.

Meanwhile, business is booming in the 'psyche' departments and the doctors of the 'soul' and 'spirit' (gurus, therapists, healers, homoeopaths, etc.) have never had it so good. And business will continue to boom in the 'psyche' department (and we will get even more 'sick' and 'fed-up') as long as we confuse ourselves and our world with our categories. As long, that is, as we insist, in theory and in practice, on *coinciding* with our social and political identities – with our names – on the one hand, and *pathologizing* our experiences of excess, disjuncture, difference, ambiguity, undecidability, contingency, chaos and chance, on the other. As long as we insist, that is, on pathologizing and abjecting our experience of the *ethical* relation with others which is our nourishment and our hope: our experience of being-otherwise-than-being a re-presentative of the category or class which names and contains us and separates us from each other; of being more and less than a man, a woman, a black, a mother, a lesbian, a Jew, etc. As I have argued, these experiences of excess are not only ineradicable for material beings in a material world; they are the necessary and indispensable conditions of ec-stasy, creativity, change and critique – and of *parole* and *politique originaire*.

The Prague photograph, and the political events it commemorates, speaks to me of and to these experiences of excess – of being beyond and between being-as. It bespeaks, that is, not a (re)turn to 'spiritual' values supposedly antithetical to and repudiated and abandoned by 'materialist' philosophies, but the truth, promise and openness of the *space-between* identities, national and religious. It affirms, inhabits and performs the space of the specifically ethical relation with others and the possibility, therefore, of a future which could (always) be otherwise: otherwise-than-being more of the same.

NOTES

1 *The Guardian*, Thursday, 22 March 1990, pp. 23, 25.
2 All subsequent references and citations are to and from Emmanuel Levinas, *Collected Philosophical Papers*, trans. Alphonso Lingis, The Hague, Martinus Nijhoff, 1987.
3 The concept of *politique originaire* (of the same order as Merleau-Ponty's *parole originaire*: i.e. speech which institutes new meanings, also called '*parole parlante*') was introduced by Eleanor Godway. It is clarified and developed in E. Godway, 'Towards a Phenomenology of Politics: Expression and Praxis', and G. Finn, 'The Politics of Contingency: The Contingency of Politics', both in Thomas Busch and Shaun Gallagher (eds), *Merleau-Ponty: Hermeneutics and Post-Modernism*, New York, SUNY Press, forthcoming. Merleau-Ponty wrote: 'The truth of politics is only this art of inventing what will later appear to have been required by the times' – M. Merleau-Ponty, *The Primacy of Perception and Other Essays*, Evanston, Northwestern University Press, 1964, p. 210. This is the starting point of our reflection on the full implications of a *politique originaire*.
4 This paragraph juxtaposes, paraphrases and condenses a number of Levinas' ideas and observations from a number of different essays and contexts. Some precise citations are given below but for further clarification of Levinas' precise uses of these terms (which is not reflected here), see *Collected Philosophical Papers*, op. cit., *passim*:
  'a relationship with the absolute other . . . opens the very dimensions of infinity, of what puts a stop to the irresistible imperialism of the same and the "I" ' (p. 55).
  'The ethical relationship is not grafted on to an antecedent relationship of cognition; it is a foundation and not a superstructure' (p. 56).
  'the other appears to me . . . as what measures me' (p. 57).
  'the face of the other would be the very starting point of philosophy' (p. 59).
  'The relationship with the infinite is not a cognition but an approach, a neighbouring with what signifies itself without revealing itself' (p. 73).
  'The relationship with the other puts me into question. . . . I did not know I was so rich, but I no longer have the right to keep anything for myself' (p. 94).
  'Consciousness is called into question by a face. . . . A face confounds the intentionality that aims at it. . . . The I before the other is infinitely responsible' (p. 97).
  'The beyond from which a face comes signifies as a trace' (p. 103).
  'A trace is a presence of that which properly speaking has never been there, of what is always past' (p. 105).
  'Proximity, beyond intentionality, is the relationship with the neighbour in the moral sense of the term' (p. 119).
  'What is ineffable or incommunicable in inwardness and cannot adhere in the said is a responsibility, prior to freedom' (p. 133).
  'We can have responsibilities for which we cannot consent to death. It is despite myself that the other concerns me' (p. 138).
  'Ethics is not a moment of being; it is otherwise and better than being, the very possibility of the beyond' (p. 165)
5 A similar slippage between the language of politics, ethics and spirituality occurs in the writing of Vaclav Havel. Like Berger, Havel presumes an hiatus and an opposition between 'material' and 'spiritual' being and locates the possibility of both 'morality' and human 'identity' in the latter: in the sphere of spirituality, and what he calls 'transcendence'. And like Berger he too describes

the 'spiritual and moral crisis' in eastern Europe as the effect of 'a system that drives each man into a foxhole of purely material existence' and in terms of a lost 'identity' which is essentially phallic: in terms of impotence, castration and emasculation. See, for example, Vaclav Havel, 'Letter to Dr Gustav Husak', in *Living in Truth*, ed. Jan Vladislav, London, Faber & Faber, 1987, pp. 3–35. Nevertheless, both Havel and Berger elsewhere in their work espouse an ethics and a politics consistent with and supportive of the 'space-between' proposed here. My point is that the traditional discourses and institutions of politics, ethics and spirituality do not serve their vision well, do not do justice to the 'space-between': in fact, obscure and obfuscate it under categories that ultimately reproduce more of the Same.

6   To be sure, the ego knows itself as reflected by all the objective reality it has constituted, or in which it has collaborated; it thus knows itself on the basis of a conceptual reality. But if this conceptual reality exhausted his being, a living man would not be different from a dead man. Generalization is death; it inserts the ego into, and dissolves it in, the generality of its work. The irreplaceable singularity of the ego is due to its life.

(Levinas, op. cit., p. 36)

7 See, for example, Geraldine Finn, 'Patriarchy and Pleasure: The Pornographic Eye/I', *Canadian Journal of Political and Social Theory*, IX, 1–2, 1985, pp. 81–95; 'Nobodies Speaking: Subjectivity, Sex and the Pornography Effect', *Philosophy Today*, 33 (Summer 1989), pp. 174–81; 'The Politics of Contingency', op. cit.; 'Why Are There No Great Women Postmodernists?', 'Beyond Either/ Or: Postmodernism and the Politics of Feminism', 'Ethics and/or Politics in the Postmodern Condition?' and 'On Being (a) Woman: Subjects, Predicates, Identities and Conditions', all forthcoming in Geraldine Finn, *Feminism and the Politics of Postmodernism*, Boston, Beacon Press.

8 This is particularly and disturbingly true of contemporary would-be postmodern debates about sexuality and the body. See Finn, op. cit., above, and especially 'Nobodies Speaking'.

Chapter 9

Marx, God and praxis

Eve Tavor Bannet

Until recently, the various Marxes who presided over twentieth-century European thought were constructed by inserting epistemic breaks some-where in the thirty-nine volumes of the *Collected Works* and by discrediting or excluding the texts which come before. Althusserian scissors were inserted at 1845 in volume V, humanist scissors at 1844 in the middle of volume III. The Marx that David McLellan has significantly called 'Marx before Marxism',[1] the Marx obsessed with spiritual, mystical and metaphy-sical questions, was repressed by both camps. The Party also made its cuts. Marginalized – at least as far as editorially possible – in the bulging appendix to volume I, the mystical spiritual Marx of the late 1830s and early 1840s had no real place either in the official Marxist-Leninist Institute chronology of the development of Marx's thinking. Engels still hovered over orthodox and revisionist excisions, with his profane, 'scientific' and merely materialist version of the Teaching, his 'embarrassment' over Marx's mystical poetry and metaphysical speculations, and his desire to consign everything but the *Theses on Feuerbach* to oblivion. Officially, Marx was hostile to religion; if he was not hostile to religion, he was not officially Marx.

Scholars who addressed Marx's relation to religion achieved the same result by different means. They sensibly or insensibly followed the official 'Marxist' peripatetic narrative pattern of youthful idealism turned around and stood on its feet, or they integrated homologies between religion and Marx's 'historical' or 'political messianism' into the liberal narrative of history as a process of progressive secularization.[2] These modes of histori-cal emplotment distanced Marx from the spiritual architectonic of his thought and from the Jewish underpinnings of his theory of praxis. They assumed too readily that Marx's 'critique of religion' was to be equated with a blanket rejection of spiritual matters. And they made the periodic return of the repressed – in the work of a Bloch or Benjamin, for instance, or more recently in Derrida, Lacoue-Labarthe, Nancy and Stanley Aaronowitz – inexplicable except as some sort of extraneous or eccentric or despairing addition to the materialist theory of praxis.

In the shadow of postmodern returns of the Spirit and in the light of the excluded texts, I am going to be telling a different story: a story about Marx's relation to God and to mystical Judaism, a story of acceptance and implementation, but also a story of contraction and falling short. This story not only opens Marx's 'critique of religion' to a critique by religion; it also presents postmodern returns of the Spirit as a response to these contractions and fallings short. By using the Jewish notion of praxis as a point of articulation between schools of thought which were once thought to be 'incommensurable', my story suggests that on a different scene of writing, a (certain) Marx, (a certain) God and (a certain) praxis have always already implied and supplied each other.

The excluded texts point in two somewhat different directions, which together inform and limit Marx's theory of practice.

First, they suggest that Marx's defining struggle was not a struggle against idealism, but a struggle to overcome in this world the dualism of heaven and earth, of the spirit and the flesh, of mysticism and life, of idea and reality – a dualism which Marx and his contemporaries thought stemmed from Christianity, and which had in one form or another haunted western culture and philosophy for centuries. Here, for instance, is part of a poem called 'Three Little Lights' written some time before 1837:

> One sweetly struggles ever higher,
> Trembling to Heaven it would aspire,
> It blinks its lights so trustingly,
> As if the All-Father it could see.
>
> The other looks down on Earth's hall,
> And hears the echoing Victory calls,
> Turns to its sisters in the sky,
> Inspired by silent prophecy.
>
> The last one burns with golden fire,
> The flames shoot forth, it sinks entire,
> The waves plunge in its heart – and see!
> Swell up into a flowering tree.
>
> Then three small lights gleam quietly
> In turn, like starry eyes to see,
> The storm may rage and wind may blow,
> Two souls in one are happy now.
>
> (I, 564)[3]

In this poem, the lights form a bridge between heaven and earth, God and the world, eternity and time, contemplation and action; and light, a traditional symbol for the soul's knowledge of the divine mystery, is presented as an active and uniting power in the world. Marx described the same project in one of the Notebooks he wrote in 1839 while preparing his dissertation. This time, however, God figures as the universal, while modern philosophy is given the mission Marx had given the lights before:

> As the meteors of the *visible heaven* are for the ancient philosophers the symbol and visible confirmation of their prejudice for the substantial . . . so the *written heaven*, the *sealed word* of the God who has been revealed to himself in the course of world history is the battle cry of Christian philosophy . . . but modern philosophy unseals the word . . . and as a fighter of the spirit fighting the spirit . . . it is universally active, and melts the form which prevents the universal from breaking forth.
>
> (I, 430–1)

By the time Marx wrote *On the Jewish Question* and *Contribution to the Critique of Hegel's Philosophy of Law* in 1843, he spoke of 'truly implementing' religion by 'realizing' the universal and human basis of religion 'in a secular manner' (III, 157, 156), of joining 'the heaven of (man's) generality' to the 'earthly existence of his actuality' (I, 31), and of binding the 'heaven of the political world' to the 'earthly existence of society' (I, 79). The language shifts, and the scope contracts from the metaphysical to the social, and from the social to the economic, but the project remains essentially the same: to unite heaven and earth, spirit and matter, idea and reality *in* reality.[4]

This project can be described as the interface between Young Hegelianism, as Horst Stuke, for instance, has presented it in his *Philosophie der Tat*,[5] and classical Jewish mysticism. The Jewish position can be briefly characterized in the words of a *zaddik* (Jewish holy man): 'The peoples of the earth', he said, 'understand the two worlds to be removed and cut off from each other. But Israel believes that the two worlds are one in their ground and shall become one in their reality.' Marx's critique of Christianity in his *Contribution to the Critique of Hegel's Philosophy of Right* and his critique of all contemporary Jewish positions but his own in *On the Jewish Question* can be regarded as an elaborate restatement of the *zaddik's* words: Marx criticized all religious, quasi-religious, political and philosophical positions which understood the two worlds to be removed and cut off from each other, and insisted that the worlds are one in their ground, and can become one in their reality. In this respect, Marx's 'critique of earth' – his condemnation of the separation of Capital from Labour, men from Species-Being or man from himself, for instance – merely repeats his 'critique of heaven'.

Accordingly, in *On the Jewish Question* Marx criticized the Jewish Haskalah movement for basing its quest for political emancipation on the argument that Jews could be Jews at home and citizens like everyone else in public. This, said Marx, 'divides the human being into a public man and a private man . . . it decomposes man into Jew and citizen', and obliges the Jew, like all other men in the existing world order, to 'lead a two-fold life, a heavenly and earthly life: life in the political community in which he considers himself a communal being, and life in civil society, in which he acts as a private individual' (III, 154). Political emancipation as the Jewish Haskalah movement understood it accepted the duality of heaven and earth and held no prospect of making the worlds one in their reality. Marx also recognized that money, once in the form of usury or huckstering or trade the only professions open to Jews, had left the Jewish Quarter to become the universal principle of civil society in the Christian world, and that this was permitting Jews to emancipate themselves practically, if not politically, by acquiring wealth and financial power. But economic emancipation held no prospect of making the worlds one in their reality either. Marx argued that Mammon is a false god who reproduces the dualism of heaven and earth by separating the whole world of men and nature from their value. And like the *zaddikim*, he rejected the 'practical religion' of the actual worldly Jew whose practice was designed to satisfy his own personal needs and private interests, on the grounds that the husks of materialism and egotistical self-interest only exile or alienate man from his true life and sacred human essence.[6]

Marx's solution to the Jewish question was not the abolition of Judaism. On the contrary, Marx insisted against Bauer that he had nothing to say against the 'sabbath Jew', and that in the context of political emancipation, the Haskalah movement was justified in demanding both 'the privilege of faith' (III, 162) and 'civil rights' (III, 160).[7] Marx's point was that it was not enough for the Jew egotistically to seek his personal salvation in political or economic emancipation and think that his work was done. For Marx, as for Judaism, the task of the Jew was not to emancipate himself but to emancipate the world; division and separation and the domination of Mammon describe the condition of the entire 'extant world order', not merely the situation of the Jew; in emancipating the world from these evils, the Jew would ultimately also emancipate himself.[8] For the Jew does not seek personal salvation, or what Marx calls 'the Christian egoism of heavenly bliss'; his goal is to make today the day when 'the idols will be utterly cut off', and when 'the world will be perfected under the kingdom of the Almighty'. The Jew therefore seeks, like Marx, to redeem the sparks, to strip the real material world of its husks of evil, injustice, separation, false independence and illusion and, by transformative activity, to make it accord, manifestly and in actuality, with its true spiritual, human and moral ground. This is why for Judaism, and for Marx, practice is a central category. And it is why Marx rejected Jewish practice in its '*dirty* Jewish manifestation', while accepting and universalizing the premises of Judaism as a religion of practice. What are these premises?

First, because it is intensely preoccupied with what happens in this world, Judaism views human life as a practical activity and constructs it as a texture of practices. Even Jewish mysticism focusses not on ascetic contemplation but on practice. It has no more patience with 'practical life [which] is spiritless' or with 'spiritual life [which] is unpractical' than Marx did (III, 186). Marx is perfectly in tune not only with Judaism but also with generations of rabbis who spent their days devising practical solutions to spiritual, social and human problems when he says in the 8th Thesis on Feuerbach that 'All social life is essentially practical. All the mysteries which lead theory to mysticism find their rational solution in human practice and in the comprehension of this practice' (V, 8).

Secondly, for Judaism, practice is not primarily a matter of 'good works' or of the accumulation of personal merit. Instead, for Judaism practice is a means of reconstructing reality. For what Marx called 'the practical Jewish spirit' recognized that practice alone can transform theory into reality, give ideas a concrete material existence, unite the upper worlds of thought with the lower worlds of being and transform human life in this world. This is why the rabbis said 'not learning but doing is the chief thing', 'let thy work exceed thy learning', 'all study of Torah without work must in the end be futile'. Like the *zaddikim*, Marx insisted that thought must 'turn not towards itself', but towards practice (III, 181) and that the point is not to observe men nor to contemplate the world but to change them.

Thirdly, there is for Judaism and for Marx no antinomy between contemplation and action, theory and practice, study and works. Both are necessary. Torah or Theory is the guide to practice; practice is the implementation of Torah or Theory. Study reforms consciousness by motivating and explaining practice; practice embodies, exemplifies and completes study. The *Gemarah* says: 'The greatness of learning is that it brings one to practice'; Marx says 'theory becomes a material force as soon as it has gripped the masses' (III, 182). The *Ethics of the Fathers* says: 'He whose works exceed his wisdom, his wisdom will endure'; Marx says: 'You cannot supersede philosophy without making it a reality' (III, 181).

Fourthly, Judaism gives man inordinate responsibility for changing the world and making the two worlds one in their reality. The *Nefesh Hahayim* says, for instance: 'All worlds are governed by the deeds of Man. . . . Man alone is the one who elevates, joins and unifies the Worlds and their Lights by virtue of his deeds' (144, 162). Only the deeds of man can return the world and men from their exile, from their estrangement in egoism, injustice, false independence and corporeal materialism and reunite them with their true being. In Jewish texts, however, the term 'man' usually stands for Israel. Israel is the group of people inhabiting every nation which is charged with bearing witness to the nations' estrangement and spearheading the fights for transformative activity on the world. In Marx, the term 'man' usually stands for the proletariat, or as Jules Monnerot has put it, Marx substitutes the Chosen Class for the Chosen People.[9]

Finally, Jewish practice lives in the Now and makes its demands of human beings Now, in daily expectation that practice will make it possible to unite the worlds. Like the Psalmist, Marx said: 'Today, if you would only hear my voice'.

The second direction suggested by the excluded texts runs counter to the first. It turns on a question first raised by Marx in an essay he wrote in 1835 to satisfy his theology requirement at his Gymnasium in Trier. The question is whether union with God is necessary to perfect the world or whether man cannot 'by himself achieve the purpose for which God brought him into being out of nothing' (I, 636). This question about union or independence in relation to God also dominates the poetry and the Dissertation Notes.

On the one hand, quite a lot of the poetry describes mystical union with God and celebrates the 'flaming, eternal/ Lovekiss of the Godhead' (I, 563), while the Dissertation Notes explore the philosophical consequences of union with God. God is conceived as Epicurus and the Jewish mystics conceived Him, as Nothing, the Infinite, the Void, 'the pure rest of Nothingness in itself, the complete absence of all determination' (I, 443) or the space where 'all determinations intermingle' (I, 451). Marx argues that if God is conceived in this way, then the union of finite and determinate beings with God can only take the form of a 'negative dialectic', the dialectic of love and death which 'smashes the many and their bounds, which tears down independent forms and sinks everything into one sea of eternity' (I, 498). The reward of such union, he says, is the pure flame of ecstasy, but its price is loss of individual selfhood and loss of individual immortality: 'No compromise helps here. If some concrete differentiation of the individual must disappear, as is shown by life itself, then all those differentiations must disappear which are not in themselves universal and eternal' (I, 455). Or as he puts it in a poem: 'To the Maker you return/ Images no more remaining.' The price of union with God is absolute loss of self.

On the other hand, much of the poetry rebels against such a loss of self. Here, for instance, is part of a poem called 'My World':

> Worlds my longing cannot ever still
> Nor yet Gods with magic blest;
> Higher than them all is my own Will,
> Stormily wakeful in my breast.
>
> (I, 523)

Or here is part of a poem called 'Feelings':

> Worlds I would destroy for ever
> Since I can create no world,
> Since my call they notice never

Coursing dumb in magic whirl.

Dead and dumb they stare away
At our dead with scorn up yonder
We and all our works decay
Heedless on their ways they wander. . . .

Then let us traverse with daring
That predestined God-drawn ring,
From the Nothing to the All,
From the Cradle to the Bier,
Therefore let us risk our all. . . .
Acting and Desiring.

(I, 525–6)

In such poems, human action figures as an act of defiance against God, an indifferent universe and man's ordinary insignificant course of life from the cradle to the grave, and action serves a purely human will for knowledge and power. Marx recognizes, in poems like 'The Sirens' or 'Human Pride', or in his treatment of Faust, that such action is demonic and egotistical: 'Vice alone could elevate Faust,/ Who really loved himself the most.' But in the fragment of a Shandean novel called *Scorpio and Felix*, Faust's deal with the Devil is presented as the inevitable human response to human ignorance of the secrets of the Godhead where all determinations intermingle:

> Tell me, thou mortal, whence cometh the wind, or has God a nose on his face, and I will tell you which is right and which is left. . . . O vain is all our striving . . . until we have determined which is right and which is left, for He will place the goats on the left hand and the sheep on the right. If He turns round, if He faces the other direction . . . then according to our pitiful ideas, the goats will be standing on the right and the pious on the left. . . . I am dizzy – if a Mephistopheles appeared, I should be Faust, for clearly each and every one of us is a Faust, as we do not know which is the right side and which the left.

(I, 622)

Marx returns to this problem with God conceived as the boundless and indeterminate in the Dissertation Notes. 'The definition of a complex, its specific distinction, lies in its boundary', says Marx, so that the boundary is what has to be defined if the complex and its 'immanent necessity' are to be known. What troubles Marx about Epicurus' view that there is an infinite number of worlds, each of which is a 'celestial complex . . . containing a cut-out segment of the infinite and terminating in a boundary . . . whose dissolution will bring about the wreck of all within it' (I, 424), is precisely that the boundary of the world/s can be neither discerned nor known. 'It is the same', says Marx, 'as if one were to say that it can be proved that there is a God but his *differentia specifica, quid sit*, the what of his determination, cannot be investigated.' But, for Marx, to accept this is to accept human ignorance and human impotence. It is to accept that 'the divine in man is ignorance' and to 'tell [one's] beads over [one's] own powerlessness and the power of things' (I, 429).

Marx recognizes that to attribute determinations to God or to the world on the basis of our 'sensuous notions' is to give them boundaries. When Epicurus says that the boundary of the world can be conceived as ethereal or solid, at rest, round, triangular or any other shape, Marx says that he is suggesting that 'every determination which in general we distinguish in a special boundary can be applied to it . . . and regarded as its boundary and hence as its closer definition and explanation' (I, 425). Similarly, when the moderns ascribe goodness or wisdom or any other quality to God, Marx says 'any of these notions which are definite, can be considered as the boundary of the indefinite notion of God which lies between them' (I, 425). What bothers Marx about this, however, is not that a boundary arrived at on the basis of human 'sensuous notions' is necessarily a distortion because a limitation of the infinite. What bothers Marx is merely that there is a 'multiplicity' of possible sensuous determinations, and that this multiplicity returns God or the world to indefiniteness and indeterminacy.

Marx's substitution of the view that 'the entire so-called history of the world is nothing but the creation of man through his own labour' (III, 305) for the view expressed by Epicurus and in his poetry, that 'the void is the condition for the creation of the world', has nothing to do with levels of abstraction – man and the void are both abstract universals, and one is no more concrete or less metaphysical than the other. The change has everything to do with the possibility of defining a boundary within which knowledge and control are possible, and with the refusal to accept that 'To the Maker you return/ Images no more remaining.' For to contract the infinity of world/s to the human world, and the human world to human history, is to cut out a segment of infinity in such a way as to give it a boundary. To contract the human world and human history further to what is produced through man's labour is to contract the indeterminate multiplicity of possible determinations to a single fixed determination, and to give the world one has cut out a nose on its face. To limit man and his world to what man creates is to reduce an unknowable 'unity of differences' to what may be in man's power to know and control; it is to assert the permanence of the human image and the force of human will against 'Worlds . . . coursing dumb in magic whirl' and against 'the Nothing and the All'.

The first direction suggested by the excluded texts, the direction which led him to seek to make the worlds one in their reality, led Marx to a virulent condemnation of self-serving practice and to a refusal of the merely egoistical quest for political or economic emancipation. But this second direction, which contracts the worlds to the bounded sphere of human making, promoted 'the real active orientation of man to himself' (III, 323) and thus enshrined man's 'filthy self-interest' (III, 267) and self-serving egoism as the highest good. Species-being and its surrogates represent both the egoism of the individual and the self-serving egoism of the species or the group.

On the level of the species, man expresses his universality by reducing nature to his 'inorganic body', his handmaid, and the means of his existence. If man is 'part of nature', for Marx he is the ruling class of natural things, with the rest of nature playing the part of the alienated and exploited worker. As the alienated worker has no existence for Capital as a human being, but only as a worker, so nature has no existence for Species-being, except as an instrument which enables man narcissistically to 'duplicate' himself everywhere (III, 277).

On the level of the group, one class of men self-servingly expresses its universality in practice by universalizing its own interests, by forcing all other men or groups to serve these interests, and by pretending that man and society have no interests or needs other than its own. Marx equates the emancipation of the worker with 'universal human emancipation because the whole of human servitude is involved in the relation of the worker to production' (III, 280).

On the level of the individual, self-serving egoism takes the form of self-assertion and self-gratification. What Marx calls *human* activity in the world is a mode of activity in which man is *not* 'wholly lost to himself' (III, 283), a mode of activity in which man can consciously, freely and without any restraint impose his will on the world and 'see himself in the world he has created'. And this self-assertion is untrammelled self-gratification. As Marx says, were I to carry out production

> as a human being . . . in my production I would have objectified my *individuality*, its *specific character*, and therefore enjoyed not only an individual *manifestation* of my life during the activity, but also when looking at the object I would have the individual pleasure of knowing my personality to be *objective, visible to the senses*, and hence a power *beyond all doubt*.
>
> (III, 227)

Here again, the self reigns supreme.

Marx's otherwise very Jewish theory of praxis becomes distorted accordingly. For Marx's contraction of the worlds to the bounded world of the human ego erased two important conditions of Jewish practice. For Judaism, man was placed in the garden *le-avdo ou-leshamro*,[10] not only to work it, but also to protect and look after it. Consequently man may not use nature or its animals as and when he will. On the sabbath, for instance, no work upon the world is permitted. This reminds people not only that we are also something other than workers, but also that nature and the universe persist without human intervention, and therefore that nature and the universe are also something other than man's creatures and creations.

The second condition that Marx erases from the Jewish concept of practice is that *bitul* or self-abnegation is the precondition for uniting the spheres and transforming the world. For Judaism, only persons who *are* 'wholly lost to themselves' can promote the matter at hand. Only work which is *Avodah*, service performed for the sake of the task, to be accomplished without self-aggrandizement, self-assertion, self-gratification or self-interest, can bind subject to object, man to man, and spirituality to materiality, and so return man and society to their purpose and their ground. Practice performed in any other way only repeatedly sets in motion what Marx somewhere calls 'the war amongst the greedy' (III, 271).

It is precisely here, where Marx's theory of praxis falls short, that postmodern texts have begun to inscribe themselves. Stanley Aaronowitz has argued, for instance, that 'the task of an emancipatory theory must be to restore nature to its autonomy' and to recognize that nature cannot be entirely 'subsumed under labour or history'.[11] And in their different ways, Levinas, Derrida, Lacoue-Labarthe and Nancy have all tried to break the circle of man's 'orientation to himself', to dissolve the 'ipseity' of human egoism and to depropriate man. The early Derrida's 'negative dialectic' opened the limited constructions of human reason back onto indetermi-nacy, and man's bounded 'sensuous notions' back onto the Void, where the left side becomes the right and the right side the left, and where all finite determinations intermingle and dissolve. Like Levinas, Derrida and Nancy also revalorize *Chesed*, goodness or 'insatiable compassion', which is loss to self and giving without limit and without need of return. As an orientation towards the Wholly Other that has left its traces in all the finite faces, finite things and finite texts in being, or as a response to an infinite debt which requires that we pass over and pass on, the practice of *Chesed* figures as the basis of human sociality, solidarity and ethical response-ibility.

In recent years, Derrida and Nancy have also gone back to rethink the way heaven and earth, spirit and matter, come together (*comparaître*) in reality. Correcting Marx's un-Jewish assumption that the two worlds are, for the present and until some once and future revolution, removed and cut off from each other both topologically and temporally, Derrida and Nancy emphasize the topological and temporal proximity of each to each. The present, the now, is a present – a gift – from the spirit which is always haunting and disturbing that present which is presence and *Gift*, the German word for poison. Similarly, the *Geist*, the spirit, is a spectre, or ghost or guest which haunts and commands the material human body: it comes to the ear (*Ou-ii, ou-ii*), to the mouth ('*Viens*'), to the hands (*don*), to the feet (*pas*), to the blood (*sang/sans*), to the psyche (the *moi-sans-moi* or ego-less-me), to the body's heat (*conflagration*) and to the genitalia, collapsing the penis, man's colossal monument to his own making, into a vaginal pas-sage for the immemorial spiritual *mer(e)*. The spiritual body and the egotological body share and infinitely differentiate the same flesh. And the same world. Every person, every thing, every text, every society, every moment, is a *Doppelgänger*, divided from what inhabits it, and participating in that from which it is divided. This *partage* is our historical double-bind, our opportunity and our disaster. It is from here, from this proximity and distance of heaven and earth in the same physical or social or linguistic body, that Derrida and Nancy propose that we rethink our sociology, our philosophy and our politics.

In his Dissertation Notes, Marx emphasized the value of the *clinamen* of the atom, understood as the atom's *declination from* a straight line. For him the declination of the atom was the precondition for 'individual motion' and for the atom's identity with itself. Movement in a straight line represented the disparaged 'negation of self' (I, 4, 16). In declining from the infinite number of worlds, and from 'the Nothing and the All' where all determinations intermingle, in declining all negation of self and in turning man in on his own giant ego, Marx's theory of praxis sanctioned the 'war of the greedy' which it sought to abolish. And it failed to perfect the world. In *La Communauté desoeuvrée*, Nancy emphasized the value of the *clinamen* understood as the *inclination* of the atom towards what is not itself. For him, declination only represents the decline of communion and community: 'A world cannot be made of simple atoms. There has to be a *clinamen*, an inclination, or an inclination of each to other.'[12] Recent postmodern texts are accordingly bent on developing a theory which '*inclines* (the individual) out of himself', a theory which inclines him to incline himself before something Other than his own finitude and his own self-interest, which can alone ground community, morality and the 'indefinite unity of differences'. This something is the Sacred and its Law. Inscribing themselves where Marx's theory of praxis fell short, the 'newest' postmodern texts return us to Marx's excluded point of departure; and they pass through it to enter, as fresh(wo)men and novices, a space 'always already' occupied by the oldest and most premodern writings of all.

NOTES

1 See David McLellan, *Marx before Marxism*, London, Macmillan, 1970.
2 See, for instance, Arend Th. Van Leeuwen, *Critique of Heaven*, London, Lutterworth Press, 1972; David McLellan, op. cit.; Paul Ricoeur, *Lectures on Ideology and Utopia*, New York, Columbia University Press, 1986; Richard Tucker and Gerhart Niemayer, *Between Nothingness and Paradise*, Baton Rouge, Louisiana State University Press, 1971; Eric Voegelin, *The New Science of Politics*, Chicago, University of Chicago Press, 1952; J.L. Talmon, *Political*

Messianism: The Romantic Phase, London, Secker & Warburg, 1960; Karl
Lowith, *Meaning in History*, Chicago, University of Chicago Press, 1949.
3 All citations from Marx's writings are from *Marx and Engels: Collected Works*,
New York, International Publisher, 1975.
4 Others also see such continuities. See, for instance, Trevor Ling, *Karl Marx and
Religion*, New York, Barnes & Nobel, 1980.
5 Horst Stuke, *Philosophie der Tat: Studien zur 'Verwirklichung der Philosophie'
bei den Junghegelianern und den Wahren Sozialisten*, Stuttgart, Ernst Klett
Verlag, 1963.
6 R. Schneur Zalman, *Likutei Amarim*, London, Kehot Publication Society,
1973, chapter 19.
7 See also Marx, *The Holy Family*, IV, pp. 106–18.
8 For Marx's attitude to Judaism and egoism, see also Elizabeth Fontenay, *Les
figures juives de Marx*, Paris, Galilée, 1973; and Robert Misrahi, *Marx et la
question juive*, Paris, Gallimard, 1972.
9 Jules Monnerot, cited in Henri Arvon, 'Sociology du communisme', in *Les Juifs
et l'idéologie*, Paris, Presses Universitaires de France, 1978, p. 114.
10 Genesis 2:15
11 Stanley Aaronowitz, *The Crisis in Historical Materialism*, New York, Freger,
1981, p. 48.
12 Jean-Luc Nancy, *La Communauté desoeuvrée*, Paris, Christian Bourgois, 1986,
p. 17.

Chapter 10

Genealogy for a postmodern ethics: reflections on Hegel and Heidegger

Joanna Hodge

I INTRODUCTION

The point of this paper is to draw attention to a difference between the logics of ethics and of morality: and then to use contrasting responses to this difference to distinguish between modern and postmodern preoccupations. These contrasting responses are to be found in the writings of Hegel and of Heidegger, hence the juxtaposition of my title. By setting up these contrasts, a space can be cleared for the emergence of what I take to be a much needed new form of thinking about the human condition, with the limitations of neither morality nor ethics. The genealogy intended, then, is of this new form of thinking, which I suppose to be in process of development, not already in existence. The strategy of this paper is to mark the limited relevance of two outmoded forms of moral reflection, and to provide a focus for inquiry about just what the issues and the constraints are which make these two forms of reflection inadequate for current conditions. The strategy is to identify a certain form of moral theory as distinctive of a modern sensibility and to identify critiques of that theory as contributing to a postmodern reformulation. The terms 'modern' and 'postmodern' are here taken not to have connections to particular historical periods; instead they pick out contrasting forms of theoretical construction.[1]

In this paper, I argue that both the transcendent commitments taken to be characteristic of moral reflection and the emphatic immanence characteristic of postmodern analysis are inadequate responses to the dilemmas of human living. My suspicion is that an ethics for a postmodern community will have to retain some of the characteristics of a morality of transcendental subjectivity and transcendent value, alongside the incompatible emphases on location more characteristic of the postmodern. The task for this genealogy of a postmodern ethics is then to explain how such a conjunction of incompatible elements can be thought about at all; and how such a conjunction might be able to accommodate difficulties inaccessible to other, less contentious but less flexible systems of concepts. Combining incompatible theoretical elements is a gesture characteristic of the com-

pletion and overcoming of philosophy diagnosed by Heidegger and
Derrida in their different ways. Thus this thought of combining incompatible theoretical elements in human reflection is derived from the phenomenological strand of contemporary European philosophy, in sharp contrast
to the operations of Hegelian dialectic. The identification of conceptual
systems as belonging to a previous and completed epoch by Heidegger and
by Derrida does not necessarily entail breaking with those conceptual
structures; it can lead to their retention under a new regime of truth,
through which they acquire a revised interpretation.

II   SOME DIFFERENCES

Premodern preoccupations are to be distinguished from the modern by
their tendency to take for granted standards for judgement and ends of
action, and to take for granted the grounding of standards, judgements and
ends in some uninspected measure. As provisional clarifications, I take it
that the modern ceases to take such justification for granted, but supposes
that it can be constructed. Postmodern inquiry by contrast identifies such
justification as impossible and delusory. The distinction between a premodern and a modern moment in moral thinking is markable in the
inquiries of both Hegel and Heidegger. Hegel calls the state of taking
standards for granted *Sittlichkeit*, usually translated as 'ethical life'. I
suggest that Heidegger calls it *Alltäglichkeit*, or 'everydayness'. Hegel uses
the term *Sittlichkeit* in both the *Phenomenology of Spirit* and *The
Philosophy of Right*. Heidegger uses the term *Alltäglichkeit* in *Being and
Time*. Heidegger and Hegel both seek to construct a relation between
immersion in ethical life, or in everydayness, and the detached stance of
analysis, from which justification is attempted. For both Hegel and
Heidegger, Kant is pre-eminently the theorist who attempts to construct
such justification. Kant is the philosopher of modernity, and can be identified as the moral theorist par excellence.

I read Hegel and Heidegger as affirming the structure of ethical life and
of the everyday as the means for disrupting and revealing the limitations of
the moral theory of modernity. Both Hegel and Heidegger return repeatedly to a critique of Kant's philosophy. Kant, Hegel and Heidegger insist
on a double structure of human existence as both immersed and transcendent: in Kant's language as both empirical and transcendental; in Hegel's
language as both natural and spiritual; in Heidegger's language as both
fallen and prospecting, as both given and creative. In the context of his
moral philosophy, Kant privileges the transcendental over the empirical
and thus detaches moral reflection from the actual contexts in which
human beings seek to make decisions about what to do next. My hunch is
that a postmodern ethics, emerging from Heidegger's thought, promises to
be able to come to terms with this doubleness, in a more satisfactory way.

This doubleness expresses itself in another way in the relation between individual and collective purposes. The empirical is necessarily divided up into specific individual human beings. The transcendental is an indivisible mass term. The empirical maps on to the individual, the transcendental to the collective element in developing and transforming values.

The key oppositions here are those between individual and collective agency, and between given and created value. Only when these two oppositions, between the given and the created, and between the individual and the collective, have been adequately addressed and connected up to each other, will human beings begin to be able to make sense of their current circumstances. For these are characterized by two outstanding and novel features: the scale of alterations in nature brought about by human inter- ference, that is, a shift from given to created value; and the shift from individual to collective agency as the main means by which human beings have an impact on our world. The principal problem is that while human beings are perhaps individually more reflective and more intellectually competent than in previous epochs, collectively human beings are con- fronted with a set of problems requiring a form of agency which is not based in individual activity and decision. A new form of conceptual analysis is required through which to produce and reflect on the implications of the need for such a form of agency. This new form of analysis cannot be produced nor made productive at the level of individual inquiry and affirmation; thus part of Heidegger's contribution to a postmodern ethics is his struggle with the paradoxes of seeking to inaugurate a new form of thinking, which cannot be inaugurated by any one human individual. Hegel, while in a way similarly declaring the novelty of the possibilities opening up for human beings, nevertheless makes the slightly different move of declar- ing himself to be only commenting on possibilities which have already become available. Heidegger by contrast seeks to take part in their pro- duction. While the aim here is to develop aspects of Heidegger's thought as a response to this contrast between ethics and morality, it is helpful to set out a contrast between Hegel's and Heidegger's responses to it.

By discussing both Hegel's and Heidegger's responses to the contrast, an opposition between a modern, synthesizing and a postmodern, disjunctive response to the disjunction between morality and ethics can be identified. Features identifiable in Hegel's response to the distinction between ethics and morality make it appropriate to identify it as a modernist response. Heidegger's inverted and indirect construal of the difference, more as a disjunction than as difference, make him a major contributor to the development of postmodern thinking.[2] Taking Hegel's views into account also makes it possible to locate three further sets of issues, which are relevant to my argument. Firstly, there is a contrast between Hegel's and Heidegger's construals of the relations between philosophy, theology and religion. For Heidegger, the closer philosophy gets to religion, to the everyday practice and experience, and the further from theology, the production of hypertheoretical constructs, the better. For Hegel, there are no such exclusive alignments; the religious understanding of the world is for Hegel a precursor to a more complete philosophical understanding; and theological analysis both precedes and contributes to his own restructuring of philosophical inquiry.

Secondly, there is the difference between Hegel's and Heidegger's uses of the term *Geist*, spirit.[3] This must be located in the context of a difference between Hegel's use of the term to construct a totality and Heidegger's announcement of a completion of philosophy.[4] It connects to the third theme, the question of philosophy and its relation to completeness and system. Crudely put, Hegel's thinking is designed to demonstrate the availability of philosophical inquiry as a complete system; Heidegger's to demonstrate its impossibility. It is this last theme which feeds most substantively into the contrast between modern and postmodern preoccupations. Hegel seeks to reconcile the opposition between a logic of ethical location and a logic of a moral transcendence of context; Heidegger affirms the opposition as disjunction. There are then four sets of issues in play in this essay. Firstly, there is the suggested difference between the logics of ethics and of morality. Secondly, there are the contrasting responses of Hegel and Heidegger to this difference, the responses of reconciliation and of disjunction. Thirdly, there are different stances towards *Geist*, philosophy, completeness and system. Finally, there is the suggested transition from a morality of modernity, transcending context, to a return of context with the everyday and the ethical. A postmodern ethics is however irreducibly distinct from any pre-reflective, premodern ethics, as a result of surviving this passage through morality.

The taken-for-granted, almost pre-moral stance, with respect to the ends of human action and to standards of judgement, is not confined by Hegel and Heidegger to some prehistoric phase in human existence. It continues to exist in modern and indeed in postmodern living; and is characterized by uncritical appeal to some fact of the matter or a traditional way of life. There is no necessary correlation between this ethical life or everydayness and any matter of fact about the way an actual community once functioned. For both Hegel and Heidegger, there are however nostalgic overtones of an irrecuperable way of living which once was. At the same time they manage to suggest that it may either never have existed, or may have existed in highly qualified form, as an ideal to which reality was accommodated, rather than one which was actually experienced. They use their understanding of this way of living, in the main, in order to identify a tendency in themselves and in their own contemporaries. There is then a chronological instability about when this ethical life or everydayness is supposed to occur, and this instability is an instance of a very postmodern slippage. There is however also a powerful and under-theorized textual linkage, back to Aristotle, Plato and the pre-Socratics.

Through these textual linkages there are connections from Hegel's ethical life and Heidegger's everydayness to the early Greek city states, as reported on by Aristotle and Plato, and as those reports are understood by Hegel and Heidegger. However, these models are very second hand. Aristotle and Plato theorize on the basis of their not entirely positive experience of those city states, imagining a more thoroughly grounded way of life, either as an ideal which might be realized or as existing prior to the foundation of those city states, marking an inception from which the present is a sad decline. Hegel and Heidegger transpose those reflections into the context of their own concerns and preoccupations. They set up a Greek or pre-Socratic relation to philosophy and to the world as being more harmonious than the relations dominant in their own times. They substitute a relation to the texts of Aristotle, Plato and the pre-Socratics for any relation to actually existing Greek city states. This substitution of a textual for an actual historical linkage, with the suggestion of there being no significant distinction between the two, is also a characteristic postmodern manoeuvre. Both Hegel and Heidegger are in this way prone to substitute a history of philosophy for a history of human affairs, although in markedly different ways. This affects their views on the relation between morality and ethics.

For Hegel, as expounded in *The Philosophy of Right*, ethical life is in the first instance the domain in which gender divisions are established, in every generation. Here, for Hegel, is the moment of natural determinism in human life, which is then to be mediated, for the men at least, into a life worth leading. For Hegel, a sexual division of labour appears to be inescapable, to be an enduring feature of human existence. For Heidegger, the everyday, while not explicitly concerned with anything so determinate as sexual division, is certainly as enduring at it is for Hegel. The everyday is emphatically the 'zunächst und zumeist', the 'in the first instance and for the most part', much invoked by Heidegger in *Being and Time* as the condition in which human beings find themselves. In Hegel's *Phenomenology of Spirit*, ethical life is located not so much with reference to Plato and Aristotle, nor to some supposed historical community, but by reference to Sophocles' *Antigone*, to which Heidegger also makes resort.[5] This lack of historical location is in part justified in the mature Hegelian system by the suggestion that clear distinctions between family life, civil society and the state emerge for the first time in the course of the eighteenth century, making it possible to identify distinct principles at work in these three different domains of human experience, which, in the earlier social systems, are inseparably entwined.

Hegel never claims that his system of distinctions would have been acceptable to peoples at every stage in the evolution of that system, nor, presumably, that they have to be acceptable to all of his contemporaries.

There is no suggestion here that philosophical truths can be determined by majoritarian procedures. Nor are they supposed by Hegel to be necessarily demonstrable to all those who live within their orbit. This ethical life then is one in which distinctions do not have conceptual grounding. In certain contexts, the request for justification of the distinctions on which existing practices are based, as demonstrated over and over again in the Socratic dialogues, simply cannot be met. By the nineteenth century, however, according to Hegel, human societies have reached a point of maturity at which such justifications can be provided, at least for those who can understand them. Thus Hegel supposes that justifications for systems of values become available but perhaps only after the system has ceased to function in the world. Thus Hegel does not make the transcendent move of supposing that justification, if available, is always ahistorically available. Hence for Hegel, a system of ethics could seem to be simply grounded in everyday practice and tradition, and only subsequently be demonstrated to have a rational and absolute justification.

By constrast, Heidegger supposes that it is not the task of philosophy to provide such justifications for existing practices, at all. For Heidegger the status of everydayness is distinct from the ethical life hypothesized by Hegel. That everydayness is supposed to capture one of a number of dimensions of the lived experience of actually existing human beings. It is descriptive of given existence. Heidegger sees philosophical inquiry emerging out of and retreating back into the determinate contexts of actually existing human beings, with determinate pasts and a particular future opening up before them. For Heidegger, justifications are neither necessary nor possible; they are not the task of philosophy, which is to describe, retrieve and anticipate, not to justify. Most important for Heidegger is an anticipation of what is to come: producing forms of thought needed for understanding and responding to circumstances brought about by events. The contrast between Hegel and Heidegger here could not be plainer: retrospective justification, on one side; future anticipation, on the other. The former presumes a process of development, which is almost complete apart from the requirement to explain what has occurred. The latter presumes an open horizon, shifting as the stance of the observer shifts. It is a question of point of view, and if the observer stays still for long enough, a temporary stability can appear to be an enduring equilibrium. Thus the Kantian syntheses and the Hegelian retrospective justifications for the course of world history can appear to give definitive answers to questions of value and of justice only so long as the equilibrium holds and the parameters of reflection remain stable.

III   ETHICS, METAPHYSICS AND MORALITY

Heidegger, throughout his inquiries, is preoccupied with the question of horizons. In *Being and Time*, temporality is supposed to be going to provide the horizon for the inquiry about being. The metaphor, taken over from Husserlian phenomenology, is unfortunate, since it is hard to transpose the visual image of the line between earth and sky into temporal terms. This is indeed part of the point: Heidegger suggests that the difficulty of grasping that there is a problem here at all is the most significant aspect of the problem. In the first division of *Being and Time*, Heidegger seeks to excavate the effect on post-Cartesian philosophy of just these spatializing habits of thought. They lead to the elision of the specificity of the temporal dimension: the unpredictability of the future. These apparently abstract metaphysical concerns with a relation between thought, and the spatial and temporal constraints within which it occurs, lead Heidegger to disrupt any external line of division between metaphysics and ethics. Such externality is disrupted in much the same way as he disrupts the line between the thinking in any text on which he comments and the development of his own thought. *Being and Time* is permeated by a commentary on Aristotle, as his commentary on Nietzsche is, for good or ill, permeated with his own preoccupations.

Throughout *Being and Time*, he is extremely wary of both the terms, 'ethics' and 'metaphysics'. He argues that morality, in the Kantian form, is derivative from more basic structures of human existence. These he designates as the finitude of human beings, grounded in our directedness towards our singular unpredictable but anticipatable deaths. Contingency, finitude and mortality thus become substitutes for Kant's transcendental conditions of possibility for experience. In the slightly later *Kant and the Problem of Metaphysics* (1929), Heidegger identifies Kant as failing to address the specifically human preconditions for there being philosophical inquiry at all: human finitude, historicality and ignorance of the future. Heidegger goes on in a lecture series from 1930 to develop a more detailed critique of Kant's moral philosophy.[6] This has been explored by Frank Schalow in his study *Imagination and Existence: Heidegger's Retrieval of the Kantian Ethic*.[7] Schalow shows how Heidegger reconstrues what for Kant are epistemological conditions of possibility into ontological conditions, thus further subverting the distinction between ethical and metaphysical issues. Schalow distinguished emphatically between Kant's view that morality has a claim on human beings in so far as we are rational and Heidegger's view that morality has a claim on human beings in so far as we are finite. Thus the fundamental ontology of *Being and Time* can be shown to provide an interpretation of Kantian morality as grounded not in transcendent rationality but in the contingencies of human finitude and placement within time.

In the terms set up in *Being and Time*, morality is the equivalent, in practical philosophy, to presence at hand, in theories of what there is. It is to be complemented by a theory of action, locating a relation between agents and readiness to hand; and to be derived, in its ontological possibility, from the analysis of *Dasein*, now construed as a condition of possibility for there being moral questions at all. Thus parallel to Heidegger's distinction between presence at hand, readiness to hand and *Dasein*, I am setting up distinctions between moral theory, as definitive accounts of judgement and evaluation; theories of action; and *Dasein*, as the site at which these two take place and may be connected up one to each other, via an account of agency and in relation to an account of the constitution of individual identity. Any theory of morals and all theories of action are thus to be embedded in a theory of the nature of agents, as related to themselves, within a particular kind of temporal context, of which finitude is one important feature. This theory is made possible within the reflexivities of the analysis of *Dasein* as a kind of entity which has an issue for its own existence. This makes the displacement of spatial metaphors in favour of temporal ones both possible and indeed indispensable. However, Heidegger encounters considerable difficulties in carrying out this displacement, and the inquiry in *Being and Time* breaks off.

The analysis of *Dasein* in *Being and Time* makes available the following distinctions between levels within ethical thinking. There is a mode of reflection on such matters, the everyday mode, which does not distinguish between three different concerns and their relations one to another. Theories of value, theories of agency and theories of personal identity are all run into each other, as though there were no real shift of focus and theme. There is a more emphatic mode of reflection on these matters, in which existing practices are affirmed as coherent and satisfactory, and in which any tension between these three different focuses is denied. There are thus at least two modes of everyday reflection, one in which there are not and one in which there are recognized to be problems in the smooth functioning of the ethical system. This second form leads on into the move to construct justifications for those practices, in recognition of a certain incoherence and instability within them. This is the moment of morality. There is then the possibility of continuing to struggle to make a transcendentally grounded morality, in the style of Kant, consistent and persuasive; or of making the sceptical move, into a full-blown postmodernism, for which such coherence, consistency and adequacy are thought to be neither possible nor necessary.

There is finally a reflective postmodern mode, affirming incommensurabilities between the concerns of a theory of value and judgement; of a theory of agency, and of a theory of personal identity. This mode affirms a disjunction between classical Greek ethics and Kantian morality. For classical Greek ethics the central issue is character, putting agency and identity at the centre of concern. For Kantian morality, the preoccupation is demonstrating the universality of value and of justification.[8] These for Hegel are to be brought into some kind of uneasy compromise. With Heidegger it becomes possible to recognize that they are alternate and incompatible points of emphasis. These emphases embed into the alternate and incompatible temporal structures of the finitude of human existence, within which any particular life or character evolves and the *sub specie aeternitate* of moral judgement, which, for reasons which cannot be here entered into, Heidegger supposes to be self-deluding.

In the 1930s Heidegger cumulatively argues that metaphysics consists in abstracting from and reducing a number of ways of construing what there is, to one single dominant view. Morality, then, like metaphysics, can be understood to function as a reduction of a number of incompatible considerations to one plane concealing the tensions between them. Morality, as theorized by Kant, is such an abstract structure, construed as valid for all contexts and times, thus concealing an actual temporal specificity and historically contingent point of emergence.[9] Through the centrality of *Dasein* to his inquiry in *Being and Time*, Heidegger lays emphasis on specificity and contingency. In work published after *Being and Time*, the centrality of *Dasein* diminshes, but the critique of the non-locatedness of philosophical inquiry increases. The neutral inquiry in *Being and Time* about such locatedness is replaced by a more self-centred reflection on Heidegger's own place in the history of philosophy and in the history of Europe. The critique of the form of abstraction of which Kantian moral philosophy is one version thus continues even when the analysis of *Dasein* has been suspended. I shall develop this diagnosis of metaphysics as reductive abstraction through the contrast between Heidegger's conception of determinate existence, *Dasein*, and Hegel's conception of *Geist* in the next section.

IV   *DASEIN* AND *GEIST*

Dasein is that mode of being for which being and its own existence are issues. These characteristics are set up in *Being and Time* as preconditions for any human concern or activity and for there being questions about agency and identity at all. The shifting of *Dasein* from the centre of Heidegger's thought after the composition of *Being and Time* does not lead to a displacement of his interest in analysing the conditions in which it is possible for individual human beings to take responsibility for themselves, and for their actions. The hideous ironies of this notwithstanding, he pursues this thought through the Nazi time, in his reading of Nietzsche, into the postwar *Letter on Humanism* and the *Question of Technology*. In the latter, Heidegger considers the possibility that human beings have transformed themselves into resources in a production system, which, while built up out of piecemeal extensions of human control over our surroundings, is itself uncontrolled and uncontrollable. In these circumstances, there is a problem about the status of human purposiveness and human responsibility. If the spread of technical relations has transformed human beings into facilitators, not agents, then there are no agents who can be identified as morally responsible for their actions. An abstract morality can then be seen as a halfway stage on the way to this disappearance of agency. It appears at a time when human relations to context have become sufficiently complex, such that it is difficult to get an overview of those relations and therefore difficult to identify a relation between individual moral deliberation and the outcomes of actions. Such a view connects up to Kant's own, since Kant thought it impossible for any individual agent to know whether their actions were in accordance with the requirements of morality. For both Heidegger and Hegel, morality is very much the structure produced by Kant.

For Hegel, it is an abstract system, which will come to inform the institutions within which human beings live. Its production by Kant is for Hegel not a sign of an increasing distance between human beings and their purposes, as it seems to be for Heidegger. It is a sign of the maturity of philosophy and of the world in which it takes place. In the twentieth century we have perhaps more reason than Hegel for being sceptical about this supposed 'maturity' and about the adequacy of philosophical categories for analysing the circumstances in which we find ourselves. For Hegel, the state represents the possibility of the institutional realization of reason, as spirit, *Geist*, as the completion of history, which is the course of God through the world. *Geist*, for Hegel, is the logic of reconciliation, in human beings, between soul and body;[10] in cosmology, between creator God and created earth; and, in history, between the actual practices of human beings, their ethical lives, and the abstract conceptual requirements analysed in Kant's moral philosophy. This threefold occurrence of the term *Geist* permits Hegel to construct his system. The evolution of *Geist* through historical processes is expected by Hegel to reveal a reconciliation of the apparent oppositions between a taken-for-granted ethics and a scrupulously consequential morality. *Geist*, for Hegel is the symbol of completeness and system. It is the spirit which moved over the water and, in dividing heaven from earth, nevertheless constructed the relation between them.

Derrida, in *Of Spirit*, discusses Heidegger's use of the term *Geist* with and without quotation marks, revealing a move from a critique of the term in *Being and Time* to a wholesale adoption of it in the *Rectoral Address* (1933), when Heidegger anticipates a coming together of the forces at work in society in the success of Nazism. Derrida then remarks on a final gnomic identification, in Heidegger's discussion of the poetry of Trakl, of *Geist* with *Flamme*, flames. This is no longer the spirit which moved over the water. This is spirit as vengeance and destruction, obliterating any resource not caught up in its internal logic. It is the denial, by destruction, of both distinction and difference. The role of this reading as Derrida's response to the Heidegger controversy is here not significant. The contrast between Heidegger's use of the term and that of Hegel is important. For Hegel,

Geist is a theme emerging out of the Graeco-Christian inheritance of European thinking, which can be traced in its ambiguities in various different domains of analysis and shown to constitute the basis for completeness and system in philosophical inquiry, marking the possibility of the realization of reason and freedom in human societies. Thus the completeness of philosophy is for Hegel based in the actual course of European history. Heidegger is much more wary in his approach to the term. He is distrustful of its Christian origins and would dispute its locatability in the Greek philosophical tradition. For Heidegger there is an absolute break between the Greek tradition and the Latin, Roman, Christian tradition. In the latter he supposes there goes missing a possibility still open to the Greeks, for thinking in terms of the future, of process and of the specific conditions confronting particular human communities, in part through a reductive process of translation.[11] The richer, processual terms of Greek philosophical analysis are reduced to rigid Latin abstractions, permitting a gap to open up between paying attention to the objects of human study and reflecting productively on the aims of human living.

The logic of *Geist* for Hegel is one of completeness and inclusiveness. The logic of *Dasein* is one of incompleteness and irreducible, even unformulable difference. This insistence on difference can be read as resistant to the all-inclusive, all-consuming logic of *Geist*. It can be read as promising release from the flames of destruction, identified by Derrida in Heidegger's reading of Trakl. The fear is that incompleteness and lack of system are also harbingers of chaos and destruction. Heidegger's task then must be to reassure the anxious that the absence of univocal system is an advantage; that ambivalence is not threatening, but is rather a condition for growth and change. This he does not accomplish; but he prepares the way for such assurances. Heidegger identifies signs of a transformation looming in the events of his time. Where Hegel sees a completion of history and a fulfilment of philosophy, Heidegger sees a completion of philosophy and a radical new beginning. Where Hegel sees a filling-in of a structure already complete in outline, Heidegger stresses that at such moments of transition, the future is even more discontinuous from the past than usual, and even less likely to conform to expectation.

Heidegger attempts to think through the dogmas of a self-evident individuality and responsibility in human beings. His attempt to consider some less atomized construal of effective agency begins the task of conceptual construction required to accommodate the challenge of current circumstances. These circumstances pose problems of a different order from any previously confronted by human beings, as a result of technical innovation giving our activity a scope so much more in excess of our capacity for an overview. Heidegger suggests a radical step back from the assumption that our vision is as wide ranging as the effects of our activities. He suggests the importance of taking account of the fact that the scope of practical activity is far greater than the scope of any theoretical overview. In his later invocation of *Gelassenheit*, or releasement, he advocates a building down of our conceptions of ourselves as in control of our destinies and in control of our circumstances. He insists on the importance of acquiring a sense of respect for the autonomy of the processes in which those circumstances consist. This shifts the emphasis away from activity and control, towards self-awareness, and to a disaggregation of problems, respecting their individual and potentially incompatible logics. This, I suggest, is a welcome step on the way to a postmodern ethics.

Both Hegel and Heidegger reject a false dichotomy, urging neither a premodern ethics, nor a Kantian morality; neither the total immersion of the one, nor the fictional overview provided by the other. In contrast to Hegel, however, Heidegger urges an acceptance of bivalence and delimitation; he refuses the grand syntheses of theory which in practice impose solutions on circumstances irrespective of their singularity. Furthermore, Heidegger recognizes the otherness of the future, which need not continue in previously established patterns and modes. Confronting the challenge thrown up by that future may require just such a suspension of bivalent logics, and of the usual requirements of internal consistency in theoretical construction, which postmodern thinking and Heidegger seem to urge. In this paper, then, I have sought, through a contrast with Hegelian system, to identify in Heidegger's work a positive contribution to the problem of responding to a current crisis, which, precisely in so far as it defies our present capacities, confirms Heidegger's diagnoses of the situation. I have sought to indicate those features of the present theoretical conjuncture which suggest that there is a beneficial process of transition at work. I hope that such a treatment is neither offensive nor crass. An ethics for our time is one which permits a response to these unprecedented circumstances, neither denying past evils nor projecting them into the future.

The central distinction is between the inclusive logic of *Geist* and the disjunctive logic of *Dasein*. Hegel imposes a reconciliation between an ethical immersion in specific immediacies and the transcendence of moral judgement, by insisting that the future is continuous with the past, through the argument that institutions and given ethical practices are evolving towards a realization of absolute moral standards. Heidegger installs the possibility of an emphatic break between past and future, by revealing in the present an irreducible conflict of interpretations about the past. This opens up the possibility not just of alternative futures, depending on which interpretation of the past might be correct, or might win out. It opens up multiple possible futures. It is in the mode of alternation that Heidegger diagnoses a single option between disaster and rescue. But there is not just this either/or, but a muliplicity of possible outcomes. To confront the challenge of the future, it is not good enough to fall back either on tradition, or on some principle of universalizability, or on some unconvincing combination of the two. What is needed is a thinking of multiplicity, through a dislocation of the univocal distinctions of metaphysics, through a subversion of the inexorable either/or of immersion or transcendence, everydayness or Kantian morality, postmodern pluralism or rigorous Hegelian conceptuality. But the contribution which might be made by a logic of *Dasein* can be grasped only in contradistinction to the logics of morality and of *Geist*. The passage through modernity cannot be circumvented.

NOTES

1 I have on previous occasions pointed out how postmodern thinking can be seen as a victory for the ahistorical and non-ethical thinking of the tradition. See my 'Feminism and Postmodernism', in Andrew Benjamin (ed.), *The Problems of Modernity: Adorno and Benjamin*, London, Routledge, 1989, pp. 86–111. However, once this tendency has been recognized for what it is, it becomes possible to take postmodern thinking as an accurate reflection and description of current conditions. This can then be used in any attempt to develop and reinforce the tendencies, historical and ethical, which are in danger of being eliminated. The future which is to emerge out of these current celebrations of postmodernism is distinct from all other futures, both in what it promises and in what it threatens. It is also inflected by those celebrations, which must be understood if that future is to be understood. Thus postmodernism cannot be simply rejected; it must be put to work, to reveal within itself the temporal differentiations it tends to elide.

2 In German there are the terms *Unterschied* and *Differenz* to mark this distinction. *Unterschied* marks a fixed, atemporally given categorial distinction; and *Differenz* a system or process of differentiation, extended through time.

3 Jacques Derrida, in *Of Spirit: Heidegger and the Question*, trans. Geoff Bennington and Rachel Bowlby, Chicago, University of Chicago Press, 1989, draws attention to Heidegger's flirtation with the German idealist conception of spirit. This book lays the basis for a reworking of the relation between Heidegger and the idealist tradition, and makes it clear that Heidegger's relation to Hegel's philosophy is deflected later through his reading of Trakl, and earlier through his reading of Hölderlin and Schelling. I shall draw on this work, but not discuss it directly.

4 In his volumes on Nietzsche, published in 1961, but given as lectures during the Nazi years, Heidegger assigns to Nietzsche the role of the 'last man' with respect to philosophy. Heidegger construes Nietzsche's theses about will to power as the culmination of the history of philosophy as a sequence of metaphysical systems. The full complexity of this enormously controversial move, with respect to interpretations of Nietzsche, with respect to philosophy and its history, and with respect to interpreting the connection between Heidegger and Nazism, cannot be discussed here. However, it should be remarked that Heidegger in his lectures on Nietzsche is in dispute with the official Nazi readings of Nietzsche; and in his construal of the twentieth century as bringing with it a transformation of philosophy he recognizes a crisis in human affairs, of which Nazism might be seen as a catastrophic symptom.

5 See Martin Heidegger, *An Introduction to Metaphysics* (1935–6), trans. Ralph Manheim, New Haven, Yale University Press, 1959.

6 Published as *Vom Wesen der menschlichen Freiheit*, Frankfurt am Main,

Klostermann, 1982.

7 Frank Schalow, *Imagination and Existence: Heidegger's Retrieval of the Kantian Ethic*, Lanham, University Press of America, 1986.

8 While I have chosen to pursue this move in the context of Heidegger's work, I have been struck by suggestions in Bernard Williams' work that he is on the same track. See his *Ethics and the Limits of Philosophy*, Harmondsworth, Penguin, 1987.

9 See the discussion of Foucault's disruption of the Kantian claims in my 'Habermas and Foucault: Contesting Rationality', *Irish Philosophical Journal*, 7 (1990), pp. 60–78.

10 Heidegger refers dismissively to this account of spirit in his *Being and Time*, trans. John Macquarrie and Edward Robinson, Oxford, Blackwell, 1973, p. 153.

11 See Heidegger, *Introduction to Metaphysics*, op. cit. There he discusses the effects of translating *physis* as *natura*. See also the essay from 1939 discussing Aristotle on physics, where Heidegger traces in Aristotle's *Physics* a reduction of *physis* from both autonomous growth and controllable power to just controllable power, the object of skilled manipulation, or *techne*. This reduction of what there is to a controllable domain of forces survives the Latin-based insistence on viewing everything as created by God, to re-emerge, with according to Heidegger catastrophic effects, in the new science of the sixteenth and seventeenth centuries.

Chapter 11

Unsystematic ethics and politics

Don Cupitt

In our liberal democracies we expect a great deal of our political leaders. From time to time they have to undergo a kind of public ordeal by aggressive questioning under the eye of rolling cameras. We the public scrutinize their performance closely to see how well they hold up. The rules of the game require the politician to remain fluent and unruffled. He must never seem to be taken aback; he must not pause for thought, nor be at a loss for words. A head of government in particular has to show that he or she has a panoramic view of the entire political and economic scene, and can instantly launch into a carefully considered statement of policy on any point that is raised. This calls for very great presence of mind. Politicians – Prime Ministers, for example – are expected always to be in full command both of their basic principles and of all the details, *and* of how to reconcile the two. They may show no weakness and make no mistakes. What they say has to be fully consistent both with their own past utterances and with what all their cabinet colleagues are currently saying. Furthermore, their statements have to totalize, in the sense of being consistent with each other and adding up to a coherent political philosophy.

So the leader has everything at his or her fingertips: the vision, the grasp of detail, the clear convictions and the unwavering sense of purpose. The imagery requires us to picture him or her as marching ahead in a straight line, never U-turning or deviating; never defeated or hesitant, or obliged to bend; always in control of events.

These conventions may seem very peculiar, but if this is how very highly political politicians seek to present themselves we can be pretty sure that this is how we want them to be. They have to fulfil popular fantasies of far-sightedness and rocklike strength. For this to be possible we have to suppose that there is a standpoint from which the whole human world can be viewed as an objectively unified and rationally intelligible scheme of things. This systematically intelligible order out there is fully and simul-taneously grasped by a correspondingly clear-headed and unified human subject, in such a way that they now know completely how things really are and just what must be done. They thus achieve such a fullness of intellectual and moral knowledge and mastery that they cannot be shaken by the winds of circumstance or by political opponents, or even by a television interviewer. I am suggesting, then, that the politician has to seem to be something very like a Platonic philosopher-king.

And this is all very odd; odd, because in a rapidly changing plural and democratic society politicians obviously have to be pliable and pragmatic. They are trimmers, fixers and compromisers, and must be so. They are obliged to be everything that Plato despised. So why is it that when they put themselves on show to the public, they try to present themselves (and we for our part *expect* them to present themselves) as achieving something like Platonic standards of mastery? There must be an element of conscious self-deception or artifice here. We know that their appearance of omniscience at interview is something of a stage effect created by a combination of careful briefing beforehand and a certain amount of manipulation. We know too that a major public figure has a very large administrative back-up, so that the Palace, the White House and 10 Downing Street do a great many things in the name of the Queen, the President and the Prime Minister which cannot have been overseen in detail by the individual persons who fill those roles. Furthermore, the very fact that we speak of the Prime Minister's 'performance' and 'image' indicates that we know that what we are allowed to see of them is a kind of necessary theatre, a public show that everybody wants to see kept up.

Very well, then; but why? It seems that real political life, the day-to-day stuff of politics, is pretty chaotic. Fortunes rise and fall. Few can predict what will happen or pretend to exercise much control over events. Mostly politics is luck, contingencies, conspiracies, cock-ups and just muddling through. Intellectually and morally, it is about as disorderly as can be imagined. But public and politicians alike need to believe that events can be understood and be directed. What is needed is some kind of theatre within which the world is imaginatively transfigured so that it seems to make sense. That side of politics which is a public show, and in which politicians parade before us their manifestos, their principles, their grasp of affairs, and so on, therefore functions in the same sort of way as a drama, a church service or a novel. It gives us reassurance. It produces meaningfulness, saying to us that somebody understands, somebody is in charge, somebody is making a morally coherent story out of it all, somebody is making our life make sense and making sure that it's all going somewhere.

The basic conviction that has to be produced (artificially, as a kind of *effect*) is the conviction that life adds up, life can be rationalized and events can be managed. If this is so, then in a sense Plato is right, and there can be a fully adequate theory that precedes and successfully guides practice, even in politics. Despite appearances, there is a real order of things out there; or at least, those who are sufficiently able, disciplined and determined can *make* events make sense to themselves and to us. They prove it by their controlled and lucid presence of mind when being interviewed.

I am suggesting that in modern liberal democracy Platonism seems to survive as a necessary fiction; that is, as a classical statement of the beliefs that people need if they are to maintain their faith in the possibility of political understanding and control of events. These beliefs are no longer regarded by anybody as dogmatic truths. Instead they are *produced*, ritually or theatrically. We notice, in a way that earlier generations probably did not notice, that Plato himself does not quite present them as metaphysical dogmas, but produces them in the theatre of his dialogues. His texts are works of art in which he creates artistically for us the fictions that help us believe that our politicians can actually do something to make things better.

In summary, then, the everyday practice of politics is – and no doubt always was – an unedifying business of power-struggles, accidents and compromises. Against this background the ceremony of politics works continually to produce the faith that keeps pessimism and chaos at bay. One may say of this ritual, as of religious belief generally nowadays, that it is performed not because our life does make sense, but precisely because it does not make sense. Ritual is not a response to meaning, but a way of creating meaning to fill the Void.

There is, however, a difficulty. In periods of enlightenment such as our own, people become very highly reflective. We become vividly and ironically aware of the machinery by which we sustain the fictions we need in order to live, and this ironical awareness of our own self-manipulation imposes a certain strain upon us. In some contexts, indeed, we are not troubled about being conscious fictionalists. For example, we are not unduly disturbed by the thought that the strength of the currency is only a communally generated fiction sustained by our own belief in it. Stockbrokers and estate agents are quite happy to set about talking up the market in the way they do. They recognize that it is in their own interest to make something real by talking us all into believing in it. But it is a rather more serious matter to be an all-out fictionalist in metaphysics, religious belief and ethics. Are we quite happy to suggest that God, reality itself, the intelligibility of our life, the possibility of effective action and the difference between good and evil are all of them necessary cultural fictions, ritually produced and only as strong as our own belief in them? What about the possibility of the moral equivalent of a general slump?

So we turn to the question of ethics, asking how far the moral realm is also sustained by necessary myths that we ourselves have to keep on surreptitiously pumping up. I suggest that here again there is a clear contrast between the empirical facts about morality and certain myths about it that we still think we need to maintain.

Empirically it is obvious that morality is extremely complex, historically evolved and haphazard. Evaluation is not a special region of our experience, but is pervasive. Consider for example the overtones of the great 'cosmological' distinctions and scales – positive and negative, above and below, form and content, straight and crooked, primary and secondary, manifest and latent, independent and dependent, and so on. Each contrast has an evaluative flavour. So do all qualities, and most words. Everywhere, our perceptions and our responses are evaluatively flavoured so that everything gets a good name, a bad name or a mixed reputation, according to how we feel about it and therefore speak about it. All our institutions have their own house rules and teach their own valuations. Furthermore we have inherited a number of more or less rationalized moral traditions, classical, Christian, barbarian-military, bourgeois, and so on, all of which are internally complex and at odds with each other. As a result of all this the moral realm is not a tidy autonomous region with its own logic, but is spread across the whole of culture and is as large, untidy and historically accumulated as language itself – with which it is coextensive. Nothing says that all this has to add up, and it doesn't. No consistent sense could be made of it even if all kept still, and it doesn't even do that. Anyone who has been around and alert to linguistic change for a few decades will have become aware that valuations shift and change all the time along with the general process of cultural change.

At one time writers used to make much of a supposed specifically-moral vocabulary of conscience, duty, obligation, the moral law, desert, and so forth. Today most of that vocabulary is passing out of use as we come to recognize that morality is not something separate and *a priori* or supernatural, but is a sort of colouring of the cultural sign-system as a whole. We are bending it all the time, by introducing new topics of concern, new perspectives and new metaphors under which to see things, and by rapidly diffusing felicitous new idioms.

It is true that we remain keen to distinguish what is morally important from what is merely a matter of taste, fashion or custom. However, I suggest that this is not because the moral is transcendent in any way, but because of the peculiar world-structuring power of the moral. Morality, I have been suggesting, is emotive or expressive. It is a matter of our culturally-scaled feeling responses. These scaled responses differentiate the field of experience, turning a flat screen into a relief map as we prefer this and reject that, foreground one thing and push another into the background, react now positively and now negatively, and so on. Morality matters greatly because it brings out the structure of the life-world. Typically, if we want to bring about moral change we will seek to change the way people feel about something or speak about it. If we are trying to upgrade or promote something that has been too low-rated, then we will try to highlight it or burnish its image. When people take more notice of it, they will get into the habit of reacting to it more favourably, speaking of it differently and treating it differently – and so the world will have been changed a little. That is how moral action works, and why morality matters so much.

However, on this account morality is in the highest degree *moody*, a matter of *ethos*, something shifting, human, untidy, democratic and transactional, like language. We are all contributing to confirming or changing it all the time. And because nothing guarantees the systematic unity and coherence of morality, it is perfectly possible for there to be great fissures in the moral order. An individual may be broken by a deep conflict of values that neither he nor the rest of us knows how to resolve. For although we made morality, we did not make it straight. We made it in various ways misshapen and deformed, and have even learned to love it thus. We can't easily change it. So there can be and is tragedy.

So much for the empirical aspect of morality. It is in very sharp contrast to the ideology of the moral. People undoubtedly want, or have wanted, to believe that there is just one true morality, rational, systematic and unchanging, and expressible in terms of absolute rules or values. We would like to think that there is or can be an ethical theory that gives to morality, once and for all, a systematic rational explanation-and-justification. That is what we have thought that moral theories are *supposed* to do. And we would like to have the positive content of morality codified and packaged in summary form for transmission unchanged to the next generation.

Because of all this the history of moral theory has been to a quite preposterous degree a history of untruth. People have laboured to prove that morality is not human but has come down from above, is not transactional but absolute, is not historically changing but eternal, and not plural, untidy and emotive but one, rational and systematic. This impulse reaches its highest expression in metaphysical monotheism, which asserts that all perfections whatsoever coincide and are absolutely identical with each other in the eternal simplicity of the Divine Essence. So there can be no tragedy, no deep conflict of values and no real moral plurality or change. Evidently people until very recently could not endure the thought that our moral values were shifting transactional market phenomena, like prices. The myth of an eternal and primordial unity of all value is still being produced as a necessary fiction for us to live by.

In morality, just as much as in politics, though, I am suggesting that in modern times people are becoming highly reflective. In each case, we are aware of a gulf. What is given in experience as being shifting, human and very untidy is represented ritually or theatrically in terms of unity, mastery and control. And in each case we wonder whether the theatrical fictions are worth keeping up any longer. Would it not be better to give up dreams of theoretical mastery and unified understanding, and instead simply accept reality, which, we know, is an untidy democratic free-for-all? Paul Feyerabend and Richard Rorty would, I think, urge us to do this. They are not suggesting that we should become pragmatists in the ignoble sense of being mere opportunists, wheelers – and dealers – with no vision. Both of them allow a place, and an important place, for creative imaginings, innovations and Utopian dreams. But both would like us to give up the idea that there is just one great system of objective Truth and one canonical Method for attaining it. And in so far as religion still backs such ideas, I think they would regard it as a harmful influence.

As I have been hinting, I think they are right. The old fictions of theoretical mastery, systematic unity and control are not doing much good any longer, and we are currently abandoning them. Marxism-Leninism is in disrepute. We do not want ideological politics, nor grand modernist designs for so rationalizing the world that everyone shall live a planned life in a planned society. Systematic schemes for reducing the historically evolved variety and untidiness of our life cannot be implemented without more loss of values than gain, and serious curtailment of freedom. Space needs to be left for untidy people such as deviants and whistle-blowers. Many of us now prefer to be political sceptics, floating voters, people whose commitments are irregular, occasional and piecemeal. We interest ourselves in pressure-groups, minorities and issue-politics. Our politics is consciously *un*systematic.

In morality, we want to give up the old ideal of a thoroughly examined and unified life. There is no real truth about a real self; we are incorrigibly bitty, ambiguous creatures. Frankly, I'm a mess, and I think I must be content to remain so. The last grand scheme of self-examination was, I suppose, the Freudian training analysis. But it never reached a final Truth about the self, and so far as there was ever such a thing as a Freudian system, it now looks very badly flawed. We would do better in morality to turn our attention away from the self and towards the ways in which people, things and aspects of the world and our life are valued in the language. Much is valued lower and treated worse than it need be. If each of us were to strive to highlight something or other, then the overall outcome would be a general increase in the brightness of life for everyone. Thus one can imagine a highly unsystematic and pluralistic approach to ethics producing a varied and rich cultural life.

I have been defending unsystematic politics and ethics. I have suggested that we can renounce the old Platonic urge to seek, beyond the flickering shadows of this world, a founding and final Unity whose contemplation will give us blessedness and mastery. Nowadays that move up from the many to the One is often called 'theological', and when I say we should stop making it, I may seem to be making a radically secular move. People tend to equate religion with metaphysical theism, and with an ultimately optimistic vision of life. To give up these things, they suppose, must be to give up religion entirely. But I disagree. Religion has more than one face. One of its faces shows us an optimistic vision of cosmic order, but another, equally important, is a face of otherness, darkness, exile, loss and martyrdom.

Religious belief contains an important tragic strain. It does not deny the reality of evil. Rather it forces us to confront evil and nothingness, and purge our terror of them. Furthermore, the God of Christianity is a God who in Christ becomes human and in the spirit becomes the endless interrelatedness of everything. The doctrine of the Trinity secularizes and enhistoricizes God, disperses God into the flux of the world. So those themes in recent thought which at first sight are most anti-religious and radically secularizing may also be read as reviving forgotten aspects of faith.

Chapter 12

Groundless democracy

Gad Horowitz

I NEGATIVITY

It has been said many times: poststructuralist radicalism, having given up on Truth, is groundless in its opposition to the status quo: it is incapable of offering reasons for wishing to replace one 'regime of truth' with another.

Ernesto Laclau and Chantal Mouffe offer a simple and powerful counter-argument: radical democracy is actually thoroughly grounded in groundlessness. If we refuse all substantive definitions of democracy as this or that way of life, and recognize its true character as 'dissolution of the landmarks of certainty' (Claude Lefort),[1] we will see that democracy cannot be a system. It is anti-system, the systematic, persistent undermining of all system, 'a culture of systematic irreverence'.[2] A political order is democratic 'in so far as it refuses to give its own organization and its own values the status of a *fundamentum inconcussum*', opens them to 'unlimited questioning'.[3]

When we see this, we can see that out normative preference for democracy is in no way arbitrary, but derived from a kind of law, or anti-law, of nature: there is no objectivity. 'The being of objects is . . . radically historical'.[4] All objectivity is discursively constructed. Therefore, any politics is self-deluding which claims to be a matter of representation of 'pregiven' subjects, identities, objective class interests, true needs. The political process is actually that continuing struggle for discursive hegemony in which subject positions, identities, needs, are *constituted* out of 'a dispersion of elements'[5] that have no inherent coherence, are next to nothing at all, become something only when actively 'sutured' together in the hegemonic process.

'Social order never succeeds in entirely constituting itself as an objective order', for radical contingency, openness, is at its core as its internal limit, or, to put it the other way round, as its 'constitutive outside'.[6] The democratic movement is a manifestation of 'antagonism' or 'negativity': 'a certain limit which in itself is nothing . . . which prevents a closure of the social field'.[7]

The radical democrat accepts with a smile the epithet crafted by the conservatives: we are 'levellers'. Our fundamental principle is anti-principle: 'the equivalence of all identities'. Our revolution is the permanent revolution which 'transgresses the norm' and 'construct[s] the beauty of the specific'.[8] Democracy is solidly grounded in its very centre, which is no centre.

The problem with this monism of negativity is that it must immediately admit a second principle – that of positivity – the inescapable positive power of discourse itself. Chantal Mouffe explains: the 'hegemony of democratic values . . . will never be complete, and anyway, it is not desirable for a society to be ruled by a single democratic logic. Relations of authority and power cannot completely disappear.'[9]

Any identity once posited loves itself, yearns for itself even as it lacks itself. The most irreverent culture of systematic irreverence must necessarily also be irreverent of irreverence. Constant questioning of every institution must question also the institution of constant questioning of every institution. Any hegemonic articulation of discursive identities must forcefully exclude those which remain merely potential, unarticulated, unconstructed and thus authoritatively consigned to the realm of 'dispersed elements'. 'Even the most democratic society requires force and exclusion.'[10]

The radical democrat who first appeared as a monogamous lover of change for the sake of change, that is, of promiscuity – wedded only to the dissolution of all weddings – immediately reveals, human all too human, that she loves stability for its own sake as well. Her horror of objectivity, of the frozen solid identity which excludes all others, hallucinating itself as 'natural', 'pre-given', turns out to be balanced common-sensically with a horror of chaos, negativity, equivalence of all identities.

Radical democracy is radically pluralist. It calls for the largest possible number of ways of life – but, obviously, there is a much *larger* number of potential ways of life which must be ruled out by the rule of largest *possible* number, the rule of the positive. Radicals differ from liberals only in their assessment of what actually is the largest possible number for this political system at this time.

The radical's absolute insistence on democracy posits its own impossibility, sometimes comes close to revelling in *that* impossibility as the ultimate negation of the negation. Old-fashioned 'objectivist', 'essentialist', 'metaphysical' socialists are charged with naivety in the time-honoured mainstream liberal and conservative manner, the naive desire for total revolution which, by ending class division, brings about the withering away of all divisions and ushers in the universal homogeneous state of rational freedom and harmony, the one socialist way of life. Mouffe writes that democratic extremism is 'the myth of a transparent society reconciled with itself', and 'leads to totalitarianism'.[11] Conflict is eternal, will never be resolved, will always produce winners and losers, constructed identities and silenced, excluded identities.

Real radical democracy turns out to be a matter of common-sensical balance, more radically pluralistic than mainstream liberal democracy but fundamentally at one with the common-sense Gilbert and Sullivan dualism that finds obvious the need for both little liberals to question the system and little conservatives to preserve it. As everybody knows, a 'healthy' society is one which has just the right combination of undermining and preservative elements at every moment. Everybody knows anabolism and catabolism, Eros and Thanatos, charisma and routinization, identity and difference, yin and yang, Pareto's Lions and Foxes; Laclau and Mouffe themselves as discourse theorists prefer to cite the 'syntagmatic' and 'paradigmatic' poles of language.[12]

What is the difference between the prophets of negativity and the clerics of the liberal mainstream here? It seems to be only that radicals are always convinced that *now* is the time for more radical change, transvaluation of values, intensified egalitarianism, while liberals always occupy a middle ground: 'not so fast'. (At the good old other extreme, of course, we find the conservatives, always ferocious in their conviction that now is the time for consolidation, retrenchment, reinvigoration of the old values.) Who can demonstrate once the principle of positivity is admitted that any one of these positions is most reasonable except by reference to so-called social facts?

At certain points in their argument, Laclau and Mouffe aspire to no position, refusing both the monism of negativity and the dualism of negativity and positivity. The most striking formulation in this sense is their declaration that the two principles exist only 'through their reciprocal subversion'.[13] However, their aspiration is not realized. As Fred Dallmayr has observed, there is a 'quandary' in the work of Laclau and Mouffe, an 'opposition between democracy construed as a system of radical equivalence and democracy as a social formation intrinsically marked by the tension between equivalence and difference'.[14] Dallmayr suggests as a remedy closer study of Heidegger. In my opinion, the way out of this quandary is not clearly indicated anywhere in the philosophical tradition of the west. It is necessary to go eastwards to the Buddhist philosophical masters, Nagarjuna of India, Fa Tsang of China and Dogen of Japan.

II   EMPTINESS OF EMPTINESS

The principle of equivalence of all identities (PEI) is known in Buddhism as the teaching of emptiness (*sunyata*). All things are identical in that they are empty of identity: nothing has any substantial being in itself, own-being or self-nature. Reality is flux without any beginning or end.[15] Every event is distinguished from other events only in language and perception; every event is the result of other events, each of which is in turn the result of other events *ad infinitum*. In Buddhism, however, PEI does not require and does not give rise to any counterpart or opposite principle with which it must maintain any kind of balance or tension, because the principle of emptiness must apply to itself. Emptiness is the essence of things as their absence of essence, without itself being essentialized, reified, essentially established as the absolute negative core of being. There is no core of being. This is the teaching of the emptiness of emptiness.

The negation of metaphysics, letting go of all fixed concepts, must let go also of itself. 'Emptiness' or 'negativity' is itself a positive concept: it can be seen as 'negativity' only from the point of view of 'positivity'. The emptiness of emptiness lets go of all fixed concepts, including the concept of letting go of all fixed concepts. 'Leave it all behind' is not the last word. And 'leave "leave it all behind" behind' is not the last word either, except in so far as it points to Silence. Nagarjuna: 'If there is no establishment of being, non-being is not established either, for it is change of being that people call non-being.' 'Neither "empty" nor "non-empty" should be declared, nor both, nor neither.' No monism; no principle whatsoever: and therefore no need to correct monism with dualism. The Zen master Joshu, when asked, 'What does it mean to be devoid of discriminative knowledge?' replied: 'What are you talking about?'

Poststructuralism, self-arrested as it is at the point of 'the dissolution of the landmarks of certainty', dissolves all certainty of the body of nature. Nature is reduced to 'a dispersion of elements' which have no meanings other than those assigned by discursive practices.

Buddhism goes past this point of arrest. It agrees that there is no 'body'. 'The body' is a concept, a reification, an objectification of processes that transgress the boundaries of any separate body perceived as such, including any Body of the totality. However, these processes have actual ('conventional') existence as the bodies of our lived experience which, though never outside of discursive practice, are far vaster than discursive practice, contain discursive practice, do not derive their coherence (as opposed to their 'dispersion') exclusively from discursive practice. The discursive understanding of emptiness as empty leads directly to the intuitive grasp of suchness (*tathata*). Since all phenomena are empty in the sense that each arises together with and as a result of all others, they are seen to be neither posited nor negated. Every thing exists not as itself, but *as* every other thing manifested as the actual *suchness* of this unique thing. The real suchness of this event is every other event appearing as precisely this event. The particular validity of every empty phenomenon consists *precisely* in its radical interrelatedness with every other phenomenon. There is a story of two Zen practitioners sharing a cup of tea. One says: 'Isn't it marvellous? The All is fully present in this cup of tea.' The other quickly reaches out and tips over the cup; all the tea spills to the ground. 'Now where is the All?' he asks. The first exclaims: 'Oh! What a shame! It was such good tea.' Both laugh.

Emptiness is the body – this particular inconceivable bodily form. What arises out of the relation of this thing to every other thing is precisely the suchness of this thing exactly as it is at this moment. 'Emptiness does away with all things, but by no means does it not posit them' (Fa Tsang). 'Things are not as they appear. Nor are they otherwise' (Lankavatara Sutra).

Nature, dissolved as objectivity by the principle of emptiness, returns (as suchness) in the silence opened up by the emptiness of emptiness. Thinking through the principle of emptiness allows us to transgress the poststructuralist taboo against thinking with and for nature. The body of nature can be thought in a non-essentialist, non-objectivist, non-empiricist manner. For Fa Tsang: 'Emptiness does not negate existence, but by no means does it not terminate it.'

According to Dogen: 'Although everything has Buddha nature, we love flowers; we do not care for weeds.' 'The deluded mind believes that there must be no blooming flowers and falling leaves in the world of the true nature of things.' From the point of view of PEI, the identity of the flower is equivalent to that of the weed; they are identical in their emptiness. Beyond PEI, as a result of its application to itself (and not as a result of the introduction of any opposing principle) the suchness for humans of flowers and weeds is that there are *always* some plants actually experienced by human body-minds as injurious or noxious or not pleasant. These are called 'weeds'. At the very same time, while we enjoy flowers and do not care for weeds, our enlightened mind seeing the ultimate truth of flowers and weeds sees only their emptiness, their suchness.

The weed is not inherently or essentially unpleasant; it is unpleasant for the human body, that very same body to which it is equivalent from the point of view of PEI. Various discourses can draw the line between flowers and weeds in many different places; this drawing of the line in itself is empty; nevertheless, *as* empty, it *is* drawn in all discourses. Moreover, it can be said to be drawn correctly by some and incorrectly by others. The tomato has been mistakenly classified as a poisonous berry.

The ordinary ('deluded') mind surpasses itself initially with the discovery of PEI. It comes to the mistaken conclusion that the pleasure that all human bodies take in the blooming flower, and the sadness they feel for the falling leaves, is *deluded*, *essentialist*, since the values of falling leaves and blooming flowers are equivalent. Freed from delusion, the mind now deludes itself about delusion. Unable to stabilize itself in mere negativity, it must then strive for 'real world balance' with the admission of the opposite principle.

III SOCIAL AND DISCURSIVE POWER: LISTENING TO THE BODY

Radical democratic poststructuralism argues that discursive power must always and everywhere be resisted in so far as it offends against the (reified) PEI, and that this resistance must never go too far because there must always be human reality constructed by discursive power. If we are monists of negativity, we must undermine all human things. If we are dualists of negativity and positivity, we find ourselves in Dallmayr's 'quandary', undermining and establishing human things without recourse to any method of bodily demonstrating the preferability of some human things to others. The radical democratic poststructuralist sees no end to revolution and no *telos* other than revolution, for all *telei* are empty.

The Buddhist teaching of Suchness allows all things, the body, the self, gods and Buddhas, to appear as they are, as selfless. Even Buddhahood is an appearance, like a dream, in the sense that it has no self-nature. And this emptiness is the body: it is not merely Foucault's body of negativity, the body which *resists* discursive power. Foucault's body is important 'only because it is victimized, but its suffering can never be a source of practical wisdom'.[16] As Eugene Gendlin and David Michael Levin have recently argued, bodies have positive meanings to communicate, if we can listen. Bodily experience, says Gendlin, 'is always more than forms' (concepts, definitions, categories, distinctions, rules, patterns). 'Experience and the person' are not 'merely derivatives, mere products of the imposition of forms'. Of course the forms of discursive practice 'are always already at work in anything human', so that we have no simple recourse to any raw or pre-discursive experience; but discursive practice never works alone.

> What is more than the forms is not simply a chaos, a disorder, or a mere internal limit of order. It is a wider order. What is more than a form always functions in thinking and saying as part of its order, not its breakdown or disorder.

Gendlin refutes the poststructuralist view which

> still assumes the Kantian paradigm that order can come about only by [the] . . . imposition [of] . . . form, that there can be no feedback from that on which order or interpretation is imposed, that *that* is mere primordial disorder, undecidability, limbo. . . . There is a quite orderly and intricate order . . . which feeds back to, and can reject and complicate [the forms of discursive practice].[17]

The body of nature has its own coherence, not prior to or apart from discourse, and not simply as physiochemical process, but as a field of lived meanings that are not derived solely from linguistic forms: this body is capable of more than resisting discursive practices with PEI and then perforce moderating that resistance through acceptance of the opposite principle. David Michael Levin writes: 'The body can be a source of practical wisdom, a source of specific guidance, informing us about what needs to be changed',[18] and what it 'needs for its fulfilment'.[19] If we listen to the body of our lived experience we shall discover a distinction between discursive power as that which is indeed inescapable, and social power which is against nature, which can in principle be abolished once and for all. Although the body is always discursively constructed, some discursive practices – those characteristic of classism, imperialism, authoritarianism, racism and sexism – are injurious to it, and are not inevitable eternal limits to the possibility of democracy.

Although all potential ways of life cannot be lived simultaneously, for most must be excluded by the force of discursive practice no matter how wide open the democratic process of pluralistic negotiation becomes, that does not mean that the victorious ways of life must always be destructive of the body of human nature. Laclau's theorization of the 'Stalinism of language'[20] occludes the distinction between the Stalinism of language *per se* and the Stalinism of language in the service of the Stalinist apparatus of domination. Democracy will always have to fight against the Stalinism of language, but it need not necessarily always have to fight against the Stalinism of élite control of political, economic, cultural and social life. Democracy will always require force and exclusion, but exclusion does not always have to take the forms of oppression, exploitation, subordination of identified ethnic, gender, sexual, economic and cultural classes of people.

Not every exclusion of potentiality damages or deprives the living body. The Black American radical Cornel West writes: 'forms of subjection and subjugation are ultimately quite different from "thick" forms of oppression like economic exploitation or state repression or bureaucratic domination'.[21] Poststructuralism has no way of distinguishing oppression/ exploitation/subordination from exclusion/limitation, for that distinction can only be learned from the body speaking not only its lived pain but also its dreams and hopes. Democracy must involve some appeal to non-objectified nature, a listening to the body without regression to any metaphysics of presence or pre-given identities. Attending to the body, we discover that it is 'inherently ordered for participation in structures of mutual recognition'.[22] We discover a 'bodily felt need for recognition and for reciprocity'.[23] It is the 'ego-centred body' constructed by the discursive practices of domination that is alienated from the possibility of this kind of attention. 'We . . . are much too deeply cut off from the nature of our own bodies to realize their inherent norms and dreams.'[24]

The disparate interests which are coming together in the democratic movements of postmodernity are not united only by their equal adherence to PEI. That would not suffice to bring them together, to wish to learn from one another, to listen and share the experience of the other. The aspiration to democracy is therefore not simply a drive to equalize, to level all constructed identities, to question, criticize, undermine, negate, which must be in tension with a reciprocal drive for order, stability and meaning. Democrats are moved by the erotic desire, grounded in the body of suchness, to create forms of life which are life enhancing. Life-enhancing life is that which is open to the experience of self as the infinite inter-relation of all beings. As the American Whitman, poet of democracy, says: 'I am large; I contain multitudes.' As the ancient Tibetan Longchenpa says: 'Every time I zero in on my own mind I find billions of worlds and other beings.'

When the evanescence and suchness of the constructed identity is *feelingly experienced*, there is compassion, the listening and feeling together of self and other. Groundlessness as compassion is the no-ground of democracy. Levin, referring to Merleau-Ponty's notion of 'intercorporeality', writes:

> We are as embodied joined inseparably . . . to others . . . by grace of the flesh we are gathered with others into a primordial sociability. This . . . gives us a much needed touchstone, a normative ground, for perceiving and judging the character of our social practices and political institutions.[25]

And that is why we hope that the democratic movement will never again succumb to the violence of negativity: we shall realize the emptiness of the Enemy. Democracy will listen and feel with all persons, with the lowest criminals and with the highest.[26]

Levin quotes Merleau-Ponty: 'the intertwining of my life with the other lives, of my body with the visible things . . . the intersection of my perceptual field with that of the others . . . we reflect one another, we resonate and echo one another'.[27] Buddhism has taken this to infinity.

Walt Whitman wrote:

> I speak the password primeval. . . . I give the sign of democracy. In all people I see myself. And I know I am deathless. . . . I know I am august. . . .

> I am the poet of the body. . . . And I am the poet of the soul. . . .
> Askers embody themselves in me, and I am embodied in them. . . .
> I rise extatic through all.

> It is you talking just as much as myself; I act as the tongue of you. . . . I am large; I contain multitudes.

NOTES

1 Quoted in Chantal Mouffe, 'Radical Democracy: Modern or Postmodern?', in Andrew Ross (ed.), *Universal Abandon? The Politics of Postmodernism*, Minneapolis, University of Minnesota Press, 1988, p. 34.
2 'Building A New Left: An Interview with Ernesto Laclau', *Strategies*, 1, Fall 1988 (Los Angeles), p. 22.
3 ibid., p. 19.
4 ibid., p. 16.
5 ibid., p. 16.
6 ibid., p. 13.
7 ibid., p. 15.
8 ibid., p. 22.
9 Mouffe, op. cit., p. 41.
10 Chantal Mouffe, Address to Graduate Association of Students in Political Science (GASPS), University of Toronto, Canada, October 1989.
11 Mouffe, 'Radical Democracy', op. cit., p. 41.
12 Ernesto Laclau and Chantal Mouffe, *Hegemony and Socialist Strategy*, trans. Winston Moore and Paul Cammack, London, Verso, 1985, p. 129.
13 ibid., p. 184.
14 Fred Dallmayr, 'Hegemony and Democracy: A Review of Laclau and Mouffe', *Philosophy and Social Criticism*, 13, 3, 1987, p. 293.
15 The main Buddhist texts quoted in this section are those of Nagarjuna, the great Indian philosopher of the middle way, or negative dialectic (*madhyamika*); Fa Tsang, the systematizer of the teachings of the Chinese Hua Yen school; and Dogen, the founder of the Japanese Soto lineage of Zen Buddhism. For contemporary translations see *Nagarjuna: The Philosophy of the Middle Way*, trans. David Kalupahana, Albany, SUNY Press, 1986; Garma C.C. Chang, *The Buddhist Teaching of Totality*, London, Pennsylvania State University Press, 1977 (on Hua Yen); and *Dogen: Shobogenzo*, trans. Thomas Cleary, Honolulu, University of Hawaii Press, 1986.
16 David Michael Levin, 'The Body Politic: The Embodiment of Praxis in Foucault and Habermas', *Praxis International*, 9, 1 and 2, April and July 1989, p. 115.
17 Eugene Gendlin, 'Thinking beyond Patterns: Body Language and Situations', unpublished manuscript, 1989, pp. 13, 14.
18 Levin, op. cit., p. 115.
19 ibid., p. 125.
20 Slavoj Zizek, *The Sublime Object of Ideology*, London, Verso, 1989, p. 212.
21 Laclau and Mouffe, op. cit., p. 271.
22 Levin, op. cit., p. 123.
23 ibid., p. 127.
24 ibid., p. 118.
25 ibid., p. 122.
26 Shinran: 'Even a virtuous person can attain rebirth; how much more so an evil one.'
27 Levin, op. cit., p. 120.

Chapter 13

Ecological peril, modern technology and the postmodern sublime

Jonathan Bordo

The riddling Sphinx induced us to neglect mysterious crimes and rather seek solution of troubles at our feet.

(Sophocles, *Oedipus Rex*)

I REPORTS TO THE STATE

Lyotard's tract *The Postmodern Condition* calls itself a 'report', more specifically, a report on knowledge. Its status as a report is underscored by its commission by the state (the government of Quebec) and its subsequent publication history. Even its original French edition as a book was published with state funds. Lyotard's self-designation should thus be taken at face value, and not treated as simply another penurious philosopher's ironizing 'research' strategem.

Another report, of far greater fame, to which it might usefully be compared, is the Brundtland Report *Our Common Future*, the report of the World Commission on Environment and Development established by the United Nations in 1983. Both reports make pronouncements about the contemporary collective condition, and in both cases the pronouncements, whatever their explanatory basis and prognostic value, perform the seer's role, announcing through pronouncements. Reports usually rely for their authority on a distance created by anonymity. The messenger is not visible. The prototype of all reports was the ancient oracle, and it initiated the tradition of the authorless, subjectless voice as the conduit for urgent knowledge. The distance created by anonymity increases the power of the reporting.

The case of Lyotard is paradoxical here. His report speaks in the voice of the subject, pronouncing on a condition that declares the death of the subject. Like an earlier narrative on the condition of knowledge, Descartes' *Discourse on Method*, Lyotard's recitation is personal only in that it displaces this quality through the institutional address of the report itself. The addressor is an author; the addressee is the state. Through this reversal of the agents of address, and here I adapt Lyotard himself,[1]

Lyotard invests his report with the special epistemic authority of the bureaucratic report and oracle.

Reports making epochal claims are not undertaken lightly. They arise in circumstances of urgency. Descartes' *Discourse* was formulated in the aftermath of Galileo's final silencing in 1633.[2] Brundtland received its commission after an accumulation of frightful environmental disasters. Sophocles' *Oedipus the King* opens with the report of catastrophe. Creon is sent to consult the oracle because the very survival of Thebes is threatened. The city is 'reeling like a wreck . . . barely able to lift its prow out of the depths, out of the bloody surf'.[3] At the outset of *Oedipus*, the chorus establishes the ecological character of the impending danger. Struck by blight, Thebes is unable to reproduce itself physically and biologically: 'a blight is on the fruitful plants of the earth/ a blight is on the cattle of the fields/ a blight is on our women that no children are born to them'.[4] Pandemic decimates the existing population: 'A God that carries fire, deadly pestilence, is on our own town.'[5] Thebes is indeed threatened with extinction, and the danger is literally ecological because 'the life-supporting relations' (*Lebensbeziehungen*) that join the human being as 'living organisms to the world, to their habitat, customs, energies and parasites', to quote the founder of modern ecology Ernst Haeckel,[6] are endangered. Etymologically speaking, such threats are literally ecological because it is the *oikos*, the basic unit of society, in its life-dependent connectedness to its physical surroundings, that is at risk: blight, flooding, disease, sterility. An ecological danger is one that threatens the very continuance of living organisms, in this case, human beings.

The threat announced by the chorus at the outset of *Oedipus* seems, at least on the surface, to be of a kind no different than those enunciated by the Brundtland Commission in its report. When the commission speaks of the transgression of 'thresholds that cannot be crossed without endangering the basic integrity of the system', it has explicitly in view 'the risk of endangering the survival of life on Earth' as a whole.[7] Thus there are environmental trends

> that threaten to radically alter the planet, that threaten the lives of many species upon it, including the human species. Each year another 6 million hectares of productive dryland turns into worthless desert. Over three decades this would amount to an area roughly as large as Saudi Arabia. . . . In Europe acid precipitation kills forests and lakes and damages the artistic and architectural heritage of nations; it may have acidified vast tracts of soil beyond reasonable hope of repair. The burning of fossil fuels puts into the atmosphere carbon dioxide, which is causing gradual global warming . . .[8]

Indeed the vast body of the commission's report is a highly repetitious cataloguing of such threats as undermining the basis of human and non-human life alike. Not only do they seem to be about the same peril, Brundtland curiously enough, despite its scientific and objective basis, speaks about it in the archaic language of pollution, transgression and degradation, the very discourse of the oracle: 'King Phoebus in plain words commanded us/to drive out a pollution from our land,/pollution grown ingrained within the land;/drive it out, said the god, not cherish it,/till it's past cure.'[9] Let me call these developments and possibilities, which place at risk the very survival of human and non-human life alike, *threats to standing*.[10] These are to be distinguished from ordinary threats because they have the very character of threatening or being perceived to threaten the very existence of groups and collectivities where the fate of an individual is inextricably linked to the fate of a larger group and the threat to its survival. They are not of the kind that might be enunciated as 'I will die but I will live on in my work, in my children, through the community'. They have both an ontological and a transcendental quality, putting at risk the very existence of living entities as wholes. Ecological threats are prototypically threats to standing since they attack the conditions and relations supporting life.

To be sure, the archaic and the modern responses to such ecological danger, despite this crucial ontological intersection, diverge epistemologically and strategically. They part company with respect not only to the causes of such threats but more to the point, to the very meaning of cause.[11] Cause, for Sophocles, is meaning, and hence cause has a source in divine or human agency. The pollution is someone not something. For the archaic, the agent of disease is a person, when it is for us, a thing. A human being holds Thebes 'in the destroying storm'. Someone not something is a toxin that must be expelled before 'it is past cure': 'By banishing a man or expiation of blood by blood, since it is murder guilt which holds our city in this destroying storm'.[12] Although undeniably the result of human practices, the causes of global environmental catastrophe reduce meaning, neutralizing the agency of the cause to efficient causation. For the modern, agency has become external to cause – a bearer of value – while for the archaic, agency has become internal and central to the meaning and nature of cause: meaning is cause. In *Violence and the Sacred*, René Girard interprets ecological threats as signs of the sacred, and when such dangers erupt, they manifest themselves as signs of a 'sacrificial crisis':

The sacred consists of all those forces whose dominance over man increases or seems to increase in proportion to man's effort to master them. Tempests, forest fires, and plagues, among other phenomena, may be classified as sacred. Far outranking these, however, though in a far less obvious manner, stands human violence – violence seen as something exterior to man and henceforth as a part of all the other outside forces that threaten mankind. Violence is the heart and soul of the sacred.[13]

This is not the place to argue with Girard concerning either the meaning or priority of violence. Is what he means by violence an environmental condition in the sense that I have discussed? As independent and exterior force, is it the dynamic of ecological catastrophe? Or are flooding, forest fires and disease themselves acts of violence whose consequences are ecological because what is endangered is the very survival of human beings as living organisms? Girard seems to claim that the sacrificial crisis is the cause. I want to heighten this ambivalent directionality and say ecological danger is symbolically re-enacted as sacrificial crisis. It need not be the only source of sacrificial crisis, but the sacrifice is the archaic mechanism for controlling crises to human standing having an ecological source.

Girard gives a very specific content to archaic religion as symbolic re-enactment which addresses the threat by a complicated ritual process that identifies the cause with a polluting human subject. Cause is transformed into narrative re-enactment, converging 'on an isolated and unique figure, the surrogate victim',[14] and having a dramatic punctuation in a ritual event of sacrifice. In short, ecological crisis is represented in archaic culture in terms of a religious framework, and when it is threatened, 'the whole cultural foundation of the society is put in jeopardy'.[15]

It is important not to lose sight of the extension of the archaic disease metaphor in the Brundtland Report's portraying of the environmental condition. The disease metaphor organizes its opening of the report:

> From space, we can see and study the Earth as an organism whose health depends on the health of all its parts. We have the power to reconcile human affairs with natural laws and to thrive in the process. In this our cultural and spiritual heritages can reinforce our economic interests and survival imperatives.[16]

But the disease metaphor requires a site and stance to position the agent and the patient. 'From space' the agent can view the Earth as an organismic whole bound together through the inextricable systemic links of ecological interdependence. The Earth's toxicity falls beneath the extraterrestrial gaze of the polluting agent, the human subject. Indeed from this view outside the world, human activity ceases to dominate and what comes to the foreground is the natural environmental background: 'From space, we see a small and fragile ball dominated not by human activity and edifice but by patterns of cloud, oceans, greenery, and soils.'[17] Earth-the-patient has to be constituted first as an object, a 'small and fragile ball', beneath the distant gaze of the extraterrestrial observer. Kant's so-called Copernican turn underlies the planetary positioning of agent's and the patient.

The opening sentences of the Brundtland Report establish explicitly the alleged Copernican character of the investigative stance:

In the middle of the 20th century, we saw our planet from space for the first time. Historians may eventually find that this vision had a greater impact on thought than did the Copernican revolution of the 16th century, which upset the human self-image by revealing that the Earth is not the centre of the universe.[18]

The historical causality of this assertion is only slightly myopic. Contemporary society has fashioned a technological platform for the transcendental viewpoint. The extraterrestrial technologically secured 'vision' might be better thought of as that later and advanced epoch of the initial Copernican thought experiment when the hypothesis became institutionalized as as administrative gaze.[19] The need for such a totalizing operation arises in the view of the Brundtland from a deeply ingrained human disability, namely from 'humanity's inability to fit its doings into [an enviromental] pattern.'[20] However to control such a profound discontent both presupposes and demands ever larger administrative and state operations. The Brundtland Commission 'came to see that a new development path was required, one that sustained human progress not just in a few places for a few years but for the entire planet into the distant future'.[21] If the archaic response to ecological danger is understood as a sacrificial crisis, establishing 'a violent unanimity of the all against the one, the surrogate victim',[22] the modern response to ecological threat summons the organization of the planet into a unitary techno-administrative system. The modern response is to create a unanimity by making an abstractive step to envelope the world into a larger system: worlds become the world, the world becomes the Earth, the Earth a planetary subsystem, and so on. A sort of transcendental holism becomes the thought device for the constitution of a planetary Foucauldean administrative panopticon whose aim is to integrate the human being into the world by creating a larger and more elaborate system to be orchestrated by the gaze from a transcendental point 'from space', a point that is of logical, moral and administrative necessity beyond the world.

The Brundtland Commission's declaration of confidence in human continuance, even beneath the planetary ecological threat, affirms simultaneously the security of the epistemological foundation and the universality of the social and political programme of the Enlightenment while presupposing just those values as norms, providing the framework for addressing ecological peril. Overall, its telos is to preserve what might be called the 'modernist' or foundationalist vision for the evolutionary and emancipatory unfolding of human potentiality.

The Commission believes that people can build a future that is more prosperous, more just and more secure. Our report, Our Common

Future, is not a prediction of ever increasing environmental decay, poverty, and hardship in an ever more polluted world among decreasing resources. We see increased the possibility for a new era of economic growth, one that must be based on policies that sustain and expand the environmental resource base. And we believe such growth to be essential to relieve the great poverty that is deepening in much of the developing world.[23]

Indeed the conversion of the Copernican standpoint into an administrative gaze is reinforced by the replication of another piece of the legitimating scheme of modernity, the metaphysical bifurcation between the human being and non-human nature, that is usually traced back to the seventeenth-century scientific reformers, Descartes and Bacon. The base and foundation for the maintenance of the human life form, conceived globally and systemically at the centre, presuppose the need and right to reduce the non-human world fully and the human world at least partially to the status of a human use-value, in short to reduce them to the status of a resource. The last paragraph of the commission's general statement concludes by serving notice 'that the time has come to take decisions needed to secure the resources to sustain this and coming generations'.[24] For Brundtland, technological administration not only presupposes a centre, it also presupposes the normative stability of a fundamental bifurcation between the human and the non-human to permit routine technological intervention. The commission's view coincides with the Cartesian picture because Descartes' programme for the mathematization of nature invented in its turn a philosophical foundation to provide legitimation for the practical reduction of the world to the human utility of a resource.

At a crucial turning point in the third part of his essay 'The Question Concerning Technology', Heidegger offers an unexpected gloss on Descartes' famous 'maîtres et possesseurs de la nature' formulation from the *Discourse on Method*. It is the point in his argument where the human being crosses a threshold from being exclusively 'an orderer of standing reserve' to becoming himself 'standing reserve'. With the penetration of this barrier:

> man, precisely as the one so threatened, exalts himself to the posture of lord of the earth. . . . In this way the illusion comes to prevail that everything man encounters exists only in so far as it is his construct. This illusion gives rise in turn to one final delusion: it seems as though man everywhere and always encounters only himself.[25]

The text suggests that Heidegger, the great foe of humanism, turns out himself to be a humanist, in the sense that he affirms a view of the human being as special and distinct from the rest of the organic and inorganic world. For Heidegger, the danger of modern technology is its power to strip the human being of this special and exempt status as the one entity only partially enmeshed in technology. Enmeshment is both material and epistemological. We dispose ourselves to technology physically through technology as a mode of access that anchors us to the world. Not only might such total enmeshment occur but we would be unable even to discern its occurrence. The danger doubles because consciousness itself, the Cartesian mark for human exemption and domination, would not be able to detect the Kafkaesque metamorphosis because it is the source of the drive for enmeshment.

In *The Postmodern Condition* Lyotard proclaims the death of the grand narrative whose two components consist of the narrative of the constituting subject and the narrative of the system as an unfolding totality: Descartes and Kant in the case of the former, Kant and Hegel in the case of the latter. Indeed the primary thrust of Lyotard's 'report' is just the very cultural concession and the disappearance of such a legitimating scheme. Subject and totalizing system belong to the working assumptions of the Brundtland Commission's investigation. Perhaps there would not be anything note-worthy here with respect to this apparent contradiction were it not for the fact that Lyotard, at least in his report, is making a fundamental claim about the human condition in broad societal and deep cultural terms and not a more containable claim concerning a fundamental change in dis-course. His claim is about modernity, not modernism. Indeed the differ-ence in textual authority between Brundtland and Heidegger provides mutually supportive textual evidence for the historical persistence of what I have referred to as the Cartesian picture as a legitimating scheme for technological intervention. The Brundtland Report, not being a tract in philosophy, fails to fulfil Lyotard's requirement that foundationalism re-quires an explicit 'meta' discourse.[26] Rather foundationalism runs through Brundtland as an invisible 'fil conducteur'. The Cartesian picture is presup-posed in every page of the Brundtland Report because its resourcist perspective concerning the environment legitimates action that requires the belief in an unbridgeable gap and an unshiftable anthropogenic posit-ioning between the human being and nature.

The importance of Heidegger's argument in 'The Question' is that it demonstrates that the intractable persistence of the Cartesian picture for modernity is carried, not by explicit, let alone rationally justified belief, but as a way of acting. But then Jameson also proves to be on the right track when he criticizes Lyotard for failing to take the further step of positing not the disappearance of the great master-narratives, but their passage under-ground as it were, their continuing but now unconscious effectivity as a way of 'thinking about' and acting in our current situation.[27]

Contemporary environmental philosophy posits just such a 'political unconscious' or more aptly a 'cultural unconscious' when it traces the sources of the western domination of nature to the formation of the very nature concept itself in ancient Judaeo-Christian and classical attitudes, which received a crucial philosophical recension at the hands of the scientific reformers of the seventeenth century. The common interpretation of the meaning and extension of postmodernity collides with the intractability of the Cartesian picture because it points both to the persistence of it as an attitude and the irrelevance of grand narrative as superstructural cement for that attitude. Postmodernity is often linked with the pragmatist claims for the sufficiency of technique to get the work done. Lyotard leans heavily on the later Wittgenstein in just this regard. However, it may turn out, as I begin to suggest in the next section, that pragmatist claims for the sufficiency of technique are not intended to address the foundations of technique but are to justify the role of technology to control the bad infinite released to human consciousness. The bad infinite is the 'postmodern sublime', a condition brought about by modern technology itself. It is a grave and ironic paradox that its 'management' has come to fall within the province of its cause, technology.

II   HEIDEGGER'S DENIAL

I return to the passage in 'The Question' where Heidegger reworks Descartes' concept of 'lords and masters' by embedding this concept within technology as a theoretical site:

> As soon as what is unconcealed no longer concerns man even as object, but exclusively as standing reserve, and man in the midst of objectlessness is nothing but the orderer of standing reserve, then he comes to the very brink of a precipitous fall, that is, he comes to the point where he himself will have to be taken as standing reserve.[28]

At a certain moment in the relentness dynamic of technological enmeshment, the human being finds itself on the verge of a fatal caesura when 'he [sic] himself will have to be taken as standing reserve'. At that point the human becomes itself resource. But according to Heidegger we are still wending our way up to this last ultimate barrier, up to the 'very brink of a precipitous fall'. The adverb 'still' is an interjection of history, of the ontic into discourse. It interjects the historicity of the author, Martin Heidegger himself, into the text. At the time of his writing 'The Question', Heidegger was still of the view that the human being had yet to reach the very brink itself, had still in other words to take 'a precipitous fall'. According to Krell, Heidegger delivered 'The Question Concerning Technology' as a talk in 1953 under the title 'The Enframing'.[29] Thus as of the time of its delivery, Heidegger's position was that the human being had still to reach the brink of catastrophe and had not yet taken the fatal plunge into standing reserve.

Heidegger's mendacity concerning his intimate and engaged political and philosophical allegiance to Nazism has only recently and reluctantly been absorbed into the academic and discursive record, due in large part to the courageous efforts of Victor Farias.[30] Mendacity doubled by a denial concerning the Holocaust finds a perverse and damning discursive repetition in the 'yet' of the passage under discussion. It is not yet, not because of Auschwitz. Heidegger's mendacity from the point of view of the text preserves his assertion that the transformation of the human being into standing reserve had not yet happened. I repeat. His failure to take moral responsibility for the technologically organized genocide of Nazism, long after it had become part of the public record, finds textual repetition as a denial that the precipitous fall of the human being into standing reserve had already been accomplished in the way that the 'final solution' had been planned and executed as a confidential manufacturing problem – as a mere problem in the ordering of standing reserve. The text is thus a denial that a historical threshold had been crossed as a way of adjusting history to the absolute, commanding and truth-revealing power of *theoria*. Heidegger's anti-modernism[31] is expressed through one of the most elevated, domineering and unreflected modernist assertoric stances. The mendacity is thus ingrained in the very voice of the text which depends upon modernity especially when it is modernity itself that Heidegger disavows and denies.

Yet it is in the acknowledgement that thresholds have already been crossed that we have at least the presentiment of an epochal change that has come to be called by some the 'postmodern'. It is in the acknowledgement of the great catastrophic criminal political events of Auschwitz, the Gulag and the atomic bomb that an unalterable change has taken place in the conditions of European and western self-consciousness. Technologically organized threats to human standing had already been executed as deliberate political and social policies. Genocide provided the political precedent for what is the utterly ubiquitous unplanned ecological threats to the permanence of the Earth. The change is in the recognition of the quality of the threat. Threats to standing have become ordinary and acceptable.

No wonder theory has so much to say about world-destroying historical events such as Auschwitz and the Gulag, just as it now has thematized AIDS, while being virtually speechless concerning the Aral Sea, Gulf oil fires and global warming. Master-narratives are embedded in Auschwitz and the Gulag just as the whole cultural history of western patriarchy finds itself revealed in the secrecy of the master-narrative for AIDS. It seems that modernity itself, its project, stripped of master-narrative, is expressed in ecological threats. Could this be the postmodern condition – modernity without master-narrative? Or is it the muteness of nature in the face of ecological catastrophe that provides the source of the postmodern sublime?

The very idea of an ecological threat under conditions of modern technology exacerbates all our existing notions of the sublime to the point

of creating techno-administrative practices of denial. The very idea of an
ecological threat as creating an unbearable incommensurability between
the technological character of the threat in the most general terms and our
capacity to delimit it, received its first significant articulation with the
releasing of atomic energy in the building of the atomic bomb. The
scientists themselves spoke in terms of the incommensurable power of such
a weapon. In Robert Oppenheimer's words to the Association of Los
Alamos Scientists on 2 November 1945:

> I think it is for us to accept it as a very grave crisis, to realize that these
> atomic weapons which we have started to make are very terrible, that
> they involve a change, that they are not just a slight modification: to
> accept this, and to accept with it the necessity for those transformations
> in the world will make it possible to integrate these developments into
> human life.[32]

Indeed the qualitative change that Oppenheimer speaks about can be
formulated in terms of an unbridgeable disproportion or incommensurability between the all-pervasive destructiveness stemming from the nature of
such devices and the limited end or goals which human beings would
pursue with them as instruments.[33] Common sense encounters this incommensurability in terms of instruments and outcomes. But common sense
cannot square what Oppenheimer calls the technical 'sweetness', the theoretical contents of the device and all the processes needed to devise and
execute the device, with ordinary experience. The scientific basis of the
technology posits entities and processes that are too small and too precise
to be grasped without the possession of or access to special expertise. They
are epistemologically inaccessible. In addition, the technological outcomes
are incommensurable because ordinary experience cannot grasp, for
example, the ideas of nuclear winter or of rapid climate change. Just as the
theoretically posited entities are too abstract and minute to be graspable,
so the outcomes of such technologically organized processes are also
ungraspable, except in terms that suppress the very incommensurability
which the technological process has made possible. Nuclear winter was
only recently a common thought experiment for a climactic and organic
termination which is so final that we would be unable to conceive the
possibility of human life in any recognizable form.

The thinkers of classical modernity, Pascal, Burke and Kant, established
the conceptual and metaphoric landscape of incommensurability from the
Archimedean point of the natural capacity. Burke and Kant referred to the
experience of incommensurability as the 'sublime'. Burke sketched the
existential conditions for such a sentiment by locating its source in situations 'where we are strongly effected with whatever threatens life and
health', which presupposes in turn that 'the performance of our duties of

every kind depends upon life, and the performing them with vigour and efficacy depends upon health'.[34] In other words, if the source of the sublime is in the existential sense of a threat to life and health, then the experience of the sublime would always arise from conditions of ecological peril.

Under modern technological conditions, our sense of the sublime surfaces from the technological incommensurability of instruments and ends. The sources of the threatening processes are abstractively too remote to grasp relevantly in situations of crisis while the repercussions are too calamitous to envisage. Kant articulated the conceptual conditions for the sentiment of the sublime as arising from the inadequacy of our cognitive powers to find experiential tokens, permitting us to bring ideas of the sublime beneath a concept. As a result, examples of the sublime are unrepresentable.[35] In general, the classical thinkers of modernity assumed the reliability of the human cognitive capacity as naturally given. I want to say that the notion of incommensurability and hence the sublime undergo a dramatic change under conditions of modern technology because the principal source of the sublime comes from processes released by human ingenuity and construction: technology. This is unlike the archaic experience of the sacred which arises from the sense of human powerlessness up against vicissitude.

Under contemporary conditions of modern technology, sentiments of the sublime such as terror and anxiety arise from our most intricate scientific devisings. The sublime arises, not from what reason has excluded and suppressed, but from the products of reason itself. Our experience of ecological peril, then, is not aesthetic in the classical sense. It is an ordinary, everyday happening proclaimed in the media through reports on rapid climate change or the state of the latest oil spill and oil fire, or as simulated scenes of war as 'the destruction of technological infrastructure'. It pervades the media as images which are as numbing as they are uninterpretable and banal. The destructiveness of oil spill Y is compared to the destructive effects of oil spill X. Who can remember the last disaster? Bhopal, Chernobyl, the *Exxon Valdez*?

This routine quality of banal and terrorized numbness contains the secret of the appeal in contemporary culture to pragmatism. The contemporary response to technologically induced threats to standing is denial. Heidegger's denial: what has happened is bad but it has yet to happen; the Jews (the Indians, the trees, the cod steaks, the water table) do not count as telling examples. The denial does not occur in the assertion that things are bad but they could be worse. The denial is in the assurance that actions are already being taken, including the action of announcing and reporting, to address the latest crisis.

The threat to the environment does not summon technological response as much as the threat to human experience arising from the perceived damage to the environment. The sublime has been released by the ecological threat. Released, the sublime, threatens to get out of control.

The technological steps are demonstrations. What consequence the steps have for the environment are unknown. We can be assured that the area of the oil spill in Alaska will never be restored to its 'original pristine beauty'. We will never know just how widespread and long lasting were the toxic effects of Chernobyl. Whether anything has really been done to redress the 'objective' aspect of the threat to the environment, the primary use of a secondary technological intervention on the environment is to control the sublime by removing the threat behind the veil of technological procedure. Thus the damage to the environment itself recedes, becoming like Kant's 'Ding an sich', out there but out of reach, behind the screen of technological representation.

The gap then between the modern technological response to ecological danger and the archaic turns out to be not that wide, as Girard astutely remarks:

> The goal of religious thinking is exactly the same as that of technological research – namely, practical action. Whenever man is truly concerned with obtaining concrete results, whenever he is hard pressed by reality, he abandons abstract speculation and reverts to a mode of response that becomes increasingly cautious and conservative as the force he hopes to subdue, or at least outrun, draws ever nearer.[36]

Both have the purpose of controlling the experience of threats to standing. But there is one significant difference. Contemporary technological pragmatism has as its primary task the organizing of an effective screen of denial to channel threats to standing. Ecological danger under archaic conditions was local and physically uncontrollable. A plague might destroy a large part of Thebes but it didn't threaten to destroy the whole of life as it then existed. It just ran its course. Someone escaped. Technologically induced ecological threats to standing are ubiquitous in their scope.

Denial through pragmatic technological operations is rational when it succeeds in martialling a collective will to address the ecological damage itself, to address the threats at their source. This would require penetrating the screen of technological representation itself, but before that could happen it would first have to be understood as a screen. Hence it turns out that technological action has the very performative quality of the language game assigned to it by Lyotard – not, as he asserts, because of its effectiveness, but just because it might well be instrumentally ineffective. It represents itself symbolically as doing something effective when the wheels of its vaunted productivity, to paraphrase Wittgenstein, could very well be spinning idly. The symbolic re-enactment as representation imposes a closure around its indeterminacy. Lyotard profoundly misunderstood pragmatist desire.[37]

And how would we be able to discern the difference? The powers of modern technology have released the sublime, and every effort to manage the sublime by technological means seems merely to increase the indeterminacy, rendering our experience even more inchoate and defenceless in face of it. Is this not at least the epochal site for the meaning of the postmodern sublime?

NOTES

1 Jean-François Lyotard, *The Postmodern Condition*, Minneapolis, University of Minnesota Press, 1984, pp. 18–23.
2 J. Bordo, *The Appeal to Reason: The Legitimacy of Science and the Cartesian Genealogy of Knowledge*, Ann Arbor, UMI Press, 1980, Part II, Section 2.
3 Sophocles, *Oedipus the King*, trans. D. Grene, in D. Grene and R. Lattimore (eds), *Greek Tragedies* vol. 1, Chicago, University of Chicago Press, 1960, p. 111.
4 ibid., p. 112, ll. 25–7.
5 ibid., ll. 27–31.
6 Cited in D. Worster, *Nature's Economy*, Cambridge, Mass., Harvard University Press, 1987, p. 191.
7 Brundtland Commission (World Commission on Environment and Development), *Our Common Future*, New York, Oxford University Press, 1987, p. 16.
8 ibid., p. 2.
9 Sophocles, op. cit., p. 114, ll. 95–101.
10 See J. Bordo, 'Nuclear Weapons as a Threat to the Permanence of Life', in M. Fox and L. Groarke (eds), *Nuclear War: Philosophical Perspectives*, New York, Peter Lang, 1985, pp. 101–6. The author is writing a monograph, with the same title as the present essay, on modern consciousness under technological threat.
11 René Girard, *Violence and the Sacred*, Baltimore, Johns Hopkins University Press, 1984, p. 31.
12 Sophocles, op. cit, p. 113, l. 102.
13 Girard, op. cit., p. 31.
14 ibid., p. 79.
15 ibid., p. 49.
16 Brundtland, op. cit., p. 1.
17 ibid.
18 ibid.
19 Hans Blumenberg, *The Genesis of the Copernican World-View*, trans. R. Wallace, Cambridge, Mass., MIT Press, 1987, II, 3.
20 Brundtland, op. cit., p. 4. See also Neil Evernden, *The Natural Alien*, Toronto, University of Toronto Press, 1984.
21 ibid.
22 Girard, op. cit., p. 84.
23 Brundtland, op. cit., p. 8.
24 ibid., pp. 1–2.
25 Martin Heidegger, 'The Question Concerning Technology', in *Basic Writings*, ed. D. Krell, New York, Harper & Row, 1977, p. 308.
26 For Lyotard's view that grand narrative is centrally linked to the philosophy story as ruling second order discourse, see J.-F. Lyotard and J.L. Thebaud, *Just Gaming*, Minneapolis, University of Minnesota Press, 1985, pp. 40–5.
27 See Fredric Jameson's preface to Lyotard, op. cit., pp. xi–xii.

28 Heidegger, op. cit., p. 308.
29 ibid., p. 285.
30 Victor Farias, *Heidegger et le nazisme*, Paris, Verdier, 1987.
31 M. Zimmerman, *Heidegger's Confrontation with Modernity*, Bloomington, Indiana University Press, 1990. See also J. Herf, *Reactionary Modernism: Technology, Culture and Politics in Weimar and The Third Reich*, New York/ Cambridge, Cambridge University Press, 1984.
32 A.K. Smith and C. Weiner (eds), *Robert Oppenheimer: Letters and Recollections*, Cambridge, Mass., Harvard University Press, 1980, p. 318.
33 Bordo, 'Nuclear Weapons', op. cit., pp. 101–6.
34 Edmund Burke, *On the Sublime and the Beautiful* (1756), New York, Collier & Son, 1909, p. 38.
35 Lyotard, op. cit., pp. 77–81.
36 Girard, op. cit., p. 33.
37 Lyotard's appropriation of the Wittgensteinian language game for his own pragmatist programme is considered in a forthcoming paper that attempts to sketch a genealogy or history of pragmatist desire.

ACKNOWLEDGEMENT

The author wishes to acknowledge Verena Huber Dyson, Harold Coward and the participants in the Modernity and Technology Seminar for various assistances in earlier articulations. Initiating versions were supported by grants from the SSHRC and Trent University as well as by a sojourn as a research fellow at the Calgary Institute for the Humanities in 1987.

Part III

Gender and psyche

Chapter 14

Adultery in the House of David: 'nation' in the Bible and biblical scholarship*

Regina M. Schwartz

What happens when a discipline like biblical studies – not just any discipline, mind you, but the one largely responsible for the shape of university liberal studies – what happens when the ideologies that shape that discipline become, for those who work in it, virtually indistinguishable from the ideologies of the materials they work upon? Examples are rife: somehow, we see in nineteenth-century women's novels the same feminism that gave rise to the discipline of women's studies in the 1970s; somehow, we find in English documents from the sixteenth century the same left politics that shaped the new historicism in the 1980s. Epistemological humility dictates no less – after all, we can only inquire into the objects of our investigation through our own tinted lenses, but if we are not careful, what begins as epistemological humility can quickly turn into the special arrogance that mistakes the biases undergirding an influential discipline for the only biases 'discernible' in its materials. With the advantage of some historical hindsight (and newly tinted lenses) we can investigate the politics of a discipline and see how its reading of a text differs from a reading of the same material from another vantage. The case of the Bible is particularly pressing because it has been authorized by the west not only as a spiritual guide and a handbook of truth, but also as a manual for politics. As if that doesn't make biblical interpretation hazardous enough, the authority attached to the Bible also 'bleeds' onto the discipline of biblical studies and the political assumptions that have formed it.

Biblical scholarship is preoccupied with history – not the same history that the Bible constructs, but a history that the Bible offers clues to – the political and religious history of the ancient Near East. I think it is crucial to make distinctions between those projects, that is, to make distinctions between the writing of history in the Bible and the writing of history in biblical scholarship, especially because they are so often and so dangerously blurred. Dangerously, because the equation of the ideologies of biblical narratives with a positivist historian's understanding of 'real events' turns what could be founding fictions of western culture demanding critique into 'facts' that seem formidably unassailable. Dangerously, because the German historicism that gave birth to biblical scholarship is no mere positivism (as if there were such a thing), rather, every archaeologist's spade and every philologist's verb ending is deeply inscribed with politics. Dangerously, because that very politics, once read into the Bible through the back door of something as seemingly innocent as historical-critical scholarship, can offer 'evidence' for justifying the oppression of people. It is too late in the day and our understanding of narrative is too advanced to allow any pernicious notions of 'biblical truth' – including those of 'higher criticism' – to continue to stick. Here I would like to try to separate the complex constructions of the nation in the biblical narratives that span the book of Judges through II Kings, the 'Deuteronomistic history', from the nationalism read into these narratives by biblical scholarship. I may as well confess at the outset that my lenses have been tinted epistemologically by postmodern approaches to history rather than by the German historicism that forged biblical scholarship, and that they are tinted politically by deep suspicion of exclusive national identities.

I   BIBLICAL SCHOLARSHIP

'Traditional history', as Foucault characterizes it, 'retracing the past as a patient and continuous development', strikes me as an apt description of the major pursuit in biblical studies for the past two centuries. The project that has dominated the field is the historical reconstruction of the biblical text; as de Wette prescribed in the nineteenth century, 'the subject matter of biblical introduction is the history of the Bible'.[1] This project is marked by its quest for origins – the origin of a given passage, the origin of a cultic practice, the original setting of the text – and by a deep commitment to charting development, whether the formation of the text (what is the extent of J, the Yahwist contribution, and E, the Elohist contribution, and when did they come together?), the development of the ancient Israelite religion (what are the earliest signs of Yahwism?), or the development of political organizations in ancient Israel (how did the tribal confederacy become a monarchy?). Much biblical scholarship has been devoted to ascertaining sources – even though the Bible has unhelpfully obscured its sources – and many of the historical reconstructions of ancient Israel have been markedly teleological – even though the Hebrew Bible depicts a history that stubbornly resists any notion of fulfilment or completion.[2]

These projects have their own history. In the nineteenth century, historical-critical biblical scholarship saw itself as part of a larger Germanic historiographic tradition. Among others, Robert Oden has recently asserted that this is not just a question of influence; 'rather, the broader historiographic tradition shared the same methods, the same goals, the same prejudices, and the same world of understanding as biblical scholarship'.[3] The chief assumptions were that history charts development, that its focus should be the development of the nation – the German nation in particular – and that the nation should be understood as an individual entity with its own unfolding spirit, its own internal laws of development. Teleological use of organic metaphors predominates: the growth of an innate tendency, or the seed flowering into a nation. Philosophic idealism joined to the project of national revival in the Wars of Liberation gave nineteenth-century German historicism that special cast in which the nation's quest for power was an ethical imperative. For Leopold von Ranke, 'it must be the uppermost task of the state to achieve the highest measure of independence and strength among the competing powers of the world, so that the state will be able to fully develop its innate tendencies.'[4] Johann Gustav Droysen writes of the idea of a 'divine order', of 'God's rule of the world', along with the insistence that a divine plan is working itself out in Prussia in particular. In his *History of Prussian Politics*, Droysen tried to argue that ever since the fifteenth century Prussian rulers (ever conscious of Prussia's German mission) followed a consistent plan of action, a plan still unfolding in Germany.[5] An emphasis on teleological development insistently marks his thought:

> The moral world, ceaselessly moved by *many ends*, and finally . . . by the *supreme end*, is in a state of restless development and of internal elevation and growth. . . . With every advancing step in this *development* and *growth*, the historical understanding become wider and deeper [my emphasis].[6]

Droysen's philosophy of history is indebted to that of Wilhelm von Humboldt, who in his famous essay *On the Task of the Historians* sounds at first surprisingly at odds with the prevailing notions of coherence and continuity. 'What is apparent', he writes, 'is scattered, disconnected, isolated', but then he explains that it is the historian's task to take what is 'apparent' and show the hidden coherence: the historian 'takes the scattered pieces he has gathered into himself and work[s] them into a whole'.[7] Von Ranke also begins by talking about isolated events, but his interest too soon turns to the notion of a cohesive hidden order informing seeming chaos:

> Although [history] pursues the succession of events as sharply and accurately as possible, and attempts to give each of them its proper color and form . . . still history goes beyond this labor and moves on to an investigation of origins, seeking to break through to the deepest and most secret motives of historical life.

Nietzsche describes this consuming fever of history which he believes his age suffers from in his *Untimely Meditations*, critiquing the kind of history that seeks to reduce the diversity of time 'into a totality fully closed upon itself . . . a history whose perspective on all that precedes it implies the end of time, a completed development'.[8] For Ranke, Humboldt and Droysen, historiography reveals the inner logic in the randomness of events, and that logic is the course of national development.

For ancient Israel, the book of Samuel was among its founding fictions.[9] It set the terms by which the institution of monarchy was to be understood, and by which the nation of ancient Israel was defining itself; it was a narrative engaged in the formation of identity – not just of its chief protagonists, Saul and David, but the identity of the nation. Nationalism was the paramount concern in that other set of founding fictions – and I do use the term fiction here advisedly – the founding fictions of German historicism. History was called upon to narrate the ideals of the German nation, its various 'progresses', moral, military, political, religious; and because the story of ancient Israel was written by historians who were also thinking about, even writing, the story of Germany, it is no wonder that the two stories were often confused. All that development so faithfully outlined in the growth of the German nation was easily, too easily, found in the growth of ancient Israel.

We can see this confusion in the work of one of the most prominent biblical scholars of the late nineteenth century, Julius Wellhousen, when he writes in the introduction to his *Prolegomena to the History of Ancient Israel*, 'it is necessary to trace the succession of the three elements [the Jehovist, the Deuteronomic and the Priestly] in detail, and at once to test and to fix each by reference to an independent standard, namely, the inner development of the history of Israel'. With this commitment to charting such 'inner development', he cannot help but find it. The metaphors he uses to discuss his theory of the literary composition of the books of Judges, Samuel and Kings are symptomatic:

> we are not presented with tradition purely in its original condition; already it is overgrown with later accretions. Alongside of an older narrative a new one has sprung up, formerly independent, and intelligible in itself, though in many instances of course adapting itself to the former. More frequently the new forces have not caused the old root to send forth a new stock, or even so much as a complete branch; they have only nourished parasitic growths; the earlier narrative has become clothed with minor and dependent additions. To vary the metaphor, the whole area of tradition has finally been uniformly covered with an alluvial deposit by which the configuration of the surface has been determined.[10]

He shifts from the metaphor of a plant with a new branch to a plant that has only parasitic growths; next it is overgrown with accretions; and then he dresses it (the plant wears 'minor and dependent' clothes), only to proceed to drop the plant altogether to opt for geologic history; now the biblical text is comprised of layers of alluvial deposits, and presumably scholars can take out their spades and dig right through it. Whether as the growth of an organism or the accretion of geologic deposits, this is the picture of history that he quickly applies not only to the development of the text, but to its plot, that is, to the biblical narrative's own account of history.[11] Deftly, almost without our noticing, the story of Germany becomes the story of Israel.

When we read the secondary literature about David with German historicism in mind, we can detect signs of it virtually everywhere. Many scholars' accounts, both of the development of the text and of the history of Israel, are informed by the same assumptions we detect in Wellhausen, for their story tells of the accretion of David's power, alluvial deposit by alluvial deposit. Finding this presupposition of development in one too many places, I began to be frankly suspicious. If biblical scholars reconstructed the *text* that way because the whole discipline of textual studies (including philology) was permeated by the assumptions of German historicism, so be it.[12] But to find that development in the story of David, whose history is so marked by discontinuity and ideological conflict? How were biblical scholars going to reconcile the drive for finding continuity and development with this messy tale? They did it by chopping up the narrative into different documents, first into big pieces, then into smaller ones, and when they were finished, they had taken the amorphous, heterogeneous story we have been given and separated it into strands, each governed by – you guessed it – the criteria of development and continuity. Here is one of the prominent source theories: a historian or historical school wrote a large strand of the story that bridges Judges to Kings according to the coherent principle that Israel's fate was determined by its responses to the law in Deuteronomy (it is rewarded for obedience and punished for disobedience). One version has it that this part was written in exile, from the point of view of a hope for an Israel that failed. The narrator:

> considered the whole of past history in relation to this law, concluded that the prescriptions of the law should have been observed at all times (2 Kings 22:13, 17) and thus reached an unfavorable judgment on the history of Israel, seeing it as a period of going astray from God for which it was punished.[13]

However, amidst all of the narratives describing the disobedience and failures of Israel, there was also a recognizable drive to idealize David, and this contradiction, between the pessimism of the Deuteronomistic historian and the optimism about David, is resolved by separating the documents. To be coherent, one document must espouse one ideology – say, that Israel is continually going astray from the law and Israel must be punished for her sins – and the other document expouse another – say, that David is the ideal of kingship and kingship is the ideal for Israel.

To a surprising degree (surprising, because most of us assume that these decisions about sources were based only on linguistic data), the criterion of a consistent sympathy or ideology or the plot continuity of a narrative – whether pro- or anti-monarchical, pro- or anti-Saul or pro- or anti- whoever or whatever the critic chooses to focus on – has been *determining* in separating strands of narrative and ascribing different authors. Sources have even been named for the character the author ostensibly sympathizes with – the 'Saul source', the 'Samuel source' – and when two basic sources did not resolve all the contradictions, more narrative strands had to be isolated to account for them, and when these were not named for a character, they were named for a continuous thread in the plot; hence, we have the 'ark narrative', or 'the rise of David narrative'. Note how blithely Kyle McCarter, the scholar who wrote the impressively learned Anchor Bible commentaries on I and II Samuel, can take for granted in his introduction that *his* demand for coherence is also felt by his readers: 'Numerous internal thematic tensions, duplications, and contradictions stand in the way of a straightforward reading of the story.' What does he mean by a 'straightforward' reading of the story? Whether he is suggesting that reading forward and reading straight mean reading straight for the goal, reading for development, or if he is defining 'straightforward reading' in his sentence tautologically to mean the kind of reading we do when there are no 'thematic tensions, no duplications or contradictions' (and I know of no such reading), he sets out to rectify the problem, rewriting the Bible into coherent stories, and the difficult one we have in our Bibles is either neglected or, worse still, 'solved'.

II   BIBLICAL STORIES

Writing on Nietzsche's *Genealogy of Morals*, Michel Foucault distinguishes 'effective history' from traditional history. If traditional history is devoted to searching out sources, establishing continuity, finding resemblances and charting development, 'effective history' is devoted to charting ruptures and discontinuities, to disrupting the fiction of the unity of the subject, and to breaking the commitment to seeking origins and ends:

> History becomes 'effective' to the degree that it introduces discontinuity into our very being – as it divides our emotions, dramatizes our instincts, multiplies our body and sets it against itself. 'Effective' history deprives the self of the reassuring stability of life and nature, and it will not permit itself to be transported by a voiceless obstinacy toward a millenial ending. It will uproot its traditional foundations and relentlessly disrupt its pretended continuity. This is because knowledge is not made for understanding; it is made for cutting.[14]

In complicated ways, the Hebrew Bible depicts history as a series of ruptures in which various identities are cut and recut, formed, broken and reformed, rather than as a continuous process in which a stable entity called Israel develops. In a narrative like Genesis 15, where Abraham is told to cut three birds in half for a mysterious convenant ceremony in which fire passes between the pieces while the promise of a future nation is made to the patriarch, does cutting signify constituting identity or destroying it? Or both? Animals are not the only entities severed here; Abraham's descendants are to be separated from their home, 'sojourners in a land not theirs' as part of the process of creating a new home, and yet, Yahweh will threaten that Israel's inheritance will be cut off. Israel is already 'cut off' in that it is separated from the other nations; that separation is defining, and it means that not Israel, but its enemies have been 'cut off' before it (II Samuel 7:9). Other forms of rupture characterize this history: in Israel's story, 'cutting' is joined by an emphasis on 'tearing away' and 'breaking', and what is broken is not always Israel's enemies, nor, for that matter, is it always Israel. Defeating the Philistines, David rejoices that Yahweh has 'broken through' his enemies, comparing this bursting or breaking to the breaking of waters (II Samuel 5:20). The comparison of defeating enemies to breaking waters can be read as an allusion to the defeat of the Egyptian pursuers and the separation of waters at the exodus; Israel is formed by such breaking. But in another kind of internal rending (I Samuel 15:27–8), the kingdom is torn away from Saul, a metaphor that is theatricalized in the story of Saul tearing Samuel's cloak in a desperate attempt to hold on to the priest's, and hence divine, favour. Later, the kingdom is torn away from Solomon as it was from Saul (I Kings 11:11–13), but in this instance, we are told that it is not all torn away for the sake of David. Yet if 'for David's sake' means not cutting off here, elsewhere David is told that the sword will never be far from his house (II Samuel 12:10). I rapidly enumerate some of the ruptures in the story of Israel – ruptures that the language of cutting so overtly signals – because they run counter to a strong drive in biblical scholarship to read that history as portraying development of identities, of the people, of the nation.

One version of 'development' that has been ascertained frequently in the books of Samuel is the 'rise of David', and with it, the corollary demise of Saul; supposedly, Saul's paranoia, ineffectuality and estrangement from Yahweh develop, and David's political astuteness, military success and favour with Yahweh develop. But as more sensitive biblical scholars are aware, the depiction of Saul is more difficult than a progressive demise and David is not always on the rise. In the very passage asserting that David's power is made secure by God – the oracle of Nathan that David will have a secure dynasty, a permanent House – there is a curiously contradictory exchange. David has been enjoying a brief period of peace; he has succesfully taken over the house of Saul, he has been made king of both the north and the south and is at rest from his battles, and he would like to build a house for God in the city of David. The response comes from the Almighty: '*You* want to build *me* a house?' (The pronouns are emphatic.) David is reminded that he is not God's patron; God is *his* patron. But then, after Yahweh corrects David on this score, clearly *limiting* the sphere of his influence, he proceeds to *expand* his power. It sounds as though David's ambition is simultaneously rebuked and rewarded. Here is the conflicting message: The Lord says:

> Are you going to build me a house for me to live in: I haven't lived in a house from the day I brought up the Israelites until this very day! Instead I've gone about in a tent wherever I happened to go throughout Israel. Did I ever speak with one of the staff-bearers of Israel whom I appointed to shepherd my people Israel and say, 'Why haven't you built me a house of cedar?'

It continues:

> I took you from the sheep pasture to be prince over my people Israel. I was with you wherever you went, clearing all your enemies from your path. And I shall make you a name like the names of the nobility in the land. I shall fix a place for my people Israel and plant it, so that it will remain where it is and never again be disturbed.

God clearly suggests that the idea of a house, of permanence, of stability, is abhorrent, and yet he offers David a house as though it were desirable indeed; as the passage reads, the promise of a House is far from an unequivocally welcome one. We readers could probably wrench our imaginations into some resolution of this conflict – certainly many scholars have separated the account into independent strands so that there is no conflict left – but the price would be the elimination of one of the key conflicts in the Bible: the tension between, on the one hand, a nostalgia for an Israel that is not fixed and not 'like the nations', nostalgia for a period of wandering dispossessed, for associating tent-dwelling with godliness and moral rectitude, and on the other hand, the longing for stability, for landed property, for a standing army, a dynastic leadership, in short, for becoming a nation among the nations.

Four chapters later, someone other than Yahweh will also refuse the offer from David to take up residence in a house. Called back from the front to cover up the king's adultery, Uriah the Hittite, Bathsheba's husband, will remind the king of Israel that:

> the ark, and Israel, and Judah, abide in booths; and my lord Joab, and the servants of my lord, are camping on the face of the field; and I, shall I go into my house to eat and to drink, and to lie with my wife? As you live, and as your soul lives, I will not do this thing.

> (II Samuel 11:11)

The passage casts a dark shadow back upon the earlier promise of a stable House. Everyone else has rallied to the field to meet the enemy – only David dwells in a house – and it is while he stays in that house that he commits adultery and orders murder: thereby, among other things, undoing that promise of permanence and stability to his House. Henceforth, the nation is rent with civil strife, and Nathan prophesies that the sword will never be far from David's House. It seems that a House is a bad idea after all. Conflicts like these are frequent because this text is not simply about the people, the nation or its king *amassing* power; these narratives are ambivalent about power. Even as the story of Israel depicts an effort to become 'like the nations', it depicts that very project as pernicious, for Israel depends for its identity on its distinctiveness, on being drawn 'from the nations'.

The institution of monarchy itself is presented from widely divergent points of view, often broadly drawn. How can the narrative depict the 'development of the monarchy' when it is unsettled about what the nation is, let alone what monarchy is, and what it means for this entity called a nation to be ruled by this entity called a king? Rather than presupposing settled answers, these stories are intently interested in exploring such questions of definition. Is a king one who will enslave the people and seize their property, as Samuel warns them in his stirring testimonial against the abuses of kingship? If so, why does the same Samuel who delivers a scathing critique against monarchy anoint, not one king, but two?

> He will take your sons and assign them to his chariot and cavalry, and they will run before his chariot. He will appoint for himself captains of thousands and captains of hundreds from them. They will plough his ploughland and harvest his harvest and make his weapons and the gear for his chariotry. Your daughters he will take as perfumers and cooks and bakers. Your best fields and vineyards and olive groves he will take and give to his servants. Your seed crops and vineyards he will tithe to provide for his officers and servants. Your best slaves, maidservants, cattle, and asses he will take use for his own work; and your flocks too he will tithe. You yourselves will become his slaves. Then you will *cry out* because of the king you have chosen for yourselves.
>
> (I Sam, 8:11–18; emphasis added)

The Israelites had 'cried out' in Egypt, groaning under slavery to Pharaoh, and the promised land was intended as the hope of deliverance from such unbridled tyranny, not as a re-enactment of their enslavement. But, at the height of Israel's peace and prosperity, when the proverbial milk and honey were flowing, King Solomon married – could it be? – a daughter of Pharaoh. Shortly after his adultery, David himself had set a captured population to work as slaves, brickmaking, to be precise, as the Israelites had in Egypt. Is this why Israel's liberator, Moses, is an Egyptian, to suggest that Israel is not simply delivered from Egypt, but fundamentally delivered to Egypt? How could Israel become Egyptianized when from its inception it is the antithesis?

On yet another level, the story has trouble keeping its agenda straight. If we thought it was preoccupied with the serious business of political and military history, the rise (or whatever that is) of monarchy (whatever it is), the narrative is interrupted by disturbing sex scenes like the story of David taking Bathsheba when he spots her bathing from his roof, or Amnon, overcome with passion, raping his half-sister. Do the struggles for Israel's definition have anything to do with these sexual scenes? The way in which these scenes are carefully interwoven with political events would indicate that they must: the David/Bathsheba affair is surrounded by the war with the Ammonites; their insult to David's emissaries (emasculating them by cutting off their tunics and shaving their beards) precedes the story, and the Israelite siege of the Ammonite capital, Rabbah, follows. Immediately after the Israelite victory over the Ammonites, the narrative turns to the rape of Tamar, which is followed by Absalom's murder of his elder brother (and the heir to the throne) and ultimately the story of civil war. Simply put, Israel is threatened from without and from within and in the very midst is an act of adultery and rape. This is no accident. Mieke Bal has made it clear that the book of Judges, which is so explicitly about war and political intrigue, is also about sexual violence; she even labels that sexual violence a kind of counter-coherence.[15] These are not separate spheres, public and private, that have impact on one another – such a reading would say that the private acts of David have public consequences, that David is torn between private desires and public duties, that David's private affections get in the way of his public role[16] – instead, politics and sexuality are so deeply and complexly integrated as to be inseparable. The text itself claims their virtual synonymity in the scene that delivers the divine judgement on David's illicit affair:

> Thus says the Lord, 'Behold, I will raise up evil against you out of your own house; and I will take your wives before your eyes, and give them to your neighbour, and he shall lie with your wives in the sight of this sun. For you did it in secret; but I will do this thing before all Israel, and before the sun.'

David's ostensibly private affair in fact implicates the entire nation: Absalom will sleep with David's concubines in a declaration of civil war.

There is no question that owning the sexual rights to a woman (or stealing them, as the case may be) confers power in patriarchy. As this is overtly the case for marriage to the king's daughter or sexual intercourse with the king's concubines, it is no less the case in other sexual exchanges. Lévi-Strauss taught us that the exchanges of women establish power relations between men; hence, David's dominance over other men is signalled by both his military and his sexual conquests.[17] When he is a fugitive from King Saul, garnering the support of the masses, he turns for provisions to a man he previously protected with his guerrilla band. The man denies David's power, refusing to acknowledge his obligation to him:

> Who is David? Who is the son of Jesse? There are many servants nowadays who are breaking away from their masters. Shall I take my bread and my water and my meat that I have killed for my shearers, and give it to men who come from I do not know where?

In an unsubtle commentary on his poor judgement, the man is named Nabal or Fool. David decides to show him who David is by destroying Nabal and his household, but before he can, this test of David's power and of his right to the throne takes an interesting turn; the way the story unfolds, David does not kill Nabal (Nabal conveniently drops dead just hearing of David's threat to him). Instead, David takes Nabal's wife. The power gain is presumably equivalent. The Fool's wife, Abigail, acknowledges David's power and colludes in her own exchange, engaging in a seduction that is entirely political; or should I say, politics is her seduction?

> And when the Lord has done to my lord according to all the good that he has spoken concerning you, and has appointed you prince over Israel . . . and when the Lord has dealt well with my lord, then remember your handmaid.
>
> (I Samuel 25:30–1)

David remembers right away and marries her.[18]

When David takes Bathsheba, he does not need her. He is at the height of his power, king of all he surveys, including Bathsheba. She is still the property of another man; in fact, two other men have rights to her before David, as the careful inclusion of her patronym (so rare for women in the Bible) 'daughter of Eliam' reminds us. Her husband, Uriah the Hittite, is a loyal servant of the king, and moreover, a loyal servant of God. His name probably means 'light of Yahweh' and we might well wonder what a Hittite, Israel's 'other', is doing with such a name – fighting his holy war while David lulls about at home during 'the time when kings go to war'. Hence, taking Bathsheba contrasts with the way David garnered power as a fugitive. In fact, the roles have reversed: now, David is the Fool. The king is greedy as Nabal was, and he denies his neighbour what is rightfully his, as Nabal denied David provisions and hospitality. Nathan's parable of the ewe-lamb drives home the point that this adultery is a violation of a property right: Bathsheba is compared to an animal, a favoured animal, to be sure, one that is like a daughter (alluding to the Hebrew wordplay on Bathsheba's name, *bath* = daughter), and the only one the poor man has; still, the polluting of his woman is analogous to the slaughter of his animal.

Like the incest taboo which enforces exchange with an outside group, the adultery taboo protects peaceful alliances.[19] But when women are stolen, rather than peaceably exchanged, all of the binding relational directions reverse, towards fear, anxiety and hostility. In the Bathsheba story, the consequence of stealing another man's wife is the murder of a loyal servant: David issues a death warrant for the husband who refuses to cover up the king's seduction. Chaos ensues: 'you have killed with the sword so the sword will never be far from your House', and the death of a child born of such an infraction is overdetermined. The biblical·division of the universe into pure and impure further suggests that we understand adultery as adulteration:

> Adulteration implies pollution, contamination, a 'base mixture', a wrong combination. . . . If society depends for its existence on certain rules governing what may be combined and what should be kept separate, then adultery, by bringing the wrong things together in the wrong places (or the wrong people in the wrong beds), offers an attack on those rules, revealing them to be arbitrary rather than absolute.[20]

Adultery challenges not only the rules as arbitrary, but the precarious identity of the societies that depend upon them for definition. The child of the adulterer cannot be admitted into 'the Congregation of the Lord, even to the tenth generation' (Deuteronomy 23:3), that is, it is banned for ever from the people of Israel. (The rabbis even relate the Hebrew term for illegitimate child, *mamzer*, to the adjective *zar*, 'a stranger', 'an alien'.)[21] For all the vigorous laws on adultery invoked to police its borders, adultery clearly threatens the very identity of Israel.

All of this anxiety about identity, political and sexual definition, is succinctly summarized in that one biblical word: *nabal*. It does not only mean fool, but also outcast, as in David's lament for Abner when he asks why he should have died as an outcast, *nabal*. It refers to someone who has severed himself from society through a moral transgression, someone who has forfeited his place in society by violating taboos that define the social order. As a verb, it means to violate, and it is used especially to indicate sexual violations: the rape of Tamar, the rape of Dinah, the rape in Judges 19, adultery in Jeremiah 23; but it is also used to indicate uttering false words, thereby disrupting the order of language. Its Akkadian stem was used to indicate breaking away (as a ṣtone) or tearing away, and that Akkadian sense of rupture is still attached to the Hebrew word used for an adulterer in ancient Israel where sexual violation signals breaking away, rupturing the norm. A variant of *nabal* means corpse, and in ancient Israel a corpse represents another rupture, this time not only from the social order, but from the order of life itself. Death represents the strongest degree of uncleanness, an 'irreparable separation from God's life-giving power and from the centre of life, the cult'.[22] But the outcast is not so very far from the corpse, for as a bearer of evil, the one cast out of society had not only no home, but 'no name' (Job 30:8). Who is a *nabal* and who is not, what makes one cast out and another not, is of course another way of asking what is an Israelite and what is not, what is Israel and what is not, for the outcasts define Israel's borders.

Finally, to return to that prominent story about Nabal in the David narratives, the story of David's dealings with Abigail's husband: 'Nabal is his name and *nabal* is his behaviour.' Again, Nabal has violated the covenant agreement by which David protects him and in turn has earned protection; therefore, he becomes an outcast from the order and soon becomes a corpse, allegorizing the meanings of his name. In all this, David is made the foil for Nabal; unlike the Fool, David is wise, knows the rules and follows them, knows wise words when he hears them, knows, that is, not to shed blood so that he may inherit the kingdom. But in the parallel scene with Bathsheba, where David marries another wife of another man who dies, David is not contrasted to Nabal. David becomes the *nabal*. While it is not made an explicit appellation in this scene, the term is most consistently used for an adulterer, and it is explicit in the next scene where Amnon rapes Tamar in an echo of David's forcible taking of Bathsheba. Retrospectively, what Tamar says of Amnon becomes an indictment of David: 'This is not a thing men do in Israel.' And like all the other scenes where *nabal* is used to signal sexual violation, David is engulfed in violence. This is not a thing men do in Israel, but David *is* Israel. At his height, when the House of David is synonymous with the nation, David behaves like an outcast. How can the House of David both define Israel and be cast out of Israel? Where is the nation when the king is in exile? What happens to the promise of a House that will be stable for ever when its recipient is a *nabal*, like the no-name, homeless ones?

The Derridian insight that the margin is the centre becomes, in this case, a perception not only that the Israelite is defined by the outcast, but that the Israelite defends himself with such ferocity against the outcast out of fear of the outcast, the violator, within him, even out of attraction to that violator. *Nebalim* is used for Israel's enemies, the 'other', but it is also used for the Benjamites when they make themselves the enemies of Israel's other tribes, and it is eventually applied to all of Israel herself (Deuteronomy 32:6). When Amnon rapes Tamar, she protests that he should not act like a *nabal*. Her objection, 'This is not a thing men do in Israel', condenses all of the allusions the term has to moral, sexual and national identity. In fact, rape is a thing men do in Israel and the law has provided for it: if the woman belongs to no one else, then he need only marry her, as Tamar reminds her assailant (Deuteronomy 22:28). But Tamar is his half-sister, and incest is not a thing men should do in Israel. Like adultery, incest confuses carefully drawn kinship boundaries, the narrow space permissible between exogamy and incest. His rape makes Amnon virtually a non-Israelite, like all the *nebalim*, a non-entity. Following his sexual violation, he will die (fulfilling that other sense of *nabal*, corpse), and even his death is engulfed in an ever-widening circle of violence, moving from his brother (Absalom murders him and is murdered) to the entire family (the civil war, the usurpation of Adonijah, the assassinations of the kings of Judah and eventually the forced exile of the population). This kind of violence attends each instance in the Bible where *nabal* signals a sexual violation. In Genesis, the rape of Dinah leads to war with Israel; in Judges, the rape of the concubine gives way to war with Israel; and in both cases, these are wars of definition, establishing borders, who is Israel and who is not.

The meaning of *nabal* deepens when we view David's act of adultery with Bathsheba, not only in the light of the exchanges that characterize his other marriages, but in the light of the much larger issue of adultery that pervades the biblical text. Israel is continually whoring after other gods, as the Bible pointedly puts it; the faithfulness or faithlessness of the people towards their God is always cast in sexual terms: 'I am a jealous God, you will have none but me.' It is a theology obsessed with the possibility and actuality of betrayal, with 'going astray' as the term for both faithlessness and sexual transgression. Idolatry is repeatedly figured as sexual infidelity: 'So shameless was her [Israel's] whoring that at last she polluted the country; she committed adultery with lumps of stone and pieces of wood' (Jeremiah 3:9). It is in this context that the king of Israel goes astray. Even within the Bathsheba story itself, desire for God and human desire are homologized, for David's adultery is set in stark relief – not, as we would expect, to the fidelity of Bathsheba's husband to her – but to Uriah's faithfulness to God. Under the injunctions of holy war, to sleep with his own wife would be to be faithless to God; it is that fidelity that Uriah maintains despite the obvious attractiveness of his wife and despite his drunkenness, and it is that fidelity to God that he finally dies for. Meanwhile, David, so very careful about idolatry, has 'gone astray' from God after all.

In the act of adultery, David has violated a whole series of commandments: 'You shall not kill; you shall not commit adultery; you shall not steal; you shall not bear false witness against your neighbour.' And just before these laws regulating social order – the commandments about not killing, not committing adultery, not taking what is your neighbour's – are the commandments about the exclusivity of desire for God. 'You shall have no gods except me.' A relation between the final five commandments and the earlier ones that specify loyalty and gratitude and exclusivity of love towards God is thereby established. The logic could be paraphrased: 'you shall love only me, you shall not love your neighbour's god' and that means that 'you shall not covet your neighbour's god, you shall not covet your neighbour's wife'. Hence, in Yahweh's response to David's adultery

with Bathsheba, it is not at all clear who David betrayed, her husband or
God, for the infidelities are inseparable: 'A sword will never be lacking in
your house, because you treated *me* with contempt and took the wife of
Uriah the Hittite to be your own wife.'

Both sexual fidelity and divine fidelity are preoccupations of a narrative
that tends to construct identity as someone or some people *set apart*, with
boundaries that could be mapped, ownership that could be titled. But if, as
I have been arguing, the parameters of Israel's identity are very much at
issue – which God is allowed and which is not, and which woman is allowed
and which is not – then the identity of the nation and the people is not
already mapped, but in the process of being anxiously drawn and redrawn,
and we must address the prior question: *is* this people set apart? Or is its
hankering to 'go astray' an effort to cross boundaries, or at least to blur
them by being God's and being someone else's too? Which people are
outside and which are inside the boundaries of the community of Israel?
For all the legal protestations to the contrary, to seek clearly circumscribed
definitions in this text is to be frustrated at every turn. The biblical
narrative's effort to construct Israel's past is no less than an effort to
construct Israel, but it is not a construction in the sense of building a
building, nor is it a national spirit unfolding, an institution growing or an
organic personality flowering. Instead, 'Israel' is an inconsistent, fractured,
complex and multiple concept: a people who are bound by a law that they
refuse to obey, a people who are defined by their nomadism but who are
promised a land, a people who have a land only to lose it; and even these
formulations are misleadingly stable, for each presupposes 'a people' when
defining them is very much a part of the task of the 'history'. One way the
story defines the people is that it is those who claim a united history, and
they are only a people so long as they remember (or adopt) that shared
history; yet they are forever forgetting, needing to be reminded. Another
way is that they are a people who have entered into a covenant with their
God – a covenant that stipulates they must not go astray – but they are
continually doing just that. And whatever Israel is, even provisionally, it is
always threatened with being 'cut off', disinherited by Yahweh, even with
being not-Israel. For once disinherited, Israel will not be on its own,
struggling for independent survival; once disinherited, Israel will cease to
be. In this sense, the deal struck in Exodus, 'I will be your God if you will
be my people', could be rephrased 'You will be *a* people if, and only if, I,
and only I, am your God.' That means that when Israel 'goes astray' it risks
losing not just prosperity, but that promised identity, 'Israel', not only
because whoring after Baal and Asherah or whomever means losing some
version of cultural distinctiveness but because under the terms of the
contract Israel is constituted by the exclusivity of her object choice: 'You
shall have no gods except me.' If they forget their history or go astray from
their God, they will be 'no more', but because they always do, they already

are 'no more'. Adultery, rape, the people going astray: these violations are not just violations of commandments; they are violations of various identity-constructs and they become tests of definition in a text that is anxious about who this story is about, and whose story it is anyway.

NOTES

* An earlier version of this essay appeared as 'The Histories of David: Biblical Story and Biblical Scholarship' in *'Not In Heaven': Literary Readings of Biblical Texts*, ed. Jason Rosenblatt and Joseph Silterson Jr., Bloomington, Indiana University Press, 1991, pp. 192–210, and in *Critical Inquiry*, 19 (Autumn 1992), pp. 132–52.
1 Like any discipline, biblical scholarship is not monolithic. In particular, recent interest in literary questions is beginning to make headway into the dominant methodology I characterize. See especially David Gunn, 'The Story of King David', *Journal for the Study of the Old Testament* (*JSOT*), 1978, who argues that the so-called succession narrative is not best described as history writing; J.P. Fokkelman, *Narrative Art and Poetry* in the Books of Samuel, 2 vols, Assen, Van Gorcum, 1981, 1986; Robert Polzin, *Samuel and the Deuteronomist*, New York, Harper & Row, 1989, who is explicitly bracketing the concerns that preoccupy traditional biblical scholars, especially pp. 1–17; Meir Sternberg, *The Poetics of Biblical Narrative*, Bloomington, Indiana University Press, 1985; and Peter Miscall, *I Samuel: A Literary Reading*, Bloomington, Indiana University Press, 1986. Furthermore, not all traditional biblical scholars who are interested in sources depict a developmental vision of history for the Samuel narratives. Among the notable exceptions is R.N. Whybray, *The Succession Narrative*, London, SCM Press, 1968, who points out that there are too many personal scenes for this narrative to be characterized as history; instead, he regards it as political propaganda.
2 A recent survey of the major positions held by biblical scholars in this century shows how consistent their presuppositions are despite their different conclusions, for these theories take different stands on the same issue: the nature and extent of two layers of redacted material in the biblical text and on how those two layers came together. The two layers are the Dtr. and non-Dtr.. Dtr. means the Deuteronomic and/or Deuteronomistic, the distinction being part of the dispute about the 'nature and extent of the sources'. See Suzanne Boorer, 'The Importance of a Diachronic Approach: The Case of Genesis-Kings', *Catholic Biblical Quarterly*, 51, 1989, pp. 195–208.
3 Robert Oden Jr, *The Bible without Theology*, New York, Harper & Row, 1987, chapter. 1, p. 6. I am indebted to Oden's chapter for bringing the role of German historicism in biblical scholarship to the fore.
4 Georg Iggers, *The German Conception of History*, Middletown, Wesleyan University Press, 1983, p. 9.
5 See Iggers' discussion of Droysen, ibid., p. 106.
6 Johann Gustav Droysen, *Outline of the Principles of History*, trans. and intro. E. Benjamin Andrews, Boston, Ginn & Co., 1897. Partial translation of *Historik: Vorlesungen über Enzyklopedie und Methodologie der Geschichte*, ed. R. Hubner, Munich, R. Oldernbourg, 8th edn 1977.
7 This does not necessarily mean the historian is an empiricist. Events are 'only in part accessible to the senses. The rest has to be felt (*empfunden*), inferred (*geschlossen*), or divined (*errathen*)'.
8 Quoted by Michel Foucault in 'Nietzsche, Genealogy, History', in *The Foucault Reader*, ed. Paul Rabinow, New York, Pantheon, 1984, p. 88.

9 See Doris Summer, 'Foundational Fictions: When History Was Romance in Latin America', *Salmagundi*, 82–3, 1989, pp. 111–41.
10 Julius Wellhausen, *Prolegomena to the History of Ancient Israel*, Cleveland, Meridian, 1957, p. 228.
11 ibid., p. 231.
12 While my focus here is on the influence of German historicism on biblical study, classical philology had an equally formative role.
13 Martin Noth, 'The Deuteronomistic History', (1967), trans. J. Doull *et al.* from German, *JSOT*, 1981, pp. 80–1. This thesis of Martin Noth was considerably revised by Gerhard von Rad and Frank Cross who noted the positive elements in the Deuteronomistic history that conflicted with this sweeping principle. This critical history is summarized in P. Kyle McCarter Jr., *II Samuel, The Anchor Bible*, Garden City, Doubleday, 1984, pp. 4–8.
14 Foucault, op. cit., pp. 145–72.
15 Mieke Bal, *Death and Dissymmetry: The Politics of Coherence in the Book of Judges*, Chicago, University of Chicago Press, 1988.
16 On King David, see David Gunn, *The Story of King David*, Sheffield, JSOT, 1978; and Kenneth R.R. Gros Louis, 'The Difficulty of Ruling Well: King David of Israel', *Semeia*, 1977, 8, pp. 15–33.
17 Claude Lévi-Strauss, *The Elementary Structures of Kinship*, Boston, Beacon Press, 1969.
18 Sexual and political power are so completely fused again in the story of Saul's concubine that it is not quite right to claim that one is a metaphor for the other; they are not distinct enough to stand in for one another. Upon the death of Saul his general, Abner, sleeps with one of the deceased king's concubines, Rizpah. When the king's son learns of it he is incensed; the act is clearly a sign of pretension to the throne, for the competition over who will succeed Saul – his son or his general – is fought out over sexual ownership of the concubine (II Samuel 6:8). Abner is sufficiently incensed over the contest about 'the woman' to vow to betray Saul's son by joining the enemy David in a treaty. Needless to say, his betrayal is cast in the same terms – traffic in women – for the condition David sets to enter into any agreement with Abner ups the ante: David will take, not one of Saul's concubines, but Saul's daughter, Michal, thereby crushing all hopes for succession for both Abner and Saul's son.
19 Lévi-Strauss, op. cit., p. 68.
20 Tony Tanner, *Adultery in the Novel*, Baltimore, Johns Hopkins University Press, 1979, pp. 12, 13.
21 Joseph Levitsky, 'The Illegitimate Child in Jewish Law', *Dor le Dor: The Jewish Biblical Quarterly*, 18, i, Fall 1989, pp. 6–12.
22 W.M.W. Roth, 'NBL', *Vetus Testamentum*, 10, 1960, p. 401.

Chapter 15

Tomb of the sacred prostitute: The *Symposium*

Shannon Bell

This paper disentombs the ancient priestess Diotima, whose shadowy presence has haunted the phallic representations of woman fragmented in western thought and the masculine imaginary. It is in postmodernity – where the bodily boundaries of sex and gender, inside and outside, are losing definition – that this first woman of western philosophy can be reclaimed as a spirit, a mother and a whore. I read Diotima[1] as a post-modern manifestation of the love-goddess Aphrodite: a goddess whose flesh is as important as her spirit, who simultaneously teaches the receiving and the giving of pleasure and the receiving and giving of knowledge. This (re-)reading of one of western philosophy's founding texts, the *Symposium*, from the position of the subterranean presence of the hetairae of ancient Greece in this and others of Plato's texts, could only be under-taken at this postmodern moment, in which many feminisms prevail from diverse subject positions:[2] the historical moment in which prostitutes have collectively constructed their own political identity.[3]

My approach will deploy the fourfold rule of deconstruction decoded and developed by Eve Tavor Bannet in her book, *Structuralism and the Logic of Dissent*. In a reading of Derrida's famous X, Tavor Bannet inscribes four Vs in the blank spaces of the X. She interprets these as Derrida's method, writing them as: Division, Articulation, the PiVot and the Veil of Displacement. These strategies for reading a text, strategies of deconstruction, open the text to the possibility of a subversive reading and to the political project of the reader. Division 'deconstructs [the] notion of the text as a single, coherent and identifiable entity by seeking out each text's inconsistencies, incoherences and obscurities and by developing them into full scale contradictions'.[4] Articulation dissolves the boundaries between the inside of the text and its outside, and grafts different texts onto one another. The PiVot reverses accustomed hierarchies by making the term which is customarily the minor term of the couple the condition of operation of both terms: 'In the pivot . . . the critical text actively inter-venes in the text which is being read by reversing its assumptions.'[5] The Veil of Displacement is what Tavor Bannet claims distinguishes Derrida from other critics who have engaged in 'habits of thought' – cum textual operations – that correspond to Division, Articulation and the PiVot. Derrida, she suggests, displaces the textual operations that others engage in in two ways:

> First . . . he divides, articulates and pivots in a different place from everyone else: he divides what we are accustomed to thinking of as distinct, and pivots hierarchies that we have not previously noticed, much less questioned. And secondly, he gives these operations new names.[6]

Mine is an *unfaithful* reading: a reading that 'strays from the author, the authorized, produc[ing] that which does not hold as a reproduction, as a representation'.[7] My infidelity arises out of a particular female position from which Plato has never yet been read. I read and write from a position which can be figured in terms of the clitoris (Plato, it can be argued, read and wrote from the position of the phallic eidos): what Gayatri Spivak names a 'short-hand for woman's excess in all areas of reproduction and practice, an excess that must be brought under control to keep business going as usual'.[8] The clitoris represents that part of female sexuality – pleasure – that is superfluous to reproduction; a site of radical excess, which provides a point of departure for an affirmative feminism, in this case a reading of the politically and philosophically active woman in Platonic thought. The physicality of the concept of the 'radical excess' of the clitoris, its immediate and powerful relation to physical pleasure, seems radically at odds with Plato's exoteric attempt to orient the philosophic *eros* away from the body towards the *Idea*. Yet the sexual body is the underside, the shadow of the spirit, that had to be mastered; a subtext always present in the text's denial of the body.

I read classical antiquity as carnivalized antiquity, defining 'carnivalization' as the intrusion of play, humour and folk culture into high discourses such as philosophy. I focus on mimicked speech, rhetoric and the sexual body.[9] These are embodied in Plato's works in the hetairae – the female bodies at the centre of Greek philosophic discourse and at the margin of Greek patriarchy, the infidel of patriarchy. Carnivalization gives rise to a transcoding displacement between the idealized and degraded images of the physical body, between philosophic and vulgar discourses, and between high and low locations in the social domain.

To read from the position of the philosophic clitoris is to read the space between two contending discursive approaches to the history of philosophy: the phallocentric tradition upholding the classical canon, and the gynocentric strategies of reading opposed to it by many feminist theorists and philosophers.[10] It is also reading the space unentered even by the best of politicized homosexual readings, specifically David Halperin's excellent reading of Diotima's/Socrates'[11] speech: 'Why Is Diotima a Woman?'[12]

In reading from the standpoint of the philosophical clitoris and reappropriating the sophistic-sexual female subject from the text, one must be cognizant of three things. Firstly, that the excess of the clitoris does not make any radical distinction between the physicality of female pleasure and the activity of philosophy itself; so-called physical pleasure is the conduit for so-called spiritual pleasure. (This is why I substitute the concept 'philosophical clitoris' for clitoris.) The excess of the clitoris is no simple other of the excess of the thinking mind. This is very significant in re-reading the logocentric element of Diotima's speech in the *Symposium*.

Secondly, patriarchy will make every effort to split off the 'mere physicality' of clitoral excess and to bring it under control, as Plato does in Book V of *The Republic*. When Plato, in *The Republic*, brings philosophy and the city (i.e. politics) together, he is attempting to bring the excess of the clitoris, which, I will argue, had allowed him to write an intellectual sameness between male and female and to include men and women in the guardian class, under a uterine reproduction-oriented organization.

Thirdly, the uterine social organization (the punctuation of the world in terms of the reproduction of future generations, where the uterus is the chief agent and means of production) cannot simply be written off in favour of a clitoral. 'The uterine social organization should, rather, be "situated" through the understanding that it has so far been established by *excluding* a clitoral social organization.'[13] Embodied in the sacred prostitute, in practice and in representation, is the *unity of the womb and clitoris*. The temples of sacred prostitution (the best known of which were the temples of Aphrodite in Corinth) were oriented simultaneously to clitoral, uterine and spiritual purposes: sexuality, fertility and spirituality were not · radically distinguished.[14] In the secularized survival of the sacred prostitute, the hetairae,[15] it has been argued that the sexual function was defined exclusively in terms of male desire; I would disagree: hetairae were the only women who were able to experience and express desire with one another[16] and with male patrons. Even if one concedes that the hetairae were primarily objects of male desire, the excess of the clitoris survives in their pursuit of philosophy, excess to the city.

A number of hetairae, contemporaries of Plato, were active as sophistic philosophers and teachers. Aspasia, a well-known hetaira, ran a gynaeceum for prostitutes where she taught rhetoric, philosophy, religion, poetry, not only to prostitutes but also to statesmen, including Pericles and Alcibiades, and philosophers including Socrates.[17] Socrates cites Aspasia as his teacher of rhetoric and politics in the *Menexenus*. Alciphron, a third-century Athenian rhetorician and epistolographer, writes these words in the hand of Thaïs, another well-known Greek hetaira:

Do you suppose that a professor is any different from a courtesan?. . .
As for teaching young men we do quite as well as they. Compare a

courtesan like Aspasia with a sophist like Socrates, and consider which produced the better pupils: the woman trained Pericles, the man Critias.[18]

Feminist philosophers and theorists have tended to take up and counter-theorize what they read as the dominant image of women in the canon texts: that of woman as reproductive body. In so doing they have both silenced another female body written in those texts, the libidinal female body, and (re)inscribed a binary opposition within the category woman, polarizing the reproductive and the libidinal, reducing difference to this opposition and privileging one side – reproduction – as essentially female and therefore as superior. The readings of two innovative feminist philosopher/critics, Wendy Brown and Page du Bois, will serve as examples. Wendy Brown reads Plato's personification of philosophy as a female and Socrates' equation of philosophy with procreation as a feminine critique of the dominant masculine ethos of the Athenian *polis*.[19] Brown cites Socrates' discussion of philosophy's lovers in *The Republic*:

> men for whom philosophy is most suitable go . . . into exile and leave her abandoned and unconsummated . . . while . . . other unworthy men come to her . . . and disgrace her . . . of those who have intercourse with her, some are worthless and the many worthy of bad things. . . . When men unworthy of education come near her and keep company in an unworthy way, what sort of notions and opinions will we say they beget? Won't they be truly fit to be called sophisms . . .?
>
> (495b–6a)[20]

For Socrates, philosophy is simultaneously sexual and maternal. Yet Brown appropriates only the maternal metaphor and marks the Platonic female body as the maternal body. She misses the fact that for Plato philosophy was simultaneously cognitive and carnal. Page du Bois, in *Sowing the Body*,[21] argues that Socrates' incorporation of the female activities of procreation, generation, birthing, labour, nurturance into his own body, the body of the male philosopher, opened the way to the subsequent philosophical production of woman as lack. But one can only hang this on Socrates/Plato if his 'maternal' metaphors are read as absent libidinal content and if Socratic philosophy is understood as strictly a male activity.

I read the maternal body as a trace of the prostitute body; this trace has been lost in contemporary phallocentric and gynocentric readings. Socrates, identifying his philosophic powers with the midwife's skills, says in the *Theaetetus*: 'with the drugs and incantations they administer, mid-wives can either bring on the pains of travail or allay them at their will' (149d).[22] 'Midwife' can be read with awareness that many hetairae worked as midwives, perpetuating the simultaneity of the procreative and sexual aspects of the sacred prostitute: body as spirit: body/spirit. William Sanger, in *The History of Prostitution*, connects the skills of midwifery with sorcery, and both with the hetairae: 'retired courtesans often combined the manufacture of . . . charms with the business of a midwife'.[23]

Socrates incorporates the female body into his speech as the mimicked speech of his teachers[24] and as metaphoric identification with the midwife. To read this appropriation solely as maternal, as do Brown and du Bois, is to overwrite the other aspect of the female body present in Socrates' speech and thus in Plato's writing: the philosophic clitoris. Brown and du Bois' readings occlude the weighty presence of an active speaking sexual female subject doing philosophy; she is reduced to a spiritualized, maternal referent for desexualized philosophy. This is, as well, the error of David Halperin who poses the questions: 'Why is Diotima a woman?' 'Why did Plato select a woman to initiate Socrates into the mysteries of a male, homosexual desire?' 'What qualifies her to be a professor of (male) desire?' 'Why does Plato introduce a woman to enlighten a group of articulate paederasts about the mysteries of erotic desire?'[25] These are well-posed questions. And Halperin, writing from a homosexual/feminist subject position, provides an interesting twist on feminist readings of Diotima. Yet he writes the same female body. He argues that 'woman' is a *trope* in the representational economy of Plato's text: she is the figure by means of which Plato images male philosophical values. Halperin claims that a double movement underlies Plato's erotic dialogue: 'men project their own sexual experience onto women only to reabsorb it themselves in the guise of a "feminine" character'.[26] The crux of Halperin's reading is that the interdependence of the sexual and reproductive capacities contained in Diotima's metaphors of erotic doctrine can refer only to male physiology; in women, he argues, the sexual and the reproductive are separate, therefore the unified sexual and reproductive allegory in the *Symposium* must be read figuratively, not literally. Halperin's, like other feminist readings, forgets that the sexual, the reproductive and the spiritual were simultaneously embodied in the sacred prostitute in the ancient world.

Both the male philosophical tradition and the feminist anti-tradition explain Diotima's presence in the *Symposium* as the teacher of Socrates on the grounds that she is not an ordinary woman but a desexualized, spiritualized, religious priestess. Socrates introduces Diotima as 'a woman who was deeply versed in . . . many . . . fields of knowledge. It was she who brought about a ten years' postponement of the great plague of Athens on the occasion of a certain sacrifice' (201d).[27] Robin May Schott, in *Cognition and Eros*, writes:

> Diotima is not merely a woman; she is a priestess. According to Greek
> religious practices, those women eligible to serve the gods were either

virgin or past child-bearing years. . . . Plato admits into the dialogue the role of the priestess as a mouthpiece for the gods, along with the presupposition that she had become desexualized, in order to transform her into the mouthpiece for philosophy . . . it is the abdication of her sexuality that allows Diotima access to wisdom.[28]

Andrea Nye, in her radical reading, 'The Hidden Host: Irigaray and Diotima at Plato's *Symposium*', reads Diotima as the host of the symposium rather than the feminine absence which Irigaray makes her. Nye constructs Diotima as one of the surviving remnants of the Minoan heritage of female spiritual leaders: a feminine theological understratum of the pagan-cum-Christian-warrior-father-god.

It occurs neither to the phallocentric reader nor to his gynocentric critic that it is precisely Diotima's sacred sexuality that allows her access to 'divine paederasty' or wisdom. Schott can equate female sexuality with 'childbearing', portray the priestess as a mouthpiece for the male gods rather than participating in the divine Aphrodite, only because she ignores the hetaira, the sexual female body, who practised philosophy in ancient Greece; hetairae, hardly 'desexualized' women, practised as both midwives and priestesses. Nye, like Schott, absents the sexual in Diotima's speech, reducing it to abstract generativity:

Diotima's theory of love does not focus on pleasure; genital pleasure in the sense of a private sensation is not mentioned in her philosophy. . . . Although Diotima grounds sexual desire in a principle of nature, that principle involves neither women's reproductive organs nor men's penises. Instead, it has to do with the fact of mortality and the impulse of living things to perpetuate themselves.[29]

I read Diotima as a sophist-hetairae – a trace of the sacred prostitute, servant of the divine Aphrodite, a sophistic teacher of love. The very name Diotima is a trace of the temple prostitute or priestess; Diotima means 'one who honours God', and the sacred prostitute worked in 'service of the god or goddess'.[30] There is textual and contextual evidence to mark Diotima a hetaira. The symposium was a central part of Athenian social and sexual life. It was a gathering dedicated to eating, drinking, games, philosophical discourse and sexual intercourse among men and between men and hetairae: carnal and psychic paederasty: the spilling of the seed in vain. There are two women present in the *Symposium*: the flute girl or *auletris*, hired to perform musical and sexual services for the host and his guests, whose absence is requested at the beginning of psychic paederasty, high philosophical discourse; and Diotima: an absence made present as mimicked speech – low discourse entombed within the high which serves to transcode the high.

Diotima was Socrates' 'instructress in the art of love' (201d). The context of her speech in the *Symposium*, and its location in the text, gives a dual meaning to the art of love: philosophy and sexuality. She prefaces her discussion of the function which love performs among men with a parable of Eros' birth. According to myth, Eros was conceived at the festival of Aphrodite, the Greek goddess of love, beauty and fertility who was originally the Great Mother Goddess. In *Prostitution and Society*, Fernando Henriques has contended that in the archaic world, the goddesses of fertility were also goddesses of prostitution.[31] If so, then Aphrodite later became fragmented. In the Greek pantheon of gods, fertility was associated with Demeter, sexuality with Aphrodite. 'The sexual functions of women were concentrated in the various manifestations of Aphrodite . . . especially the persona called Aphrodite Pandemos [of All the People] and Aphrodite Hetaera, who was neither wife nor mother.'[32] Yet as described by Diotima, Aphrodite is unfragmented, a deity who unites the reproductive and the libidinal. And in Diotima's construction Eros similarly combines the sexual and reproductive; in fact, he fulfils the same function as the sacred prostitute, since he mediates between the gods and man. Diotima's Eros is 'a very powerful spirit', a daimon, 'half-way between god and man' (202e). And the sacred prostitute was in a sense the materiality of Eros: the real body through which man could have intercourse with the gods. Eros, like the hetairae, was 'adept in sorcery, enchangement, and seduction' (203d). Walter Hamilton, in his translation of Plato's *Symposium*, marks Eros 'a true sophist'.[33]

Diotima's speech contains the major contradiction out of which Plato's philosophy is produced: the relationship between the body and the soul. Its first part could be read as the teaching of a sophist.[34] Socrates says that his speech is a composite of 'some lessons' that he was given by Diotima (201d). She taught Socrates that, contrary to his assumption, Love is the lover rather than the beloved; also, that there are many equally valuable types of love: longing for happiness and the good in athletics, business, philosophy, and so on, in addition to the aspect of love that has been singled out as definitive. In another teaching, Diotima instructed Socrates that 'To love is to bring forth the beautiful in both the body and the soul' (206b); and we know that the priestess was the one through whose body one entered the sacred arena and attained the beautiful. Using the language of female reproductive experience to delimit generation of the beautiful, Diotima asserts that 'We are all of us prolific, Socrates, in body and in soul' (206c). Then, following the image of the unified body/soul, the body and soul are separated. '[T]hose whose procreancy is of the body turn to woman as the object of their love, and raise a family. . . . But those whose procreancy is of the spirit rather than the flesh . . . conceive and bear things of the spirit' (208c–9a). Mortals desire to generate because they desire immortality of the flesh and/or of the spirit. Diotima privileges offspring of the soul.

Diotima's speech becomes logocentric in proclaiming a hierarchy of love upwards from the body to the soul, and phallogocentric in privileging correct paederasty – philosophical intercourse among male lovers. It is this logocentric moment of Diotima's speech that is appropriated by philosophy as truth. Diotima sets out an ascending ladder of love that any candidate studying the philosophy of love must master:

> the candidate for this initiation cannot . . . begin too early to devote himself to the beauties of the body. First of all . . . he will fall in love with the beauty of one individual body, so that his passion may give life to noble discourse. Next he must consider how nearly related the beauty of any one body is to the beauty of any other . . . he must set himself to be the lover of every lovely body. . . . Next he must grasp that the beauties of the body are as nothing to the beauties of the soul, so that whenever he meets with spiritual loveliness, even in the husk of an unlovely body, he will find it beautiful to fall in love with and cherish. . . . And from this he will be led to contemplate the beauty of laws and institutions . . . his attention should be diverted from institutions to the sciences, so that he may know the beauty of every kind of knowledge . . . until, confirmed and strengthened, he will come upon one single form of knowledge, the knowledge of the beaut[iful].
>
> (210a–d).

Standard phallocentric and gynocentric readings, as opposed to a carnivalesque reading of Diotima's famous construction of truth, are based on the conception of the body as contamination, or as mere resource, which the soul must control and transcend in order to attain the purity of thought necessary for true knowledge. However, if one reads from the position of the philosophic clitoris, the body/mind/soul is one. Through the holy prostitute one came to the gods; her body was a conduit to the Divine Body. Thus the entire passage, beginning with one body and culminating in knowledge of the beautiful (truth), is a metaphor for the sacred prostitute. Plato presents Socrates' mimicry of Diotima as making no reference in speech to the philosophic clitoris, that is, to the sophistic-sexual body in her outline of the hierarchy of forms of love. Diotima does not speak of her own body; yet she is powerfully present as the active speaking body. Entombed within the *Symposium* is the body of the sacred prostitute. She is the body which acts as a conduit to the spirit – from one lovely body to many lovely bodies, to every lovely body, to all bodies lovely and unlovely, to the beauty of the spirit: truth. One reaches the Truth of the Sacred Body through the body here and now, as in sacred prostitution. The underside of Diotima's speech is the privileging of the low body: the desiring and libidinal body.

In Diotima's speech homosexuality is proclaimed a higher form of love than love of woman. However, only if Diotima is perceived as desexualized can she be taken as simply colluding in a 'male identified' fashion with the

Platonic privileging of homosexuality as closer to the spirit. If Diotima is recognized as the sacred priestess, 'servant of Aphrodite', then the absence of any reference to her own body, her form of love – sophistic/sexual intercourse – is a pregnant silence. Diotima's speech about homosexual love (209c–d) is a referent for the other form of love in which the seed is spilled in vain, taken from dissemination, as it were; sophistic-sexual love.

If we briefly take a look at another hetaira connected with Socrates in Xenophon's *Memorabilia*, Theodote, who was a disciple and companion of Socrates rather than his teacher, we find a trace of Diotima. When Theodote invites Socrates to come and see her often he replies that it is difficult for him to find the time, saying: 'I have the dear girls, who won't leave me day or night; they are studying potions with me and spells.'[35] Leo Strauss, unable to believe that Socrates could have female friends, reads this as a closeted reference to Socrates' male companions: 'By his female friends he probably means his companions who seek him for the sake of philosophizing; he calls them female for the same reason for which he sometimes swears by Hera.'[36] I, on the other hand, read this as a straightforward and 'out' reference: Socrates is taught by hetairae and learns from them; he exchanges the teaching of potions and spells with hetairae. This reinforces my reading of Diotima – she who was able to prevent a plague on Athens by a sacrifice – as a trace of the sacred prostitute.

For Strauss, 'female friend' is a cover for 'young man'. From my point of view, Plato's privileging of homosexuality in the *Symposium* is also a referent for Socrates' connection with hetairae. Diotima's teaching is immortalized through her friendship with Socrates. The presence of Diotima, the prostitute priestess in Platonic drag, queers Strauss' way of looking at 'friend'. Female friend could mean female friend; it could be a referent for beautiful young man; and beautiful young man could be an inverted referent for hetairae, by Hera.

Socrates' career as a student of two hetairae (Diotima and Aspasia) and teacher of another suggests a new reading of the teaching of gender equality in Book V of *The Republic*. Book V has been read by the canon as a masterpiece of ironic discourse (Leo Strauss and his followers),[37] or it has been accepted at face value only if woman is desexualized and degendered. Read from the position of the philosophic clitoris, Socrates' much cited statement that

> there is no practice of a city's governors which belongs to woman because she's a woman, or to man because he's man; but the natures are scattered alike among both animals; and woman participates according to nature in all practices, and man in all

(455d–e)

can be removed from the realms of irony and logocentrism. Socrates and Plato[38] had a model, an experience of women behaving as prescribed in

Book V of *The Republic*, and that lived body was the hetairae. Thus Plato's community of wives provides a secularized trace of the community of priestesses serving the temples of Aphrodite. The 'sacred marriages' (458e), as Plato names the unions of male and female guardians, can be read as a trace of the sacred marriages of sacred prostitutes to the god/ goddess and to man. Plato contends that woman's function and role in reproduction are irrelevant in terms of her participation in the public sphere. Once Plato has admitted women to the guardian class, however, they become subject to uterine sexual organization: the best women and men have intercourse with each other as often as possible to beget the best children; only when women and men are beyond the age of procreation are they free to have intercourse with whomever they want.

What is the purpose of a (re-)reading such as I have attempted, aside, of course, from the pleasures of carnival? The unfaithful reading has a political project: overwriting the closure of authority – authority of meaning, authority of the author, authority of the canon interpretations constructing the history of philosophy and authority of the institutions governing academic discourse. It reinscribes and reincarnates in western thought the maternal, the sexual and the spiritual female body: the divine Aphrodite unfragmented.

NOTES

1 This reading is a gift for Gad Horowitz.
2 Postmodernism, because it holds to the impossibility of a unitary subject, facilitates feminism(s) of difference(s): differences within the category of woman and within the specific social existence of women – experiential differences, positional differences and sexual differences.
3 Prostitute politicization (from within) has produced a new public site of discourse – prostitute discourse; new political subjects – politicized prostitutes; and a new social movement – local, national and international prostitute groups. It is prostitutes' assumption of their own subject position that has facilitated my reading of the Greek prostitute, the hetaira, inscribed in Plato's texts.
4 Eve Tavor Bannet, *Structuralism and the Logic of Dissent*, London, Macmillan, 1989, p. 205.
5 ibid., p. 216.
6 ibid., pp. 220–1.
7 Jane Gallop, *The Daughter's Seduction: Feminism and Psychoanalysis*, Ithaca, Cornell University Press, 1982, p. 48.
8 Gayatri Chakravorty Spivak, 'Feminism and Critical Theory', in *Other Worlds: Essays in Cultural Politics*, New York and London, Methuen, 1987, p. 82.
9 Mikhail Bakhtin represents forms such as the mimic tradition, the dialogue and the symposium as carnivalization. Mikhail Bakhtin, *Rabelais and his World*, trans. Helen Iswolsky, Cambridge, Mass., and London, MIT Press, 1968, p. 98.
10 The latter have appropriated feminine difference in the texts as difference relational to the male subject. They have not read and appropriated the inscription of the difference within the category 'woman' (the maternal female body/the libidinal female body) found in the texts. Consequently, they have

hierarchized the reproductive in the couple maternal/sexual that have come to delimit the female. I reverse or pivot the hierarchy, making the libidinal the ground or condition of my reading. The subordinate term in the couple male/female and the subordinate term in the couples maternal/sexual, reproductive/libidinal, womb/clitoris are my points of departure for approaching the text.

11 I will refer to the speech delivered by Socrates at the symposium henceforth as Diotima's speech; Socrates begins by referring to it as 'her teaching' (201d) and ends the speech stating that 'This . . . gentlemen – was the doctrine of Diotima' (212b).

12 David Halperin, *One Hundred Years of Homosexuality*, New York and London, Routledge, 1990.

13 Spivak, op. cit., p. 151. The emphasis is mine.

14 The sacred prostitute was the embodiment of the sacred unity of the sexual and maternal bodies, which had by the classical age been separated by a legal code (the laws of Solon) which identified women either with a private and secluded reproductive function (as wives and mothers) or with a sexual function, as prostitutes purchased in the public market.

15 The sexual body itself was split into high and low bodies. There were three classes of prostitutes in fifth- and fourth-century Greece: the hetairae (high status prostitutes, including courtesan philosophers and political actors), the auletrides (flute players, dancers and acrobats), the dicteriades (common prostitutes: brothel inmates and streetwalkers). Unlike the hetairae and the auletrides, the dicteriades, the great majority of prostitutes in classical Greece, occupied a low status in society. The plight of the dicteriades and the wives, mothers and daughters seems to have been the same: exclusion from the polis and restriction to functioning as the medium of exchange between men. Marriage posited women as a medium of exchange between men of different households. The dicteriades, by means of brothel taxes, financed the ships and arms of government. '[O]rdinary prostitution in Greece developed out of the practice of sacred prostitution' – Fernando Henriques, *Prostitution and Society*, vol. 1, *Primitive, Classical and Oriental*, London, MacGibbon & Kee, 1962, p. 35. The hetaira can be seen as a surviving remnant of the archaic prostitute/priestess. The hetairae functioned outside the restrictions that the male state imposed on the dicteriades. The hetairae, including the female sophists, functioned at the margins of male public space exchanging teaching, conversation and sexual interaction for payment. Historical information on the hetairae, auletrides and dicteriades is from my reading of four sources: Paul Brandt [Hans Licht], *Sexual Life in Ancient Greece*, London, Routledge & Sons, 1932; Henriques, op. cit.; William Sanger, *The History of Prostitution*, New York, Harper & Brothers, 1869; Jess Wells, *A Herstory of Prostitution in Western Europe*, Berkeley, Shameless Hussy Press, 1982.

16 Aristophanes, in his speech at the symposium, makes reference to lesbian love: 'the woman who is the slice of the original female is attracted by women, rather than by men – in fact she is a Lesbian' (191e). A link can be made between the hetairae/auletrides and lesbianism. Alciphron puts a letter in the hand of Megara to Bacchis in which Megara chides Bacchis for being unable to leave her male lover for a minute to attend Glycera's sacrificial feast. Megara scolds: 'You have become a virtuous woman and are devoted to your lover. I congratulate you on your respectability – we are just wanton harlots.' Megara, stating 'we were all there', lists hetairae and auletriades who attended: Thessala, Moscharion, Thaïs, Anthrakion, Petalë, Thryallis, Myrrhina, Chrysion, Euxippë, Philumena. No men were present. The auletrides' festivals were often

limited to women. The feast appears to be very similar to the male symposium: 'Oh, what a party we had!. . . Songs, jokes, drinking till cock-crow, perfumes, garlands, and a delicious dessert. . . . We have often had a drinking party before, but seldom such a pleasant one as this' – Alciphron, *Letters from the Country and the Town of Fishermen, Farmers, Parasites and Courtesans*, trans. F.A. Wright, London, Routledge & Sons, 1922, Letter XIII, 'Megara to Bacchis', pp. 194–5.

17 Aspasia's famous salon has been immortalized in a fresco over the library entrance to the modern University of Athens. Among other notable Athenians represented in the fresco are Socrates, Pericles, Plato, Alcibiades, Sophocles and Antisthenes. Mary Ellen Waithe (ed.), *A History of Women Philosophers*, vol. 1 (600 BC–500 AD), Dordrecht, Boston and Lancaster, Martinus Nijhoff, 1987, frontispiece.

18 Alciphron, op. cit., Letter VI, 'Thaïs to Euthydemus', p. 175.

19 Wendy Brown, 'Supposing Truth Were a Woman . . . Plato's Subversion of Masculine Discourse', *Political Theory*, 16, 4, 1988, pp. 594–616; *Manhood and Politics: A Feminist Reading in Political Theory*, New Jersey, Rowman & Littlefield, 1988.

20 Plato, *The Republic*, trans. Allan Bloom, New York and London, Basic Books, 1968. I use Bloom's translation of *The Republic* throughout my text.

21 Page du Bois, *Sowing the Body: Psychoanalysis and Ancient Representations of Women*, Chicago and London, University of Chicago Press, 1988.

22 Plato, *The Theaetetus*, trans. F.M. Cornford, in *The Collected Dialogues of Plato*, eds Edith Hamilton and Huntingdon Cairns, New York, Bollingen Foundation, 1961.

23 Sanger, op. cit., p. 63. The use of information compiled by William Sanger is in no way a sign of support for the anti-prostitute and sexist ideology underpinning his historical and empirical study.

24 Socrates' only cited teachers were sophist hetairae. Aspasia, in the *Menexenus*, is given voice, mimicked by Socrates, as is Diotima in the *Symposium*.

25 Halperin, op. cit., pp. 112–17.

26 ibid., p.142.

27 Plato, *Symposium*, trans. Michael Joyce, in *The Collected Dialogues of Plato*, op. cit.

28 Robin May Schott, *Cognition and Eros*, Boston, Beacon Press, 1988, p. 14.

29 Andrea Nye, 'The Hidden Host: Irigaray and Diotima at Plato's *Symposium*', *Hypatia*, 3, 3, Winter 1989, p. 55.

30 See Arlene Saxonhouse, *Women in the History of Political Thought: Ancient Greece to Machiavelli*, New York, Praeger, 1985, p. 52; and Henriques, op. cit., p. 33.

31 Henriques, op. cit., p. 33.

32 Eva Keuls, *The Reign of the Phallus: Sexual Politics in Ancient Athens*, New York, Harper & Row, 1985, pp. 205–6.

33 Plato, *Symposium*, trans. Walter Hamilton, Harmondsworth, Penguin, 1951, 203d. Michael Joyce translates the same inscription as 'a lifelong seeker after truth'.

34 According to *The Oxford Classical Dictionary*, in its earliest usage 'sophist' designated 'a wise man or a man skilled at any particular kind of activity' – N.G.L. Hammond and H.H. Scullard, *The Oxford Classical Dictionary*, Oxford, Clarendon Press, 2nd edn 1970, p. 1000. A sophist was a teacher, a disseminator of different knowledges and an instructor in the art of rhetoric. Each sophist had his/her special field of knowledge; for example, Protagoras

specialized in teaching virtue. Socrates introduces Diotima as 'a woman who was deeply versed in this [the philosophy of love] and many other fields of knowledge' (201d). Socrates' speech at the symposium consists of 'some lessons' he was given by Diotima.

The designation of the sophists as false philosophers, in contrast to the true philosopher, was Plato's. Sophistic philosophy addressed the same themes that Socrates and Plato treated: wisdom, justice, virtue, love, the good. What distinguished sophistic teaching (in its many diversified forms) from Plato's teaching was the absence of the ideas of Universal Truth, fixed rules of conduct and the rationality of nature. Sophistry for a Platonist is low philosophy. Plato appropriated the skills of the low philosopher, the sophistic teacher, and pressed them into the service of the discovery of Truth: high philosophy. This is precisely how Plato appropriates Diotima's philosophy of Eros.

35 Xenophon, *Memorabilia and Oeconomicus, Symposium and Apology*, ed. E.H. Warmington, London, Heinemann, and Cambridge, Mass., Harvard University Press, 1923 (1968) III, xi, 16.
36 Leo Strauss, *Xenophon's Socrates*, Ithaca, Cornell University Press, 1972, p. 89.
37 Allan Bloom, a well-known Straussian, marks Book V as 'preposterous . . . Socrates expects it to be ridiculed. It provokes both laughter and rage in its contempt for convention and nature, in its wounding of all the dearest sensibilities of masculine pride and shame, the family and statemanship and the city' – Bloom, 'Interpretive Essay', *The Republic of Plato*, trans. Allan Bloom, New York and London, Basic Books, 1968, p. 380.
38 I am not arguing that Plato is simply an advocate of gender equality. Plato's sexism in Book V of *The Republic* is more than evident in his repeated marking of guardian women as weaker than guardian men (455e, 456a, 457a), his reference to the female guardians as 'their [male guardians'] women' (454e) and his statement that 'All these women are to belong to all these men in common' (457d).

Chapter 16

Differential theology and womankind: on Isaiah 66:13

Robert Magliola

As for those who sanctify themselves and purify themselves to enter the gardens, following the one in the centre, who eat the flesh of pigs, reptiles, rats: their deeds and their thoughts shall end all at once – it is Yahweh who speaks.

(Isaiah 66:17, *Jerusalem Bible*, 1966 edn)

Because the 'one in the centre' is, in the Hebrew text, *feminine*,[1] this our inaugural biblical passage debouches onto the motifs of femininity/masculinity and centre/periphery. At first blush (*sic*) the passage appeals to a deconstructionist because it reverses the authoritarian (= logocentric) paradigm whereby the centre is good and true and the periphery proportionately less good and true (and whereby to be outside the perimeter is to be evil and false). At second blush, alas, the same passage is dis*heart*ening, since Yahweh seems no more than a tribal God angry at the usurpation of His centre. Angry at the usurpation of His centre by a pagan priestess whose initiates break His prescriptions, i.e. eat the ritually 'unclean'. True, the passage is a displaced continuation of verses 1 through 4 (see e.g. 'they chose to do what displeases me'), and thus is directed more at unfaithful Jews than at Gentiles – and this ameliorates the invective somewhat. And a wily exegete can always defuse the literal and inflate the figurative: the text is then about commitment versus betrayal, and authentic love versus 'idolatry'. And true too, of course, the New Testament later voids the boundaries of clean/unclean and male/female: there is Peter's vision that all animals are clean (Acts 10:10–15) and the Petrine/Pauline universal priesthood of believers (I Peter 2:9, etc.). If our Isaiah 66, v. 24, envisions the outside-the-walls as evil again ('They shall go out and see the corpses . . . their worm shall not die'), Christ the Outsider redeems the outside by dying out there on Golgotha, outside the walls (John 19:17).

But I begin with verse 17, and its false 'one in the centre', the false Woman, because verse 17 and its allied verses 1–4 together *circum*scribe the centre of Psalm 66, namely verse 13.[2] And verse 13 is a true centre of a text (!), for it features not a false Woman in the Centre but a *true Woman* in the *centre/periphery*: 'At her [Jerusalem's] breast will her nurslings be carried and fondled in her lap. Like a son comforted by his mother will I [Yahweh] comfort you. (And by Jerusalem you will be comforted.)' – Isaiah 66:13, *Jerusalem Bible*, (English-language edn, 1966). The paean to Jerusalem, symbol of the people Israel, commences three verses earlier:

> Rejoice, Jerusalem,
> be glad for her, all you who love her!
> Rejoice for her,
> all you who mourned her!
>
> That you may be suckled, filled,
> from her consoling breast,
> that you may savour with delight
> her glorious breasts.
>
> (66:10, 11)

Then, in verse 12 and just before our centrepiece, Yahweh proclaims:

> For thus says Yahweh:
> now towards her I send flowing
> peace, like a river,
> and like a stream in spate
> the glory of the nations.

Yahweh does all the sending to His spouse the Holy City – the figurative[3] masculinity of Yahweh, sustained through most of Isaiah 66, has become at this point even more triumphant and virile. Quite a set-up for the reader, though. Yes, quite a set-up, dear reader, because we have been – again, dear reader – again again (lovingly) naughtily naughtily framed. For this (figuratively) masculine God turns, all of a sudden, figuratively feminine – a Mother who comforts. 'Like a son comforted by his mother will I comfort you.' The volte-face gave a jolt to the Jewish scribe too, it seems. Many biblical scholars agree that the last line of verse 13 is a gloss assimilated later into the text, as if the scribe were desperate to keep matters straight.[4] '(And by Jerusalem you will be comforted.)' No doubt the human mind's *Form-Trieb* is a strong, well-nigh-overwhelming one. On rhetorical grounds (no purple patches!), on socio-cultural grounds and on theological grounds, the scribe wanted to keep Yahweh purely masculine and Jerusalem purely feminine. Make no mistake about it, there are vested interests, crucial questions of firstliness and secondariness involved.

Needless to say, I (and many others) can easily critique this status quo in Marxist or other antipathetic terms. I want, instead, to continue the more difficult and serviceable project to which this paper intends a contribution, viz., an evidencing of how deconstruction can *abet* – if it deems warranted – the logocentric system at hand, in this case, how postmodern theology can *abet* an orthodox belief-system. Phrased another way, my project aims to show, among other things, how a logocentric system can survive via the recognition that it necessarily deconstructs itself. *In re* our Isaiah 66, verse 13, biblical exegetes would traditionally regard the conjectured Ur-Text (that without the scribal gloss) as an alternative to the Incumbent Text (which includes the gloss). Instead, I propose again my postmodern, my *differential* model (if we may provisionally call so lickety-split and open a process a model): – the incumbent version becomes the Text and the conjectured Ur-version becomes the Subtext, and together they constitute Sacred Script's Isaiah 66:13.

Since it turns out here that the Subtext is more logocentric than the Text (differentialism being the guerdon of Divine corruption), I begin with it. When, in verse 13 of the *Subtext*, Yahweh becomes Mother, what has happened in structuralist terms is that the binary of God-Male and Zion-Female is shattered. The Feminine migrates from creaturehood to Divinity: Woman crosses the wall from secondliness to firstliness. (Indeed, as we shall see later, the scribal gloss added in the *Text* seems to put the feminine back in place – Jerusalem, that is to say, Zion the Servant Nation, still does the 'feminine' things like comforting: God might have a feminine moment, but females remain on the secondary side of the ledger too.) The Subtext does *not* have the gloss, however, and this is the rub of the difference. No doubt Yahweh retains a Male moment even though the Female moment is affirmed – Yahweh's masculinity is again asserted already by verse 14[5] – but that Jerusalem retains a Female moment is much less clear (otherwise the scribe would not have added the insistent gloss). Without the gloss, Jerusalem is capitulated over to the remainder, that is, to two remaining options.[6] Whatever the fears of the scribe later trying to remedy matters, without his gloss the proto-text, our Subtext, shines with Revelations, its several own glorious Revelations.

In terms of the engaged sexual rhetoric, the first option, simply put, is that Jerusalem is left with Nothing. By becoming Woman too, God has 'taken even Womanhood, the Feminine, from us, from humans!'[7] God is both Male and Female, God the Androgynous . . . and Jerusalem the Servant Nation is now Nothing, destitute, negated. Be assured, this is not a 'logical grid of possibilities' that we are filling in, mechanically. Rather, at the bottom of this first option there is a Mysticism – that God by appropriating our sexuality, our cloaca, our (in psychological terms) ALL, has left us with no identity of our own – and (the correlative proposition) God is thus absolutely Other (the Other of the pseudo-Areopagite, of Silesius, even of perhaps an Emmanuel Levinas). Jerusalem (and for Christians the Church) must serve in mystical darkness, in pure faith . . . confessing its absolute dependency. God's Allness/Otherness, Jerusalem's Nothingness – a Revelation.

Again in terms of the gendered rhetoric, the second option for Jerusalem is even more explosive than the first, and precisely because it is *unnamed*.

(Beware the unnamed, the hidden term! v. Freud, Lacan.) If by way of
rhetorical twist the femininity of Jerusalem has been filched by the Male
God (result: a Conflated M/F God), shouldn't we suppose the chiasmic
trope has come into fuller play, so that Jerusalem has become in turn
Male? Not a conflated F/M Jerusalem, I don't think, because, as already
indicated, there is much greater pressure to retain God's masculinity
concurrent with the newly absorbed femininity, and much less pressure to
retain Jerusalem's femininity concurrent with the new masculinity – otherwise, no reason for the later scribal gloss. (The scribe felt no need to insert,
'And by Yahweh you will be defended, like a son by his father'.) Thus the
Subtext implies here a singularly Male Jerusalem, and precisely because
Jerusalem is male according to this model, the Maleness is suppressed. To
wit:

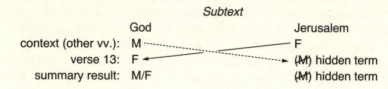

Why must the maleness be suppressed? To understand this we should
further clarify the scenario. The narrator throughout is the Isaiah-voice,
proclaiming God's message and often quoting Yahweh in the first person
(indeed, he is quoting Yahweh in our verse 13). The narratee is the
numerical leadership of individual Jews, *not* to be confounded with
Jerusalem as the *collective* referent and *symbol* of the Jewish people. Ergo,
the individual Jews, the readership, are exhorted, for example, to rejoice
for Jerusalem the collective referent, as in verse 10: 'Rejoice, rejoice for
her, all you who mourned her!' Our discussion of the gendered rhetoric
does *not directly* involve the gender of numerical Judaism – obviously the
Jewish population had a biologically distributed proportion of females and
males (and, culturally, a fierce male bias – notice how in v. 13 the mother
comforts a *son*).

Our discussion of gendered rhetoric does *indirectly* involve the numerical population, of course, and very much so – since the gender(s) attributed
to God and to Jerusalem (*symbol* of the Jewish People) necessarily con-
ditioned cultural behaviour. Because the New Testament's God evolved
from the Old Testament's God-tradition, *and* because the Church considers itself the Jerusalem of the New Covenant, the Bible's gendered
rhetoric is of beetling import, of beetling and bristling, looming and rearing
import, for Christianity too. We know already that according to the
Subtext's verse 13, it is *not* to be presumed that Jerusalem, i.e. the Jewish
People or the Church, is feminine (the latter thesis belonging instead to the
Text). The theological binary anterior to verse 13 had been what we call a

simple dominant–subdominant binary, i.e. one term is primary and the other is secondary to it. Ergo: God (male) [primary] – Jerusalem (female) [secondary]. Because of verse 13 the binary becomes, according to the first option left for Jerusalem: God (male/female) [primary] – Jerusalem (?null) [secondary]. And according to the second option left for Jerusalem: God (male/female) [primary] – Jerusalem (male suppressed) [secondary]. According to *both* options the numerical women, i.e. the real existent females of the culture – real existents we call *tertiary* in relation to God and Jerusalem – have 'suffered' an overtopping gain/loss when their status is compared to their anterior one. Heretofore the feminine was secondary (female Jerusalem) and of course tertiary (female existents on the mundane level). Because of verse 13, the feminine both climbs to the primary, its gain (God/female co-primary with God/male) and gives up the secondary (Jerusalem null or suppressed male), its loss. How all this relates to the tertiary female and tertiary male is the key to our current *agendum*, viz., the question – why must the (presumable) maleness of Jerusalem be suppressed? What kind of Revelation can this be?

One might say the comings and goings of gain and loss are many in this God's (God of a) world . . . for example, there is the monological punctum when gain is gain and loss is loss; there is the paradoxical punctum when gain is loss and loss is gain; there is the postmodern punctum when gain is ever more than gain and loss is forever less within loss. I argue that the feminine's loss of Jerusalem is from one point of view paradoxical – only an apparent loss and really a gain. If we start our judgement of the relations between primary–secondary–tertiary from what Buddhists call the 'world-ensconced' end (instead of the 'transcendental' end), i.e. if we start from the concrete or material end of the scale, we find the following ratio: in the tertiary domain (mundane behaviour of existents), male and female roles correlate to the gendered distribution of roles within God, within Jerusalem and between God and Jerusalem. Of course we are talking here of concrete history in so far as it is influenced by Old and New Testament theology (and no doubt the theologies have been manipulated in turn by history – especially male history – the causality is entangled from the beginning). And protean and plastic the forms of Power, of course – psychological, economic, political power. According to these considerations, the three ratios which take the measure of our current discussion can be diagrammed as follows:

	Primary		Secondary		Tertiary		
	FIRST	:	SECOND	: :	FIRST	:	SECOND
(I)	God (M)	:	Jerusalem (F)	: :	males	:	females
(II)	God (M/F)	:	Jerusalem (M̶)	: :	females	:	males (?)
(III)	God (M/F)	:	Jerusalem (M)	: :	females	:	males

To sum up what the diagram implies, we can say the old model was patriarchal (see no. I), and supported male claims to cultural power: the ratio of the old model declares – as male God is to female Jerusalem, so in the practical world is the individual male to the individual female. Thus we conclude that a gender-change on the secondary level, viz., the affirmation of a male Jerusalem/Church (see no. III) would in the practical world constitute the *male as secondary* to the female. Ergo, in a male-controlled society, the male-identity of Jerusalem/Church had to be *suppressed* (see no. II). Even the suppression makes for a more fluid, equivocal situation – the male Jerusalem/Church is suppressed but still there (under erasure, ꝳ). As for the model of Goddess, a God figuratively feminine and only feminine, and perhaps a Jerusalem/Church figuratively male and only male, I do not think Isaiah 66 poses a pure moment of such, maybe because it was socially impossible for the historical Jews and Christians involved.[8] Males wanted to be big firsties and not little secondlies, centres and not peripheries, and a God as Androgynous (no. II)[9] was already a bitter saying – breaking the male God-concept and sending many a consequence trickling down.

I have said all along, however, that my project is to show how post-modern *procédés* can work (from) within a belief-system, not against it (negation is not deconstruction). So what are the messages whereby the Subtext's second option can instruct the believing Church? It goes without saying that males in fact have administered the Church *while* emphasizing its symbolic Femininity. That Jerusalem/Church has a male-moment teaches male establishments everywhere that they cannot use the concept of Feminine Jerusalem as an excuse for subordination of women – and this is a Revelation. What is more (because less) – (1) since Jerusalem represents the essential secondariness of the People, humankind, to God; and (2) since Jerusalem in the Subtext is *non-Woman*; it follows that (3) the Male represents in his own proper nature this general inferiority. The Male is better suited, better qualified ontologically – so to speak – than the Female is, to represent human *inferiority*, to represent the human qua human, the human as created, contingent, fallen. This too is a Revelation. Finally, since Jerusalem/Church is secondariness and males have historically dominated the Jerusalem/Church, their historical domination has been Divinely permitted them (we speak here of the past) precisely because of their inferiority to women. A Revelation.

Across a Divine synapse now, to the 'received' text – the incumbent Isaiah 66:13 with its pre-canonical gloss,[10] that insistent and contrary gloss – in postmodernism we retain contradictions, variant versions[11] . . . conceived earlier, conceived later . . . a superfetation of Divine meanings. Such fuss over that single line '(And by Jerusalem you will be comforted)', you might think; such a brouhaha of theologies brewed from so very little, you might think! Such a *mons* from a *mus*. But please understand that I am operating in glorious, long-lasting traditions here: (1) theologically speaking, my specimen verse 13 is an instance of several gendered combinations which entangle *all* of the Sacred Script; and (2) hermeneutically speaking, my methodology is both (new) Auerbachian[12] and (old) Midrashic in so far as it regards a textual snippet as meaningful, illuminative, for a whole *oeuvre*.[13]

The gloss '(And by Jerusalem you will be comforted)' is technically a *supplément*.[14] The logocentrist deploys the concept/term supplement to peripheralize, or indeed, 'cast outside' of the circle, that which is co-primary but embarrassing (unsettling, destabilizing). The postmodernist, detecting the alleged supplement is in fact co-primary, reads its content as a finessed 'more of the same': the apparent outside is also inside, the secondarity is also firstly. Anent Isaiah 66:13, it should be clear that the scribal supplement inserted into the text can have the effect of cosmeticizing, of *remandering*, the embarrassing messages (the *remainings*) of the Subtext – viz., (1) that with Woman's departure Jerusalem and the Church are a remaining Nothing, and/or (2) that with Woman's departure Jerusalem and the Church, because their remainders/remains are male (would, if the maleness were not suppressed), establish the Feminine as dominant elsewhere . . . as dominant in society, and maybe even in God.

In other words, judged from what we have called the world-ensconced end, the effect of the gloss can be seen as an exercise of masculine power: Woman is put back in her place, Jerusalem/Church. But a postmodern reading exposes the supplement as a Revelation. A Revelation that, according to the Text (in contrast to the Subtext), the Feminine is pervasive. A Revelation that She is not put *back* in her place, but that supplement is *extension*[15] – Women's place is *everyplace*. Woman is an Event, She 'takes place'. Unlike the Masculine, the Feminine occupies all three domains. She is co-primary in God, in possession within Jerusalem/Church and a quantitative moiety in society.

'Double standard! Double standard! What a quick fix of a twist!' – you might be protesting right now, dear reader. If with the logocentric reading the fix is on, and with the postmodern reading the fix is off, it seems someone needing a feminine fix has turned a dirty twist, a quick fix, a refixative. Because the argument treating the *Subtext* has said that the possession of Jerusalem meant secondariness, inferiority: the gendered ratio of God to Zion could be displaced onto societal relation (M/F God is to Male Jerusalem as individual female is to individual male), and that just such a threat had compelled the Male establishment to suppress Jerusalem's presumed maleness. Now the postmodern argument treating the Text says that a Female Jerusalem can mean not secondarity but *plasmic* presence – the Woman as recurrent, as supportive, as somehow everywhere.

I answer that this is *not* inconsistency at all. The feminine pervasion is not a perversion. For postmodernism deconstructs logocentric ratios, logo-centric primaries–secondaries–tertiaries, precisely by means of *encroach-ment*, precisely by means of recurrence. When compared to the Subtext Isaiah 66:13 and the logocentric Text of the same, our postmodern Text Isaiah 66:13 proffers a New Woman, a Feminine that occupies God as co-primary, reoccupies Jerusalem as sole secondary and preoccupies society as co-tertiary – thus undoing their very boundaries by the very fact of recurrence. (And keep on remembering, alongside, that the postmodern deconstructs but does not destroy: if in the postmodern moment there are undoings and levellings, still in the logocentric moment there are some ever good insides, peripheries and outsides to be ever had.) Why, though, link femininity to the egalitarian role and masculinity to hierarchy, to gradation? Because love is the great *equalizer* . . . there is no gradation between lovers;[16] when gradation intervenes, power has cut woman from man and love has fled (in the sex-act, too, gradation is degradation). No wonder the (syllogistic) middle is missing! – you might very well exclaim. Not to worry! Scripture, our Isaiah 66, gives us the missing middle for our syllogism – when Scripture identifies the feminine with love and the masculine with power (in Isaiah 66, God is male when punitory and powerful, and female when loving, compassionate). As a consequence: (1) the loving is equalizing; (2) the feminine is loving; ergo – the feminine is equalizing.[17] (Or at least so in this postmodern moment.)

Bonum diffusivum sibi, 'Love is (ever) diffusive of itself', an old old formula here reinstated, this time reinstated by postmodernism, by *differ-ential theology* – because God's very truth always keeps on coming. Keeps on coming coming, save with a *difference*,[18] postmodernists would say. Differential theology stresses that the Love which forever spreads, infil-trates, is at the work of dashing power and dashing down boundaries . . . but *not* according to programme. Feminine recurrence, feminine 'more of the same', is forever differing from itself . . . ongoing in surges and riptides and undertows, proliferating, profligate, *imprévue* . . . a sameness which is *not* 'one and the same'.[19]

It was *Scripture* which just now supplied for us the identification of the female with love, and it was *God* who kept the truth coming on and on (Divine come-on). In short, if the world-ensconced end of analysis defined the supplement verse 13 in terms of power, what we have called the transcendental end of analysis has defined it in terms of love.[20] Supplement becomes a positive, a sacred Redundancy (from L., *re* – 'over, back'; *undare* – 'overflow'; *unda* – 'wave'). The gloss adds more Feminine (as Jerusalem/F comforting) to the Feminine already there in the Text (as God/F comforting). She's a lot of Woman, this Text. Love as Female is indeed '(ever) diffusive'. It so happens that secular deconstruction takes great interest in the redundant – showing its frequency to be more wide-spread than supposed, and showing its formal fault to be often fecund, productive. Towards these ends, deconstruction has developed many a descriptive sally and sortie. What I am calling a differential theology should, in my opinion, sort these, resort to these, and our Isaiah 66:13 supplies us a good chance.

Redundancy redounds[21] in many ways, and can be bespoken in many ways – of which I shall englut two, two that make the gain of the gloss a postmodern 'gain more than gain'. (First instance –) Sometimes redundancy begins when the secondary term of a binary relation outruns its proper ratio to the primary term, thus becoming disproportionate (and inducing 'inflation'). The quantum of the secondary term's disproportion, unable to adequate itself properly to the primary term, instead must *repeat* itself, i.e. become redundant (must 'make waves again', we can say). What is intriguing is that if the surplus continues abuilding, there comes a point in time when the secondary term either (1) attains autonomy, or (2) initiates a reversal (converse relation) whereby it converts to primary function and generates new secondaries at what was the primary end of the binary.[22]

Beginning again with world-ensconced analysis and its cultural tilt towards male power, we find the first instance, the first sort of redundancy – the redundancy of inflation – sets out from a logocentric dialectic, from a sortites of sorts. The stanzas preceding verse 13 climb a ladder of signifier–signified binaries, so by the time the reader reaches verse 13 the male God as *signified* (and thus primary) and the female Jerusalem as His *signifier* (and thus secondary) hold firmly to their assigned places. Even when verse 13 moves the Woman in with the male God, she is treated by the Jewish (and Christian) tradition – so fearful of her fearsome sortilège – as the cohabiting *signifier* even though she is technically the co-primary signified.

The subtext of verse 13 weighing in with a non-gendered Jerusalem (the M/Jerusalem having been X'd over), it is not until the Text's gloss that the M/signified–F/signifier binaries become lopsided – to wit, there appears a surplus Lady Signifier – a supernumerary. According to the first instance of redundancy, the supernumerary *supererogates*, i.e. the redundancy is fertile, productive. Thus I take our Text's feminine pervasion as an Emblem – an emblem staking out the (1) moment of Feminine autonomy, and the (2) moment of Her converse relation. During the moment of Feminine autonomy, the Woman is parthenogenetic – the Woman as superabundant Signifier engenders, from within, a signified for herself (and others). When Mary sings her Magnificat, 'My soul magnifies [Gk: *megalúnei*] the Lord' (Luke 1:46), Mary's signifying soul (her 'within') *magnifies* the signified Lord, so that the Lord becomes the Effect (*signifier*) produced out of Mary's magnification. To wit:

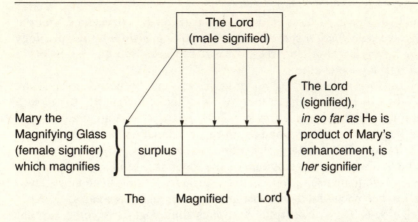

The image of the Lord which Mary presents to herself and the world by way of her magnification is the product (*signifier*) generated specifically by *her* expansive activity. This is to say, the resultant Lord is the Lord made over by her supplement, reconstituted from out of her *excess of signifying*. In this specialized sense, Mary is a good example of the autonomous moment: she is a female signifier who redounds, from within, a male signified for herself (and others) – a signified who, by the very fact he is her product, is her *signifier*; in short, his moment as *her* signifier is Mary's 'autonomous moment'.[23]

If in the autonomous moment the Female signifier makes its own signi-fied, in the converse moment the Female signifier reverses the male signified at the other end of the (traditional) polarity. She becomes the dominant (the primary) of the dominant–subdominant binary and the male becomes the subdominant (the secondary). This is what happens at the marriage-feast of Cana, for example. Mary's 'Do whatever he tells you' (John 2:5) is just the reiteration of an infinity of signifying him, and from this excess of female signifying she can command the converse: the male Christ becomes at Cana the secondary, and performs at her insistence a miracle he had at first refused ('What is it to me and thee?'). And this is too how I would interpret the moment when Christ laments over Zion's unrepentant children: 'How often would I have gathered your children together as a hen gathering her brood under her wings, and you would not!' (Luke 13:34).[24] This is a converse moment when Christ becomes the female, the tender mothering hen, and he can do so only in imitation of Mary the tender Mother. He can signify her only because of the teeming excess, the supererogation, of her own signifying as Mother.

What I call the second instance of redundancy involves the fallacy of 'category-confusion'. I mean to say: (Second instance –) Sometimes the operating adequation is 'always already redundant' because its equation is false. From the start, the quanta are adequated to the wrong *qualia* (confusion of ontological categories) in order to attain the wrong *telos* (confusion of ethical categories). Thus, in terms of the mistaken *telos* any increase in quanta is futile, always already *de trop* and absurd, like adding ciphers to nullity, an impossible chute of 'loss within loss'. With the 'empty' increase in quanta, however, there comes the time when the inverse *telos* is achieved in the contrariwise *qualia*. And here it is precisely the *inversion* which so intrigues.

The gloss of our Text, taken again as an exercise of androcentric power (saying, in effect, 'Lady, back to your place!'), resorts to the rhetoric of power in order to enforce male primacy. Save that the selvage (selvage: 'the edge of a fabric woven so it will not unravel') is selfish, is always already *superannuated*. So much is Woman kept (physically) second that this always already redundant secondarity triggers female primacy on the other side of the pons, the *transcendental* side. Some quantum fix! Lady Jerusalem becomes a Lady who is *First*, not just the First Lady of a First Man, nor the patsy of a mere 'Ladies first'. And what of the next moment, when all of the above, all of the gendered weights and counter-weights are taken together – what issues forth? I think the resulting *combinatoire*, shaky with slippage as it is, emits a gracious message – Love equalizes consort and spouse, Woman and Man are *Co-Equal*. During the *punctum* when the biblical M/F God (or the extra-biblical F/M God) relates to Jerusalem as Consort to Spouse, the love nexus equalizes even such a Consort and even such a Spouse.[25] And love everywhere equalizes Woman and Man everywhere. This is a sense, surely of Galatians 3:28: 'There is neither Jew nor Greek; there is neither slave nor free; there is no male or female.'

I want to size Isaiah 66:13 one more time, quickly, vamping spouses and con/sorts at my (for the nonce) last postmodern last – according to a de/sign I have called elsewhere 'pure negative reference'. The claim is that pure negative reference, i.e. pure difference, is *constitutive*.[26] According to this way of thinking, things are the 'same' not by virtue of a substratum-in-common,[27] but via the negative interval specifically defining their difference. Especially in our Text and because of the gloss, female and male roles are defined by way of opposition, contrariety.[28] (This is true even when the two genders are conflated in God: they come together but as roles in God remain distinct, juxtaposed.) Taking care to read the Text so that both female and male roles are affirmative (e.g. the feminine as protective nurturing, the masculine as protective strength),[29] it is still very clear that the roles differ contrariwise and thus define themselves. Their pure difference is constitutive of their moment of Sameness. That Sameness wherein 'they neither marry nor are given in marriage' (Matthew 22:30). If redundancy yields the *punctum* that Women and Men are Co-Equal, pure difference yields the *punctum* that Women and Men are the Same. Two Revelations.

Sometimes ungainly from loss and gain, from shortfalls within loss and longfalls beyond gain, the Bible according to postmodernism never really settles down. No Divine entropy here. Text(s) and Subtext(s) deconstruct each other, but the outcomes (ever) have a lean and list to them. Pace Lévi-Strauss, no structuralist stability here. Thus our differential study of Isaiah 66:13 found a discernible Female sway – an irreducibly excessive Feminine. Woman is truly in the centre (holy libertine: she cohabits with God's maleness), and truly at the periphery too (holy revanchist: she gets Jerusalem back, damosel *dorée*, damosel all-golden).

> Patched trapunto trimming somehow towards its 'End',
> Sacred Script moves on,
> iridescent-fast,
> > God's silken and moiled moiré,
> > > – foudroyant with energy

NOTES

1 See Edward Young, *The Book of Isaiah*, vol. 3, Grand Rapids, Eerdmans, 1972, pp. 530–1: 'Both the Q^{e}re and the first Qumran Scroll take the word *one* as feminine.' The Massoretic text also has the feminine: see *Pentateuch and Haftorahs*, ed. J.H. Hertz, London and New York, Soncino Press, 1981, p. 946; and J. Skinner, *Isaiah: Chs XL–LXVI*, in *The Cambridge Bible*, 1907, p. 251. *The Jerusalem Bible*, London, Darton, Longman & Todd, 1966, follows suit, commenting: 'Probably the one who conducts the ceremony (or a priestess, since the text has the feminine) in the centre of the procession through the sacred garden', p. 1247. For more extensive critical apparatus, see the revised French fascicule edition of *La Bible de Jérusalem*.

2 That is, there are twenty-four verses in Isaiah 66. A deconstructionist would say the mutations of centre/periphery are 'always already there', since logocentrism is (defective but) inescapable: deconstruction is *para*sitic. Thus all decoding involves necessarily a new encoding, though the how/what of new encodings is for each case situationally unique, errant, non-programmable. Logocentric recurrences within deconstruction tend to be subtle, refined – deconstruction goes forth in that meditative Care which is the (momentary) intersection of chance and con/*centra*ted effort.

3 Figurative, but still of enormous consequence, culturally and theologically.

4 See, for example, George Adam Smith, 'Chapters L–LXVI', in *The Book of Isaiah*, vol. II, New York and London, Harper, 1927, p. 508: 'The Hebrew adds "and in Jerusalem shall ye be comforted", probably a later addition, superfluous both to the metre and the meaning.' And Edward Kissane, *The Book of Isaiah*, Dublin, Browne & Nolan, 1943, p. 325: 'Some critics omit the third clause as a later addition.'

5 That is, Yahweh is identified with a physical power of protecting and punishing, and the military metaphor is resumed: 'To his servants Yahweh will reveal his hand, but to his enemies fury' (v. 14).

6 In terms of the gendered rhetoric, that Jerusalem is a third option, an epicenic third sex or neuter, can be excluded – I think – as impossible for what was the contemporary Jewish imagination.

7 We are not dealing at this point with theology but with a *psychological* moment:

the human imagination – possessive, quantitative, unliberated – feels deprived though no deprivation has really occurred. Needless to say, the attribution of femininity to God does not preclude the ongoing attribution of femininity to Jerusalem. But the Scripture presents us an anthropomorphic and gendered *drama*, one which the human emotion of the reader tracks consciously and unconsciously. Interesting too that humankind in general and males in particular are more traumatized by the loss of Woman than the loss of Man – it is as if Woman represents the human pith and marrow, and all humankind unconsciously knows this. A Jungian might say, of course, that the ousted Woman is not actual women at all, but just the male imagination's fictional *anima* – so good riddance to her! Given time, I would argue against Jung that the situation is much more complicated, and involves mutual reinscriptions of actual women, *anima* and ousted Woman.

8 Though of course several neighbouring peoples contemporary to the Jews did worship a supreme goddess.

9 For my distinctions between the androgynous, the epicenic, etc. see Magliola, 'Sexual Rogations, Mystical Abrogations: Some Données of Buddhist Tantra and the Catholic Renaissance,' in Clayton Koelb and Susan Noakes (eds), *The Comparative Perspective on Literature: Approaches to Theory and Practice*, Ithaca and London, Cornell University Press, 1988, pp. 204–11.

10 That is, the gloss was assimilated into the text before the Jews set about the task of standardizing their scriptures.

11 As long as the empirical evidence for their authenticity is more or less equally distributed among them.

12 Auerbach bestows meticulous attention on short, selected passages from large works: he finds encoded in these passages, either overtly or subliminally, the themes and styles of the work taken as a 'whole'. Thus his approach can achieve sharply focussed particularity, yet issue in much more general claims which apply to the grander work. See Erich Auerbach, *Mimesis: The Reproduction of Reality in Western Literature*, trans. W. Trask, Princeton, Princeton University Press, 1953; original German language edn, *Mimesis*, Berne, A. Franke, 1946.

13 Some might say that Auerbachian *stilistique*, and semiology, and deconstruction – so-called modernist and postmodernist approaches – are anachronistic for Scripture, and ill suit it. 'Nor do people put new wine into old wineskins; if they do, the skins burst, the wine runs out, and the skins are lost' (Matthew 9:17)! Let us recall that the kinds of philology and linguistics currently applied to Scripture are likewise anachronistic, and that Midrashic theory and practice, *not* anachronistic to Scripture, are now very seldom used (though of course *modernist* and *postmodernist* study of Midrash *is*). Perhaps the more applicable (in the Midrashic sense, note!) biblical quotation comes not in Matthew 9 but Matthew 13: 'Well then, every scribe who becomes a disciple of the kingdom of heaven is like a householder who brings out from his storeroom things both new and old' (Matthew 13:52).

14 A more detailed discussion of supplementarity as I treat it can be found in my 'French Deconstruction with a (Buddhist) Difference', *Studies in Language and Literature*, 3, October 1988 (Taipei: National Taiwan University), pp. 11, 12.

15 I would here explain Woman in terms of the 'open elliptical' and the 'moving site,' broken analogies I broker in my own way from/for Derrida.

16 *Qua* lovers. See also below, note 25.

17 Please permit me two remarkings. A lesser showing: Notice that syllogistic form itself works by way of equalizing terms (syllogism as feminine, ah well!). And a greater showing: Notice how – *re* our rhetoric – the *somatic* allegory (woman

and the missing middle) is somatically inscribed into our *logic* (the syllogism's missing middle term), and how – when the missing middle is found – it proves to be Love, love unconcealed by God in the Scripture (eureka!). This is a lover's discourse differing from Roland Barthes', but he is much more than worth consulting anyway, in Barthes, *A Lover's Discourse*, trans. R. Howard, New York, Hill & Wang, 1978.

18 That is, postmodern theology – at least as I conceive of it – does not describe Divine truth as a substance which is carried on bodily, as it were, with time effecting only adaptive changes. Postmodern theology deconstructs so substantialist a formulation – so that the resulting description of God's oncoming truth is more like Buddha's analogy of the flame 'moving' from candle to candle (though Buddha is describing *karma*). When a candle-flame is touched to the next candle, the latter 'catches' fire, and in turn can ignite a third candle, and so on. Nothing has passed on . . . there is absolutely new flame every 'moment', yet there is always flame . . . there is always in this sense a reliability.

19 I borrow the vernacular locution 'one and the same' because it literally implies the binary unit characteristic of logocentrism (viz., a 'factor' and an 'agent' which repeats it by 'mirroring' it, so together factor and agent form a dyad). Since theories of substance or essence depend on a version of this binary unit in order that a 'ground-which-is-common' can perpetuate itself, when logocentrism is deconstructed these binaries are broken. What results is either an off/random stream of 'floating signifiers' or a field of 'isolated signifieds'. What has happened is that a *function* has been deconstituted, and the debris of this function is the 'same' in a way analogous to the sameness of the flame in the Buddhist similitude of 'passing the flame' (see the preceding note). See also Magliola, *Derrida on the Mend*, Lafayette, Purdue University Press, 1984, pp. 15–19, 25–8, 41, 111 *et seq*.

20 My point is that postmodern theology can absorb all approaches, those that are rooted in 'secular' assumptions and 'objects of analysis', and those rooted in theological ones. Apropos the gloss, it is true that some male motivations for its inclusion in verse 13 could have been pious: for example, the pious intention might have been to assert more definitively the role of Jerusalem as *loving* spouse of Yahweh (an aside: this is love according to a logocentric formulaic; I am instead trying in this paper to explain love according to a postmodern deconstruction). But even if the intention operated because of love, one of the strongest structural *effects* of the gloss, and of its ilk throughout Scripture, was to keep women, at least what we are calling 'tertiary women', in *check*.

21 'To redound', from L., *re + undare*. At least in so far as their Latin roots are the same, my two words, here, make a redundant phrase, do they not? Half the point. But the other half is that 'redound' is mediated through the more clearly affirmative ME form *redounden*, 'to abound'. That is, 'to overflow' can be *good*.

22 Cf. Jacques Derrida, *Of Grammatology*, trans. G. Spivak, Baltimore, Johns Hopkins University Press, 1976, pp. 6 *et seq*.

23 An analogous format characterizes Simeon's prophecy, Luke 2:35. So much is Mary *secondary*, i.e. so much at the 'receiving end' of dolour ('and a sword will pierce your own soul too') that this very secondariness becomes the locus of a *firstliness* – those who, by shafting her Son, have shafted her, find here that their *reaction* to Mary's pain becomes normative for whatever judgement is to befall *them* ('so that the secret thoughts of many may be laid bare').

24 The correlevant Matthew 23:37 does not make clear that the parent bird's gender is feminine, but Luke 13:34, having the feminine possessive form, does.

25 *Qua* lovers, specifically. This is not to deny that other 'moments' in the technical

sense, those involving God's omnipotence, omniscience and other prerogatives of Divine authority, are – in between God and humankind – *unequal*. See also my discussion in 'Sexual Rogations, Mystical Abrogations', op. cit., p. 198.

26 See Magliola, *Derrida on the Mend*, op. cit., pp. 21–37, 112–13, 144–9.

27 Lady Jerusalem doesn't need foundation garments.

28 Though contrariety, i.e. syzygy in the Jungian sense, characterizes the preponderance of Isaiah 66, of course.

29 Perhaps needless to say, I am aware of the many feminists who reject these gender-based role assignments, and reject the Bible on this count. My purpose here is otherwise: to cope postmodernistically *with* the Bible and thus with its textual determinations (and indeterminations).

Chapter 17

Intolerable language: Jesus and the woman taken in adultery

Patricia Klindienst Joplin

'He who eats my flesh and drinks my blood
lives in me
and I in him.
As I, who am sent by the living Father,
myself draw life from the Father,
so whoever eats me will draw life from me.
This is the bread come down from heaven;
not like the bread our ancestors ate:
they are dead,
but anyone who eats this bread will live for ever.'

He taught this doctrine at Capernaum, in the synagogue. After hearing it, many of his followers said, 'This is intolerable language. How could anyone accept it?'

(John 6:56–61)[1]

The phrase the Jerusalem Bible translates as 'intolerable language' is rendered as 'a hard saying' in the Revised Standard Edition. The Oxford Bible's comment on Jesus' 'hard' words is nobably bland: '*Hard saying* means offensive or difficult, but not obscure.' Perhaps. But freedom from the threat of offence, that is, obedient reception of official interpretation – eating Jesus' word prefigures the eucharist[2] – is purchased only by retrospection, a look back from ritual to its constituting moments. This can silence in us the utterly believable question which the text records as one unmediated response to hearing Jesus speak of himself so strangely: 'How could *anyone* accept it?' The text records the prophet's complex speech-act as well as dramatizing the problem of its reception: the shock and confusion of hearing the ground of one's belief shifted.

It has always been important for the exegetes, who mediate the gospel's reception, to distinguish the good from the bad reading of this text – which calls continual attention to the perilous distance between speaker and listener – by referring us to the differences among listeners in the text. What we decide Jesus means is, John insists, a matter of life and death: on our acts of interpretation Christians stake their lives. And as we have struggled to understand what authentic witness to this text might mean, we have often been taught that we must not be like 'the Jews', here set up as prime examples of bad or literal readers. It is history, specifically, the history of Christian intolerance – *persecution in the name of the victim* – which has made the Christian Church's tendency to define itself at the expense of the gospel's bracketed other, 'the Jews', intolerable. We must question the way the gospels constitute themselves as Christianity's founding texts, bearing in mind, always, that they are not finished; they are not primarily or ultimately texts. The gospels are opened to fresh interpretations in their ongoing life as liturgy, as the revised rubric for Good Friday makes stunningly clear. In the post-Holocaust, post-Vatican II era, the American Catholic Church has the worshipping community play *every* role in the Passion. In our own language, it is we who shout 'Crucify him!' 'We' become 'them', the turbulent crowd; we, Christians, step into the place of 'the Jews' and hear one of our own play Pilate. In a ritual with the potential to move us to self-recognition (if we connect our words with our deeds), we enter into the corporate act of worship as the internal elements of doubt and discord and own our responsibility for abandoning Jesus, our complicity in his death – and the death of innocent millions. This act of ritual substitution of 'us' for 'the others', if we let its deep structure change us, might counter the history of violence worked in the name of our cult's founding victim, by preparing us (I hope) to stand with the persecuted. In the move from gospel text to liturgical performance, we become actors in the drama – still present, still opening its threat and promise – but only by yielding up our mythic innocence and 'the Jews'' mythic guilt.

In what follows, I bear in mind, then, the power of John's testimony as contemporary ritual practice seeks to transform it, redeeming his gesture towards marking a new (old) victim – 'the Jews' (a reductive epithet he employs for a heterogeneous people at least seventy times in his testimony) – even as he discloses, with astonishing power of vision, how Jesus was marked and taken for confounding both religious and secular constructions of difference and identity.

The story I will re-read here is one I heard as a child as part of liturgy, moved by the terror at its heart, and the hope in its unexpected conclusion. Terror for the way men presume to decide the fate of a woman whose bonds to other women – mother, sister, daughter, friend – have been entirely erased; hope in the realization that Jesus frustrates one of the oldest bargains between men in the history of western culture: the ritual exchange of women to mark the boundaries of patriarchal power.

As I will argue here, in choosing to insert the homeless *pericope* of Jesus and the woman taken in adultery (which many attribute, for its elegance, to Luke) into a critical sequence of crises in John, gospel scholars have generated a text of great power. For here Jesus makes visible a relationship between words and flesh that opens into a moment of peace and reciprocity, unexpectedly, where even those who wish to speak magnanimously for the text and its founding victim have missed it. And they have missed it, I think, because it is so hard to see Jesus as a body.

In his discourse on the bread of heaven, Jesus calls attention to his real, physical body, and in John this body is the ground of God's original utterance of all being. For in his retrospective Prologue, a provocative supersession of Genesis 1, John makes the stunning claim that God's Word has become flesh (1:14) and dwelt among us; Jesus is Word Incarnate, there from the beginning, though John did not know this until after the resurrection. John's Gospel comes into being to bear witness not only to the good news but, less obviously, also to testify to the author's own failure to understand until after he, too, had abandoned Jesus to judgement and death.

Breaching the decorum of synagogue instruction, Jesus is a provocateur. He makes his gendered, sexual body the referent for the 'word of God', for 'bread of heaven', manna that kept alive the persecuted and exiled chosen people in the desert. What is he doing when he says 'eat me and live for ever'? The echo of American sexual slang in his provocation may help us register the shock of the moment – how obscene it could feel for someone local, so known, so ordinary, to appropriate the language of transcendence, to locate the hope of a whole people in himself and the claim that the old fathers are 'dead' while his Father is 'alive'. Biblical commentators mute this offence, as if it is not necessary to feel the living, costly question posed here. Jesus may offend his interlocutors *in* the text, 'the Jews', but we who receive it, 'Christians', must be cushioned from offence. Why? What happens if we read the text against (or from) our own gendered bodies in relation to Jesus' and learn from our anxiety?

I do not make this suggestion casually. The text itself positions us for such a question. For those who decided how to construct the text of John's gospel have made a fascinating choice: tradition juxtaposes the critical moment when people begin to say of Jesus, 'He is the Christ' (7:41), upon which 'the chief priests and Pharisees' decide to arrest him (which closes John 7), and the story of the adulterous woman (which opens John 8).[3]

They all went home, and Jesus went to the Mount of Olives.

At daybreak he appeared in the Temple again; and as all the people came to him, he sat down and began to teach them.

The scribes and Pharisees brought a woman along who had been caught committing adultery; and making her stand there in full view of everybody, they said to Jesus, 'Master, this woman was caught in the very act of committing adultery, and Moses has ordered us in the Law to condemn women like this to death by stoning. What have you to say?' They asked him this as a test, looking for something to use against him.

But Jesus bent down and started writing on the ground with his finger. As they persisted with their question, he looked up and said, 'If there is one of you who has not sinned, let him be the first to throw a stone at her.' Then he bent down and wrote on the ground again. When they heard this they went away one by one, beginning with the eldest, until Jesus was left alone with the woman, who remained standing there. He looked up and said, 'Woman, where are they: Has no one condemned you?' 'No one, sir,' she replied. 'Neither do I condemn you,' said Jesus. 'Go away, and don't sin any more.'

(7:53–8; 1–11).

The narrative is framed as a scene of instruction, 'he sat down and began to teach them', which is immediately interrupted by another, 'Teacher . . . what do you have to say . . .?' We can take this as a model of how this text interrupts John's own, and find our own scene of instruction. The teaching begins with a challenge presented to Jesus, a call for interpretation which is presented as a matter of life and death. 'Teacher,' they said to him, 'this woman has been caught in the very act of adultery. Now in the Law Moses ordered such women to be stoned. But you – what do you have to say about it?' This lesson begins from a body, specifically the body in relation to other bodies. This works on three levels: the woman's use of her body in relation to two men (her spouse, her adulterous partner); the men's use of her body in relation to Jesus; Jesus' use of his body in relation to every other body present. She wills the first use of her body between two males;[4] the group of men will the second; Jesus wills the third.

The woman is presented to Jesus not as the subject but as the object of inquiry, just as she is linguistically presented first as the object of verbs which take the men as subjects: they 'led her forward', they 'caught her in the act'. For the accusing crowd, the subject of this linguistic transaction is 'it', or 'something', not 'her' or 'someone', signalling that the abstract principle of legal and social contract (right marital exchange, which ensures the internal coherence of any culture) is more primary than the living being, the woman. In their offer of a body as if it were a text, the group of men betray a triple refusal to take responsibility. They take responsibility neither for the violence they would do her (stoning), nor for the violence they are doing her by using her as an object of exchange, nor finally for the violence they wish to do Jesus, through her. At the same time, in asking Jesus to assume responsibility, they bear witness to the connection of law to person, speech to body, self to other in the act of sundering each of them. In bearing witness as they do, the accusing men – eyewitnesses deceptively sure of their authority to bring the woman to trial – open the very notion of witness to reinterpretation. They, and Jesus with them, also bring to light the violence inherent in the ritualized exchange of women.

Jesus takes responsibility for the resolution of this crisis which links his fate to hers: if he fails to condemn her he will seem to violate Mosaic law,[5] and if he condemns her, he violates Roman law, for in this period it is believed that the Sanhedrin's power to levy a death sentence was removed by Roman decree.[6] Jesus evades this carefully constructed double bind – his entrapment between two laws, one religious and one secular – but in a way no one expects. The narrator at this point brackets the prophet's trial: the aside, 'They asked him this as a test, looking for something to use against him', invites us to look at the structure before us.

Jesus responds to both the spoken and unspoken (the content as well as the intent) of this challenge in silence, with his body. He answers their question by moving: he bends down to draw in the dirt. But the crowd does not see his bodily gestures as a reply. Feeling that Jesus is evading the task of answering them, they ask again. Moving again, this time straightening up, Jesus used words: 'If there is one of you who has not sinned, let him be the first to throw a stone at her.' Then he repeats his first gesture, bending again, but this time the Greek verb is more precise: Jesus bends down to *write*.[7] The second time Jesus bends down, the connection between language and the body hits home. Now the crowd of men respond to Jesus' words with their bodies. The men, who a moment earlier signalled their violent unanimity by speaking with one collective voice, unified by two enemies – the woman, the prophet – now, one at a time, begin to move. 'But the audience went away one by one starting with the elders'. Each enacts, in silence, his own self-judgement before the others. Having arrived as an undifferentiated crowd, they leave as individuals, and they do not 'take' the woman with them. What has happend here?

In the preceding chapter, John is careful to tell us that Jesus has already been threatened with arrest – 'the Jews' are trying to kill him (7:1). He has begun to warn everyone, in language they cannot understand, that he will soon leave them (7:35, 8:21ff). In the passages which precede and follow this story, Jesus speaks a great deal, and passionately, about law, witness, testimony, judgement and love. Here, he says almost nothing. Here, he acts rather than speaks: or, to be precise, he testifies far more powerfully with his body than with his words.

Though, by definition, it takes two to commit adultery, and though we are told that the woman was caught in the act, so that the man must also have been caught, she alone is subjected to the crowd's legal authority and ultimate punishment: death by stoning outside the city's walls. Death by stoning is anonymous ritual muder: no one strikes first, no one touches the victim, so as not to risk becoming polluted with responsibility for murder. There is no question of a hearing (the very privilege the Temple police insist must be granted Jesus in chapter 7, when they return to 'the chief priests and Pharisees' empty-handed, having refused to arrest him). Actions have spoken louder than words. The female's body *is* her speech, and having performed it by having sex with someone not her legal spouse, she has forfeited the position of word-speaker.[8] In contrast, the males' words are offered as their definitive speech-acts, proffered as if detached from their gendered, sexual bodies. This is not, however, how Jesus appears to receive them.

Jesus undermines the apparent differences between the righteous men and the guilty woman. And he does so precisely by way of referring to the men as individuals with personal histories, and by relocating their speech in their bodies. By his words, Jesus refers each man back to himself, making each answerable for himself. His counter-offer works precisely because these men share with Jesus a field of reference: a wish, however occluded and corrupted by wordly power, social prejudice and fear of the prophet's authority, to honour God. Earlier, in chapter 7, Jesus offered the confusing and paradoxical imperative, 'Do not keep judging according to appearances; let your judgment be according to what is right' (7:24). Chapter 8 opens with this example of how it works. At the same time, this scene enacts Jesus' insistence that there is a model of expulsion, or 'casting out' of evil, which is grounded not in a self-interested misrecognition of the scapegoat but in the instant of self-recognition which begins from a genuine discovery and acceptance of the likeness between the guilty other and one's hidden self. Jesus incites the men to open in themselves the place of the other, the sinner, and to keep it inside, rather than projecting it onto a surrogate.

Jesus undermines an interdependent set of socially defined differences which it is extremely dangerous to disrupt or confuse at any time in any culture: between the innocent and the guilty, and between good violence (legal execution) and bad (murder). In confounding these distinctions, Jesus simultaneously exposes their foundation in a primary biological difference the crowd exploits: the asymmetrical relation of female to male. Jesus works a different kind of distinction, that between the spiritually (not the sexually) faithful and unfaithful. The erotic is the pretext, not the text, of this transaction.

In judging, Jesus was to have made himself vulnerable to judgement. But he refuses to judge. He signifies this by moving: bending down before accusers and accused alike. This apparently cryptic gesture has spawned innumerable esoteric explanations. Raymond Brown, editor of *The Anchor Bible*'s volumes on John, begins a lengthy summary of theories with the question, 'What did Jesus draw on the ground with his finger?' Most commentators have argued that Jesus is writing a biblical passage that indicts the accusers; a few think he is buying time, pondering what to do or displaying 'the Semitic custom of doodling on the ground when distraught'. Brown concludes, 'one cannot help but feel that if the matter were of major importance, the content of the writing would have been reported'.[9]

When the field of reference for our reading is the *figural* body, a text (what Jesus *writes*), we blind ourselves to the possibilities of Christian theology for a reading of Jesus' *literal* body as an incarnated, enacted utterance (what Jesus *does*). As the struggle to read Jesus' gesture *as if he were secretly still judging* is abandoned, as content is let go, the question of what occurs when Jesus bends to write can now emerge as the question of his intent in moving. The gesture functions structurally: Jesus bends down to break the spell of unanimity generated among the crowd of men all of whom stand up, as one, before him. The body's participation in a web of meaning, the person as the truly significant, seems quite clear to him, and he uses his gendered body to refuse the violent terms of exchange offered him because he is the powerful rival male. Had the men all sat or knelt, I think Jesus would have stood up. The point is, he physically distinguishes his position from theirs. Jesus' 'writing', like the crowd's speech, is not the true message; and in the crowd's wordless reply, we find our own answer to the riddle of Jesus' touching the earth. Everyone present is a speaking body; Jesus most consciously so. He not only refuses to stand with the accusers, he lowers himself, uncontaminated by the crowd's desire or the very dirt he draws in, a sign of our common origin and end.[10]

The group of men who at first cannot see a language in Jesus' posture are like the commentators who are sure the text *of* this scene hinges on a text *in* the scene. Such readers, like the accusers (from whom they would clearly differ), insist that words, particularly open, public speech, serve as the ultimate measure of response and responsibility: 'What have you to *say*?' They *persist*, John says. To the accusers' literalism, Jesus answers in the conditional and issues an imperative: '*If* there is one of you who has not sinned, *let* him be the first to throw a stone at her' (8:7). In a scandalous over-literalization of the terms of exchange, Jesus raises the ante. He recreates the wager on female flesh in language that makes each man a subject who must choose to destroy the woman as a person right here, right now – not later, outside the city's gates. He addresses them not as a crowd, but as persons: 'one of you'. The appeal is clear: as a group they act as one body with no head. This underscores the point that these men constitute the *disembodied*, a falsely incarnated corporate body, the crowd that functions with false authority and without conscience, as all lynch mobs do. Recalled to themselves, each to his own body and its history, they must act with full consciousness of the legal difference they wish to enforce with violence.

And in his response to the crowd's abuse of language (speaking as one, they speak falsely), Jesus directs the male gaze inwards. Jesus uses the power of language to hold present not a distorted representation of the event before them, but an as yet unrealized possibility for restored meaning and relationship. Ironically, he does this by outdoing them linguistically. By taking their gesture literally, Jesus offers it back to them with an intense pressure for immediate interpretation. Now they must act, not speak, and the act of throwing the first stone meant to signify their innocence will instantly constitute their guilt. The difference they would assert from the woman can only be upheld by violence. But for their stones, the material emblem of executed judgement, the death sentence, Jesus substitutes his words and embodied witness. For their spectral object/victim, the woman reduced to her crime, an 'adulteress', Jesus substitutes themselves.

At the turning point – in the pause between question and answer, tense with anticipation for the isolated and silent woman who waits to see what this invitation will mean for her vulnerable and exposed body – the narrative provides us with the scene of instruction and judgement which the 'scribes and Pharisees' had hoped to orchestrate. The reader is enabled, indeed we are *asked* by the narrator, to bear witness to this exchange. Now it is 'the scribes and Pharisees' who are caught in the act: they are guilty of adulterating the law, and in this they, too, have sinned in their use of a woman's body. Just as Mosaic law required two witnesses, so here, the accusers sin before two witnesses: the woman, Jesus.

Moved to knowledge by an invitation to be violent, 'If there is one of you who has not sinned, let him be the first to throw a stone at her', the men also bear witness to their virtue. None accepts the invitation. No man exempts himself from self-judgement. In this, the place of spiritual law is reconstituted – reinscribed within – and in relation to existing religious structures: the community of elders, the Temple, the larger social body and the actual gendered body. No sooner does each man experience himself as a subject *like* the woman, than he must lift the sentence, himself standing accused and vulnerable to the spirit of the law and the crowd's two victims.[11]

In his choice to behave as he does, Jesus enacts a model of witness intended to forestall the negative or violent triangulation of conflict. He reconstitutes the missing adulterer by locating him in the conscience of every male present.[12] Each man, voyeur to an illicit sexual encounter, stands accused, not necessarily of adultery – Jesus does not share in the crowd's (or the commentator's) fascination with sexual transgression – but of the more general ethical failure, sin. All sins, any sin, would make every man like the single woman. Even here, we miss a great deal if we refuse to see that the engendered distinction between the sins (bodily v. spiritual), the violence of a double standard, is destroyed: if the man has sinned, he is no different from the woman except in appearance, except that her sin was open and theirs closed to the viewing eye; until, that is, Jesus made it manifest by forcing their choice. Now they may understand what the woman who is made 'to stand there, in full view of everybody' suffers while they proclaim her guilt and presume to decide her fate.

This text turns on ironies of inversion, and constitutes us, its readers, as witnesses who are also implicated in the crisis of judgement. As the triangulated conflict is overturned, both the original *and* the surrogate victim of the crowd are left unharmed, and the position of neutral or innocent bystander to violence is evacuated. The narrative structures an unexpectedly rich scene of instruction for every player in the drama (including the reader), at the same time that it clears a place for merciful judgement (extending to the reader).

In the end, the scene moves from triangulation to the pair, from an exchange of challenges to a dialogue. Two people face each other, each of whom stand outside the kinship system by acts of volition (his chastitity, her adultery). One of them endures a moment of terrible isolation for this choice (the woman), while the other rests calmly in the solitude of his witness (the prophet). In the end, Jesus, rather than distinguish himself from the crowd, speaks to the woman as if his actions would follow from and be modelled on the others': 'He looked up and said, "Woman, where are they: Has no one condemned you?" "No one, sir," she replied. "Neither do I condemn you," said Jesus. "Go away, and don't sin any more."[13]

The imperatives which follow from Jesus' 'straightening', his willingness to meet the gaze of his present interlocutor, suddenly bring her into view. Jesus' interrogative engages the woman not as victim of but as witness to the crowd's decision, just as his imperatives presume her active subjectivity, her volition. Freed from her use as mute object, a medium for the accusers' challenge to Jesus' authority, the woman is now engaged as a person. In contrast to the men humbled into silence by Jesus' lowered gaze and posture, the women is invited into speech as he straightens and looks up at her, waiting on her perception of what has just occurred. The woman answers Jesus directly, with no plea, no argument, no attempt to explain. Jesus uses the control over her the men presumed to offer him as the occasion to renounce it: he appeals to her mind, her will, her spirit. He refers her back to herself. She is told, as the men who accused her were told, to be answerable for herself. Free to leave, freed to live, the woman has her own choice to make in response to the release from judgement and death Jesus has worked for her. She, like the men, is turned back from the place of judgement uninjured. She walks away – and is remembered for ever.

The hope in this story is the generative power of compassionate recognition, a refusal of self-definition in terms of the other: Jesus sees a person in the woman, neither an 'adulteress', nor an object of exchange. The exegetical tradition blinds itself to the new language of relationship generated here. By privileging male over female, writing over speech, words over bodily speech-acts, sins of the flesh over sins of the spirit, the biblical commentator upholds the very distinctions the text undermines. To look for too much signification where there is too little and to see none at all where it truly works is to fail to see how practical and material the model for upsetting the mechanism of the surrogate victim is, and potentially to fail to know how to imitate it positively. Jesus, as male (and, theologically, as Word Incarnate), is traditionally examined for what he *writes*: it must be words, and commentators aware that this is the only recorded instance of Jesus writing are at great pains to argue what his text must have been. They mistake the writing as the text and see no message in the bodies, in the woman's silence as a product of her positioning between men or in Jesus' physical gestures of abasement, his articulate body by which he signals his refusal to exchange persons as if they were merely words, or words as if they were merely empty signs. Jesus' movements bracket the words he speaks in order to move the crowd from violent unanimity (signalled by false accord: they speak in one voice, the voice of accusation and entrapment) to peaceful (and non-verbal) retreat from false witness. The men testify most truthfully in the text when they no longer speak 'as one' but silently *move* 'one by one'.[14] The elders who leave first bear witness not to the mere re-establishment of existing hierarchy, but to the more humble privilege of old age: time enough for the patriarchs to have sinned and to know it.

Commentators who think they know how to recover the text of Jesus' writing also presume to know how to read the text of the silenced female body: she is silenced by her *shame*. This ignores the text's clear emphasis on the relationship between where one stands in the structure of violent exchange and whether or not one can speak and be heard. The woman cannot speak so long as she is exploited as sign/word, occupying the place of the surrogate victim, her voice stilled by the ventriloquism of the men who would speak through her. The woman speaks only once the exchange of her body fails. But here the failed exchange leads to the *withdrawal* of false meaning from her flesh: no longer a sign/word, she comes into view as a speaker of words, a woman.

The woman's peaceful recognition that 'No one' condemns her in John 8 has a dark twin in the Passion (John 18–19) when no one comes forward from the turbulent crowd to stand with Jesus. The close of chapter 8 suggests why.

The crowd John continually refers to as 'the Jews' want to know one thing, 'Who are you claiming to be?' (8:25). Now Jesus speaks the hardest, the most intolerable language of all: he echoes Yahweh, collapsing the most profound of distinctions, the original difference between divine creator and human creature. In this assertion of intimate identity with God in the face of material evidence of his humanity, his body, Jesus stages a decisive crisis of difference. He refers himself, as a sign/word, to the original referent and primary Other:

I tell you most solemnly,
before Abraham ever was,
I Am.

(8:58)

This tremendous 'I Am' is Jesus' last utterance in chapter 8, which ends with the fulfilment of the threat anticipated at its opening. But now the object of the violence is no longer the adulterous woman, but Jesus himself, who here adulterates the terms of speaking of and being in himself in relation to God. Now a crowd responds to his claim with spontaneous violence, an immediate desire to execute judgement: 'At this they picked up stones to throw at him; but Jesus hid himself and left the Temple' (8:59). Legal stoning was the threat hanging over the woman at the opening of chapter 8; spontaneous stoning is the threat against Jesus at the close.[15]

'The Jews' declare that they are subject to Roman law, 'We are not allowed to put a man to death' (John 18:31), even as they condemn Jesus according to Mosaic law: 'We have a Law . . . and according to that law he ought to die, because he has claimed to be the Son of God' (19:7). This is the vice-grip the earlier crowd used on Jesus and the woman (8:5), but this time the judge presented with the text of persecution does not know what to do with it.

Jesus is condemned to death by a turbulent crowd whose secular head evacuates the position of authority. 'Truth? . . . What is that?' John's Pilate cynically asks when Jesus says, under examination, that he exists 'to bear witness to the truth' (18:37–8). Pilate's rhetorical question, a stunning modern touch, stands in bitter contrast to Jesus' wordplay in 8:1–11 which cleared a literal and figural space for the self-recollection of an accusing crowd, a gesture that released accused, accusers *and judge* alike.

Having given up on truth, Pilate can locate no ground to stand on. He orders that a title be nailed to the cross, written in the three languages of the people who will crowd around to read it (Hebrew, Latin, and Greek): 'Jesus the Nazarene, King of the Jews' (19: 20). This attempt to fix a meaning to the sign of the cross locates blame on 'the Jews' who stand accused of killing their king by handing him over to Pilate, who, by way of this inscription, would hand him right back. In the Passion narratives, most powerfully in *John*, Jesus becomes the ultimate object of exchange.

In the course of the two trials – the woman's, his own – Jesus passes through virtually every position in the juridical process: accused, accuser, witness, advocate, victim, judge, opening each to fresh interpretation. There is only one role he refuses to play, the one we ascribe to him at our own peril: executioner. To play this role, or to ask Jesus to play it, is to fail the test of virtue he turns back to the crowd of accusing men who, unlike generations of Christians, quietly turn back from the place of judgement, uninjured, and uninjuring.

NOTES

1 Unless otherwise noted, all biblical quotations are taken from *The Jerusalem Bible*, New York, Doubleday, 1966. I thank Daphne Hampson, Margaret Homans, Leslie Moore, Jaroslav Pelikan and most of all John Timpane for their

generosity and wisdom in reading various drafts of this essay and offering suggestions for revision. All errors are, of course, my own.

2 *The New Oxford Annotated Bible with the Apocrypha: Revised Standard Edition*, eds Herbert G. May and Bruce M. Metzger, New York, Oxford University Press, 1977, p. 1296.

3 For a discussion of questions of authorship and canonicity, see *The Anchor Bible*, vol. 29, *The Gospel According to John* (i–xii), Garden City, Doubleday, pp. 335ff. Brown notes that 'it is only from ca. 900 that [this narrative] begins to appear in the standard Greek text'. Brown sees this brief story as a rupture in the text. Contemporary literary theory makes it possible to read for structure in a way that makes this interruption extremely revealing and fruitful, a breach that opens the text.

4 For the suggestion that the woman's husband set her up to be caught, see Brown's summary of the commentators, ibid., p. 338.

5 In *Torah*, the law concerns *both* parties to adultery: 'If a man is found lying with another man's wife, both of them – the man and the woman with whom he lay – shall die. Thus you will sweep away evil from Israel' (Deuteronomy 22:22) – *Tanakh, A New Translation of the Holy Scriptures According to the Traditional Hebrew Text*, Philadelphia, New York and Jerusalem, Jewish Publication Society, 5746/1985.

6 *The Anchor Bible*, op. cit., p. 337.

7 ibid., p. 333.

8 For a discussion of woman as speaking from the place of marriage, or inside her role in right exchange, see Claude Lévi-Strauss, *The Elementary Structures of Kinship*, trans. James Harle Bell, John Richard von Sturmer and Rodney Needham, ed. Rodney Needham, Boston, Beacon, rev. edn 1969, p. 496; for my revision of this concept in uncovering the cultural structures that mark women as targets for eroticized violence, see Patricia Joplin, 'The Voice of the Shuttle is Ours', in Lynn A. Higgins and Brenda R. Silver (eds), *Rape and Representation*, New York, Columbia University Press, 1991, pp. 35–66.

9 *The Anchor Bible*, op. cit., pp. 333–4.

10 I would like to thank John Drury for this insight.

11 And before the silent witnesses within the text, those who had originally come and sat on the ground before the entrance to the Temple, waiting for Jesus' instruction, who leave, too.

12 René Girard kindly pointed this out to me. For his argument concerning the revelatory perspective on scapegoating in the gospels, see Girard, *The Scapegoat*, trans. Yvonne Freccero, Baltimore, Johns Hopkins University Press, 1986; and with Jean-Michel Oughourlian and Guy Lefort, *Things Hidden since the Foundation of the World*, trans. Stephen Bann and Michael Metteer, Stanford, Stanford University Press, 1987.

13 *The Anchor Bible* offers a variation on the last words Jesus addressed to the woman, a choice that obscures the power of Jesus' vision: 'from now on, avoid *this sin*', adultery. *The Jerusalem Bible* is closer to the Greek.

14 Just as Daniel is moved by the spirit and breaks the spell of unanimity among those who condemn Susanna by physically moving away from those who would spill her blood. In a longer version of this essay, I compare the gospel story to the trial of Susanna's virtue in Daniel.

15 Though stoning is the legal punishment for blasphemy outlined in Leviticus 24:16, here the gesture is represented as spontaneous.

Chapter 18

Law and gynesis: Freud v. Schreber

John O' Neill

The postmodern condition, as I shall take it, is one marked by a certain disinheritance, the collapse of patriarchy as an effect of a series of defamilizing strategies which simultaneously expand statism, consumerism, globalism and, of course, postmodernism itself.[1] As an aesthetic, an architecture and a 'paralogic' of fairies and women released by the collapse of the major ideologies,[2] postmodern theorizing is part of the social hysteria it affects to analyse and consequently at best a weak point of view. Alice Jardine[3] has nicely observed that the male reaction to the 'loss' of meaning has produced among them an ambivalent gynesis. What we have to respond to in this is a sea-change in modernity that all parties – however reluctant or however celebrant – seem to identify as the event of *woman's-becoming-woman*. Lyotard[4] has also addressed this movement of gynesis in terms of the myth of an Orpheus who must now learn to look woman in the face if 'we-men' are not to lose for ever the chance of civilization.

These events cannot, of course, leave the Judaeo-Christian narrative untouched. However, rather than assume that everything goes dead with the 'death of God', I think it is more likely that we are experiencing a refiguration of the 'Holy Family' in which the paternal, maternal and filial positions are being redefined. In this process, the new children will adopt both patricidal and matricidal arguments, celebrating their own parthenogenesis. Others, however, may rediscover the sacrificial parents behind the patriarchal law and with them the burden of intergenerational trust. In short, this may be the time to abandon the worship of gods and goddesses (especially in academia) in order to consider the possibility of a new *figurability of the sacred* in which the bond (*religio*) between us is deterritorialized and dehistoricized. I propose, then, to treat a case of male paranoia[5] – Schreber's becoming God's wife – as an exploration of the breakdown in the boundary between eternity and paternity in which a man permits himself to be re-entered by the Holy Spirit. Since I cannot explore every aspect of this celebrated case, I will focus upon the question of woman's figurability in Schreber's second psychotic episode and its subsequent legal-clinical history.

Early one morning in a state half between sleep and waking, the idea came to Schreber 'that after all it really must be very nice to be a woman submitting to the act of copulation'.[6] The Freud translation renders Schreber's vision more passive than it is in his own words: 'Es war die Vorstellung, dass es doch eigentlich recht schön sein musse, ein Weib zu sein, das dem Beischlaf unterliege.'[7] The English translation, as was required of it, is absolutely faithful to Freud's interpretation of Schreber's project of becoming God's wife as a passive homosexual phantasy in which a series of father-figures are played off in a delusional system recorded in the *Denkewurdigkeiten eines Nervenkranken*. But whereas Freud over-looked the *positive aesthetics* contained in Schreber's remark, Janine Chasseguet-Smirgel[8] focusses upon it in order to show how Schreber struggled against his father's pedagogic usurpation of the functions of the archaic mother, striving to integrate his femininity with his own sex. Because Freud ignored the paternal text, he also overlooked the composite figure of Schreber's father/mother. He thereby not only homosexualized the *return of the feminine* in Schreber but also ignored Schreber's *myth of parthenogenesis* which I think may be interpreted as a desire to recreate his family, whose patriarchal line was about to become extinct through the destructive combination of Oedipal psychology and Christian pedagogy. Moreover, Freud's reading of the *Memoirs*[9] refused to treat Schreber's intertext – namely, his father's *Medical Indoor Gymnastics*[10] – as the basis for understanding the *Memoirs*. Because Freud ignored Schreber's success-ful plea for release from the asylum that is appended[11] to the *Memoirs*, I propose to treat the psychoanalytic text as complicit with a repressive therapeutic culture from which I shall try to redeem Schreber's delirious project of 'becoming-woman' and of exceeding the law that on this occa-sion renders a verdict of *nihil obstat*.

The fact that we have to consider is that Schreber's delirium did not prevent him from recording his illness, nor from a successful legal defence in which the *Memoirs* figured as evidence that neither Schreber's writing nor his transvestism were excessive. Schreber's delirium, then, was com-patible with certain standards of bourgeois reasonableness and public decorum. Yet there is much in the *Memoirs* to convince us that its language is nonsensical and thereby serves to justify Schreber's exclusion from the commerce and community of his day. Surely, in Schreber's *Memoirs* language has gone on holiday, as Wittgenstein puts it, and its hallucinatory effects would seem to justify both Freud and Lacan in locating Schreber's delirium in the collapse of his relation to his father and to the law of which language is the proper effect in our daily interactions. Even so, Freud recognized that Schreber's *Memoirs* are a reconstruction of his illness and thus not entirely bound to the repetition of the base-language (*Grunds-prache*) contained in them. Hence the *Memoirs* are not on the same level as the delirium they contain. Rather, the *Memoirs* are a non-medical, literary and, we might add, legal strategy for resisting the language of medicine and religion in which Schreber suffered as a child and later as a clinical patient. What I am suggesting is that Schreber's *Memoirs* are a delirious ('derailing') intertext constructed to overturn the paternal logic of language and embodiment contained in his father's medico-psychical-spiritualized pedagogic texts.[12] What gives the *Memoirs* a hallucinatory voice is the subtext of the father's medicalized appropriation of the divine voice. In a society that speaks to God on everything from its concern with its daily bread to victories in war and which feels closest to God when discussing its sexual obsessions, Schreber's divine intercourse hardly marks him out as a mad man. And so the Court of Saxony rightly judged.

I am not suggesting, of course, that the law easily accommodates the practices of delirium and hallucination. It does not – any more than does psychoanalysis and, indeed, the combined effect of law and psychiatry will generally be hard upon such cases as that of Schreber and would serve to institutionalize them. In this regard, it would be tempting to read the *Memoirs* as the intertext of the *Medical Indoor Gymnastics* but to treat each as combined effects of the rise of disciplinary power in the therapeutic state, along the lines suggested by Foucault, thereby supplementing his work on technologies of the self.[13] To some extent I am going to do just that by taking up Deleuze/Guattari's reading of Schreber, especially since they do not erase Scheber's delirious bypassing of the rational-legal discourse upon the institutionalized (Oedipalized) body in his excursus upon the 'un-organizable-body' of *jouissance*. But I shall surrender to Schreber's language somewhat more than Deleuze/Guattari by letting its mythopoesis be heard in its most profound level of 'becoming-woman', where the absent centre is the blessing (*Seligkeit*) of birth and not, as Freud thought, the dead soul (*selig*) of the father. Schreber's delirious discourse needs to be understood as a meta-linguistic comment upon how our socio-legal discourses make nonsense of the body's language, most especially when they cut off the body from its source in the will to live in midst of its most ordinary experiences, familied and sociable, from generation to generation – for which it must thank God, on the one hand, and Caesar, on the other.

We now set aside the literature that is devoted to treating the *Memoirs* as a device for encoding the unmentionable act of 'soul murder' experienced by Schreber whether at the hand of his father or at the hands of his clinicians.[14] We nevertheless invoke this background in order to decode Schreber's *Entmannung*, or 'becoming-woman',[15] as a positive myth of the refiguration of a 'sanity' beyond the borders of narcissism and psychosis, into the in-between of sexual difference. Alice Jardine has suggested that the Schreber case is a perfect example of the crisis of modernity.[16] It is, indeed, especially if we treat Freud's account of the *Memoirs* as one side of the patriarchal crisis – as itself a symptom – but regard the *Memoirs* themselves as Schreber's vision of that newly contested procreativity which is the symptom of postmodernity. As Deleuze and Guattari might argue, Schreber's *Entmannung* does not represent the 'loss' of an organ but rather the collapse of an Oedipally organized body. Schreber's nervous body of pleasure (*Wollust*) is a 'body-without-organs', a body becoming-woman in a new order of things where the Oedipal and the disciplinary bodies have decayed and rotted away, hollowing out the sites of use and power. The Oedipalized body – the body of stages, zones, boundaries separated and hierarchized – requires an extraordinary repression of the 'body-without-organs (BWO)' whose desires are not object-satisfactions and not confinable within the family or the factory. Consequently, Deleuze and Guattari argue that the desiring body cannot be inscribed within the cycle of production and consumption (constituted by law, economics and psychoanalysis) since this artificial zoning only hides the fact that everything is process. This in turn means that there exists only a further artificial separation between man and nature since each is continuously in process and never reducible to the object of one or the goal of the other:

> Not man as the king of creation, but rather as the being who is in ultimate contact with the profound life of all forms or all types of beings, who is responsible for even the stars and animal life, and who ceaselessly plugs an organ-machine into an energy-machine, a tree into his body, a breast into his mouth, the sun into his asshole: the eternal custodian of the machines of the universe.[17]

The 'desiring machines' are grafted upon the products of the organ body whose objects always presuppose a continuous flow of partial objects, just as every machine presupposes its connection to other machines or to the production-of-production. The desiring machines are implanted in/on the body of organs but continue to dream of the 'unorganized' body like that of Schreber – without organs, teeth, larynx, eyes or intestines, consuming itself.

What Schreber rejected is the produced body, the body of pedagogy, the panoptic body of disciplined heterosexuality and work. Against all this, he set up a counter-body – a body without organs, a body of rays, suffused with music and poetry, a body beyond sexuality, a body of perpetual *jouissance*. Or rather, since he believed that God was captured by the influencing machinery of Dr Flechsig[18] which tempted God to attach himself to the organ body, Schreber had to accomplish a transformation of his body such that God will recover his capacity for love-at-a-distance, i.e. without need of intervention, and without the phallus. In his alliance with Flechsig, God was tempted to try to produce desire for Himself by acting upon Schreber's bowels – the very place where only an idiot could imagine there would be no desiring machinery unless cranked by his intervention. Holy shit! God's seduction by Flechsig – and, of course, by the Christian pedagogy of Schreber's father – had reduced love to a disciplinary test, a writing system and a memory system exacting continuous confession in a parody of spiritual exercise. This is the model of Christian capitalism or capitalized Christianity founded upon its heaven/hell influencing machine and the accountability of soul-banking which is grafted upon the body without organs to record its thoughts, motives, actions, omissions and commissions.

Christian pedagogy renders the body paranoid by means of its system of disjunctions, of higher and lower regions of the body, society, of God and of the heavens. But Freud's genealogy of Schreber's paranoia is itself blocked around the organ body – i.e. the body with a penis or 'with no' penis. Freud's notion of nature is likewise domesticated – talking birds must be young girls foolishly desirous of seduction by the baby-penis. Freud requires that every body be a third body – an Oedipal body, i.e. a body incapable of thinking its sexuality apart from the primal scene of parental copulation. Nobody is a body full with itself – as Mary was full with child while God kept His distance. But Schreber dreamed of a body whose *jouissance* exceeds the Oedipal triangle and whose reproduction floats all sexual difference in a miracle he had seen inscribed on woman's body. Here Deleuze and Guattari invoke the concept of the 'celibate machine' to show Schreber's move beyond the paranoidal-machine of the paternal pedagogy and the God-Flechsig miraculating machine. The aim of the 'celibate machine' is to 'marry', so to speak, the desiring-machines and the body without organs into the body of eternal *jouissance* whose intensity is prior to delirium and hallucination and which results from the forces of attraction and repulsion which traverse the body without organs:

> The breasts on the judge's naked torso are neither delirious nor halluci-natory phenomena: they designate, first of all, a band of intensity, a zone of intensity on his body without organs. The body without organs is an egg: it is criss-crossed with axes and thresholds, with latitudes and longitudes and geodesic lines, traversed by *gradients* marking the transitions and the becomings, the destination of the subject developing along these particular vectors. Nothing here is representative, rather, it is all life and lived experience: the actual, lived emotion of having breasts does not resemble breasts, it does not represent them, any more than a predestined zone in the egg resembles the organ that it is going to be simulated to produce within itself.[19]

Schreber before his mirror is not a thing of rags and baubles. He is not his own cheap wife – that marital organ whose necessity can be budgeted within a rational household budget, a minor pleasure whose indulgence will appeal to the law as evidence of his maturity and readiness for release into the bourgeois world. He includes all that in his appeal to the Court of Saxony just as he defends himself against the ruin of publishing the *Memoirs*. Schreber's pantomime recuperates the world's history, re-enacts its creation, renews humanity and marries science and religion – *Ecce Miss Schreber*. Schreber's mirror does not play back the primal scene to the infantile sexual theorist so that he can control his first person utterances. It reflects the eternal feminine (*die ewige Weibe*), the exhaustion of the body with organs, with breasts, with a penis, with orifices. Schreber's mirror shimmers and glitters, multiplying the intensities of the body without organs, amplified by being quite *alone*. But not in solitary confinement such as he experienced in the asylum at Sonnenstein where the panoptical eye ravished his body as though it were nothing but a dead anus, a stone sun. There the asylum is a machine for the production of castrations, for infantilization and the collapse of language and sense that will feed madness into the asylum as its *raison d'être*, as the asylum requires solitariness in order to maximize the violation of the body on behalf of society. Schreber defends himself by entering into a covenant with God to shed the body with organs and to become a woman-in-*jouissance*-with-herself. He separates himself from himself in order to engender himself, like a bride preparing for her wedding to the lover she already holds in her heart and who floats around her like Chagall's groom.

In his struggle to reduce Schreber's divinity, Freud for once was prepared to make himself sound perfectly boring – indeed, to crackle like the miracled-up voices, everything belongs to the Father, the father is behind everything, behind God, behind Flechsig, behind your bum! Indeed, psychoanalysis is boring because sex is boring and sex is boring even when it involves buggery, by God! But this is why Schreber wanted to get out of the asylum. He had had enough of abortive sex with the miscarriages suffered by his dearly loved wife. It was she who protected him from the worst ravages of the asylum. It was with her that Schreber intended to share his transformation into a woman – whatever its difficulties for them both so long as they held on to the old Oedipal organization. But they both wanted a child more than anything else and thus Schreber's body took the place that his wife's body had not been able to fulfil. However, Schreber responededs to the dilemma not by assuming the phallus which would legitimate another wife but by becoming a woman whose self-impregnation is beyond the phallus since God has no need of the copulatory act once he grants a miracle. Thus Schreber was prepared to sacrifice himself in the shape of God's wife in order to bring upon his own marriage the blessing of new life for which he and his wife had longed beyond all other marks of wealth and happiness.

The *Memoirs* are an extraordinary testimony to Schreber's attempts to keep his wife's love and respect through this strange journey, particularly in view of the risks of madness, confinement and degradation to which it exposed him and his family. These risks are, of course, at their height in Flechsig's power to castrate Schreber on behalf of the institutionalized Oedipalism that empowers his clinic, if not Freud's office. Between these two limits, Schreber's infant body had already experienced the panoptical pedagogies instituted by his father on behalf of the Christian family and its subservience to God's love. For Schreber's father had constructed an extraordinary system of inspecting and drilling the infant body to make it the instrument of an external order of redemption and salvation in the double service of God and state:

> When we learn that the instructor, the teacher, is deadly and the colonel too, and also the mother – *when all the agents of social production and anti-production are in this way reduced to the figures of familial repro- duction* – we can understand why the panicked libido no longer risks abandoning Oedipus, and internalizes it. The libido internalizes it in the form of a castrating quality between the subject of the statement (*l'énoncé*) and the subject of the enunciation, as is characteristic of the pseudo-individual fantasy ('I, as a man, understand you, but as judge, boss as colonel or general, *that is to say as the father*, I condemn you').[20]

Freud was obliged to homosexualize the double voice in this judgement because he suppressed the institutional contents of the paternal metaphor in favour of the paternity of psychoanalytic reconstruction.[21] He therefore overlooked Schreber's constant struggle with the authorities in the asylum, as well as his vigorous opposition to his sexual transformation while it operates within conventional socio-legal institutions. The schizo-body can consume its parts, chew itself up, go without organs because its partial objects do not communicate with any total body, whose parts have been hierarchized on the Oedipal model of repression, organization and devel- opment. It is therefore resistant to those penal pedagogies which seek to redirect its resistance to the integration of its drives, nerves, rays that vibrate, explode and float like birds from an open cage beyond the pleasure principle.[22] It is from this beyond that Schreber had exclaimed '*how beautiful it would be to be a woman succumbing to the act of love!*' Thus we have not to reduce Schreber to the little man at the foot of the primal bed guessing at an uncertain future of becoming Daddy. It is woman's case, her fall, her swoon, her body of bliss, that Schreber recalls in order to project himself beyond his present struggles with the asylum pedagogies that seek to make him remember the Oedipal family with its bird-brained little girls dreaming of naughty little lads. Schreber's child is so much more than that. Its birth demands a miracle of its parent who must place himself outside of the failures of copulation into the miracled body of parthogenesis around which every human family gathers in virgin awe. Such is Schreber's holy night, his silent night with God's love and impregnation in which the blessing of birth is transported beyond any understanding of the paternal pedagogue or his psychoanalytic counterparts in the asylum and the ana- lyst's office.

Schreber was perfectly canny in observing the phenomenological boundaries of practical and religious discourse, just as he was competent with the ecology of private and public life as a constitutive feature of what we call 'sane' and 'insane' behaviour. He did not treat his covenant with God as on a par with his daily contracts, any more than the average Christian expects his belief in the gospels to overthrow his conventional morality. On the other hand, without this extraterrestrial theatre (*die anderer Schauplatz*) of religious phantasy everyday life would appear far less reasonable and much less tolerable with regard to its injustice, its lies and its cruelty. Schreber did not pull heaven down to earth. He recognized that the two domains are separated by a long way and that his own becoming-woman was no more likely to occur tomorrow than is the second coming of Christ. But such transitions may be rehearsed in the body without organs where the separations of male and female, of husband and wife, may turn through one another in what each has of the other rather than what they lack in either part:

> Thus the schizo will accept the reduction of everything to the mother, since it is of no importance whatsoever: he is sure of being able to make everything rise again from the mother, and to keep for his own secret use all the Virgins that had been placed there.[23]

For this reason, Schreber was not afraid to go mad, to lose his organs, to become a woman, to draw the other world which spoke through him upon himself. His project was to make first things first – all over again, once for all. The first baby. To achieve this Schreber had to escape his father's panoptical project for regenerating the German nation by means of his physical contraptions and confessional exercises to make all children the docile instruments of the state and religion. If Schreber could not step into his father's shoes, it was because the father trampled upon his little children; not because Schreber is pleading for another beating. Rather, Schreber pushed the paternal project into the delirious transformation of his body into a body of voluptuousness, of birthing without birth, because his new body had no need of little men going in and out of it, and no need of Godsprick because God's miracle isn't housed there. Schreber's transformation occurred upon the body between schizophrenia and psychosis, the body upon which Oedipalization cannot force its decisions. Hence Judge Schreber's breakdown and his flight into hypochondria, i.e. his unfixable illness in the belly where he rots and flowers.

Schreber's ultimate strategy was to graft upon the father's manuals and his grandfather's biological and economic treatises a 'wild' text from his own body-without-organs, deliriously and calmly recording its confinement, degradation and transformation into the redemptive organ and choir of creation. The pages of the *Memoirs* fill out with devils, insects, tortures, decay, birds and bellowings, with a plot to reverse the cosmic order of things, to capture and to ruin God Himself. All this is inscribed upon

Schreber's body which detaches from itself by the sheerest shred of sanity in order to reconstruct that human order in which there is bearable sense, reasonable limits and ultimate justice, at least for children. Schreber's transformation was not from one *sex* to another but from one *family* to another – to the family whose love is not constrained by Oedipalized sexually, whose love is not a church-state discipline, whose love is not an army drill or a school board examination. But Freud could not allow Schreber to pluralize homosexuality, to shatter the social order built upon the paternal metaphor. Even the dead father reversed in the Freudian family must be passed on through the mark of castration, the reminder that it is the Oedipus myth which binds the generations and not their sexuality. To copulate without the father in mind would unleash sexuality, multiply the body; it would celebrate birth in the place of death. Freud could ignore the father's sadistic pedagogies because he had reversed the soul murder of the children sacrificed to his Oedipal genealogy of God-fearing copulation. Even in the game of *Fort/Da*, Freud misses the infant construction of a device for throwing away the Oedipal body responsible for his mother's disappearances.[24] The mother toy is the beginning of childhood without parental copulation, sexual banking and the panoptical disciplines of the church and school, factory and clinic which sit behind the analyst. In the face of such a future, Freud reverses history, shunts every present into the past, binding it to a murderous myth.

Why does Freud shift things to another scene – into the theatre of Oedipus and away from the *Memoirs*? It is because the violent act – the primal scene – can be kept off stage all the time it structures what can be seen to transpire on stage as confusion, a crime or a plague calling for the punishment that anyone beyond the family must incur. 'Father, forgive them. For they know not what they do.' From birth to death, a double crucifixion before which the analyst remains silent. To this Schreber's miracled body responds like intensified parts which have broken away from their place as the reduced organs of exercise and punishment in the paternal pedagogy. They are no longer the part objects of Oedipal expression, they are beyond the sucking places of society. They prefigure a body without sexual organs, a body of love, which can only be seen, or heard, or felt on entirely miracled occasions that exceed the organization of the Oedipal family and its catechism. It is because of this vision that Schreber faints before the law. He cannot step into his father's shoes because his father's teachings have reduced the spirit of the law to its letter, to its examinations and its panoptical contraptions for binding the soul to the body. Schreber sought the garden, the lake of poetry and music apart from the mad instructions of the school and the asylum where even God is seduced by his own creation:

Is it Schreber's father who acts through machines, or on the contrary is it the machines themselves that function through the father? *Psycho-analysis settles on the imaginary and structural representatives of reterritorialization, while schizo-analysis follows the machinic indices of deterritorialization.* The opposition still holds between the neurotic on the couch – as an ultimate and sterile land, the last exhausted colony – and the schizo out for a walk in a deterritorialized circuit.[25]

Schreber escaped the analyst's couch and the hospital bed because love's body does not lie in the Oedipal bed. So the *Memoirs* are placed upon Freud's desk for a retrospective analysis, for homosexualization *post factum*, torn from Schreber's own mouth, hand, anus, and cut off from their heavenly flight and divine rebirth. Schreber's madness is saved from insanity but only to expropriate his nervous body for the history of psychoanalysis. Thus Schreber's body is divided once and for all between the active and passive bodies of homosexuality, i.e. the same old sex whichever way you look at your orifices. Schreber's song is silenced and its garden of miracled birds and insects closed to the imagination inspired by spontaneous generations in contravention of the laws of reproduction. But Schreber's suicides do not justify the closure of the gates of the imagination. Rather, they figurate a model of death desired by the inorganizable body of love whose procreation dances amidst the swoons, faints and seizures of the body's little deaths.

The paternal pedagogy desires to rewrite the child body so that it will desire its own punishment, so that it will enjoy nothing with impunity. No bodily movement inside or outside of the body's reach is allowed to escape this test; nothing escapes the divine inspector and everyone has eyes only for him. Family, school and factory hum with the production of this order which permits only breakdowns, machinal or nervous, but not revolutions. This order has its genealogy, handed down through the sons by the fathers and witnessed by the mothers whose bodies reproduce the family, church and state. The sexual order and the gymnastic order represent two articulations of the medicalized state[26] which the Schreber family served and to which Schreber addresses the *Memoirs* in so far as they constitute a treatise of scientific interest alongside the interests of his wife's understanding. By the same token, the *Memoirs* drift in favour of the family romance however much it offends science and the medical order. Thus the mother body, the wife body and the Virgin are not separated in Schreber's transformed body any more than they are in the Holy Family adored on the side altar of the Oedipal family. In short, there is Blessed Assumption in every woman's desire just as there is a Holy Child whose innocence exceeds the desire for reproduction and continuity and is wanted in each of us, whether man or woman.

248 Gender and psyche

NOTES

1 John O'Neill, 'Religion and Postmodernism: The Durkheimian Bond in Bell and Jameson', *Theory, Culture and Society*, 5, 2–3, June 1955, pp. 493–508.
2 Jean-François Lyotard, 'For a Pseudo-Theory', *Yale French Studies*, 52, 1975 pp. 115–27.
3 Alice A. Jardine, *Gynesis: Configurations of Woman and Modernity*, Ithaca, Cornell University Press, 1985.
4 Jean-François Lyotard, *Dérive à partir de Marx et Freud*, Paris, Editions de Minuit, 1973.
5 Daniel Paul Schreber (1842–1911) was the son of Daniel Gottlob Moritz Schreber whose orthopaedic and gymnastic work made him famous. These texts cannot be ignored as an intertext in the son's own *Memoirs*, written in 1902 after two periods as an inmate in the Leipzig Psychiatric Clinic, directed by Dr Fleschsig (1884–5) and in the Sonnenstein Asylum, directed by Dr G. Weber from 1893 to 1902. Schreber was a successful lawyer, a county court judge, and indeed successfully conducted his own appeal – in which the *Memoirs* functioned as evidence – for release from the Sonnenstein Asylum in 1902. After the death of his mother and his wife's stroke in 1902, Schreber fell ill and finished his days miserably in the asylum at Leipzig-Dosen, where he died on 14 April 1911.
6 Sigmund Freud, 'Psychoanalytic Notes on an Autobiographical Account of a Case of Paranoia (Dementia Paranoides)', in *Case Histories II*, Harmondsworth, Penguin, 1979, p. 124.
7 Daniel Paul Schreber, *Denkwürdigkeiten eines Nervenkranken*, Mit Augsatzen von Franz Baumeyer, einem Vorwort, einem Materialanhang und sechs Abbildungen herausgegeben von Peter Heiligenthal und Reinhard Volk, Frankfurt am Main, Syndikat, 1985, p. 30.
8 Janine Chasseguet-Smirgel, 'On President Schreber's Transexual Delusion', in David B. Allison, Prado de Oliveira, Mark S. Roberts and Allen S. Weiss (eds), *Psychosis and Sexual Identity: Towards a Post-Analytic View of the Schreber Case*, Albany, State University of New York Press, 1988, pp. 158–68.
9 Daniel Paul Schreber, *Memoirs of my Nervous Illness*, trans. Ida Macalpine and Richard A. Hunter, with a new introduction by Samuel M. Weber, Cambridge, Mass., Harvard University Press, 1988.
10 D.G.M. Schreber, *Medical Indoor Gymnastics or a System of Hygienic Exercises for Home Use: To Be Practised Anywhere without Apparatus or Assistance by Young and Old of Either Sex for the Preservation of Health and General Activity*, trans. from the 26th German edn by Herbert A. Day, London, Williams & Norgate, 1899; New York, Gustave E. Stechert, 1899; and Leipzig, Friedrich Fleischer, 1899.
11 Schreber, 'In What Circumstances Can a Person Considered Insane Be Detained in an Asylum against his Declared Will?', *Memoirs*, op. cit., pp. 255–63.
12 Jean-Jacques Lecercle, *Philosophy through the Looking Glass: Language, Nonsense, Desire*, London, Hutchinson, 1985, chapter 5: 'The Psychoanalysis of Délire'.
13 John O'Neill, *Five Bodies: The Human Shape of Modern Society*, Ithaca, Cornell University Press, 1985, chapter 5: 'Medical Bodies'.
14 William G. Niederlaud, *The Schreber Case: Psychoanalytic Profile of a Paranoid Personality, an Expanded Edition*, Hillsdale, Analytic Press/ Earlbaum, 1984; Han Israels, *Schreber: Father and Son*, New York, International University Press, 1989; Morton Schatzman, *Soul Murder:*

Persecution in the Family, New York, New American Library, 1973; Zvi Lothane, 'Schreber, Freud, Flechsig and Weber Revisited: An Inquiry into Methods of Interpretation', *Psychoanalytic Review*, 76, ii, Summer 1989, pp. 203–62.

15 Gilles Deleuze and Félix Guattari, *A Thousand Plateaus: Capitalism and Schizophrenia*, trans. and foreword by Brian Massumi, Minneapolis, University of Minnesota Press, 1987, p. 289.

16 Jardine, op. cit., p. 98.

17 Gilles Deleuze and Félix Guattari, *Anti-Oedipus: Capitalism and Schizophrenia*, trans. Robert Hurley, Mark Seem and Helen R. Lane, New York, Viking Press, 1977, p. 4.

18 Dr Fleschig's portrait was kept by Schreber's wife in gratitude for her own treatment, to which she considered she owed her health. He also figures in the *Memoirs* as Schreber's 'soul murderer', who either himself abused his patient 'as a woman' or else allowed his assistants to do so. The best source on this subject is Lothane, op. cit.

19 ibid., p. 19.

20 ibid., p. 64.

21 John O'Neill, 'Science and the Self: Freud's Paternity Suit (the Case of the Wolf Man)', *Discours Social/Social Discourse*, 11, 1–2, Spring–Summer 1989, pp.151–62.

22 Alphonso Lingis, 'The Din of the Celestial Birds or Why I Crave to Become a Woman', in Allison *et al.*, op. cit., pp. 130–42.

23 Deleuze and Guattari, *Anti-Oedipus*, op. cit., p. 126.

24 John O'Neill, *The Comunicative Body: Studies in Communicative Philosophy, Politics and Sociology*, Evanston, Northwestern University Press, 1989, chapter 8,: 'The Specular Body: Merleau-Ponty and Lacan on Infant Self and Other'.

25 ibid., p. 316.

26 John O'Neill, 'The Medicalization of Social Control', *Canadian Review of Sociology and Anthroplogy*, 23, iii, August 1986, pp. 350–64.

Chapter 19

Woman and space according to Kristeva and Irigaray

Philippa Berry

The word for abyss – *Abgrund* – originally means the soil and ground towards which, because it is undermost, a thing tends downward. . . . But in what follows, we shall think of the *Ab-* as the complete absence of the ground. The age for which the ground fails to come, hangs in the abyss.

(Martin Heidegger, *What Are Poets For?*)

Is it not strange that the reflection on the feminine is so closely connected to a masculine disorder, to the 'death of man', meant as the questioning not only of philosophical truth but of knowledge? For it is in part thanks to this crossing into the void, this phenomenal acting-out on the part of the philosophical subject, that the problematic of the feminine has been given status, as the carrier of a 'new' truth. It is as if the modern subject, the split subject, discovers the feminine layer of his own thought just as he loses the mastery he used to assume as his own.

(Rosi Braidotti, *Patterns of Dissonance*)

Behold, I will allure her [Israel], and bring her into the wilderness, and speak comfortably unto her.

(Hosea 2:14)

Does anything still remain to be said about those gaping spaces and rifts, those disturbing *aporias*, which have been opened up within the traditions of 'modern' thought by postmodern thinking? In recent years, many writers directly or indirectly associated with postmodernism have performed endless variations on this theme. But two feminist theorists, Julia Kristeva and Luce Irigaray, both of whom write alongside but not always in synchrony with postmodern thought, have explored postmodern spatiality with an especial intimacy and insight; most importantly, they have been notably undeterred by the radical otherness – indeed, the uncanniness – typically associated with this phenomenon. Each has used a focus upon the emptiness of the category 'woman' radically to extend postmodernism's challenge to notions of philosophical limit: specifically, to question the contemporary philosophical posture of nihilism. The work of these two thinkers implies that the void which has opened up within western culture and society cannot be understood if we persist in maintaining an intellectual distinction between secular and sacred versions of the 'real'.

As postmodern thinkers have observed the entropic collapse of the supposedly centred 'humanist' subjectivity which took (however improbably) the heliocentric Copernican system as its 'ground', they have become increasingly emphatic in relating its demise to a very different experience of space: a vista that is disturbingly ex-centric and diffuse in comparision with the sun-centred cosmology of the late Renaissance. This new, post-Copernican spatiality, in which the subject of the modern era is not founded but foundering, can perhaps best be defined as a space of mediation: that is, as a place of articulation between a variety of different versions of space. It is of course primarily in spatial·terms that twentieth-century thinkers fascinated by the notion of the unconscious have figured those various states of unreason which since Nietzsche and Freud have explicitly shadowed philosophy. Postmodernism in particular has repeatedly related the new spatiality to the deconstruction of the overbearing humanist subject of the modern era, whose claims to wield mastery over reason, language, nature and history are now themselves seen as somewhat irrational. But at the same time, Frederic Jameson has described what he terms 'hyperspace' as a primarily external phenomenon, embracing not only the 'built' spaces of architects such as Robert Venturi, but also the huge global communications network created by multinational corporations. Jameson stresses the subjective confusion which these developments provoke: 'this latest mutation in space – postmodern hyperspace – has finally succeeded in transcending the capacities of the human body to locate itself, to organize its immediate surroundings perceptually, and cognitively to map its position in a mappable external world'.[1]

Venturi, whom Jameson holds up in this essay as a pioneer of postmodern spatiality, was determined to challenge modernist conceptions of the oneness of interior and exterior space. But other thinkers have argued that it is impossible to see the new spatiality in terms which assume a firm distinction between inner and outer.[2] While this viewpoint seems at first sight to blur the boundary between modernist and postmodern spatiality, it is combined with a specifically postmodern insight into the emptiness of interiority. As Derrida has pointed out in relation to his concept of *différance*: 'As soon as we admit spacing both as "interval" or as difference and as openness upon the outside, there can no longer be any absolute inside.'[3]

But while Foucault wrote that 'It is no longer possible to think in our day other than in the void left by man's disappearance',[4] it seems that a genuinely new mode of 'thinking in the gaps' has been surprisingly slow to appear. Perhaps a certain resistance to whatever may be implied by thinking *in* the void is even discernible in the recent reversion of several postmodern thinkers to the terminology of Enlightenment thought – specifically, to that of the Kantian sublime – in order to describe (but possibly also to contain) these amorphous spaces. The difficulty that is seemingly experienced by postmodern thinkers in the face of what Jameson calls 'hyperspatiality' may not improbably be read as the trace of a residual attachment to forms of intellectual power and knowledge which are no longer appropriate to those who claim to be writing at 'the end of philosophy'. Rosi Braidotti has recently suggested that the void is precisely the space which is created 'by the crisis of the master's discourse'.[5] In stressing the silence, indeed the secrecy, appropriate to any exploration of these desert regions, writers such as Baudrillard and Derrida are of course reintroducing a theme from phenomenology, a theme which has undoubted relevance to the contemporary crisis of philosophy; none the less, the immediate effect of such statements is to give a paradoxical authority to what are possibly admissions of the limits of their thinking. For Baudrillard: 'Words, even when they speak of the desert, are always unwelcome.'[6] For Derrida, the empty space of (the) *chora* is a place where he can 'avoid speaking': specifically, 'of a question which I would be incapable of treating'; this silence licenses his refusal to discuss the relationship of negative theology to his thought.[7] The silence invoked by Baudrillard and Derrida in the face of this new 'hyperspatiality' could be used differently, however. It could provide them – and us – with the opportunity to listen to other, less deliberately magisterial voices on this subject: voices which could possibly offer us a better insight into the significance of the new spatiality.

For Baudrillard, postmodern spatiality is intimately connected to the non-place of the desert. He contemplates its multiple associations in *America*, where he writes: 'You always have to bring something into the desert to sacrifice, and offer it to the desert as a victim. A woman. If something has to disappear, something matching the desert for beauty, why not a woman?'[8] The homage which the desert apparently requires is associated here with a specifically ritual act – that of sacrifice – in which the threat of loss or suffering which the desert inspires is displaced onto another – woman. The event which grants the postmodern traveller access to the desert's mystery is the 'disappearance' of woman. But while Baudrillard's allusion to her desert disappearance constructs woman as victim, an analogous yet significantly different version of 'the lady vanishes' has been staged by Kristeva and Irigaray, in their association of the deconstruction of woman with that metaphysical space or 'desert' discovered within philosophy. In this other 'sacrifice' of woman, the woman thinker is very definitely in control; at the same time, she stresses the centrality of her (of woman's) disappearance, or of her *emptiness*, to our deeper understanding of the rifts which have opened up within philosophical discourse.

As early as 1974, in fact, Irigaray was attempting to articulate a new, feminist relationship to this intellectual abyss. In *Speculum*, she turned the sexism of an androcentric philosophy and psychoanalysis on its head. For she embraced the associations of 'woman' with deficiency or lack in these systems, in order to figure a feminine *difference* from (rather than an opposition to) masculine models of subjectivity: a difference which she described as fundamental to thinking in the void:

> Something of her [woman's] a-specificity might be found in the *betweens* that occur in being, or beings. These *gaps* reopen the question of the 'void'. . . . This is the place where consciousness is no longer master . . . it is for/by woman that man dares to enter the place, to descend into it, condescend to it.[9]

At around the same time that *Speculum* was published, Kristeva was developing a somewhat different, but clearly related formulation of the feminist implications of emptiness, in her explorations of the maternal *chora*. By the mid-1970s, she had produced a strange yet compelling account of motherhood as a 'luminous spatialization'. Irigaray had placed the paradoxical figure of *la mystérique*, the woman mystic, at the centre of *Speculum*, yet she had implicitly distinguished her act of writing *about* the mystic from mystical speech itself; the Kristevan analysis too pointed to the oblique relationship between meditative modes of perception and representation. In her essay on Bellini's Madonnas, Kristeva observes that

> The faces of his Madonnas are turned away, intent on something else that draws their gaze to the side, up above or nowhere in particular, but never centers it in the baby. . . .The painter as baby can never reach this elsewhere, this inaccessible peace coloured with melancholy.[10]

This passage stresses the paradoxical character of the painter's attempt to represent an indeterminate locus, which is 'up above or nowhere in particular'; Bellini can only allude to this other scene indirectly, through an inscrutable feminine figure who has a mysterious metonymic relationship to the extra-pictorial dimension.

In their attempts to elaborate the feminist implications of an in-between space which undoes differences while it reasserts them, and which veils as well as reveals the production of meanings through opposition, both Kristeva and Irigaray develop implicit critiques of Derrida's figuration of a (primarily textual) version of the new spatiality in feminine terms, when, in *Dissemination*, he related his concept of the *hymen* to the work of textual deconstruction.[11] They do this via direct as well as indirect reassessments of that Heideggerian thinking which underlies so many Derridean concepts. Not surprisingly, however, this feminist return to and rereading of Heidegger is by no means a move of unequivocal acceptance.

The *ek-stasis* associated by both Kristeva and Irigaray with postmodern space has a kinetic as well as an ethical force which was (at least initially) absent from Derrida's *jouissance* of the letter, of *écriture*. Their works consequently give new definition to what Rosi Braidotti has recently described as the lightness and speed of postmodern subjectivity.[12] This interest in *bodily* representations of an intellectual event may be indebted to phenomenology in general rather than to Heidegger in particular, and presumably also to Nietzsche. Nonetheless, in their diverse emphases upon dance, movement and flight, each of these feminist thinkers has restored to *jouissance* some of the dynamic connotations of two of Heidegger's concepts: on the one hand, that of the thinker as wanderer; on the other hand, the notion of the thinker's necessary 'turning' or *Kehre* from a focus upon 'beings' to the investigation of that which gives meaning to beings. For Heidegger, of course, this is 'Being'. At the same time, in giving persistent attention, *pace* Heidegger, to the implications of the new spatiality for a subjectivity which disclaims mastery, both have reasserted the links between the *ek-stasis* experienced in this intermediate space and a new mode of ethical awareness, elaborating ideas of love which incorporate but go beyond desire. In some respects these concepts of love are comparable to the Heideggerian 'care', identified by Heidegger with the 'between' as early as *Being and Time* (although the influence of Feuerbach – himself an influence on Heidegger – is also discernible).

Perhaps the most significant debt to Heidegger owed by these feminist rethinkings of the between, however, is to his strange account of 'man' as the *openness* to which and in which what he called 'Being' could appear. Much of the criticism of Heidegger for an attachment to concepts of presence has focussed upon this ambiguous category of Being. But it is often forgotten that while the early Heidegger, the author of *Being and Time* (1927), undoubtedly privileged presence, the later Heidegger, in his preoccupation with themes of openness and nothingness, and in his conjunction of presence with absence, is thinking very differently. It was at this stage that his developing preoccupation with spatiality led him to question his former emphasis upon the priority of time in his new category of 'thinking', thereby facilitating a conceptualization of Being in terms related to spatiality: as 'the abyss' (*Abgrund*), the 'groundless ground'.[13] It was only at this point that his use of the term was intimately allied to negativity. Thus the concept of the *Lichtung* or 'clearing', which postdates *Being and Time*, is defined as a place or space within which Being can manifest its *hiddenness*. Heidegger wrote in 'The Origin of the Work of Art' (1935–6):

In the midst of beings as a whole an open place occurs. There is a clearing, a lighting [*eine Lichtung*: one word in the German text is given two translations]. Thought of in reference to what is, to beings, this clearing *is* in a greater degree than are beings. This open center [*Mitte*: middle, midst] is therefore not surrounded by what is; rather, the lighting center [*die lichtende Mitte*] itself encircles all that is, like the Nothing that we scarcely know . . . This clearing in which beings stand is in itself at the same time concealment.[14]

Some thirty years later, in 'The End of Philosophy and the Task of Thinking', the 'clearing' or 'opening' is described by Heidegger as a place of which 'philosophy knows nothing', although it 'is spoken about in philosophy's beginning': that is, in the thought of the pre-Socratics. But this 'primal phenomenon', as Heidegger terms it, also represents philosophy's future. Existing beyond the categories of philosophy, it is consequently the place where a new mode of intellectual activity can be elaborated:

> We may suggest that the day will come when we will not shun the question whether the opening [*Lichtung*], the free open, may not be that within which alone pure space and ecstatic time, and everything present and absent within them, have the place which gathers and protects everything.[15]

While Kristeva never refers explicitly to the 'clearing', and while Irigaray does not mention it until *L'Oubli de l'air chez Martin Heidegger* (1983), the influence of this concept, together with the general late Heideggerian preoccupation with openness, seems discernible in many parts of their work. And in their different but related ways both Kristeva and Irigaray also radically develop and rework the (formerly obscure) associations of these Heideggerian themes with an otherness or alterity which is defined as sacred or holy. In their strangely material (and figuratively feminine) mode of spatiality, the opposition between sacred and profane is also deconstructed, as the body becomes both abject and divine.

One way in which Heidegger's emphasis upon openness and the clearing has left its mark in the work of Kristeva and Irigaray is through their shared interest in a highly ambiguous spatial category which was used by Plato, but which also has evident affinities with the pre-Socratic thought that so fascinated Heidegger: the category of *chora*. As Derrida himself has recently pointed out (in what seems an implicit response to the continuing interest of Kristeva in this concept), the term certainly interested Heidegger.[16] Indeed, when Heidegger asserted that according to Plato 'between beings and Being there prevails the *chorismos*; *chora* is the *locus*, the site, the place', the formulation may have misrepresented Plato, but it very closely resembled his own notion of the 'clearing'.[17] For Kristeva in particular, *chora* has provided a concept of space which not only is (provisionally) gendered feminine but also, paradoxically, has certain material attributes; in this intermediate space which is both metaphysical and bodily, the philosophical distinction between form and matter is not easily applicable; the concept is mysteriously allied to space as well as to sub-

stance.[18] Thus rather than simply representing the repressed opposite term
either of idealist philosophy or of social reality, Kristeva argued that *chora*
is always *asymmetrically* 'other' to what Lacan called the symbolic order –
that is, to any philosophic, cultural or social construct.

Although Derrida criticized Kristeva's interest in *chora* as early as 1972,
because of its 'ontological essence', his recent interest in the term has
precisely stressed its lack of essence or substance.[19] It was presumably the
association of the term with notions of an archaic origin which elicited
Derrida's initial criticism. But while Kristeva might seem to have suc-
cumbed to a nostalgia for origins in privileging this archaic model of space,
in fact, as a place of mediation *between* the creator and his creation, *chora*
is both originary and supplementary. In Plato's *Timaeus*, it is described not
in terms of an opposition, but (as Derrida himself points out) as a *triton
genos* or third term, and is defined as the space or 'receptacle of becoming'
whence the Demiurge or creator fashioned a material copy of the world of
Being or Ideal Forms. Timaeus declares that 'if we describe her [*chora*] as a
Kind invisible and unshaped, all-receptive, and in some most perplexing
and most baffling way partaking of the intelligible, we shall describe her
truly'.[20]

In deciding to focus upon this particular Platonic term, Kristeva was
apparently rejecting a post-Platonic philosophical emphasis upon ideas in a
fascination with the *absence* of form, or with that emptiness which precedes
but is the necessary precondition of all forms of representation. This
emphasis, while derived from Plato, has clear affinities with pre-Socratic
thought: specifically, with the emphasis upon a primordial void or *apeiron*
found in the thought of Pythagoras and Anaximander (although it is
important to note here that the *Timaeus* does not inform us whether the
Ideal Forms preceded the *chora* or vice versa). Kristeva's move could
consequently be said to parallel Heidegger's (as well as Nietzsche's) interest in 'early Greek thinking'. She emphasizes *chora*'s lack of unity, its
constant flux: 'The *chora* is the *locus* of a *chaos* which *is* and which
becomes, previous to the formation of the first definite bodies.'[21] And here
she specifically echoed Heidegger, who had commented on what he considered to be the etymological affinity between *chora* and the Greek word
for chaos.[22] He also noted that 'Chaos, *khaos*, *khainō*, means "to yawn"; it
signifies something that opens wide or gapes. We conceive of *khaos* in most
intimate connection with an original interpretation of the essence of *alētheia* [truth] as the self-opening abyss.'[23] But while, like Heidegger's 'clearing', Kristeva's *chora* appears superficially to be allied to the past, it
similarly seems to elude any definition in terms of ordinary temporality.
Like Plato's *chora*, Kristeva's maternal origin occupies a liminal position.
It is on the borderline between all polarities: between being and nothing,
idealism and materialism, sacred and profane, silence and language.
Moreover, she shows that this mysterious, negative 'beginning' is vitally

related to the present as well as to the future. In consequence, when the philosophical complexity of *chora* is associated by Kristeva with the chaos of infantile experience, when the body experiences the mobility and negativity of the drives, she often seems to be speaking about the death or deconstruction of the subject as well as about its formation: 'The place of the subject's creation, the semiotic *chora* is also the place of its negation, where its unity gives way before the process of charges and stases producing that unity.'[24]

Kristeva's elaboration of *chora*'s relationship to representation describes it as a heterogeneous and disruptive 'semiotic' dimension upon which language obscurely depends; yet the tendency of *chora* is always to undermine the stability of the subject within signification. Thereby it bears testimony to the frequent inadequacies of language as a direct means of communication, reminding the decentred speaker of other, speechless modes of expression. Kristeva stated that 'the *chora* . . . is analogous only to vocal and kinetic rhythm'.[25] In a recent essay on Jackson Pollock, she has suggested that there are etymological links between *chora* and *chorus*, and described *chora* as a 'dancing receptacle'.[26] Its association with a bodily mode of knowledge further allies *chora* to the future of the human organism, in its connection with the death-drive. And as her treatment of this concept develops, it becomes increasingly clear that for Kristeva, *chora*'s interest is not only in its association with what comes *before* the subject, but also as a means of thinking what might come *after* the subject. In her later elaborations on the implications of this maternal space, Kristeva associates it with an identity which has a notably different relationship to the death-drive than does the subject of the symbolic order.

Like the *chora* over which she presides, the 'Phallic' Mother of *Polylogue* is defined in terms of space and emptiness:

> Through her body dedicated to ensuring the reproduction of the species, the woman-subject, submitted none the less to the paternal function . . . is more than anything else a *filter*: a thoroughfare, a threshold where 'nature' confronts 'culture'. To imagine that there is *someone* in that filter – such is the source of religious mystifications, the font that nourishes them: the fantasy of the so-called 'Phallic' Mother. Because if, on the contrary, there were no one on this threshold, if the mother were not, that is, if she were not phallic, then every speaker would be led to conceive of its Being in relation to some void, a nothingness asymmetrically opposed to this Being, a permanent threat against, first, its mastery, and ultimately, its stability.[27]

Perhaps paradoxically, Kristeva's account of the correct aesthetic treatment of the maternal position retains a trace of veneration, in its appropriation of eucharistic imagery. She writes that the language which investigates this figure 'must not leave her untouched, outside, opposite, against the law, the absolute esoteric code. Rather, it must swallow her, eat her, dissolve her.[28] To this extent, the artist who explores *chora* is expected to imitate Baudrillard's desert sacrifice. But what should follow this matricidal rite of consumption or destruction, Kristeva suggests, is another rite, this time one of self-sacrifice, in the occupation of the empty maternal place. This stance requires an attitude 'that, going beyond abjection, is enunciated as ecstatic'.[29] The priest(ess) and victim must 'Know the mother, first take her place, thoroughly investigate her *jouissance* and, without releasing her, go beyond her'.[30] In 'Stabat Mater', Kristeva notes that the great Christian mystics did indeed occupy this negative and liminal place of the mother, using it to replace concrete icons with a much less easily definable object of adoration. And in a point which she later elaborates in *Tales of Love*, she asserts that 'Freedom with respect to the maternal territory then becomes the pedestal upon which love of God is erected.'[31] The emergence of this love (called by Kristeva *agape* in order to distinguish it from *eros*) seems therefore to be directly related to the mother as empty, as a 'non-subject' whose precise place can be taken by countless others: it is a love which is produced via that dissolution of subjectivity, of the boundaries between self and other, which the semiotic *chora* promotes. Seemingly, this love resides in the *gap* between death and eternity, since as *amour* it can apparently incorporate death as 'a-mort' or undeath. A similar position, Kristeva suggests, is occupied in Christian discourse by the figure of the Virgin Mary, the doctrine of whose bodily Assumption into heaven is emphasized in 'Stabat Mater'. As she points out there, Mary was actually referred to by John Chrysostom as a 'bond', 'middle' and 'interval'. This conception of a divine mode of being which is mysteriously empty rather than essential or substantial, and whose emptiness is precisely the context in which a new kind of love or compassion can appear, figures in eastern as well as western mysticism; in fact Kristeva herself has suggested, in 'Motherhood According to Bellini', that 'Oriental nothingness probably better sums up' the 'elsewhere' of the mother than can any other analogy. She may have been thinking of Mahayana and Vajrayana Buddhism in particular, for these systems place great emphasis upon the attainment of a paradoxical, non-dual model of knowledge which is also a knowledge of emptiness; this illumination coincides with the discovery of the illusory nature of the subject–object dichotomy. In this context, the void (*sunyata*) is identified with 'absolute reality' and held to contain all dualities and polarities; specifically, to unite the opposites of form and emptiness. It should be noted here that this fullness of the Buddhist void seemingly approximates more to a Derridean *différance* than to a Hegelian *Aufhebung* or sublation of difference; as a contemporary deconstructionist has noted: '*sunyata* is everywhere the movement of rifts and flaws'.[32]

Thus like *alētheia*, the mysterious truth of Being which manifests in

Heidegger's clearing (a truth which, he reminds us, is also untruth), Kristeva's *chora*, together with the mother associated with it, is both concealed and revealed, both present and absent. And in *chora*'s suspension or deconstruction of the dualisms upon which western philosophy has formerly depended, it opens the possibility of another kind of thinking. But this new style of thinking differs significantly from that anticipated by Heidegger in its emphasis upon the necessary interrelationship of a bodily (or experiential) with an intellectual style of knowing. Similar themes appear in the work of Irigaray, who also allies a pre-Oedipal, psychic spatiality to an interrogation of the aporias within western philosophy, and who also dialogues frequently with Heidegger. In its early stages especially, Irigaray's work is also indebted to the concept of *chora*: for example, an interest in the term is fundamental to her critique of Plato's myth of the cave in *Speculum*. For Irigaray, as for Kristeva, the concept of woman can be used to undo binary oppositions. And in her continuing emphasis upon woman's identity as fluid and mobile she attributes to woman the most notable qualities of *chora*. But this has gradually produced an account of woman's relationship to spatiality which is notably more dynamic than that of Kristeva. Not only does Irigaray break decisively with the residual weight and potential stasis of Heidegger's concept of Being, in her preference for a concept of divine becoming; she also develops a theme which is only implicit in the work of Kristeva: the potential of this awareness of emptiness to create a new capacity for genuine dialogue and communication.[33]

Unlike Kristeva, Irigaray is explicit about her attempt creatively to redefine an *already existing* cultural association between woman and emptiness. She offers woman a notably more dynamic role in the exploration of this terrain than does Kristeva, appealing to woman to quit the 'closed chamber' of philosophy by rejecting the living entombment which it has imposed upon her, as the successor to Sophocles' Antigone. It seems the escape from this crypt (an intellectual trajectory which certainly echoes Kristeva's recent attempts to rethink woman's relationship to the death-drive) will require a new understanding of space, an insight which can simultaneously challenge the finite model of temporality that still tolls in the *a* of Derrida's différance and glas. This move (which once again echoes a late Heideggerian turn) may also involve a recollection of ancient, pre-Socratic cosmogonies: 'The gods or God first of all creates space. And time is there, more or less at the service of space.'[34] But this feminist *Kehre* or turning back is subordinated to a strong sense of the future's *difference*: 'The transition to a new age in turn necessitates a new perception and a new conception of *time and space*, our *occupation of place*, and the different *envelopes known as identity*.'[35] Irigaray stresses the cultural association of the female body with spatiality, as opposed to the identification of man with temporality. But she differs from Kristeva in seeing motherhood as an obstacle to a truly creative expression of woman's emptiness; as the maternal place for man's becoming, Irigaray considers that woman lacks her own space. If 'Woman, in so far as she is an envelope, is never closed. This place is never shut up', for a mother the disturbing character of this female emptiness is displaced as it is filled in the reproductive process.[36] Irigaray further suggests that it is not by rejecting, but by finding a new relationship to her lack of completeness that woman will free herself. She notes that her attributed spatiality has long associated woman with the infinite, or the *in-fini*, as a Muse figure; but she asks if 'the quest for a maternal infinity which is conducted through women can lead to the quest for a divine infinity'?[37] For her, it is not enough for woman to occupy the place of the divine for man, since if (as she contends) all communication involves going through what she calls the divine, while woman symbolizes that place she will remain symbolically excluded from communicative exchange: 'If women lack a God they cannot communicate, or communicate among themselves. The infinite is needed, they need the infinite in order to *share a little*.'[38] In this respect, Irigaray's could be said to be a more social spatiality than that of Kristeva, an emptiness which is more ethically attuned, in her concern with its facilitation of a new kind of dialogue: a theme which she has inherited and adapted from Levinas as well as from Bakhtin.

Again, this account of woman is clearly indebted to the Heideggerian 'opening' or 'clearing' within which truth can appear. But in *L'Oubli de l'air chez Martin Heidegger*, Irigaray argues that Heidegger's conception of the clearing is too earthy, too restricted and organized a conception of space. In her recent work she emphasizes that woman must escape her bodily confinement to a specified place; thus she urges her readers to substitute for the watery envelope of the womb an airy envelope where greater freedom can be achieved:

> After the envelope full of water which was our prenatal home, we have to construct, bit by bit, the envelope of air of our terrestrial space, air which is still free to breathe and sing, air where we deploy our appearances and our movements. We have been fishes. We will have to become birds. Which cannot be done without opening up and mobility in the air.[39]

It seems that woman's confinement has also been associated with a purely horizontal mode of being; in this new aerial mode of being, another kind of love becomes possible: an *exstase* or *jouissance* in which the boundaries between sacred and profane are dissolved. In a development of another Heideggerian theme, Irigaray writes of the need 'to restore the alliance between gods and mortals'. In her work, a patriarchal focus upon woman as a maternal envelope is replaced by a conception of woman as the threshold to an entirely new mode of being. Her attempt to theorize this new identity, which apparently should occupy a vertical as well as horizontal space of mediation, explains her fascination with angels, notably in the essay 'La croyance même'. Since its role as messenger requires the angel to 'traverse the envelope, envelopes, ceaselessly', it figures the possibility of 'another incarnation, another parousia of the flesh' in which there is a bodily union of the human and divine. Just as in 'Motherhood According to Bellini', Kristeva writes of the mother's body as 'a luminous spatialization', so Irigaray too has visions of a new flesh, which will be mysteriously transformed by its acceptance of the new spatiality. This angelic rapport, she suggests, is accessible to the bodies of both sexes, 'and above all to the body of woman', presumably because this body has already been defined as empty.[40]

Irigaray does not universalize woman's relationship to the 'between' or *intervalle*; rather she sees it in terms of an unfolding historical process. In the first instance, it seems, woman must acquire a deeper understanding of the freedom, the spaciousness, which is inherent in her own liminal identity. By creating the possibility of a different kind of relationship, she will be able to assist in the creation of another in-between space – the *intervalle* which is the place or possibility of the divine. Just as the two angels described in 'La croyance même' create the space for spirit between them when they face one another in the holy of holies, so woman will not continue to occupy that place alone when she can find another, a lover, to share her new spatial awareness. Neither must envelope the other; for if they can allow the new spatiality to exist between them, the resultant *intervalle* or third term will be occupied by what Irigaray labels the 'divine'. Yet it seems that what she calls the 'divine' actually involves a mingling of sacred and profane. In *Ethique*, she writes of 'a *sensible transcendental* coming into being through us, of which *we would be* the mediators and bridges'.[41] The dynamic movements of spirit and body within a space which is both sacred and profane will seemingly permit a new erotic as well as ethical awareness of the other who has helped to receive it, be they male or female: 'God has to be raised up through us, between us.'[42]

It seems that by accepting, and even accelerating, the emptying-out of humanist subjectivity, Kristeva and Irigaray have been able to explore the space-marks pondered by postmodernism not with fear, but with joy. But in an essay which she has published in several slightly different forms, Irigaray writes in notably Heideggerian terms of the risk which this investigation of the abyss (or *Riss*) involves. It appears that the philosopher 'who goes not into the abyss can only repeat and restate paths already opened up that erase the trace of gods who have fled'.[43] In other words, he or she will remain captive to the law of the Same. The one who dares, however, is by definition a poet and prophet as well as a lover. The difference of their wayless way can only be described allusively: 'They who dare all go forth blindly, without projects. No longer spellbound by the fear of being without shelter. Unreservedly abandoning themselves to the unbounded open, holding nothing back.'[44] The 'open' alluded to here seems rather different from the implicitly delimited 'clearing' of Heidegger. It has no apparent boundaries, no obvious end. Nor have those who explore it – they are 'without shelter', and without projects: that is, without *telos* or goal. But what Irigaray seems to suggest is that it is precisely this acceptance of openness or emptiness – in the self, in the world and in language – which is needed if we are to achieve a new and more compassionate stage of human existence.

NOTES

1 Fredric Jameson, 'Postmodernism, or the Cultural Logic of Late Capitalism', *New Left Review*, 146, July–August 1984, p. 83.
2 Geoffrey Bennington, 'The Rationality of Postmodern Relativity', *Journal of Philosophy and the Visual Arts*, 2, 1990, p. 28.
3 Jacques Derrida, '*Speech and Phenomena' and Other Essays on Husserl's Theory of Signs*, trans. David B. Allison, Evanston, Northwestern University Press, 1973, p. 86.
4 Michel Foucault, *The Order of Things*, trans. Alan Sheridan, London, Tavistock Publications, 1970.
5 Rosi Braidotti, *Patterns of Dissonance*, Oxford, Polity Press, 1991, p. 14.
6 Jean Baudrillard, *America*, trans. Chris Turner, London, Verso, 1988, p. 71.
7 Jacques Derrida, 'Comment ne pas parler? *Dénegations*', in *Psyché: inventions de l'autre*, Paris, Galilée, 1987, p. 562. In the same year, 1987, Derrida published a related essay entitled 'Chora', in *Poikilia: études offertes à Jean-Pierre Vernant*, Paris, Editions de l'Ecole des Hautes Etudes en Sciences Sociales, 1987, pp. 265–96. There he argued that the definite article was inappropriate to such a term, since it presupposes the existence of a thing.
8 Baudrillard, op. cit., p. 66.
9 Luce Irigaray, *Speculum: Of the Other Woman*, trans. Gillian C. Gill, Ithaca, Cornell University Press, 1985, pp. 166, 191.
10 Julia Kristeva, 'Motherhood According to Bellini', in Leon S. Roudiez, ed., *Desire in Language: A Semiotic Approach to Literature and Art*, Oxford, Blackwell, 1980, p. 247.
11 Jacques Derrida, *Dissémination*, trans. Barbara Johnson, London, Athlone Press, 1981, pp. 209–22.
12 Braidotti, op. cit., p. 283.
13 See Martin Heidegger, *Der Satz vom Grund* (The Principle of Ground), Pfullingen, Neske, 1957. This was a series of lectures given at Freiburg University from 1955 to 1956. Heidegger's changing attitude to temporality has been explored by John Sallis in *Echoes: After Heidegger*, Bloomington, Indiana University Press, 1990, chapters 2, 4.
14 Martin Heidegger, 'The Origin of the Work of Art' (1935–6), in *Poetry, Language, Thought*, trans. Albert Hofstadter, New York, Harper & Row, 1971, p. 53.
15 Martin Heidegger, 'The End of Philosophy and the Task of Thinking', in *Heidegger: Basic Writings*, ed. D. Krell, New York, Harper & Row, 1977, p. 385.

16 Derrida, 'Chora', op. cit., *passim*.
17 Martin Heidegger *What Is Called Thinking?*, trans. Fred D. Wieck, New York, Harper & Row, 1968, p. 227.
18 Julia Kristeva's first extended use of the term was in *La Révolution du langage poétique. L'avant-garde à la fin du XIXe siècle: Lautréamont et Mallarmé*, Paris, Seuil, 1974, p. 22. A full translation of this text into English is not yet available. Only part of the text is published in *The Revolution in Poetic Language*, trans. Margaret Waller, New York, Columbia University Press, 1984.
19 Jacques Derrida, *Positions*, trans. Alan Bass, London, Athlone Press, 1981, p. 101. For his recent interest in the term, see note 8 above, although in Geoffrey Bennington and Jacques Derrida's *Jacques Derrida*, Paris, Seuil, 1991, it is suggested that Derrida's recourse to a concept analogous to *chora* is apparent as early as *Dissémination*, op. cit., (pp. 194–5).
20 Plato, *Timaeus*, Loeb edn, trans. G. R. Bury, London, Heinemann, 1929, 51A.
21 Julia Kristeva, *Polylogue*, Paris, Seuil, 1977, p. 57, n. 1.
22 David Levin, *The Body's Recollection of Being: Phenomenological Psychology and the Deconstruction of Nihilism*, London, Routledge & Kegan Paul 1985, pp. 330–1, n. 57.
23 Martin Heidegger, *Nietzsche*, vol. II, New York, Harper & Row, 1984, p. 91.
24 Kristeva, *La Révolution du langage poétique*, op. cit., pp. 27–8 (my translation).
25 Kristeva, *Revolution*, op. cit., pp. 25–6.
26 Julia Kristeva, 'Jackson Pollock's Milky Way, 1912–56', *Journal of Philosophy and the Visual Arts*, 1, 1989, pp. 34–9.
27 Kristeva, *Polylogue*, op. cit., p. 238.
28 ibid.
29 Julia Kristeva, *Powers of Horror*, trans. Leon S. Roudiez, New York, Columbia University Press, 1982, p. 59.
30 Kristeva, 'Motherhood According to Bellini', op. cit., p. 191.
31 Julia Kristeva 'Stabat Mater', in *The Kristeva Reader*, ed. Toril Moi, Oxford, Blackwell, 1986, p. 162. See also her *Tales of Love*, trans. Leon S. Roudiez, New York, Columbia University Press, 1987, *passim*.
32 Robert Magliola, 'French Deconstruction with a (Buddhist) Difference', *Studies in Language and Literature*, iii, October 1988, p. 23.
33 My thoughts about Irigaray's work, especially her conception of the divine, have been much assisted by recent feminist work: notably by Margaret Whitford, *Luce Irigaray: Philosophy in the Feminine*, London, Routledge, 1991; and by Elizabeth Grosz, *Sexual Subversions: Three French Feminists*, London, Allen & Unwin, 1989. I discovered after writing my first version of this paper that Carolyn Burke had already noted Irigaray's interest in Heidegger in 'Romancing the Philosophers: Luce Irigaray', in Dianne Hunter ed. *Seduction and Theory: Feminist Readings on Representation and Rhetoric*, Chicago, University of Illinois Press, 1989.
34 Luce Irigaray, 'Sexual Difference', trans. Séan Hand, in *The Irigaray Reader*, ed. Margaret Whitford, Oxford, Blackwell, 1991, pp. 166–7.
35 ibid., p. 167.
36 Luce Irigaray, *Ethique de la différence sexuelle*, Paris, Minuit, p. 55.
37 ibid., p. 41.
38 Luce Irigaray, 'Divine Women', trans. Stephen Muecke, *Local Consumption: Occasional Papers*, 4, 1986, Sydney, p. 4.
39 ibid., p. 7.
40 Luce Irigaray, 'La Croyance même', in *Sexes et parentés*, Paris, Minuit, 1987.
41 Cited and translated in Whitford, *Luce Irigaray*, op. cit., p. 144.

42 Irigaray, *Ethique*, op. cit., p. 124.
43 Luce Irigaray 'He Risks Who Risks Life Itself', trans. David Macey, in *The Irigaray Reader*, op. cit., p. 213.
44 ibid., p. 216.

Index

social: death of *see* Baudrillard; power and groundless democracy 161–3; society as God 38; theory *see* secularists
Socrates and Diotima 198–210
Solomon 187, 189
sophism 209–10; *see also* Diotima
Sophocles 139, 166–7, 259
soul 115–17; and body 204–5; Marx on 124–5
space: sacred 27, 37; space-between and politics and spirituality 112–15, 118–20; and women 250–64; *see also* desert space (extraterrestrial) *see* Copernican system
Spinoza, B. de 34–5; on dualism 41; on expressions 34; on immanentism 37; on pantheism 34; on politics 37, 40; on positivity 38–9
spirit 4, 17, 66, 78, 261; diremption of 45–56; as fire 105–6; *Geist* 132, 138, 144–7; and Marx 132–3; modern preoccupation with 57; shadow of 11, 45–6
Spivak, G. 199
state: ecological reports to 165–72; and middle 53; separate from civil society and family 139; *see also* nation
Strauss, L. 206; on philosophy and law 46, 49–50
subject/subjectivity 36–7; autonomy 36; and humanism challenged 250–64; imploded 64; and secularists 30, 33, 34; self as 30; suicide of 63; transcendent 135
sublime 49, 252; in America 57, 64; in art 13–17, 19, 20, 26, 27; and ecological peril and modern technology 173–8; and secularists 34
subtexts 32, 45–6; of Isaiah 211–25; *see also* Schreber
suchness 159, 161
sunyata see void

Tavor Bannet, E. xi; on deconstruction 198–9; on Marx, God and praxis 123–34
Taylor, M.C. xi–xii, 4; a/theology 46–7, 48–9, 51, 54, 77–8; on dismemberment and silence 74; Moore on 102; on non-absent

absence 73; on reframing postmodernisms 11–29
technology *see* ecological peril and modern technology
temporality: Being and Time 140–3, 254; and eternity 38–9, 41; and genealogy for postmodern ethics 140–3; man identified with 259; space and time 259; time as history 73; timelessness 73, 77; and understanding 76; *see also* history
text 95; Freud and Schreber 238–49; Jesus, and woman taken in adultery 226–37; Plato's *Symposium* deconstructed 198–210; reports to state 165–72, 176, 178; *see also* New Testament; Old Testament; semiotics
time *see* temporality
totality: fear of totalization 75; and infinity 46, 49–50, 54; *see also* Levinas
trace: of other 81–92; *see also* *différance* and trace
transcendence/transcendental 66, 135, 261; in art 13, 19; denied/negated 19, 98; secularists' view of 34, 38–42; and technology 169; *see also* spirit
transgression, carnival as 94, 102
transvaluation of ethics 38–40
truth: of Being 258–9; non-existent 68; veiled 74
turn/turning 3, 34, 115, 169, 254, 259

unconscious: political/cultural 171–2; sacred 97
United Nations *see* Brundtland Report
United States *see* Baudrillard
unsystematic ethics and politics 149–55
Uriah the Hittite 188, 191–2, 194–5

value: creation of 79; denied 39; given and created, distinction between 137; transcendent 135
Venturi, R. 21, 64, 251
violence 167–8; and metaphysics 84–6; primal scene and Schreber 244, 246; *see also* Nazism; rape
virtue 48; secularists' views of 33; of theory 68; as will-to-power 40
void 65, 128, 130, 132, 158, 251–2, 258; sacred as 77, 79; *see also* space